Saris

Saris

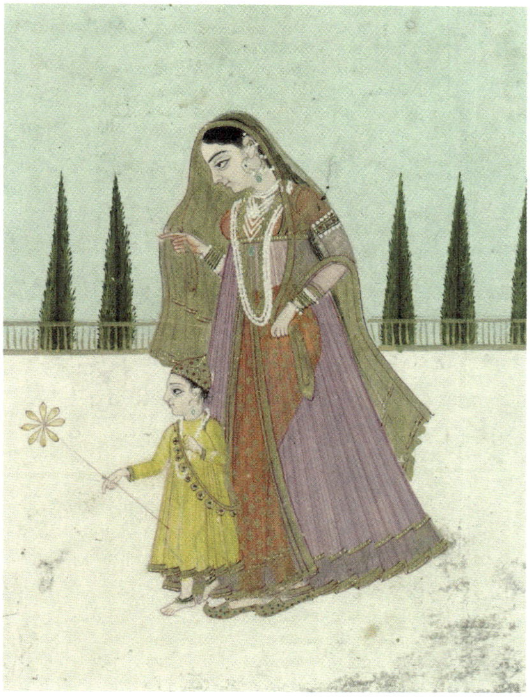

Shreya Jain

amber
BOOKS

Amber Books Ltd
United House
North Road
London N7 9DP
United Kingdom

www.amberbooks.co.uk
Facebook: amberbooks
YouTube: amberbooksltd
Instagram: amberbooksltd
X(Twitter): @amberbooks

ISBN: 978-1-83886-664-8

Editor: Anna Brownbridge
Design: Rajdip Sanghera & Mark Batley
Picture research: Terry Forshaw & Sharon Southren

Printed in China

Contents

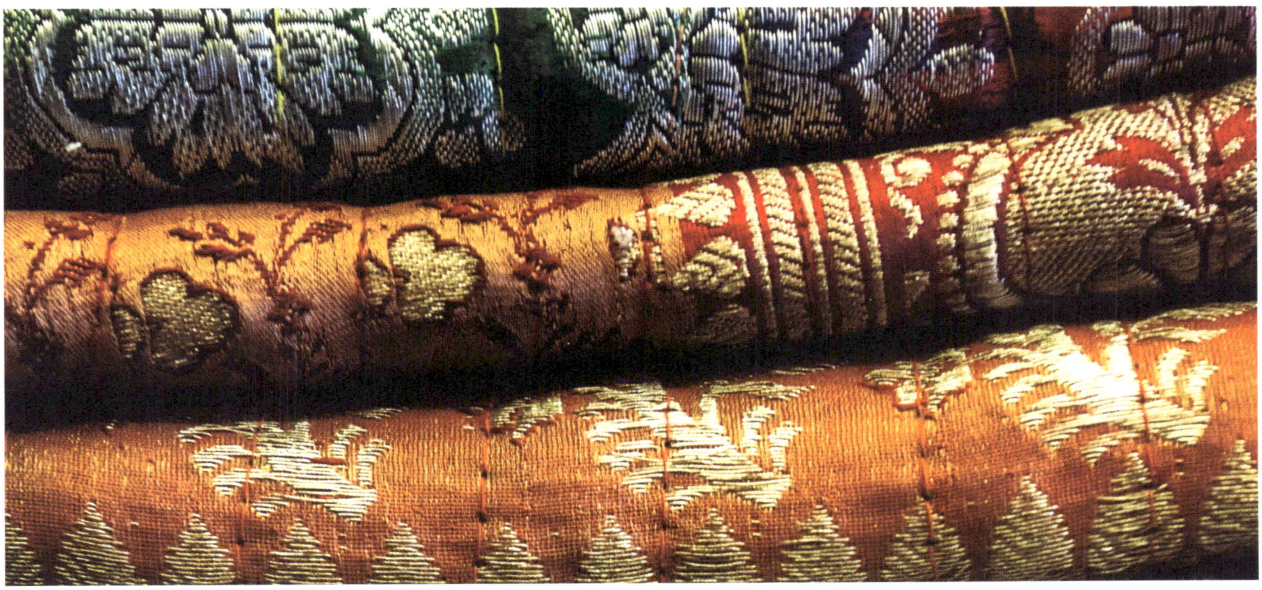

INTRODUCTION

समय के तंतु

Threads of Time: A Prologue

You're six when you find your mother's colourful dupatta.

You tie it around your waist, pull it over your head – like she does.

You watch yourself in the mirror, small, soft, becoming.

You wait to grow – a little taller, a little older – to wear those six yards.

At eighteen, it wraps around you.

Not just fabric – but a moment, a memory, a milestone.

It's your graduation.

It fits like it always knew you.

You learn to love it.

You learn to love you.

That saree – those metres of fabric – is where you come from.

And where you're going.

According to the Oxford English Dictionary, a sari is a long piece of cloth that is wrapped around the body to make a long dress, worn by women in South Asia. It is an unstitched piece of fabric, typically 4–5m (5–6 yards) long, that is draped over the body.

However, a sari is so much more than that.

It is memory, passed down in folds. It is identity, stitched into stories. It is a second skin that carries both weight and grace: the weight of lineage, the grace of reinvention.

As a child, I remember reaching for my mother's *dupatta* (scarf) and wrapping it clumsily around my tiny frame, trying to become her. Or at least become what she embodied in that moment: boldness, beauty, softness and power. In our home, the sari wasn't everyday wear. It lived quietly in cupboards lined with naphthalene balls and tissue paper, waiting for celebrations – weddings, festivals and rites of passage. When it came out, it transformed the room. The rustle of silk or the earthy fall of cotton seemed to carry joy, reverence and womanhood itself.

The sari is often simply described as just 'a garment'. Yet no other garment can hold this much life between its threads.

Every state in India has its own way of weaving, dyeing, embellishing, its own way of draping. More than a hundred styles of sari drapes exist across South Asia, each with its own language of folds and tucks, of movement and modesty. These variations are not simply aesthetic choices. They are reflections of geography, labour, climate, caste, history and personal style. The sari, in its endless adaptability, becomes a mirror – of culture, class and change.

This book begins here, at the hem of this fabric. Not only to look at what it is, but to explore what it holds.

The sari represents both presence and absence. It holds the body and also conceals it. It is at once voice and silence: what we inherit, what we reclaim. Through stories, interviews, images and personal reflections, I want to trace the sari's journey not just through time, but through memory: as heirloom, as labour, as rebellion and as ritual.

Before we begin to unravel the threads of sari history or technique, this prologue is a gesture. Like the first fold tucked into the waist, it anchors us in what the sari feels like: rich with story, yet light with possibility.

Wearing a sari

India is home to countless sari draping styles, each shaped by region, climate, and culture. From the seedha *pallu* of Gujarat to the nauvari of Maharashtra, every drape tells a different story. What follows is the most widely worn style today – the Nivi drape – simple, elegant, and adaptable across occasions.

STEP 1
Start by tucking the plain end of the sari into your petticoat at the right side of your waist. Wrap it around once, bringing it back to the front.

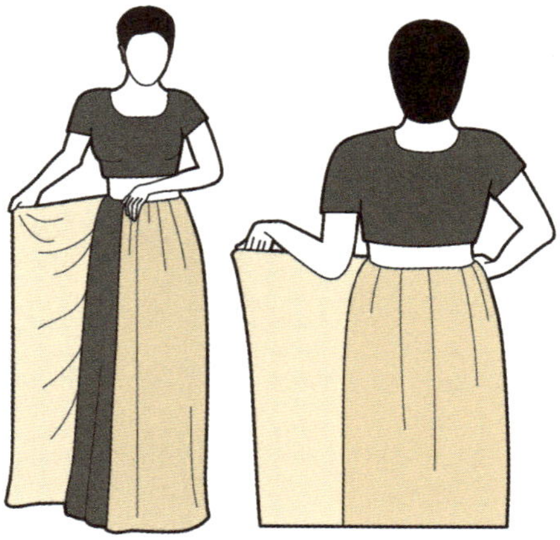

STEP 2
Continue wrapping the fabric around your waist, ensuring the lower edge just grazes the floor. Keep the drape even and smooth.

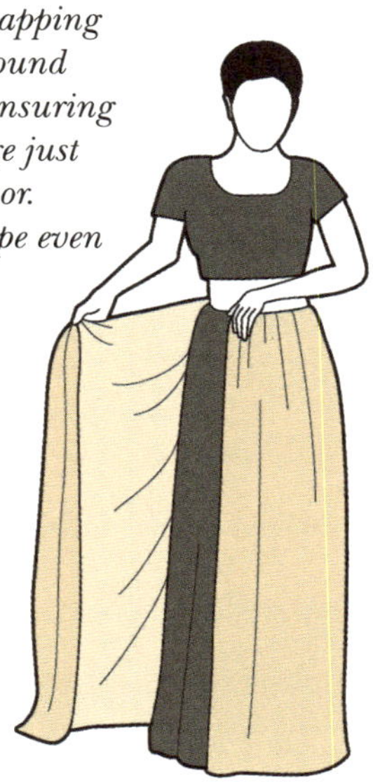

STEP 3
Begin making pleats with the remaining fabric at the front. Gather 5–7 even folds, aligning them neatly.

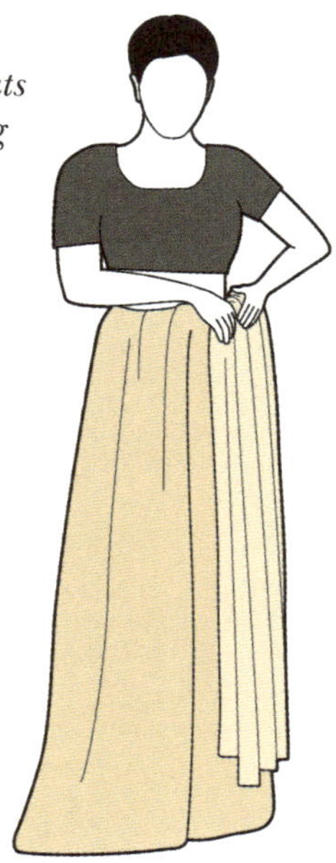

STEP 4
Tuck the pleats into the centre of your waist, ensuring they fall straight and allow ease of movement.

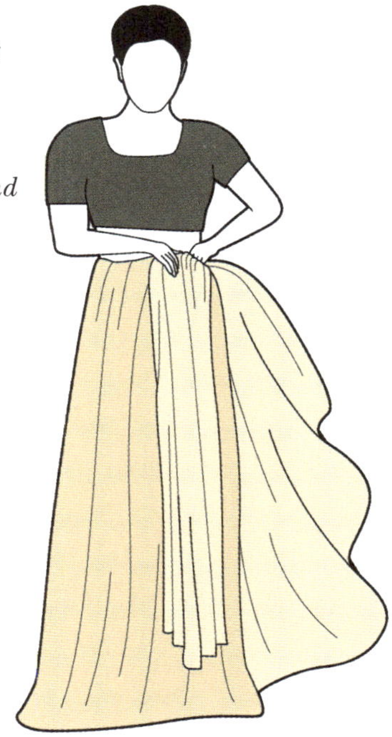

STEP 5
Take the remaining fabric around your body once more, bringing it over your left shoulder to form the pallu.

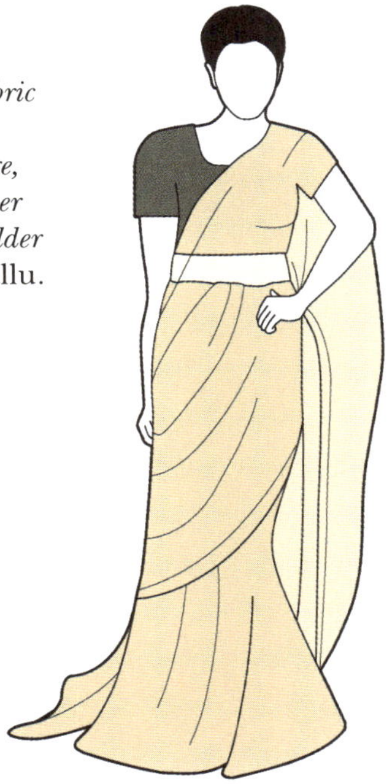

STEP 6
Adjust the length of the pallu *so it falls gracefully, either to the back of your knees or longer, depending on preference.*

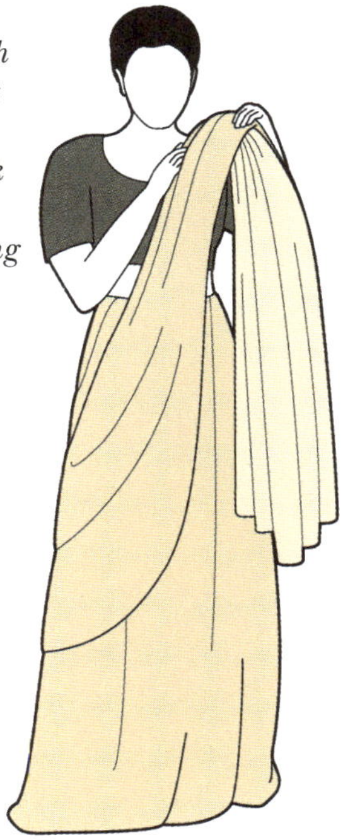

STEP 7
Neatly arrange the pallu *into pleats and secure it on your shoulder with a pin if needed. Adjust the drape so it sits comfortably and elegantly.*

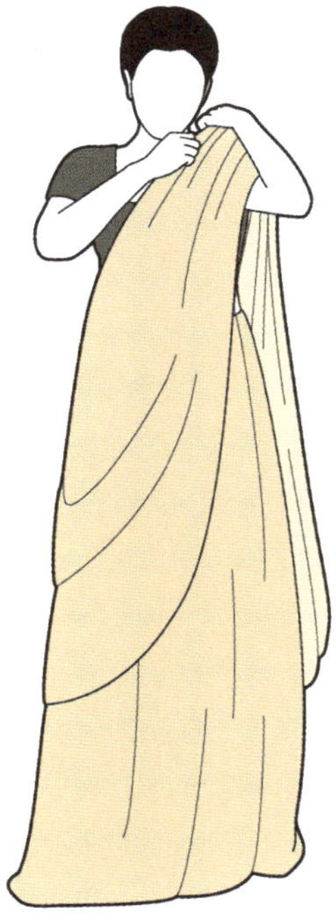

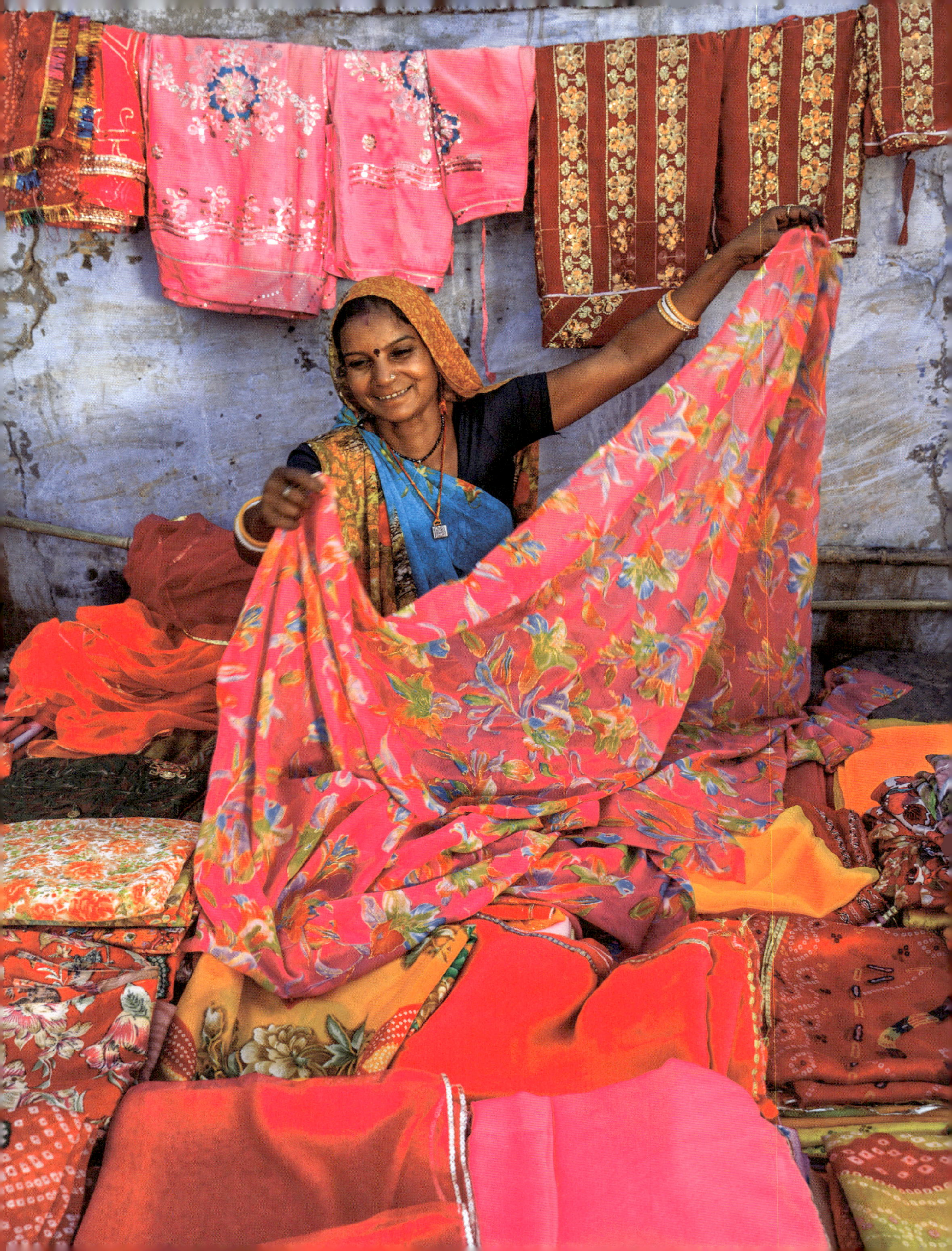

CHAPTER 1

इतहिास का करघा: अतीत की बुनावट

The Loom of History: Weaving the Past

Before it became a fashion statement or a symbol of tradition, the sari was something far more elemental: a combination of cloth and instinct. It didn't originate in boutiques or under the careful eye of a designer. It emerged in the heat of the Indian subcontinent, where modesty, climate and culture converged and women reached for a single, continuous length of fabric and wrapped it around themselves.

That was all. No cuts. No seams. Simply fabric, intention and centuries of inherited knowledge about how to fold, pleat and drape.

The sari is older than most garments still in use today. Its roots reach back to around 2800 BCE and the Indus Valley Civilization. Archaeologists have unearthed terracotta figurines and statues depicting women with garments wrapped around their lower bodies,

Woman selling colourful fabrics in a local bazaar, Jodhpur, Rajasthan, India. Jodhpur is known for its vibrant textile markets and traditional dyeing practices.

their torsos left bare, and adorned with jewellery. It wasn't called a sari then, but the impulse was the same: to use fabric not just to cover, but to express, to shape, to move.

The term sari itself comes from the Sanskrit word *sattika*, meaning a strip of cloth. Over time, *sattika* evolved into *sadi* in Prakrit, and eventually sari or saree, as we say today. But the idea remained constant: an unstitched drape worn with grace and adaptability.

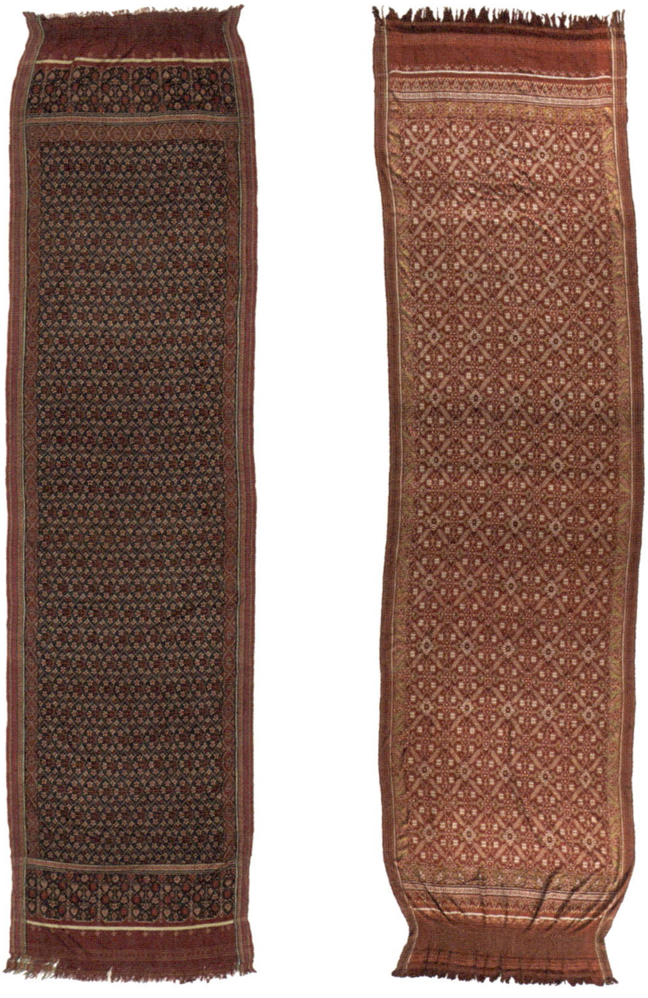

Left: Silk Patola sari, 19th century. Patola saris are double-ikat textiles, requiring precise dyeing of both warp and weft threads. Right: Woman's wedding sari, Gujarat (Patan), India, 19th century. Such saris were traditionally worn during ceremonial occasions and symbolized status and prosperity.

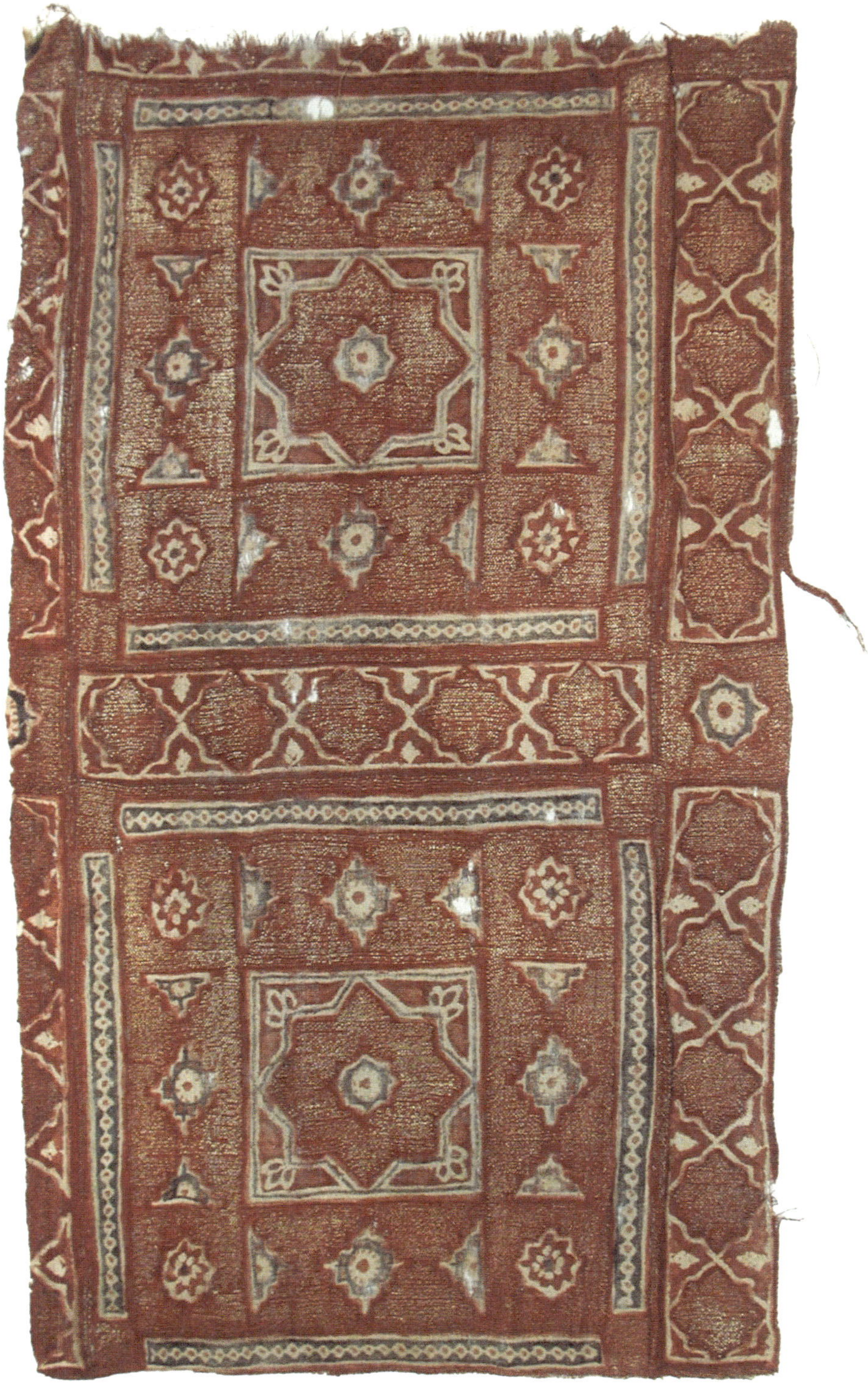

Sari, 17th century. Early saris often featured simpler weaving techniques compared to later brocaded styles

Early Iterations: *Antariya, Uttariya, Stanapatta*

The sari as we understand it today was never a single, fixed design. It was – and still is – fluid, regional and personal. In its early iterations, it was part of a three-piece ensemble: the *antariya* (lower garment), *uttariya* (a cloth worn across the shoulders or over the head) and a chest band or *stanapatta*. These evolved, merged, and transformed into a single length of cloth tailored to different bodies and customs through technique alone.

Ancient Sanskrit and Tamil works testify to this early ensemble. The *Silappadikaram*, a Sangam-era epic from Tamil Nadu, describes women wearing a single length of cloth that doubled as lower garment and head covering, leaving the midriff bare. In Kerala, Raja Ravi Varma's later paintings captured similar drapes – echoes of older traditions where

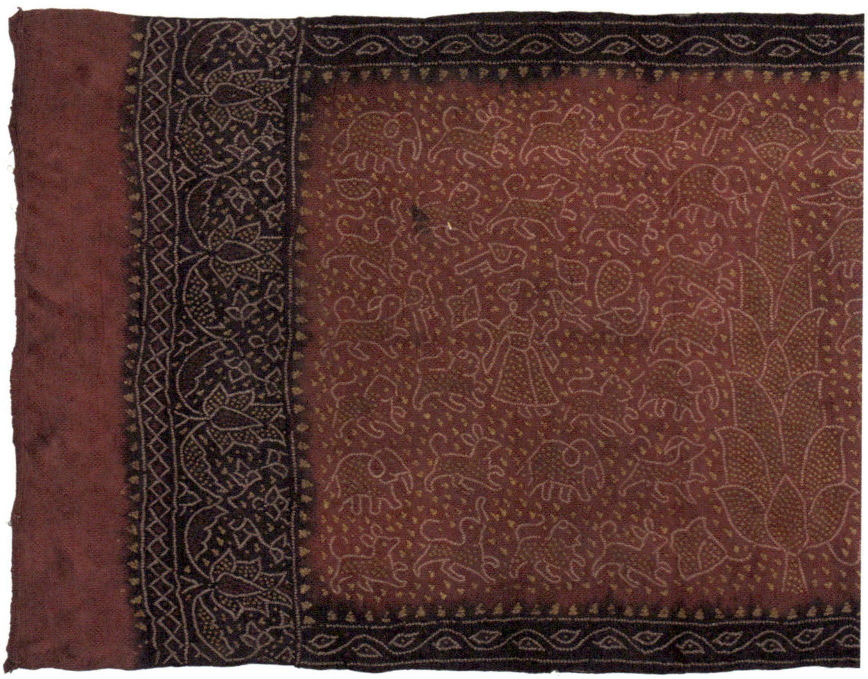

Satin sari, 19th century. Satin weaving produces a smooth, lustrous surface associated with luxury textiles.

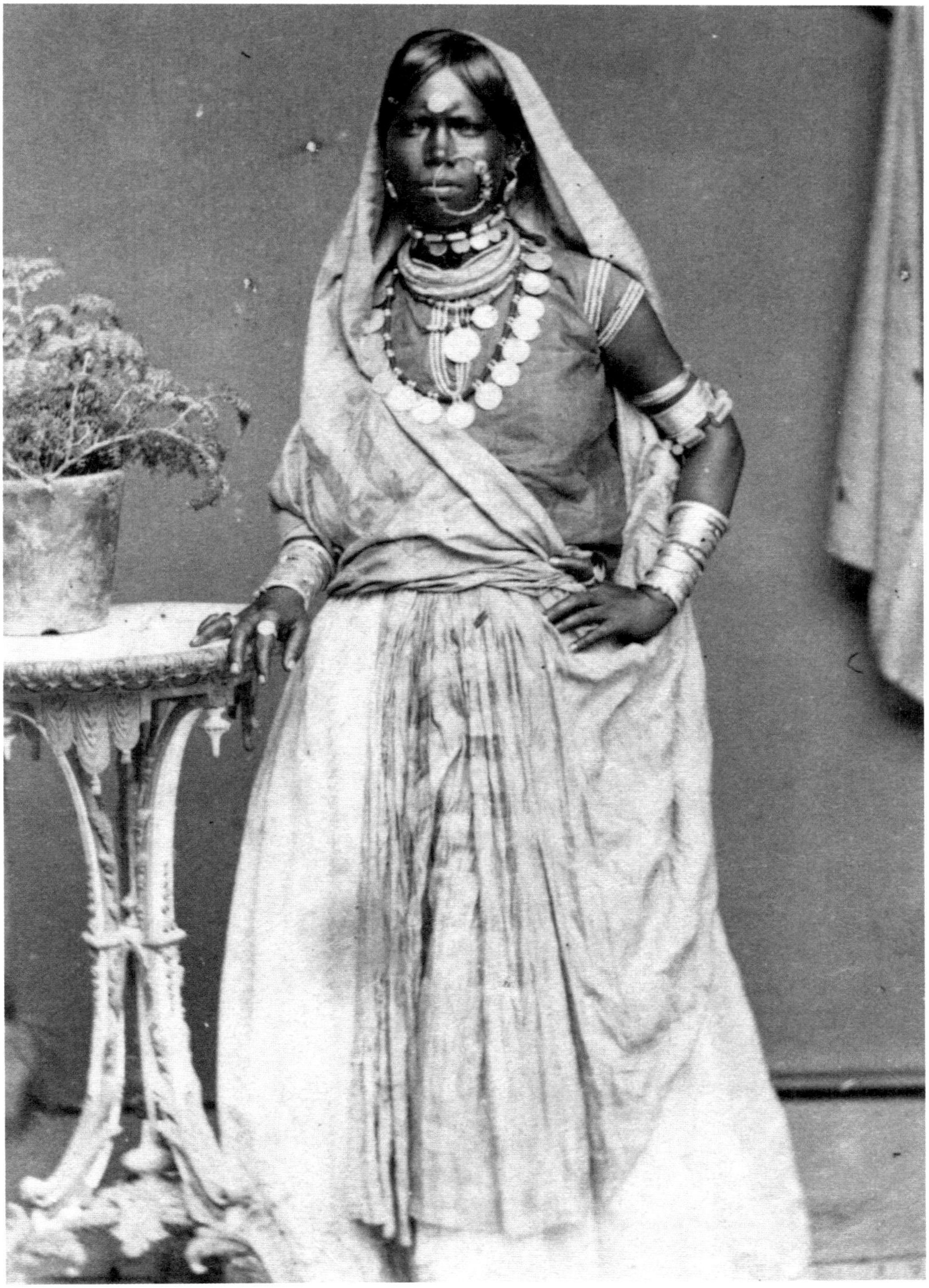

Circa 1900: An Indian woman posing in a sari and wearing ornate jewellery.
The figure's draped garment is one of the earliest known representations of textile use in South Asia.

everyday dress combined a pleated *dhoti* wrap with a *stanapatta* (breast band) and an *uttariya* (shawl for the shoulders or head). Together, these three pieces formed the *poshak* – the generic costume of the time.

The *antariya* (lower garment) resembled a *dhoti*, often tied in the fishtail style, its pleats cascading at the front. Over centuries, it evolved into the *ghagra* or *lehenga*. The *uttariya* became the *dupatta* and *ghoonghat*. The *stanapatta* transformed into the *choli* by the first century CE. By the turn of the millennium, the *antariya* and *uttariya* began merging into a single continuous cloth – the form we now recognize as the sari.

Even in these early centuries, textiles were not plain cloth. Indigo, lac, madder and turmeric were already in use – dyes so enduring that they still colour fabrics today. By 2450 BCE, silk was being reeled and woven in the subcontinent, offering sheen alongside the breathable cottons of the Indus plains.

COTTON: THE FIRST SARI FIBRE

Cotton was the backbone of early sari-making, prized for its breathability in the subcontinent's heat. Archaeological evidence from the Indus Valley shows cotton cultivation as early as 3000 BCE. Even today, everyday saris across Bengal, Andhra and Odisha rely on tightly spun cotton that softens with wear, making the sari both practical and intimate.

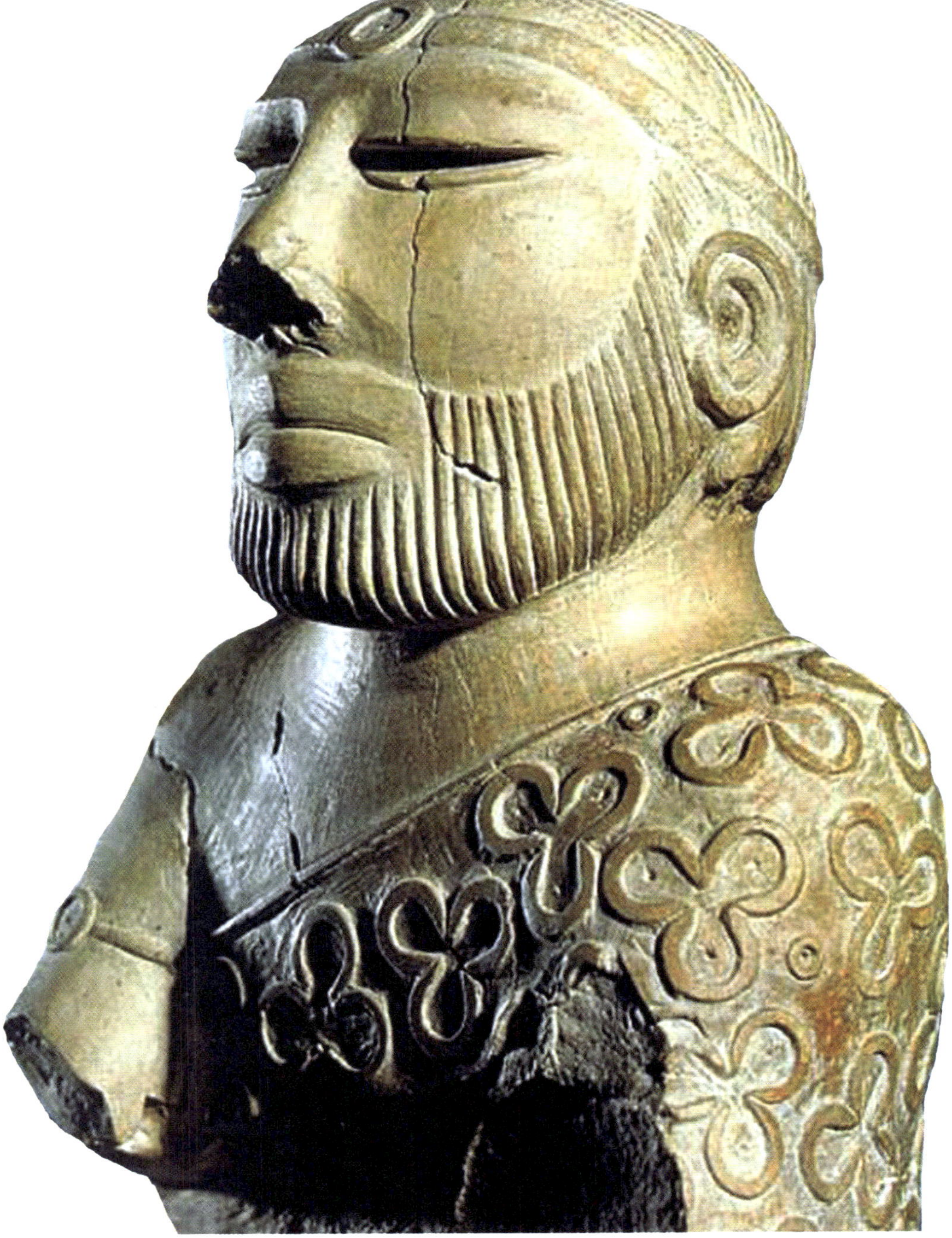

'Priest King' statue, Mohenjo-daro, Indus Valley Civilization (c. 2600 BCE), present-day Pakistan. The figure's draped garment is one of the earliest known representations of textile use in South Asia.

Mythological & Religious Origins

Long before its thread touched looms, the sari was already sacred.

One of the most enduring stories comes from the *Mahabharata*, where Draupadi, dragged into a court and humiliated, is stripped of her sari, only for the fabric to become endless – a divine intervention by Krishna. Her dignity, like the sari itself, is protected. That moment continues to echo across centuries: the sari as not just fabric, but faith. Not just adornment, but resistance.

In Hindu iconography, goddesses are rarely seen without their drapes. Durga, in fierce red, rides into battle. Lakshmi, bathed in gold, stands in a lotus bloom. Saraswati, draped in white, holds wisdom in her hands. The sari isn't just a costume here, it's symbolism: power, purity, prosperity.

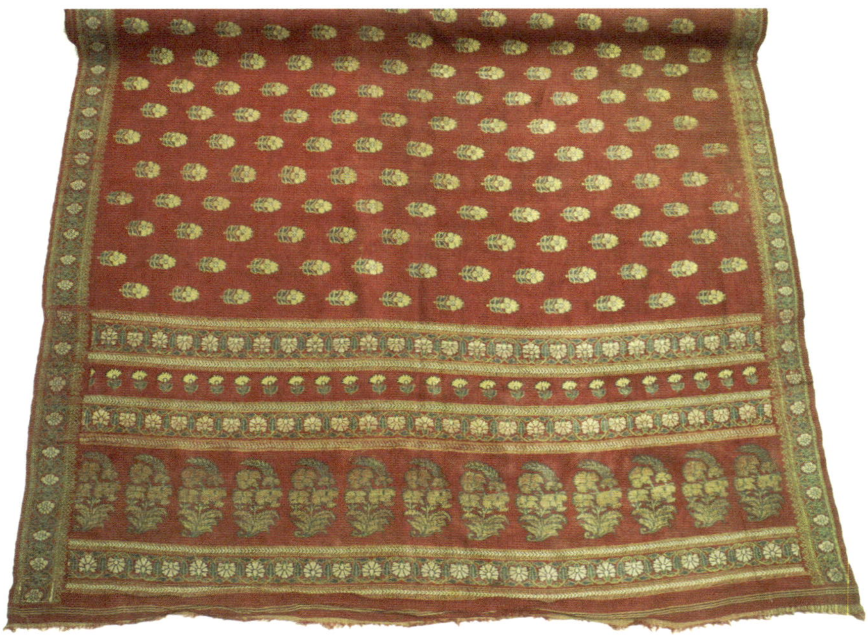

Sari, 19th century. Nineteenth-century saris often reflect regional weaving traditions and evolving decorative styles.

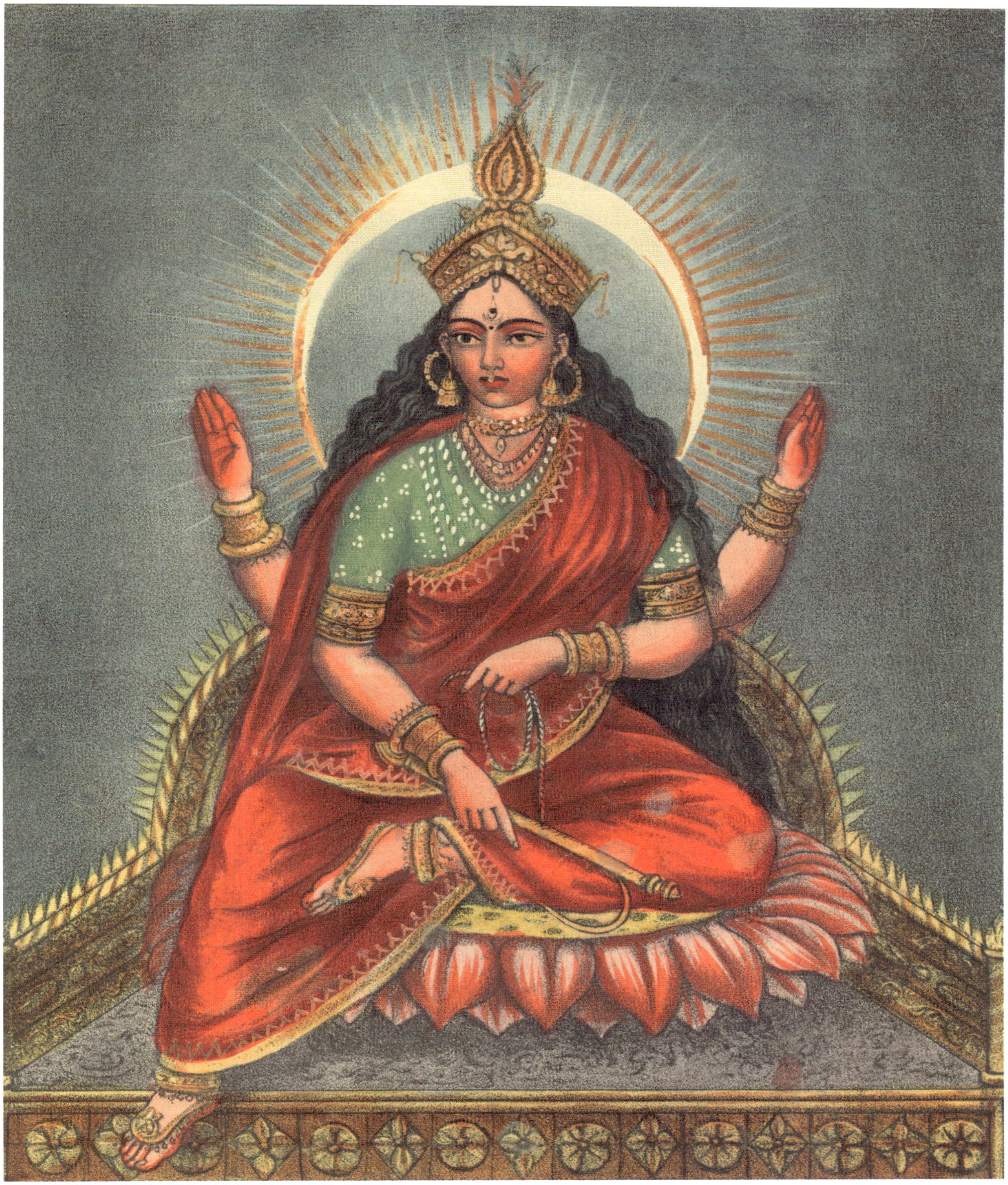

Goddess Bhuvaneshvari lithograph, Calcutta (Kolkata), West Bengal, c. 1880–1885.

Literary references deepen this sense of continuity. Banabhatta's *Kadambari* (7th century CE) describes women adorned in elaborate drapery, while Tamil epics such as the *Silappadikaram* celebrate the sari as sensual yet dignified. The Dharmashastra authors, however, insisted the navel should be concealed – a contrast to temple sculptures and the Natya Shastra, which sanctified the bare midriff as the cosmic seat of life and creativity. This tension between concealment and revelation has always been part of the sari's story, a delicate balance of modesty, movement and sacred geometry.

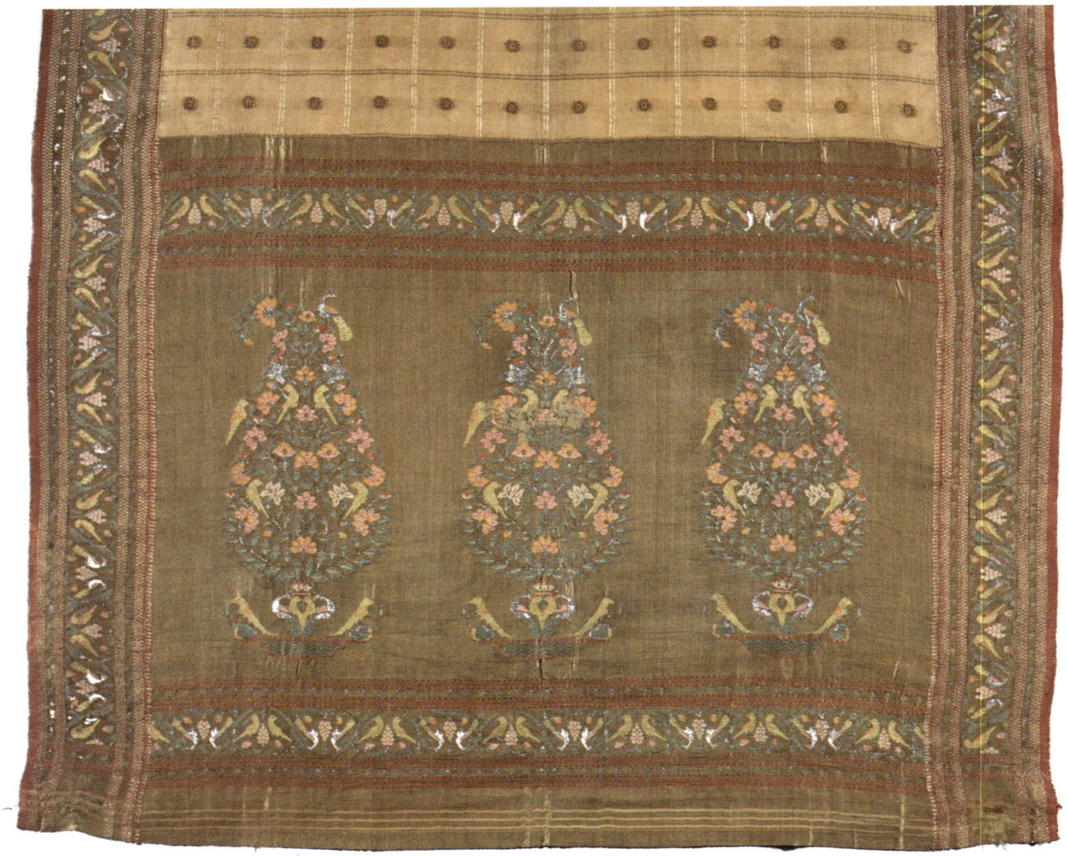

Wedding sari, India, 19th century (possibly Paithan or Chanderi).
Such saris were often woven with fine silk and metallic threads for ceremonial use.

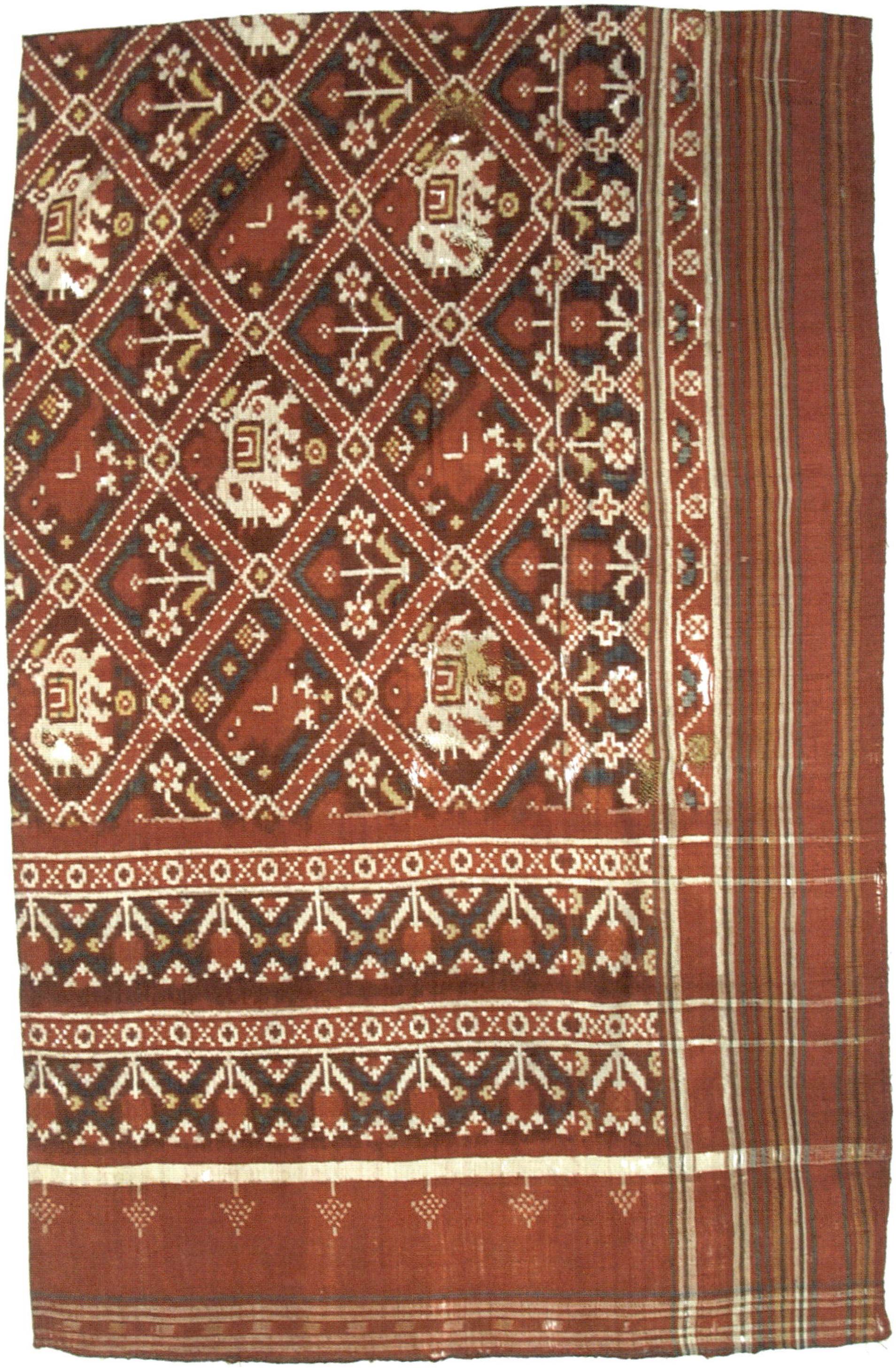

Fragment of a sari, Sindh (present-day Pakistan), 18th–19th century. Textile fragments like this help trace historical trade and weaving practices.

Across rituals – births, weddings, coming-of-age ceremonies – the sari emerges not just as clothing, but as a ceremonial object. Offered to goddesses. Passed from mother to daughter. Folded into dowries. Worn to mark both beginnings and farewells.

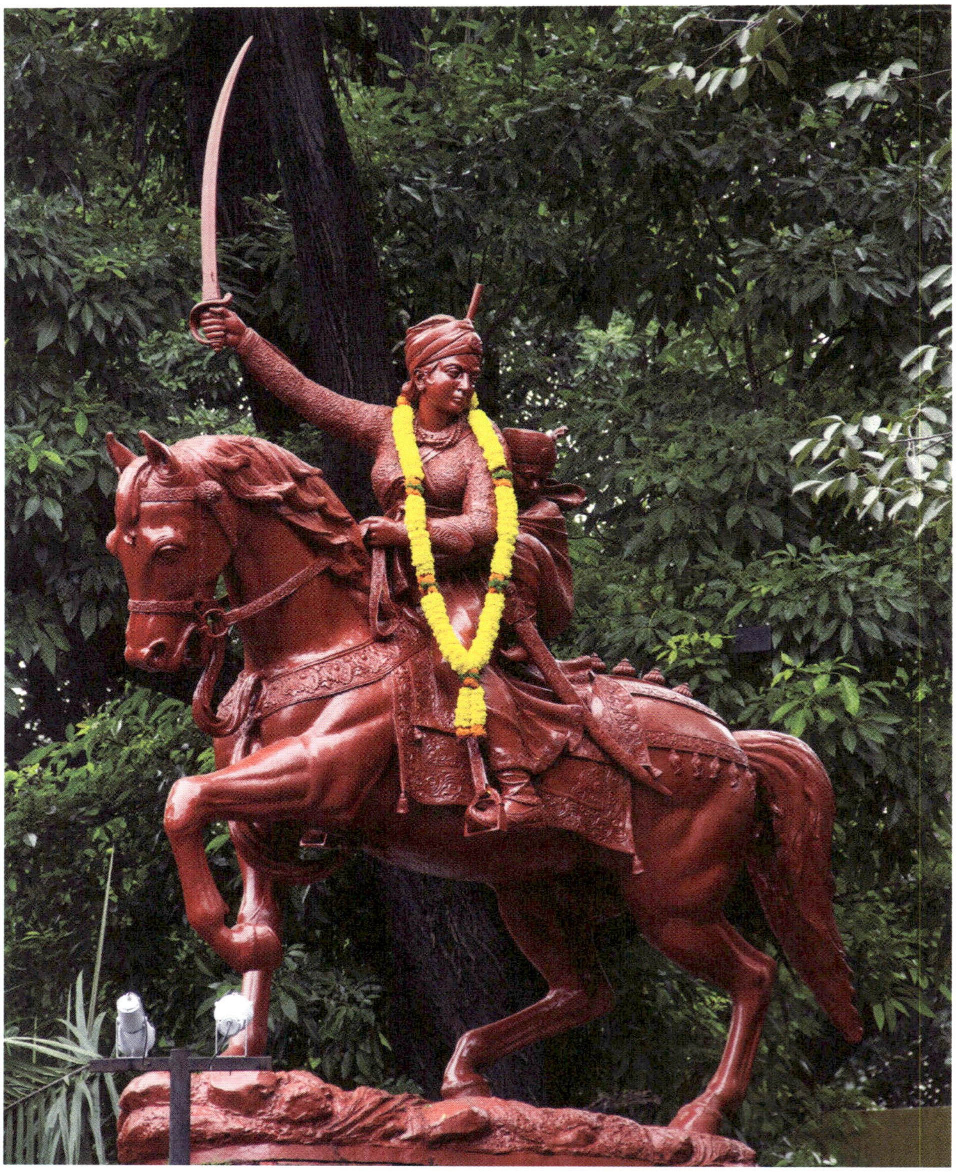

Statue of Rani Lakshmibai, Pune, India.
She was a key figure in the Indian Rebellion of 1857 and a symbol of resistance.

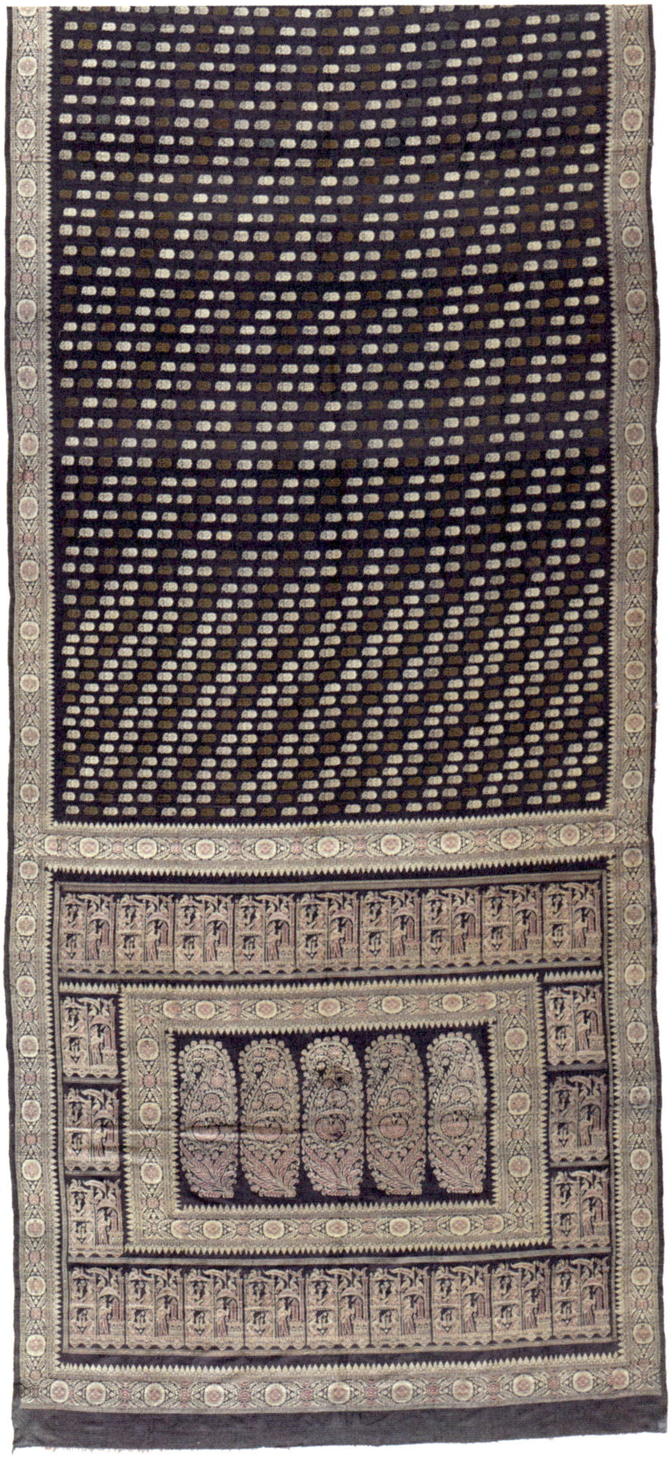

Baluchari Buttidar silk brocade sari, Murshidabad, West Bengal, late 19th century. Baluchari saris are known for their narrative motifs woven into the pallu.

Evolution Through Dynasties

As India changed hands – through empires, invaders, reformers – the sari changed with it. But it never lost its form.

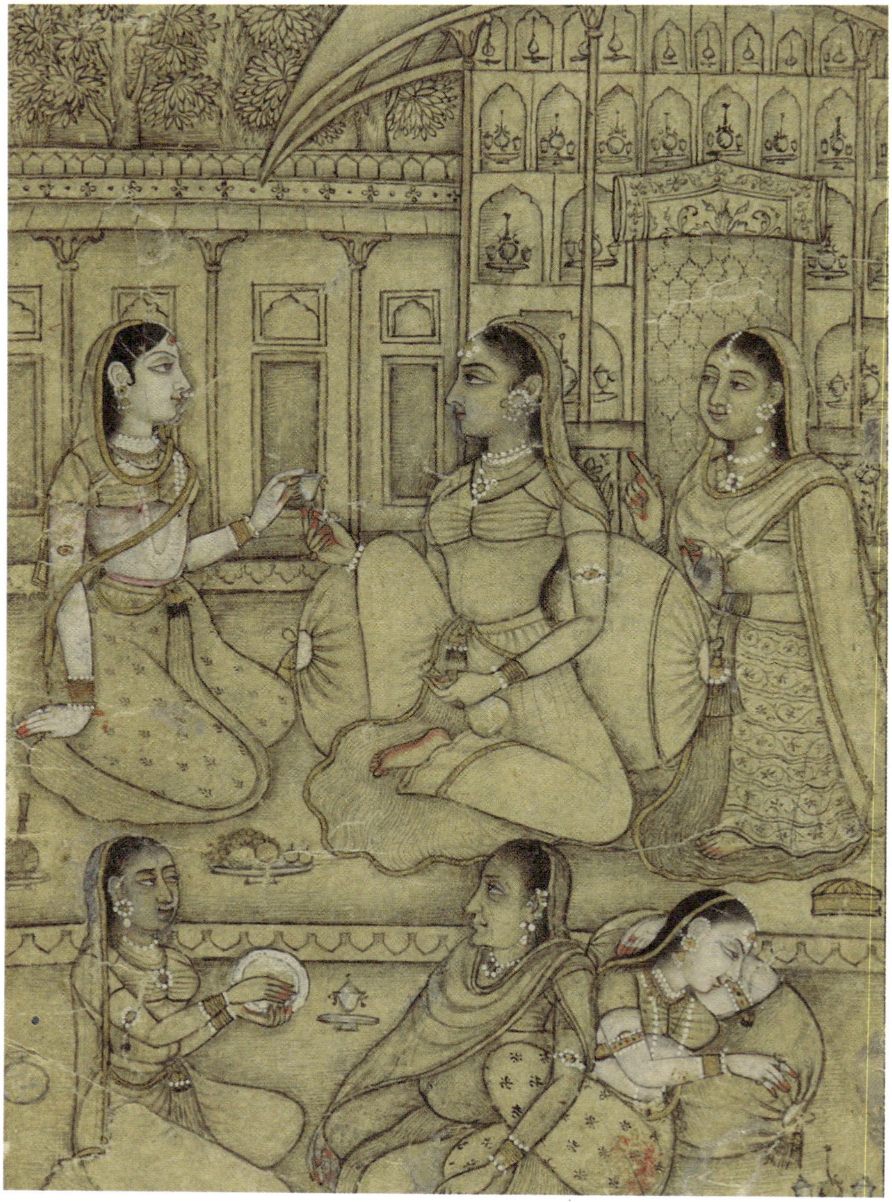

A lady and attendants seated in a courtyard, ink painting, early 18th century. Such paintings often depict domestic life and courtly settings.

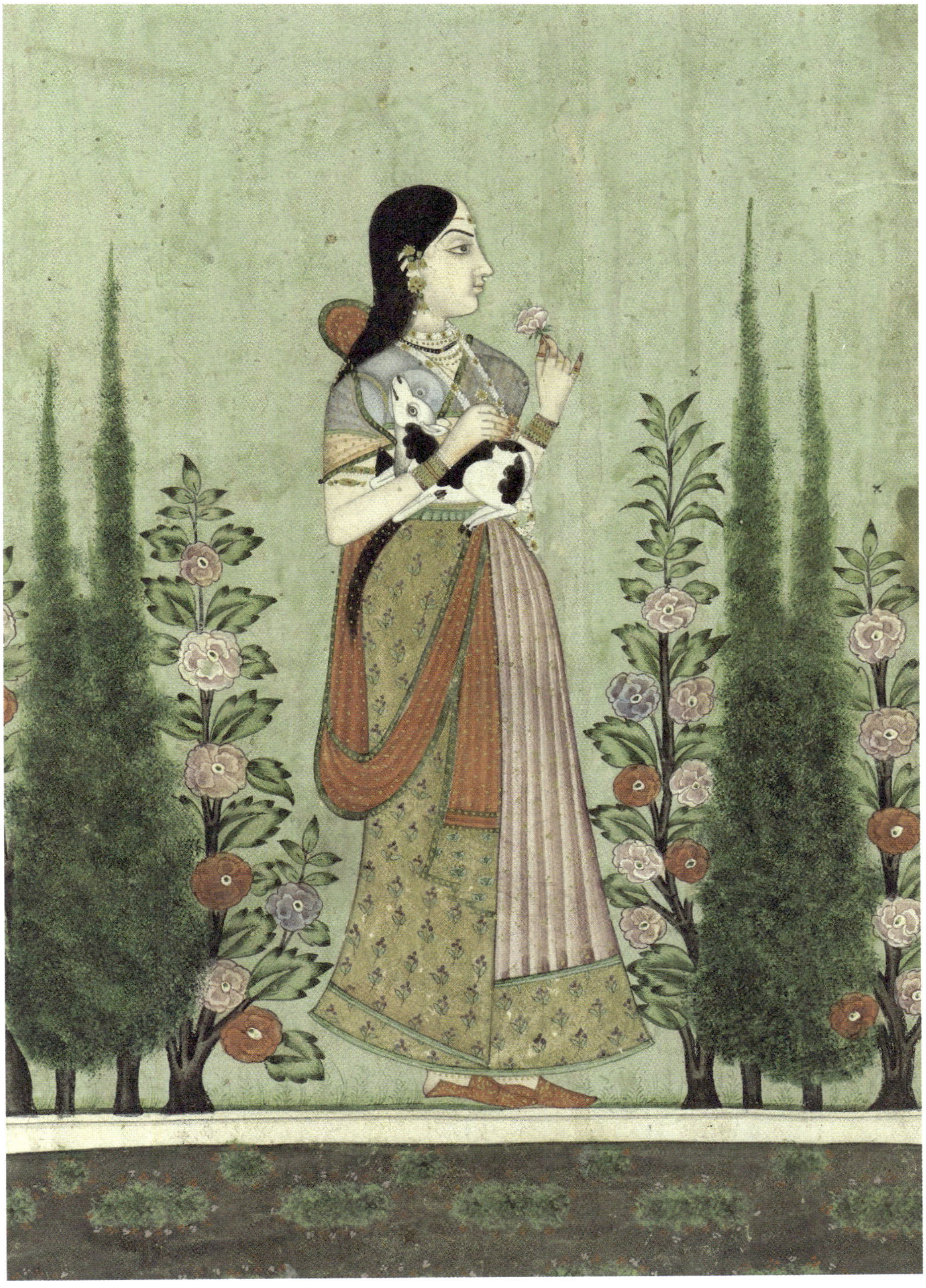

Girl with a fawn, Indian miniature painting, c. 1700–1750.
Miniature paintings frequently combine natural elements with human subjects.

The Mauryan and Gupta empires (circa 300 BCE to 600 CE) saw considerable advances in textile production. Cotton remained widespread, but silk emerged as a luxury import. Borders became more ornate. Sculptures from this era show women in graceful drapes, their garments clinging to the body, accentuating form and movement. The sari was elegance born of utility.

The Mughal Era (16th–18th century CE) ushered in a dramatic shift in aesthetics. The Persians introduced brocade, *zari* (metallic thread) and floral motifs, translating courtly elegance into everyday

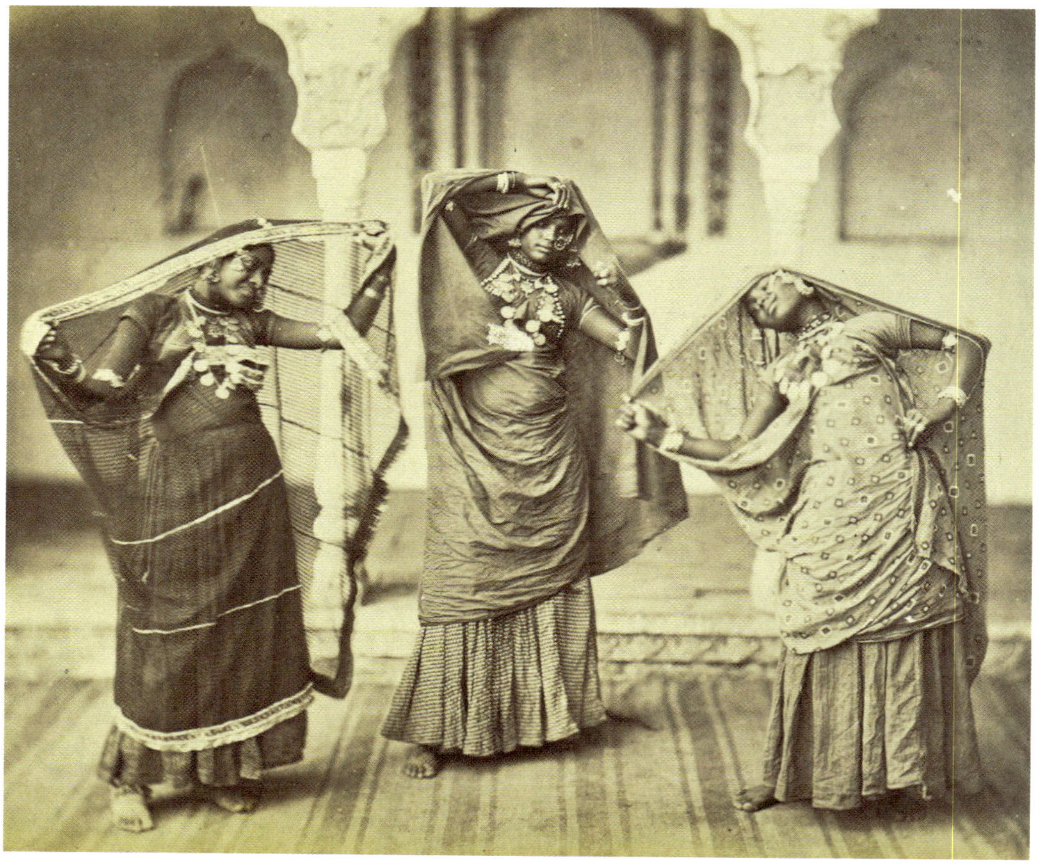

Nautch dancers posing with their saris, 1862.
Nautch dancers were professional performers associated with courtly entertainment traditions.

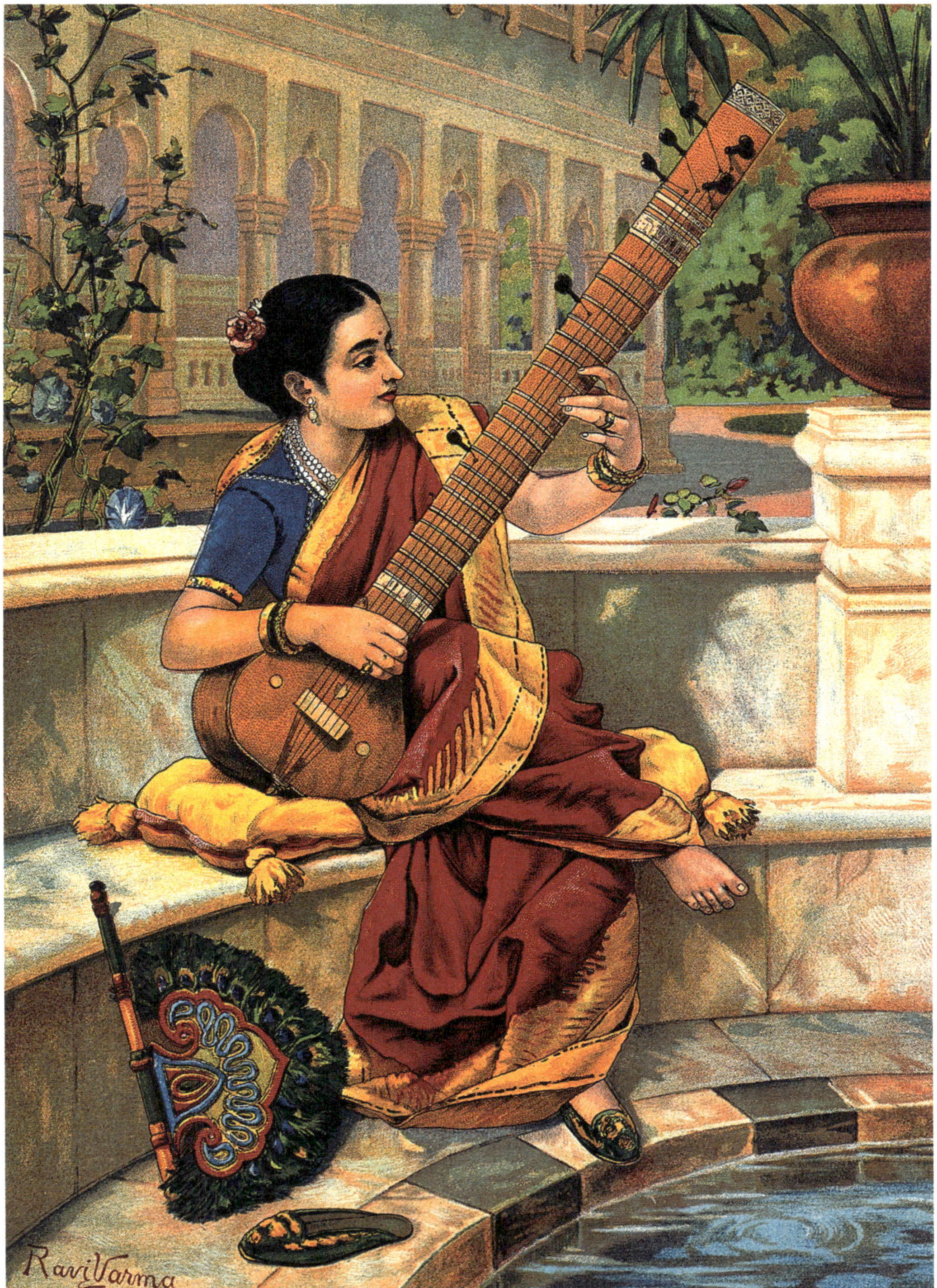

A seated Indian woman playing a sitar beside a garden pond, chromolithograph, late 19th century.

wear. Muslins and silk blends softened the drape. Stitching entered the narrative: blouses, petticoats, veils. But even as elements of the ensemble changed, the sari remained an unbroken length of cloth, a canvas that absorbed influences but stayed distinctly South Asian.

By the early medieval period, regional styles flourished. The sari became a topographical expression:

- Kanjeevarams in Tamil Nadu shimmered with gold and temple borders.
- Bandhanis in Gujarat and Rajasthan embraced tie-dye traditions and vibrant storytelling.
- Jamdani and Tant weaves in Bengal whispered of rivers, labour and revolt.

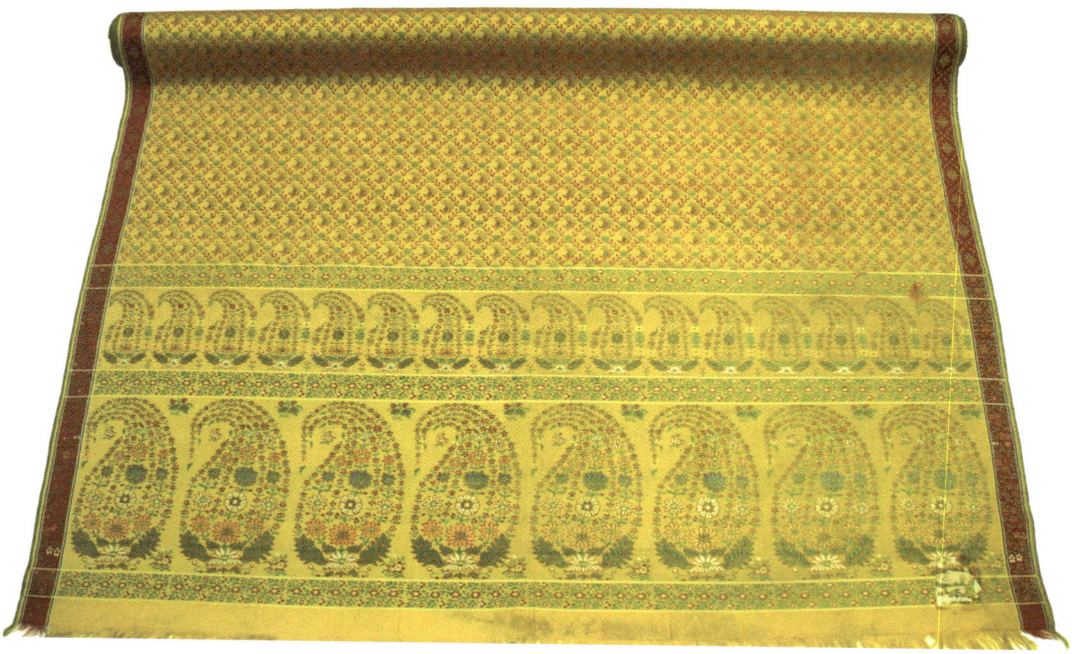

Sari, c. 1820. Textiles from this period often feature regional weaving identities.

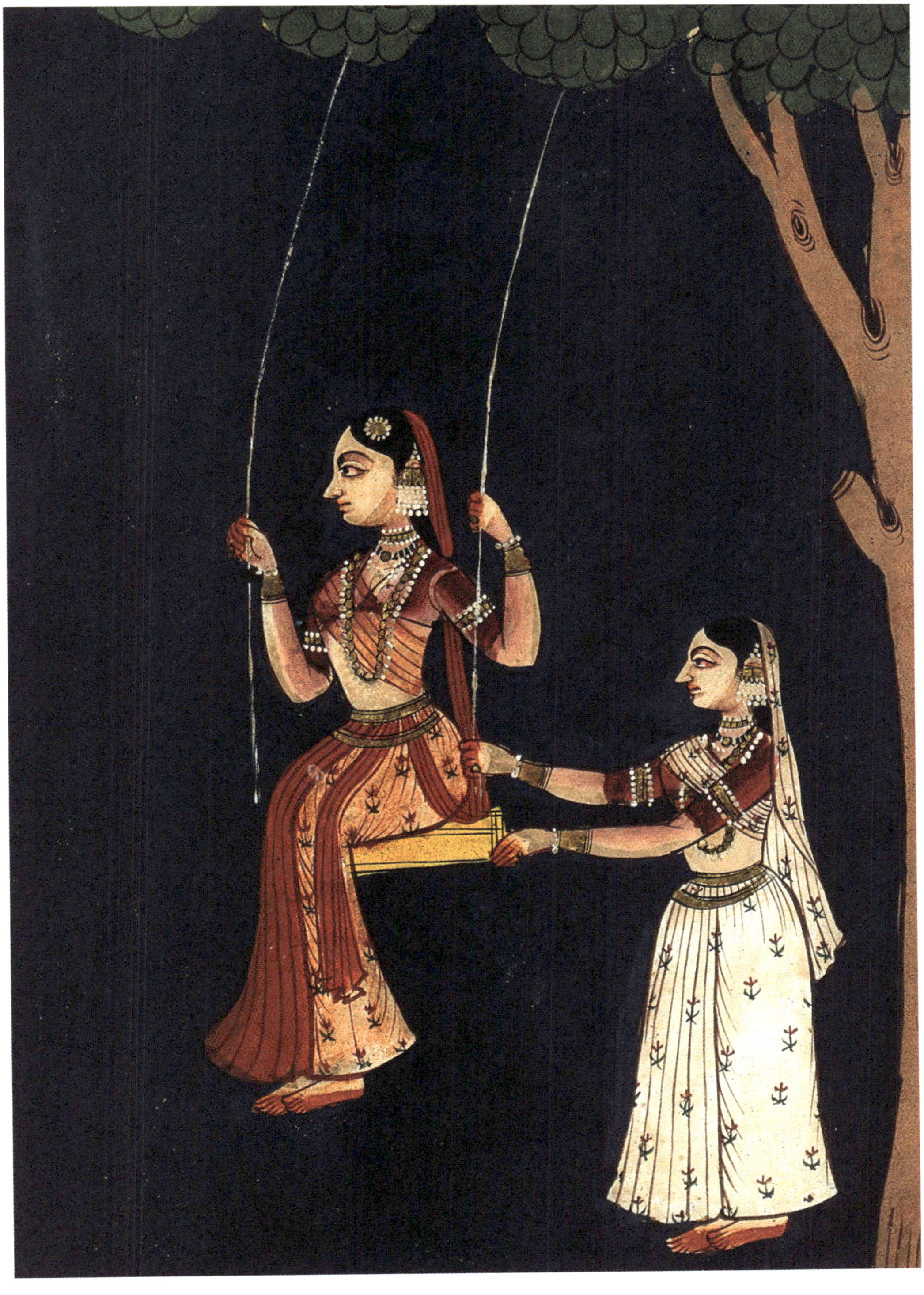

An Indian lady on a swing, gouache painting, 19th century.

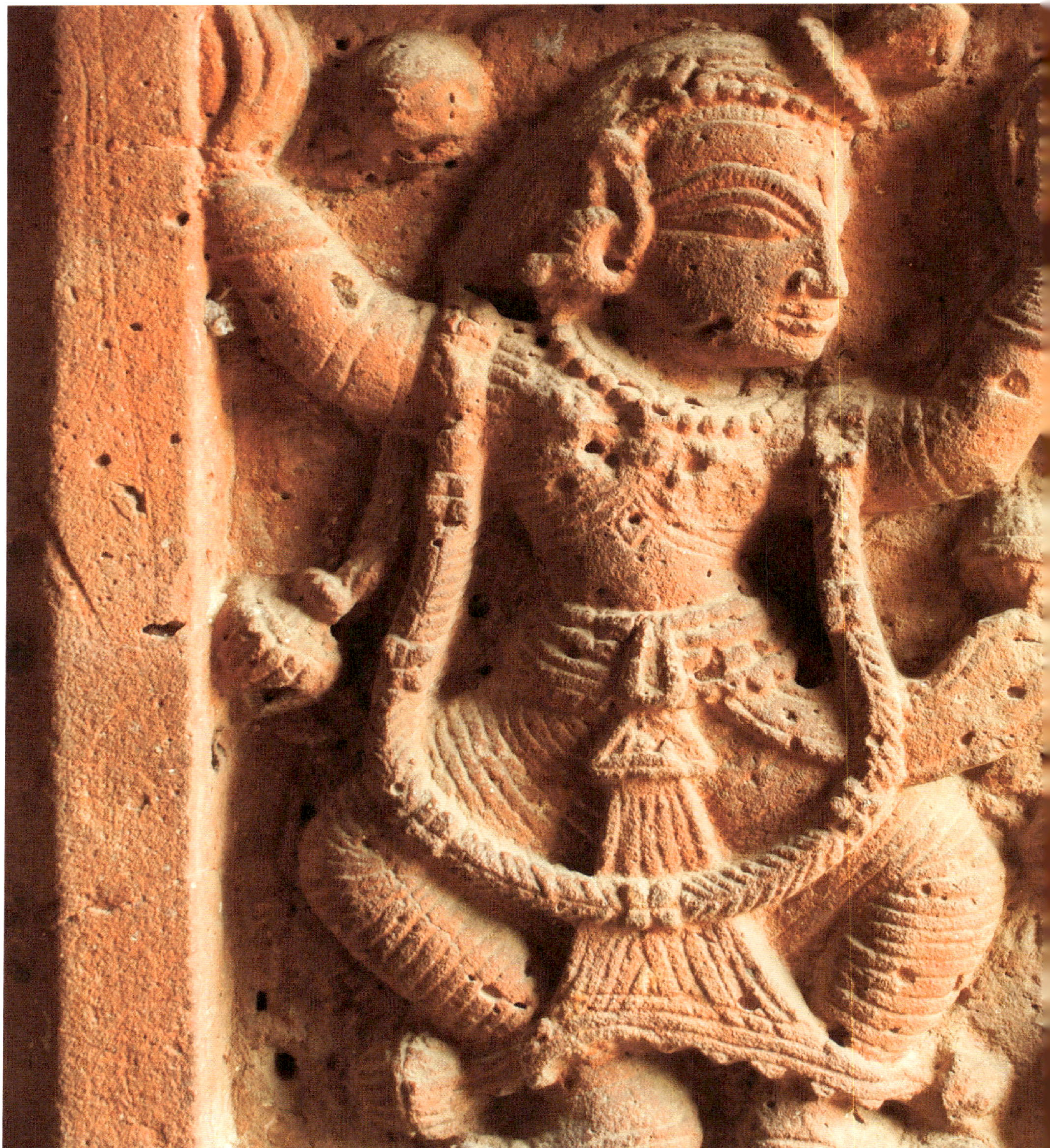

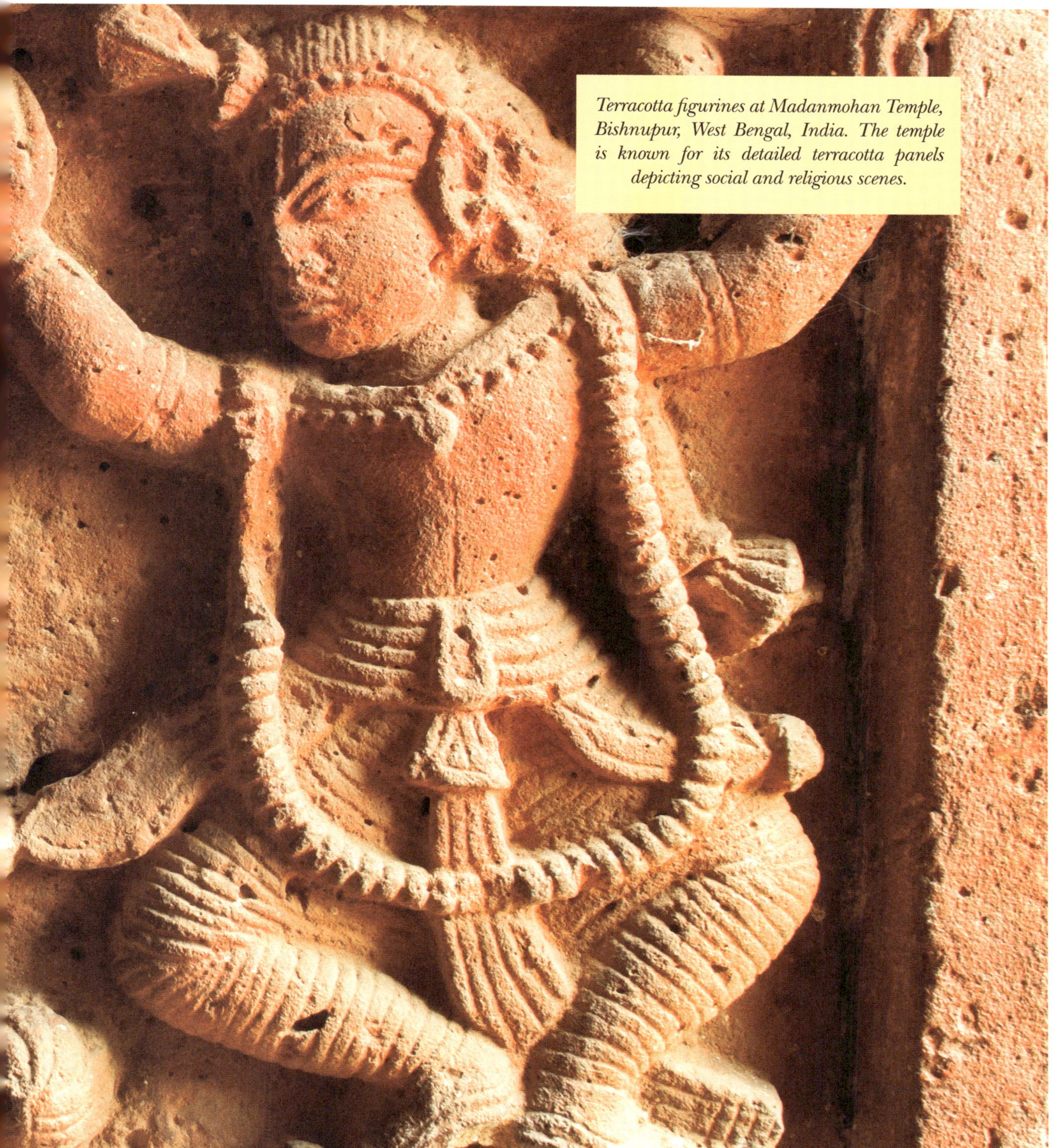

Terracotta figurines at Madanmohan Temple, Bishnupur, West Bengal, India. The temple is known for its detailed terracotta panels depicting social and religious scenes.

- Nauvari saris in Maharashtra, worn like *dhotis*, made movement possible for warriors and farmers alike.

Each drape responded to its climate, customs and geography. The sari wasn't just worn – it was lived.

Sari as Evidence of Economics and Art

The sari, in its earliest forms, was never merely clothing – it was a living ledger of the subcontinent's economy and artistry. The threads, colours and motifs woven into each length of cloth recorded trade routes, resource availability and aesthetic preferences.

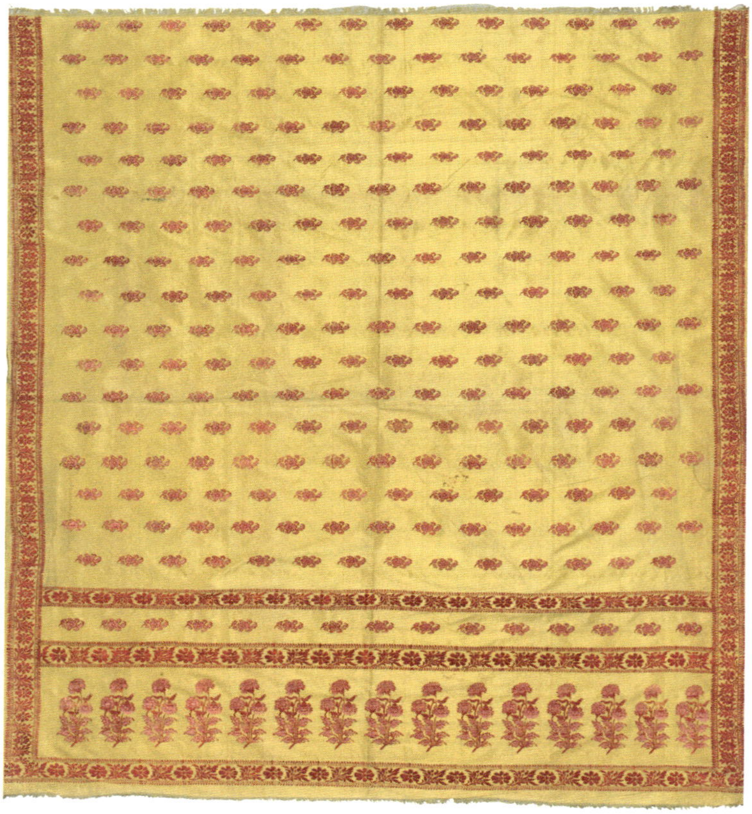

Part of a sari, Surat, India, late 19th–early 20th century.
Surat was historically a major centre for textile production and trade.

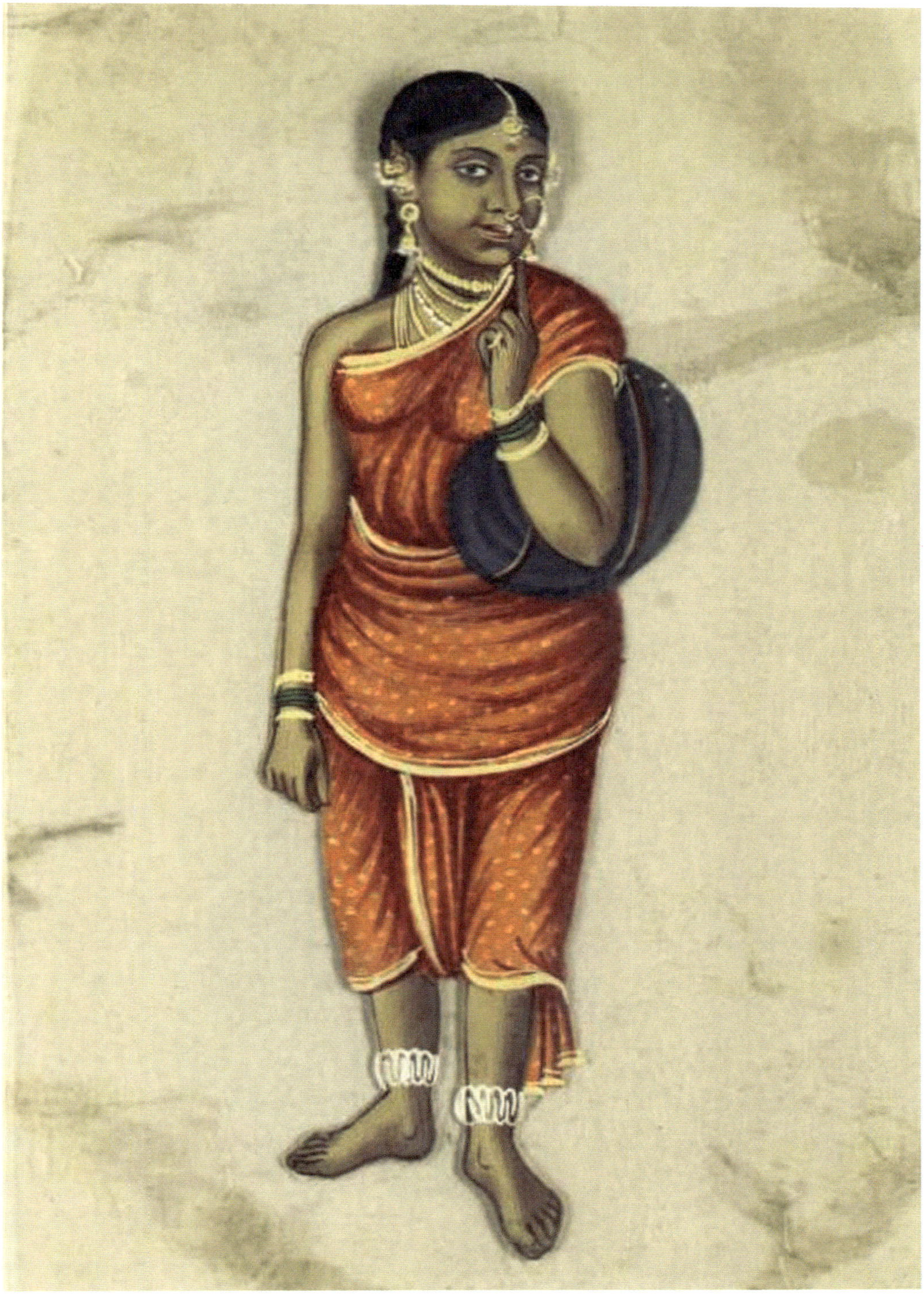

Hand-coloured mica painting of an Indian woman in sari and jewellery, from 'Seventy-two Specimens of Castes in India', Madura, 1837.

Even in the Indus Valley Civilization, dyed cottons and patterned weaves spoke of both local innovation and long-distance commerce. Indigo, madder, turmeric and lac – dyes still in use today – travelled along riverine and overland trade routes, shaping which colours dominated regional palettes. Silk, first woven around 2450 BCE, was both a luxury and a symbol of status, often reserved for elite households and ritual occasions.

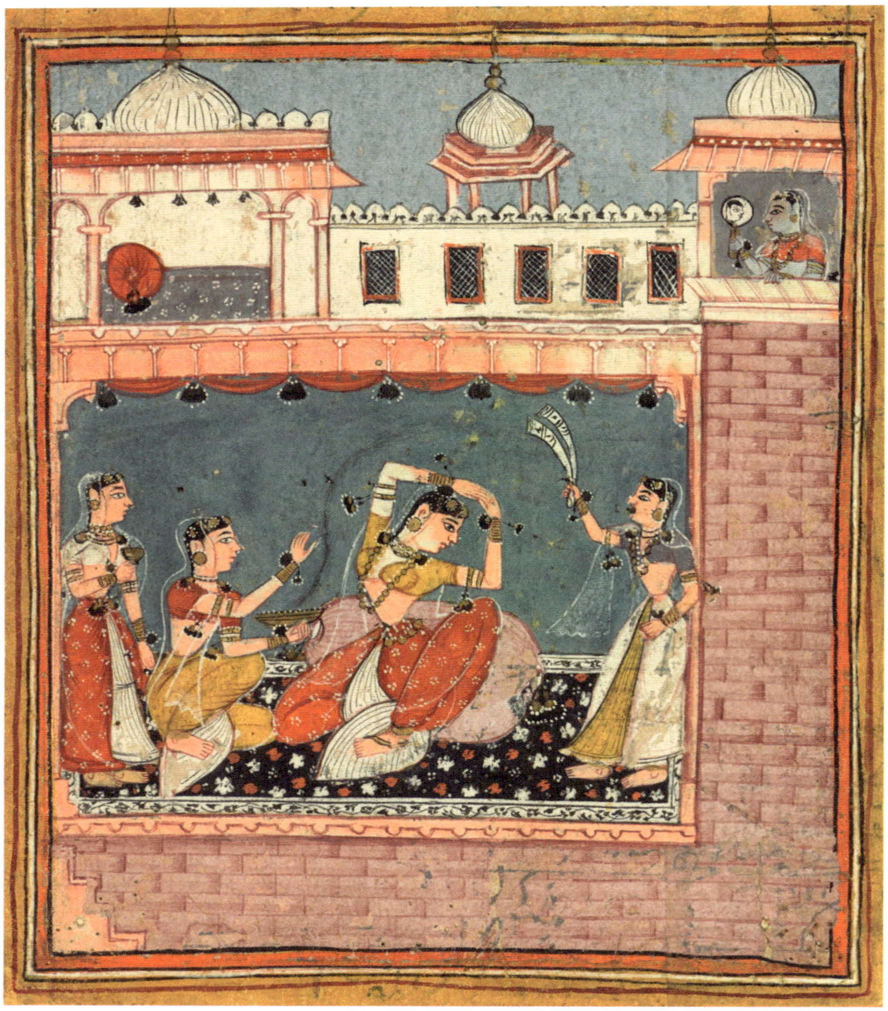

Desavarati Ragini, Marwar, Rajasthan, c. 1630.
Ragini paintings are part of a musical and visual tradition representing emotional states.

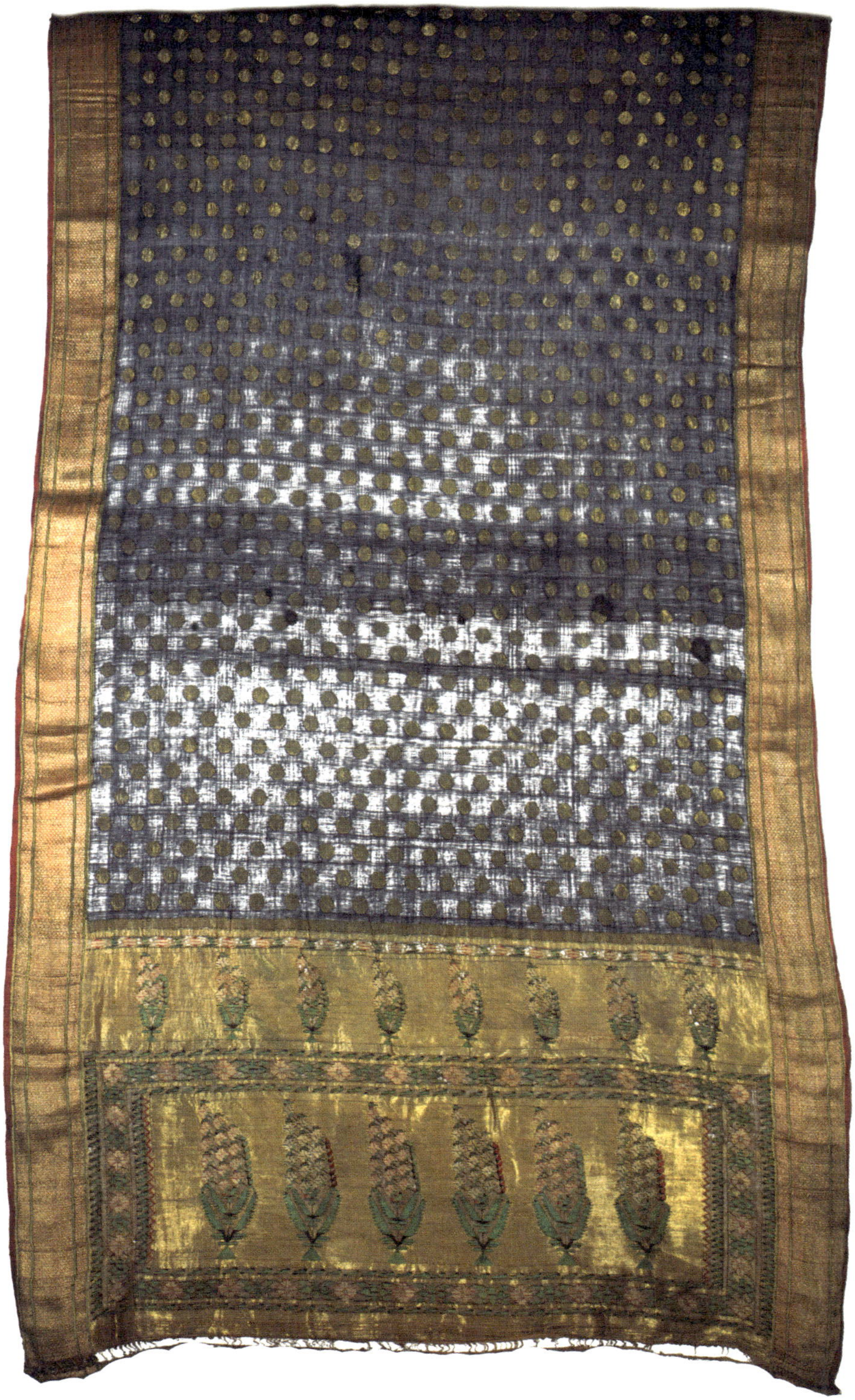

Blue patterned sari. Patterned saris often reflect regional design traditions and dyeing techniques.

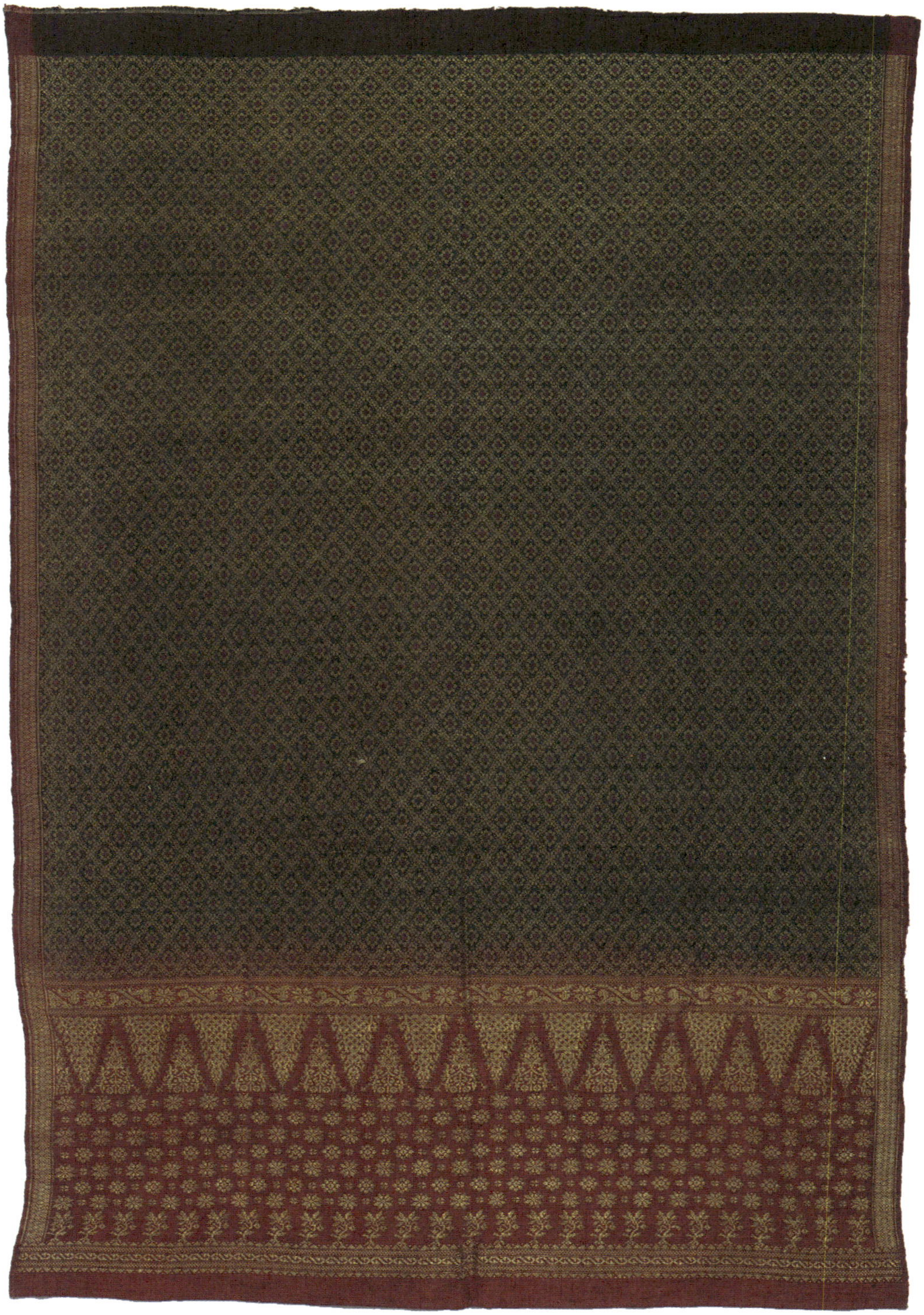

Sari fragment, 19th century. Fragments such as this one provide insight into weaving styles and material usage.

Motifs became visual languages. Geometric patterns, lotus blooms, vines and animal figures reflected both the environment and prevailing spiritual symbolism. Certain borders and motifs were tied to specific regions: Bengal's intricate Jamdani grids echoing riverine life; Gujarat's Bandhani dots mapping not only dyeing techniques, but seasonal festivals; and Kanjeevaram temple borders in Tamil Nadu connecting fabric to sacred architecture.

Patterns and pleats also carried subtle economic signals. The complexity of a weave indicated time, skill and the resources invested.

MUSLIN: WOVEN AIR OF BENGAL

Bengal muslin was once so fine it earned the name 'woven air'. Made from locally grown phuti karpas cotton, its threads were spun by hand to near-invisibility. Colonial demand and industrial disruption nearly erased the craft. Contemporary revival projects in West Bengal and Bangladesh are slowly restoring muslin's lost legacy.

A fine muslin sari of Bengal, so delicate it could pass through a ring, testified to centuries of artisan knowledge, specialized looms and a thriving textile economy. Coarser cottons for everyday wear, by contrast, reflected both practicality and local agricultural cycles.

Even colour choices mirrored availability and social value. Deep indigo and crimson were rare, expensive and often linked to

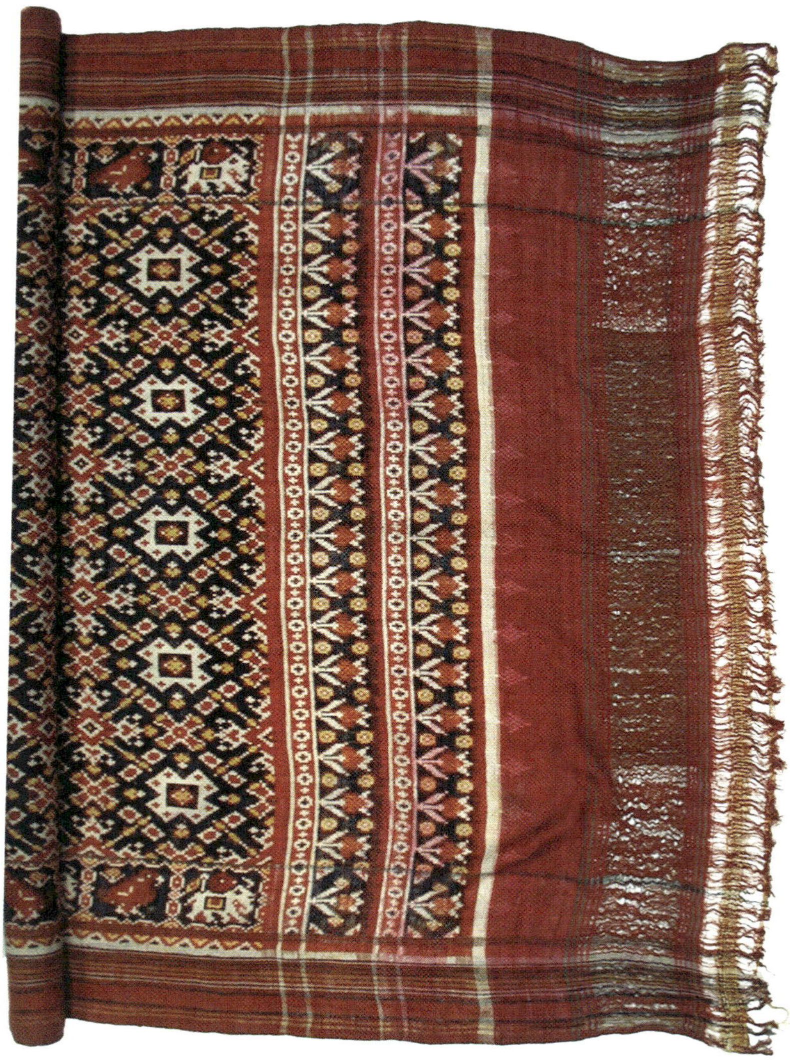

Wedding sari, Gujarat, India, 18th–19th century.
Wedding textiles were often richly decorated to signify auspiciousness.

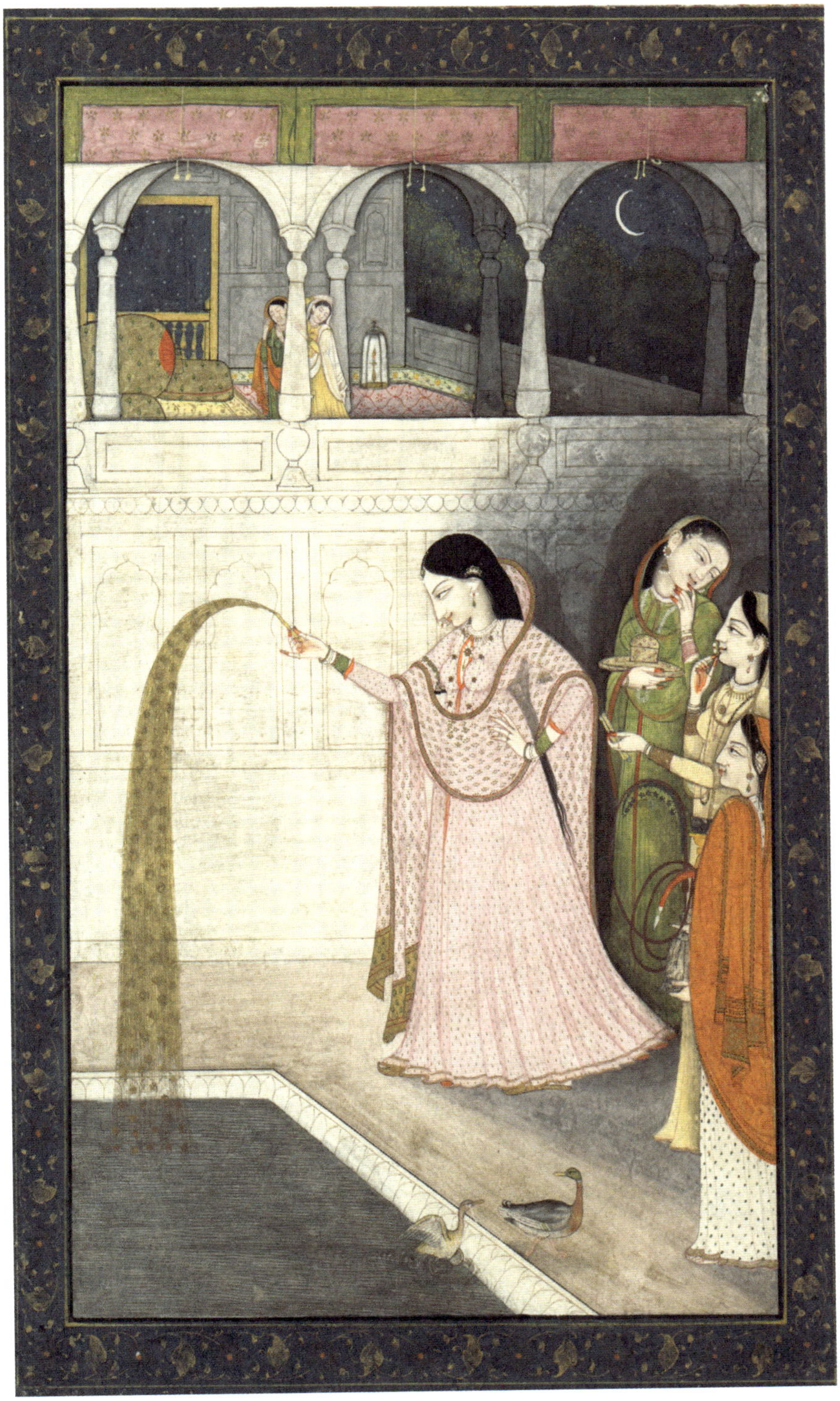

Lady holding a sparkler, ink painting, c. 1800.
Such imagery often reflects festive or celebratory contexts.

ceremonial or elite garments, while turmeric yellows and natural ochres were accessible to broader populations. In this way, the sari was both democratic and hierarchical – a fabric that could serve the daily and the divine, the commoner and the king.

Through its motifs, colours, patterns and textures, the sari became a living archive: of trade, of craft, of social and economic realities.

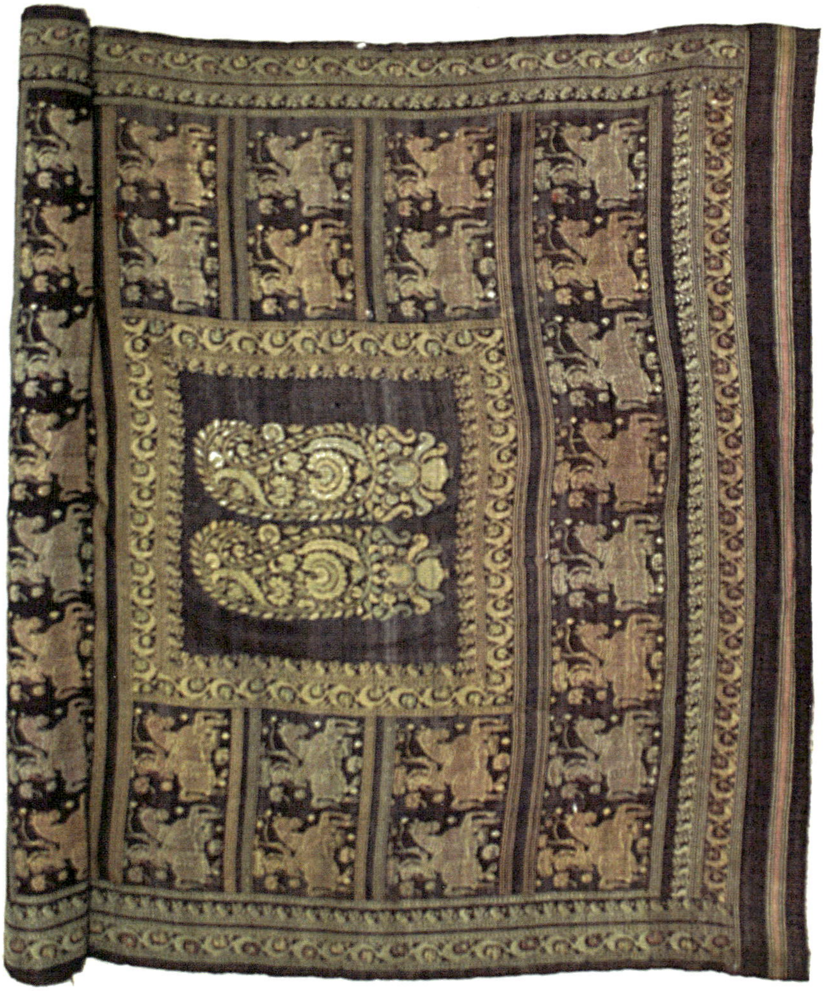

Sari, India, 18th century.
Earlier saris often used natural dyes derived from plants and minerals.

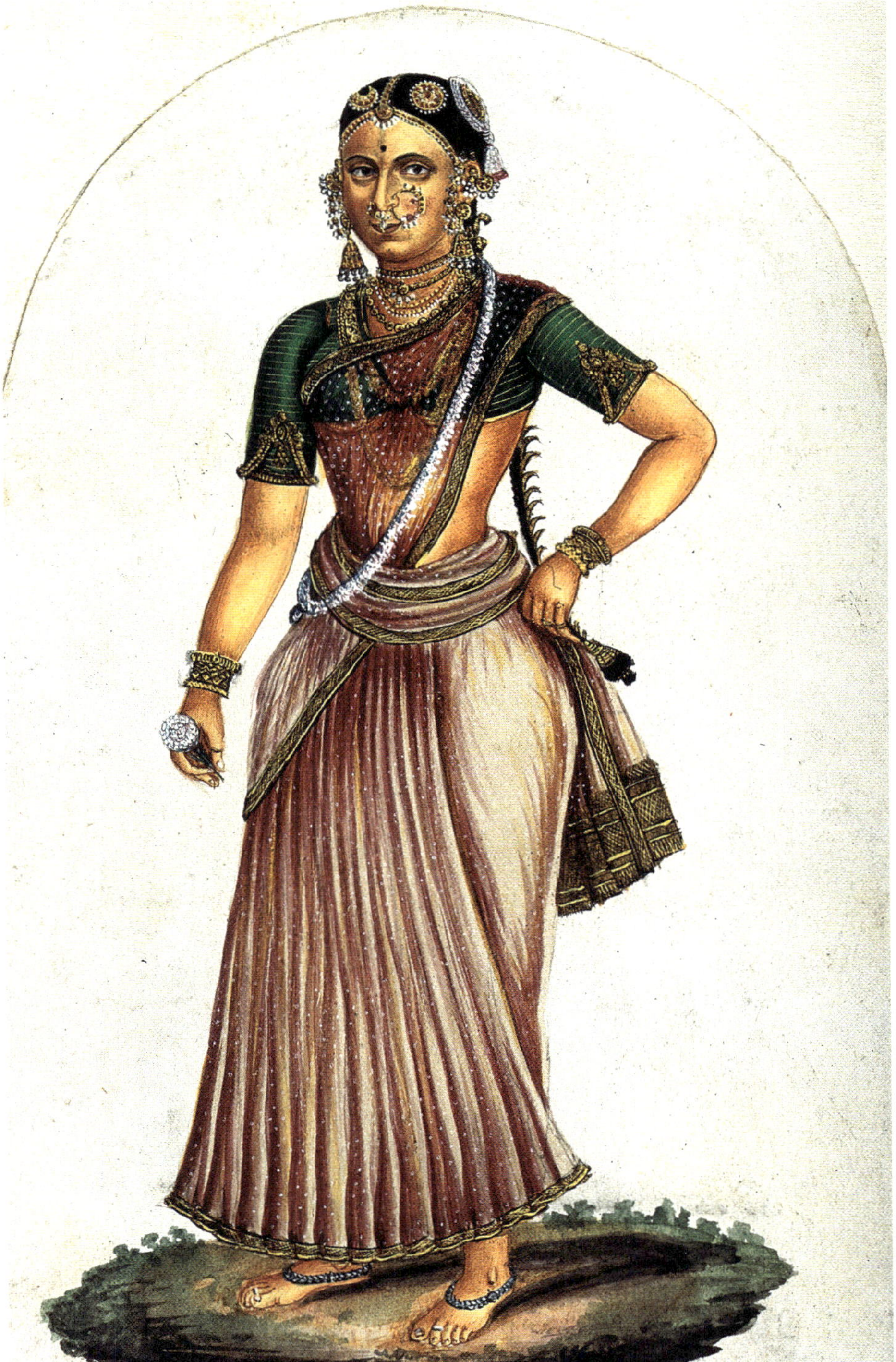

Indian woman dancer holding a flower, gouache painting, 19th century.
Dance imagery frequently appears in Indian painting traditions.

Every pleat and border was an imprint of labour, of commerce and of creativity – a testament to how economics and art were inseparable in the tapestry of Indian life.

These economic and artistic threads did not vanish with empire or invasion – they were woven into new contexts. When colonial rulers

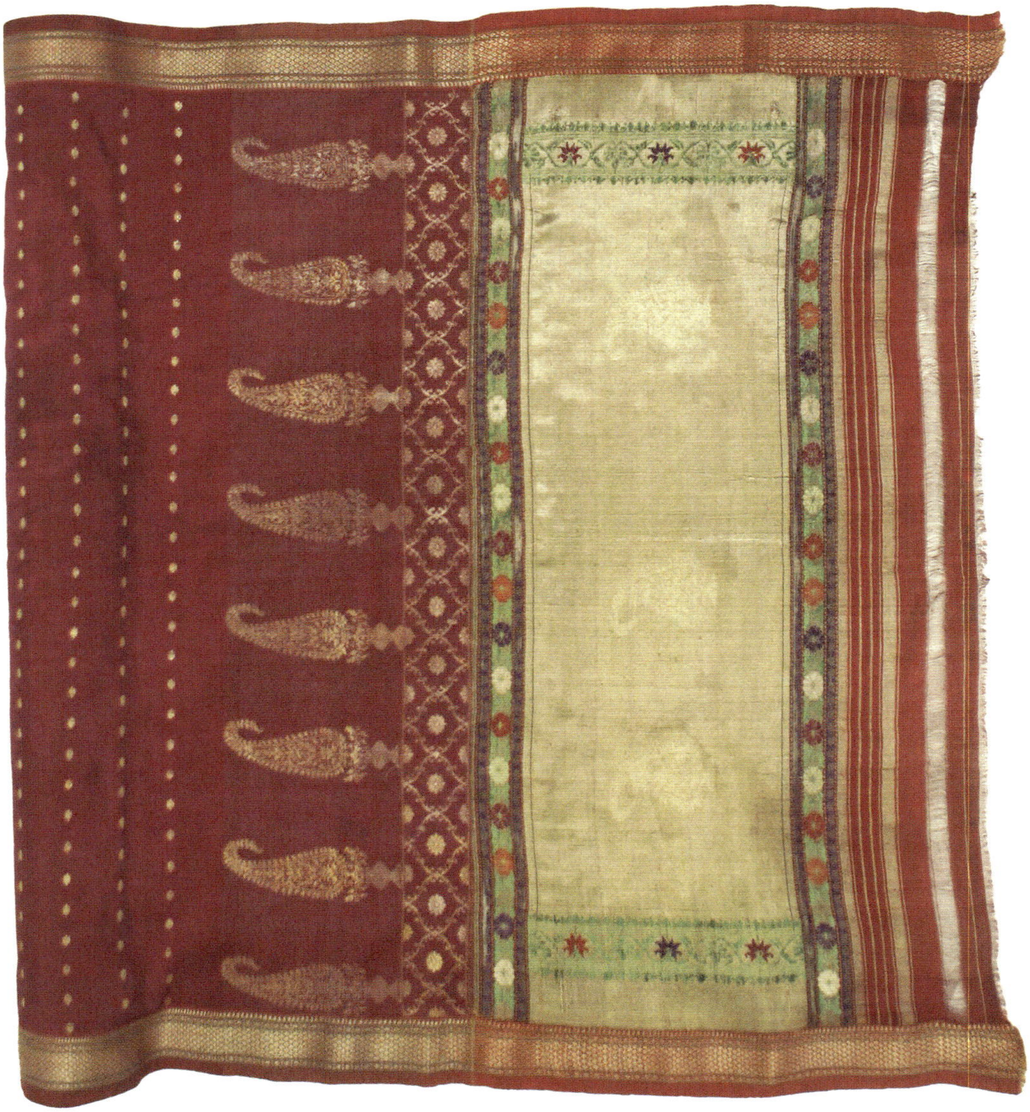

Silk sari, c. 1875. Silk weaving was associated with royal patronage and luxury textiles.

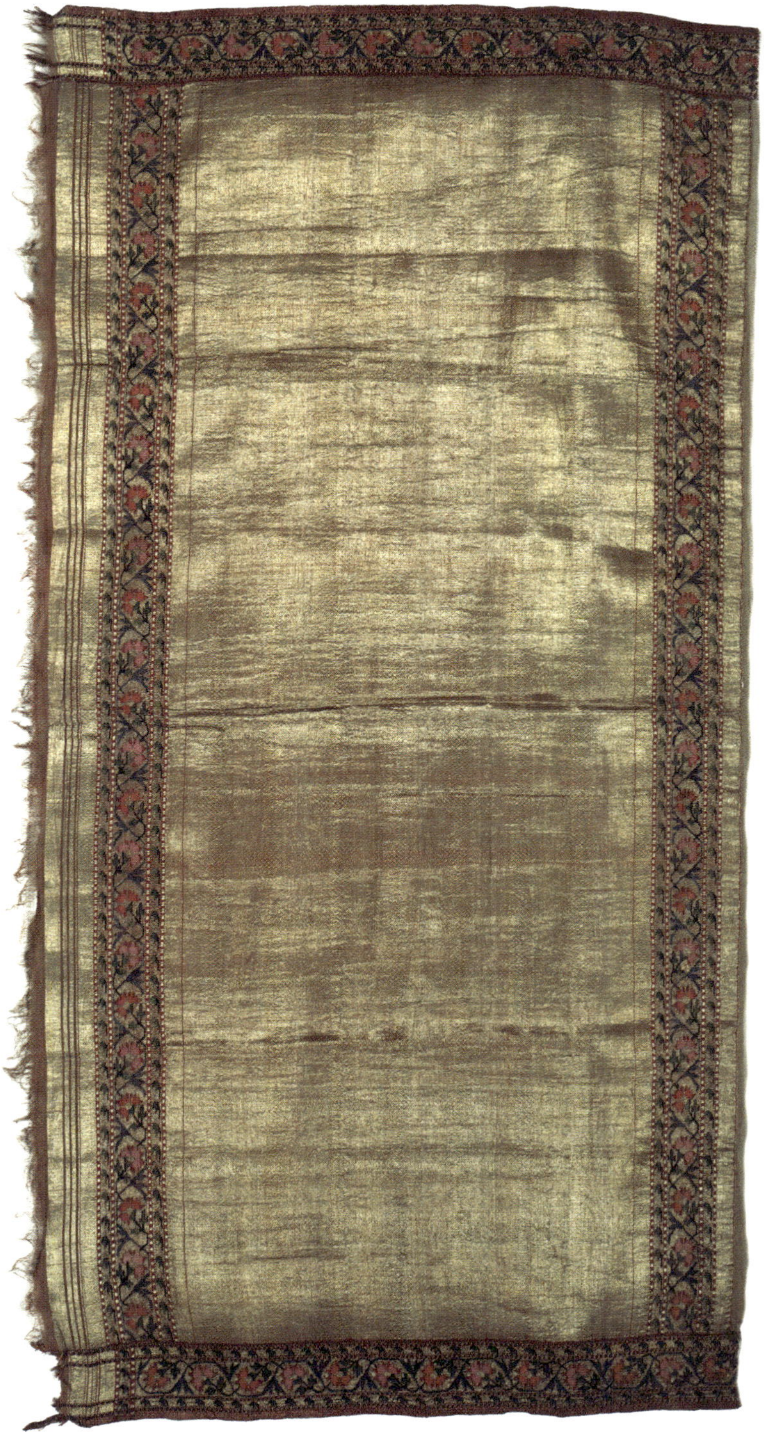

Part of a silk and metal-thread sari, 18th–19th century. Metal-thread weaving, known as zari, added decorative richness to textiles.

imposed foreign fabrics, industrial textiles and Victorian ideals of propriety, the sari absorbed and responded. Motifs, weaves and colours reflected resistance as much as beauty. Hand-spun khadi saris became statements of economic self-reliance during the Swadeshi Movement, while traditional patterns and regional weaves preserved centuries of craft and identity in

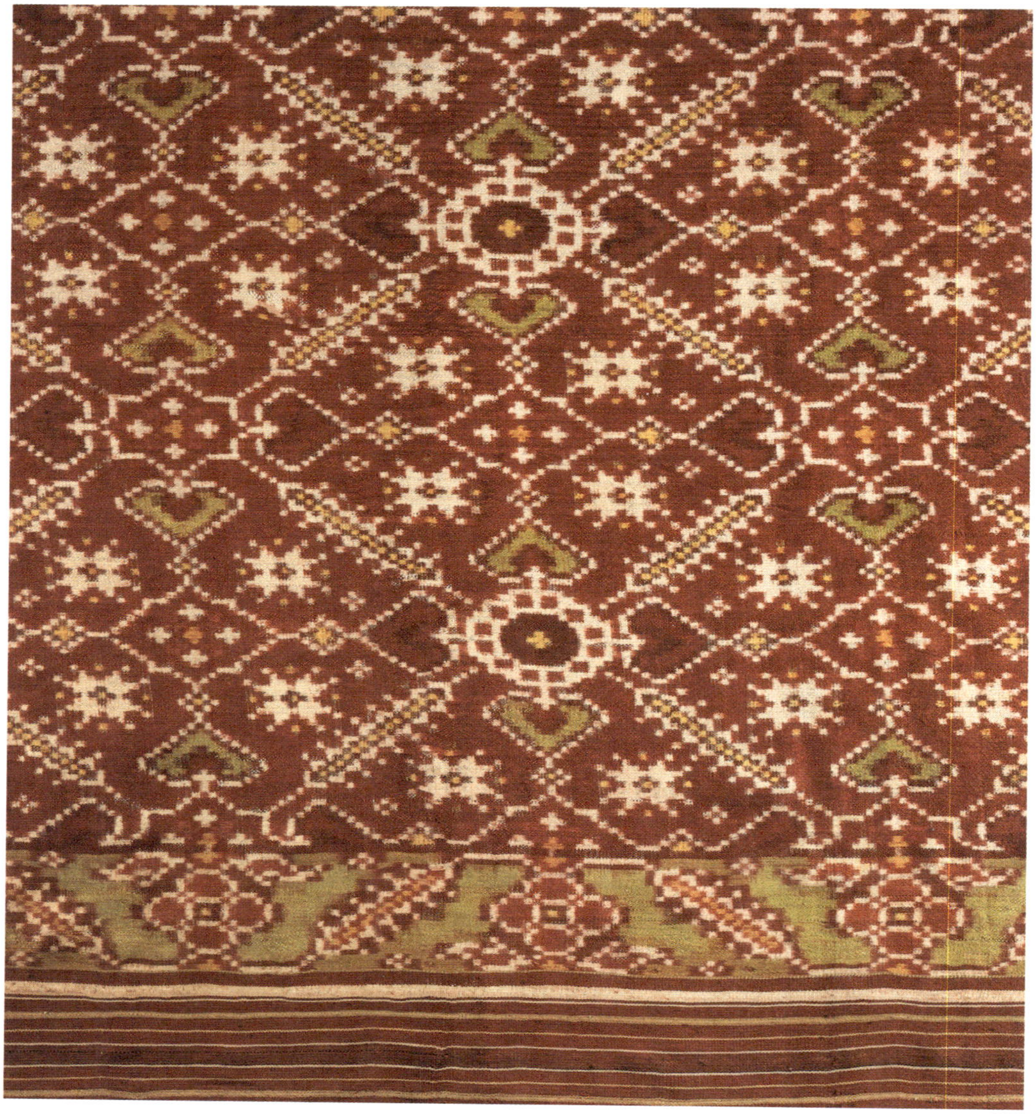

Patola silk sari with resist dye and gold thread, Patan, Gujarat, 19th century.

the face of imported materials. Post-independence, the sari continued to signal both pride and adaptability: silk borders, Jamdani grids and Bandhani dots were no longer just markers of local skill – they were symbols of national heritage, artisanal resilience and India's capacity to sustain its economy, artistry and cultural memory through cloth.

Sari as a Political Tool

With the arrival of British rule, the sari met its most complex transformation – not in design, but in meaning.

Colonial ideals, especially from Victorian England, considered the sari 'improper'. Mission schools encouraged Indian women to adopt stitched garments and cover their torsos fully. Blouses and petticoats became common not just out of convenience, but pressure.

Yet in this very era, the sari gained its sharpest political edge.

INDIGO: THE WORLD'S OLDEST BLUE

Indigo dye, extracted from the Indigofera plant, has coloured saris for millennia. India was once the world's primary indigo producer, exporting the dye across Asia and Europe. Deep indigo saris – especially in Bengal, Odisha and Rajasthan – signified durability, labour and everyday strength rather than ceremonial luxury.

During the Swadeshi Movement, Mahatma Gandhi urged Indians to boycott British textiles and embrace khadi: hand-spun, hand-woven fabric made from Indian cotton. In response, the sari evolved into a symbol of resistance. Women wore coarse, unembellished saris spun on the charkha, stepping into the political sphere for the first time – not with weapons, but with weaves.

Figures like Sarojini Naidu, Kasturba Gandhi and Kamala Nehru appeared in public wrapped in simple cotton saris. What they wore delivered a clear message: We are our own country. We will wear our own cloth.

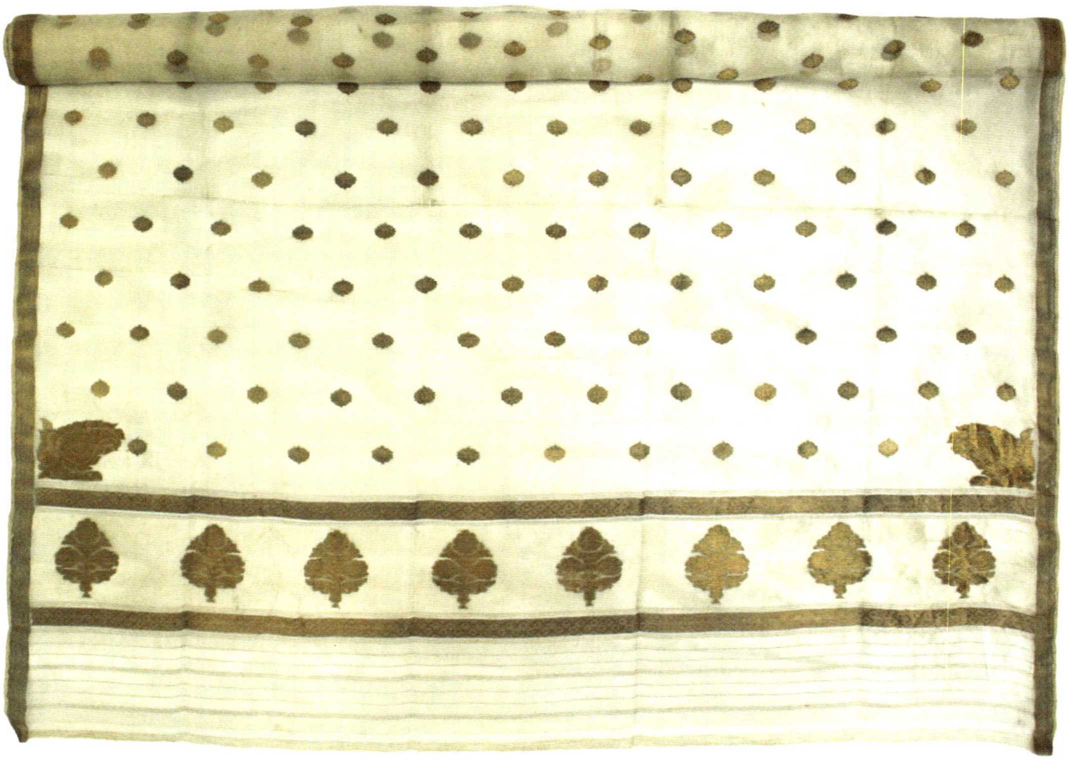

Indian sari, 19th century. Regional styles became more distinct during this period.

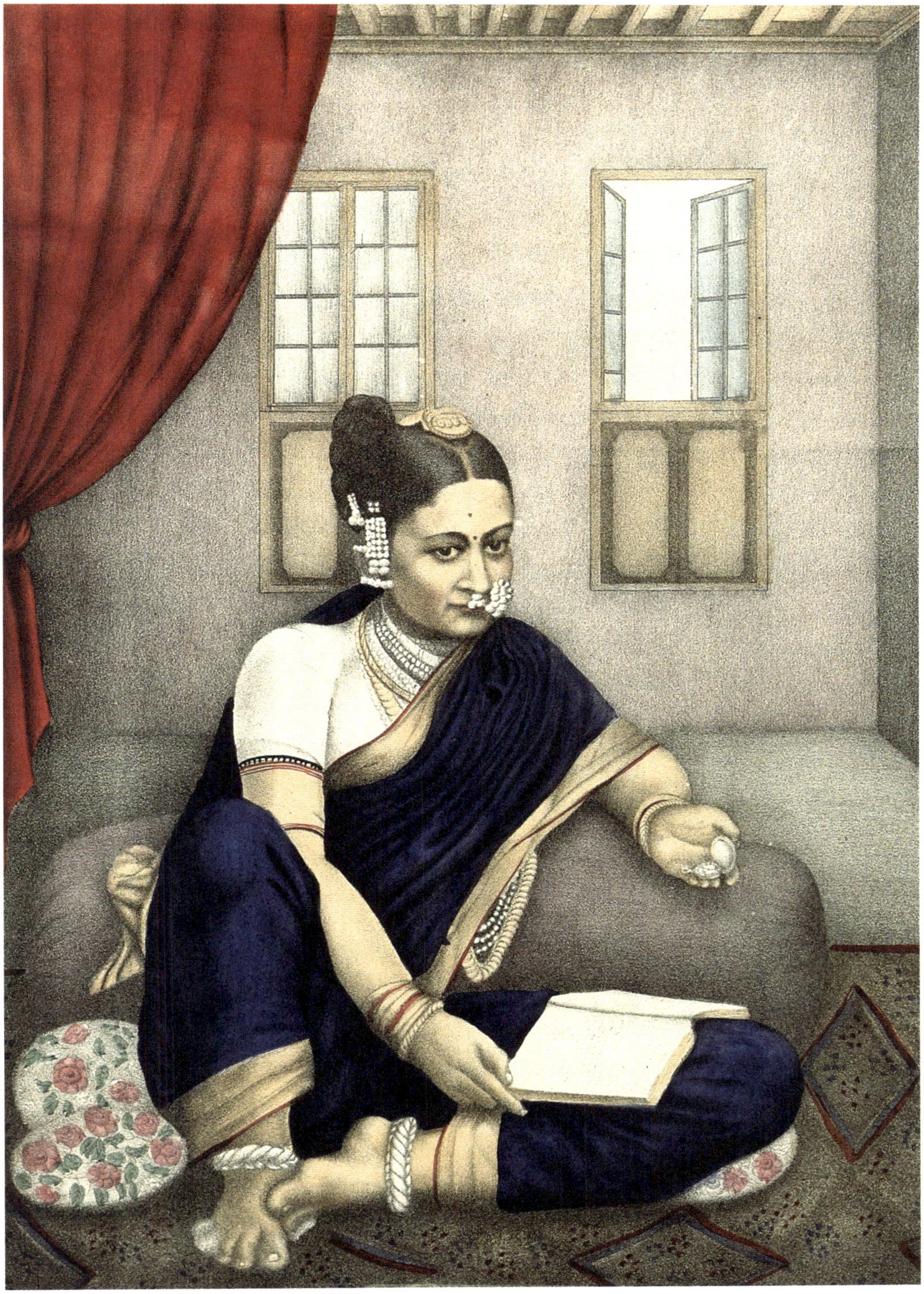

Seated Indian woman with a pocket watch, chromolithograph, late 19th century. Chromolithographs were widely used for mass-produced imagery in the colonial era.

Post-independence, this symbolism only deepened. Indira Gandhi's trademark handloom saris, often in muted shades, became a visual language of leadership. Even today, when women take to the streets in protest, or speak on global stages draped in 'six yards', they are reclaiming not just history, but space.

The sari continues to walk into courts, parliaments, protests and classrooms. It is not just tradition. It is a strategy. It is a statement.

A Living Archive

Through centuries, the sari became a canvas for more than just personal expression – it reflected class, caste, geography and climate. In the hot, dry regions of Rajasthan and Gujarat, lightweight cottons and bright dyes gave birth to Bandhani saris. In the lush, temple-studded south, Kanjeevarams

SILK BEFORE BORDERS

Silk reached India long before the Silk Road was formally established. By 2450 BCE, Indian weavers were reeling silk locally. Unlike Chinese silk, Indian silk traditions evolved independently – resulting in heavier, textured weaves like Kanjeevaram and wild silks like Tussar, which retain their natural irregularities.

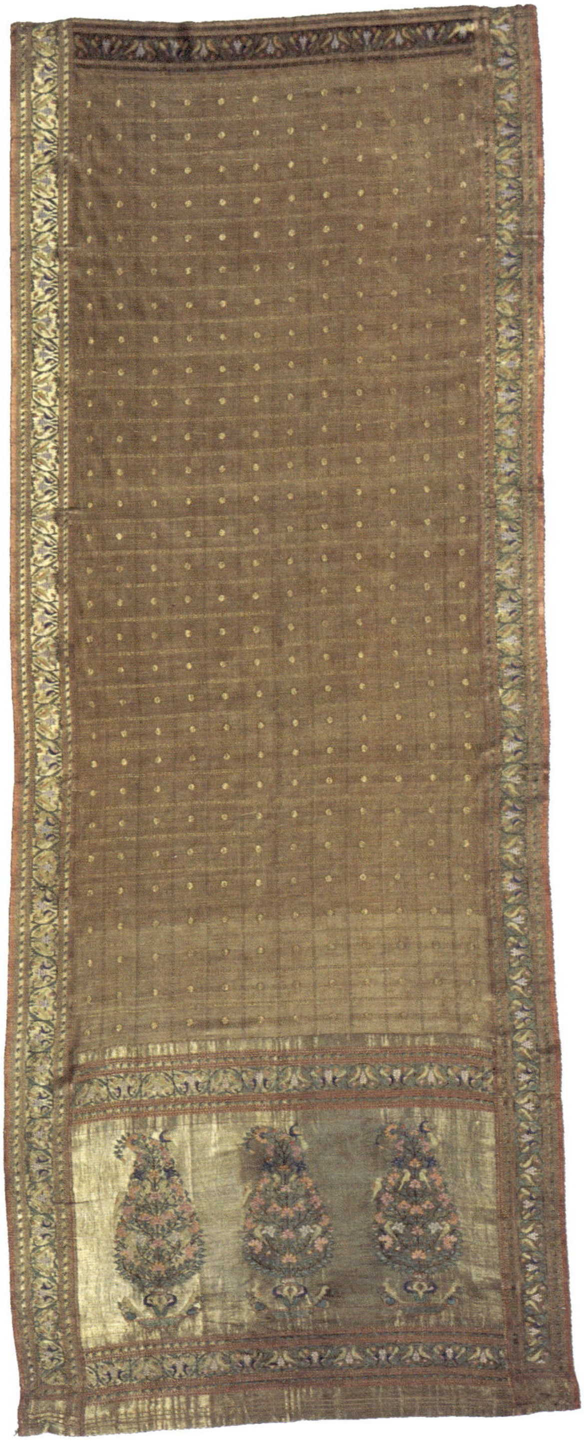

Wedding sari, India, 19th century (possibly Paithan or Chanderi). Such textiles were often passed down through generations.

shimmered in silk and gold. In Bengal, soft muslins and intricate Jamdani weaves whispered stories of river deltas and colonial resistance.

Each region, each loom, each weaver contributed to the sari's evolution.

After independence in 1947, the sari experienced a kind of revival. It wasn't just a traditional garment anymore; it was a symbol of pride, of belonging, of identity reclaimed. Films in the 1950s and '60s cemented its glamorous appeal. Actresses like Meena Kumari, Madhubala and later, Rekha, gave the sari a silver-screen permanence. In political arenas, cultural festivals and everyday life, the sari remained – evolving, yes, but always rooted.

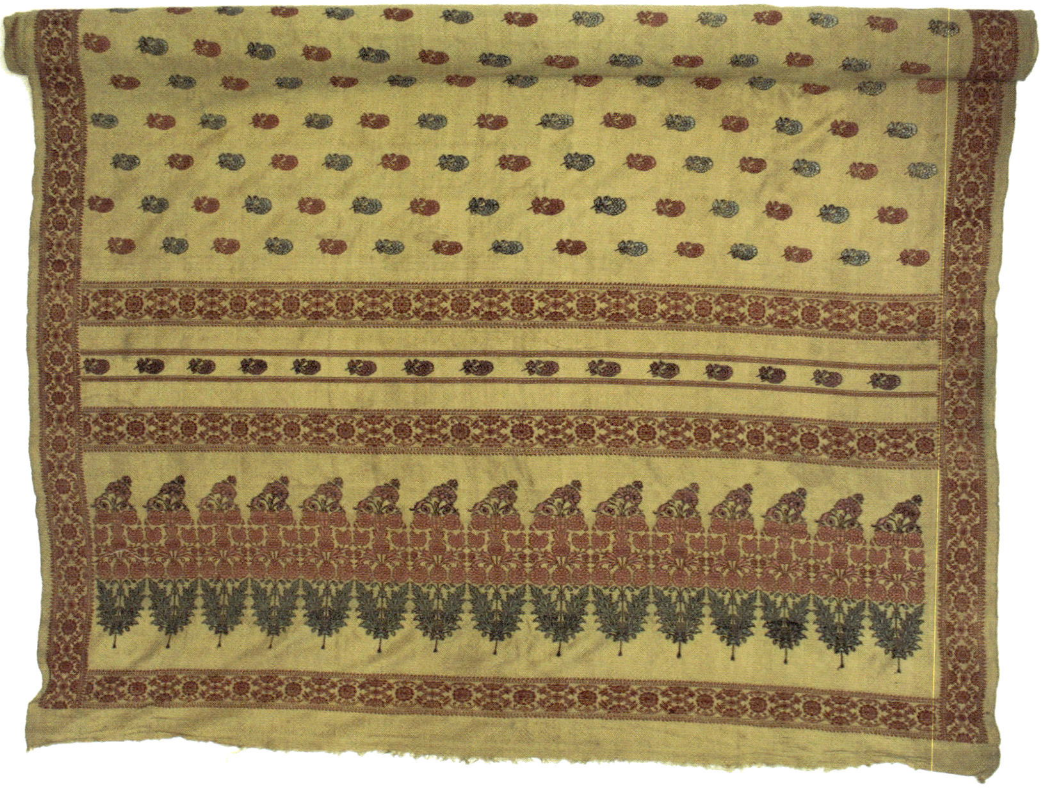

Silk sari, India, 19th century. Silk fibers allowed for finer weaving and intricate detailing.

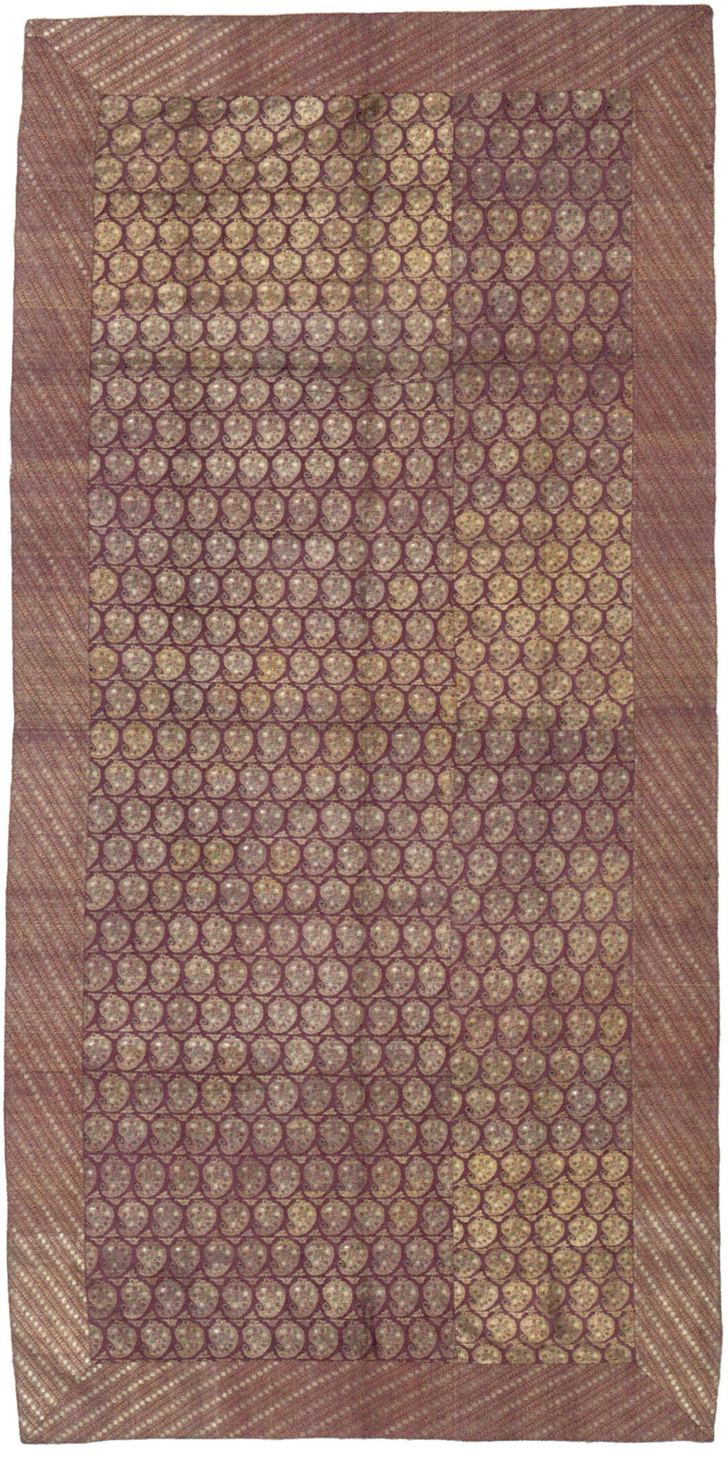

Red silk and gold sari, India, c. 1875–1900.

Survival of Ancient Styles

In Kerala, the mundum neriyathum – a *dhoti*-like lower garment with a shawl – still survives, echoing the old *antariya* and uttariya. Across southern India, literary and visual records – from the *Silappadikaram* to Raja Ravi Varma – capture drapes that reveal movement, midriff and sacred symbolism. In this continuity, we glimpse how the sari is both a descendant of ancient dress and a living garment that absorbed regional customs without severing its roots.

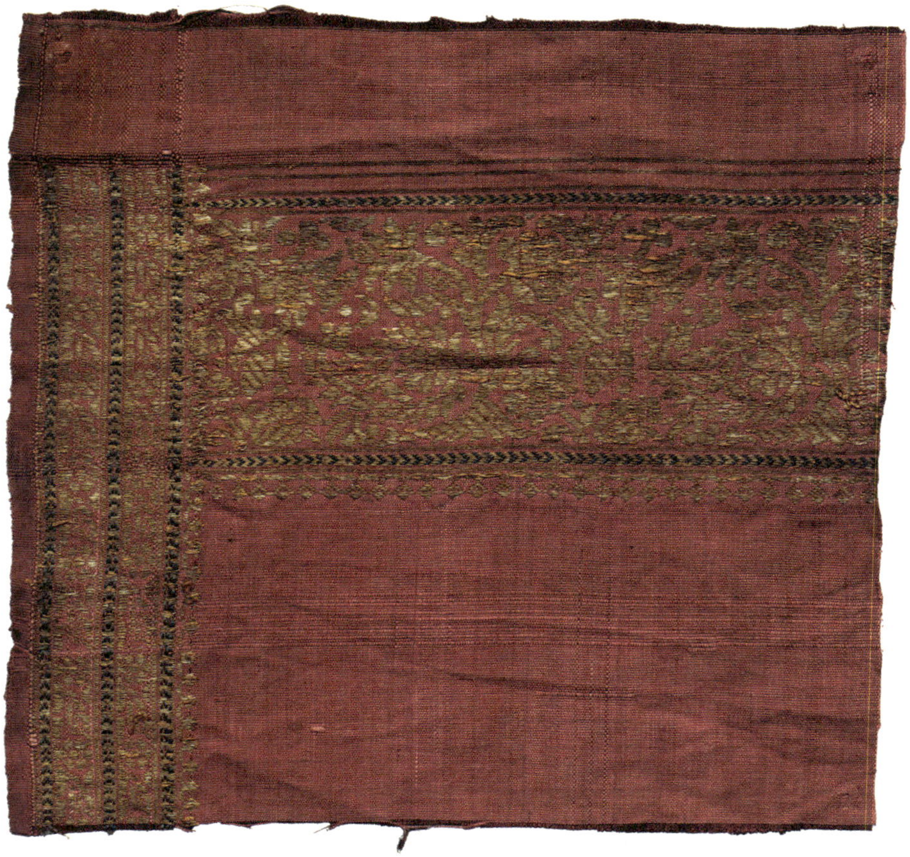

Sari fragment with silk and metal thread, 19th century. The combination of silk and metal threads indicates ceremonial use.

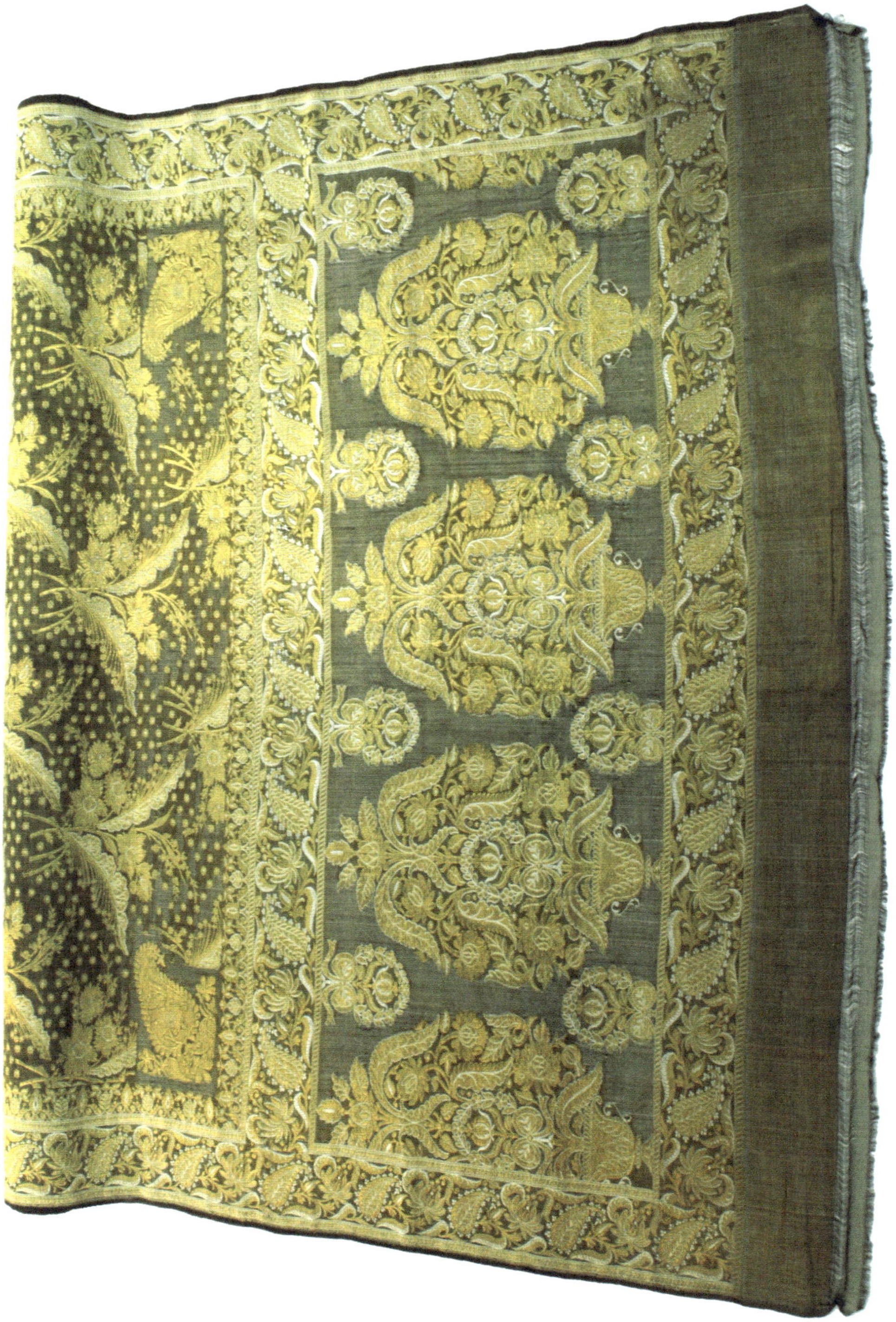

Grey sari with gold and silver leaf motifs, 19th century. Metallic motifs were commonly associated with festive attire.

A Fabric that Lives On

What is extraordinary about the sari is that despite its long journey through history, it has never needed to be 'reinvented' to stay relevant. It has quietly adapted – shifting fabrics, changing drapes, allowing for new expressions – while staying true to its original form. It has survived invasions, colonization, industrialization and globalization. And it has done so because it is both incredibly simple and endlessly complex.

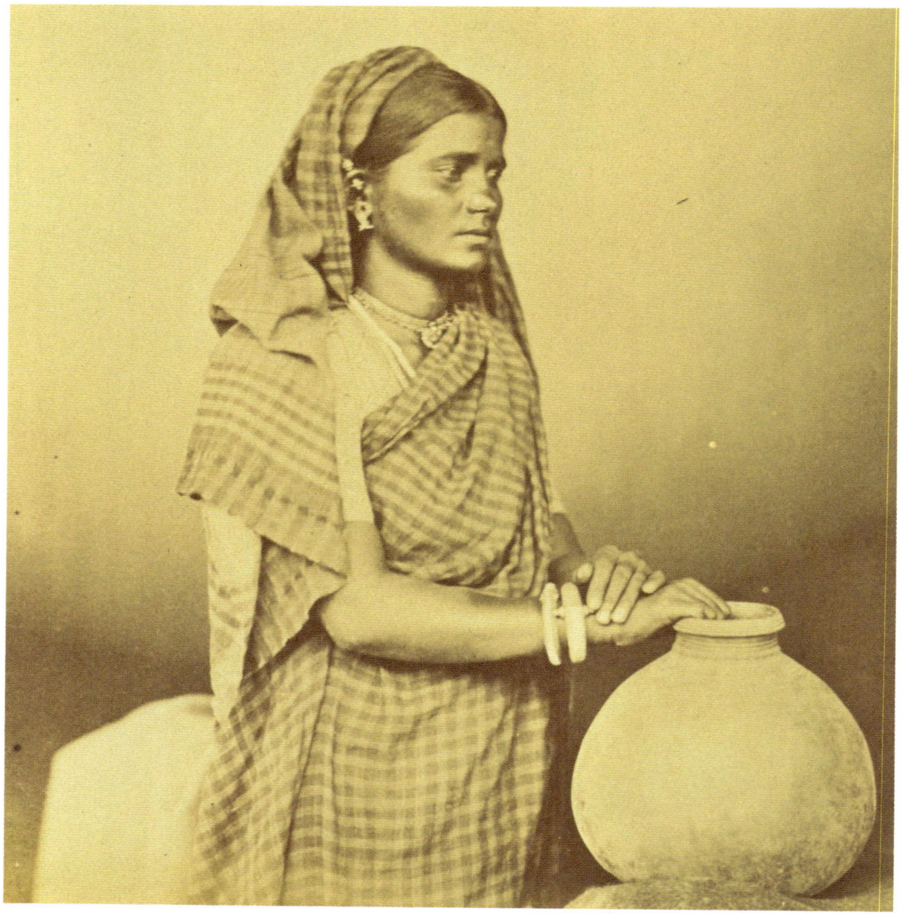

Portrait of a woman, c. 1870. Portrait photography became more common in India during the colonial period.

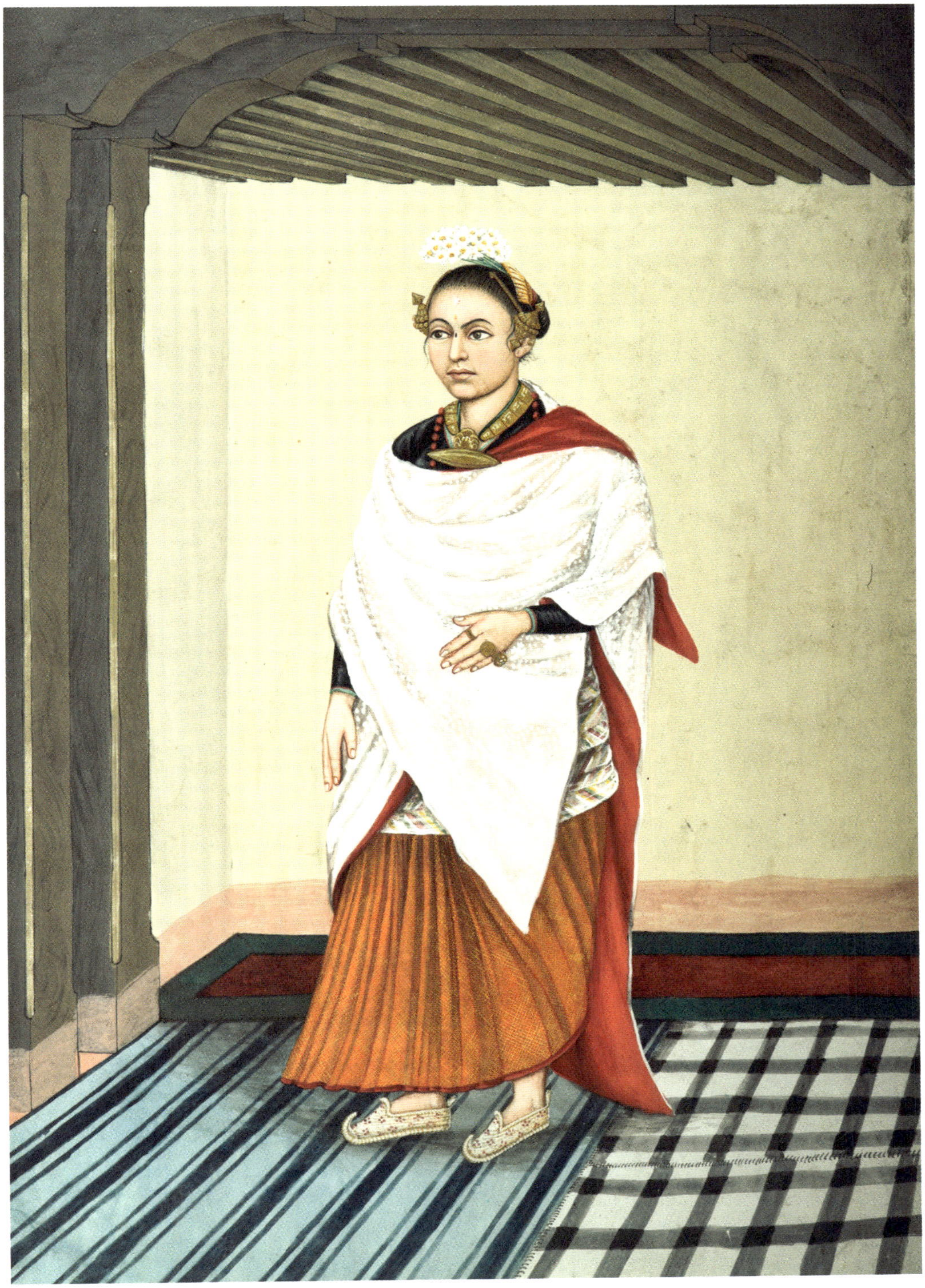

A Newar woman, Nepal, watercolour and gold on paper, c. 1860–1900.
Newar art is known for its detailed ornamentation and cultural symbolism.

However, the story of the sari is not only about who wears it: it is also about who makes it. For every historical moment it has witnessed, there have been weavers, dyers, printers and embroiderers whose skills have kept its threads alive. In every region, the sari carries the texture of local soil, the rhythm of local hands and the knowledge passed carefully from one artisan to the next.

To understand the sari fully, we must move away from the archives and venture into the workshops. Into the villages where looms hum

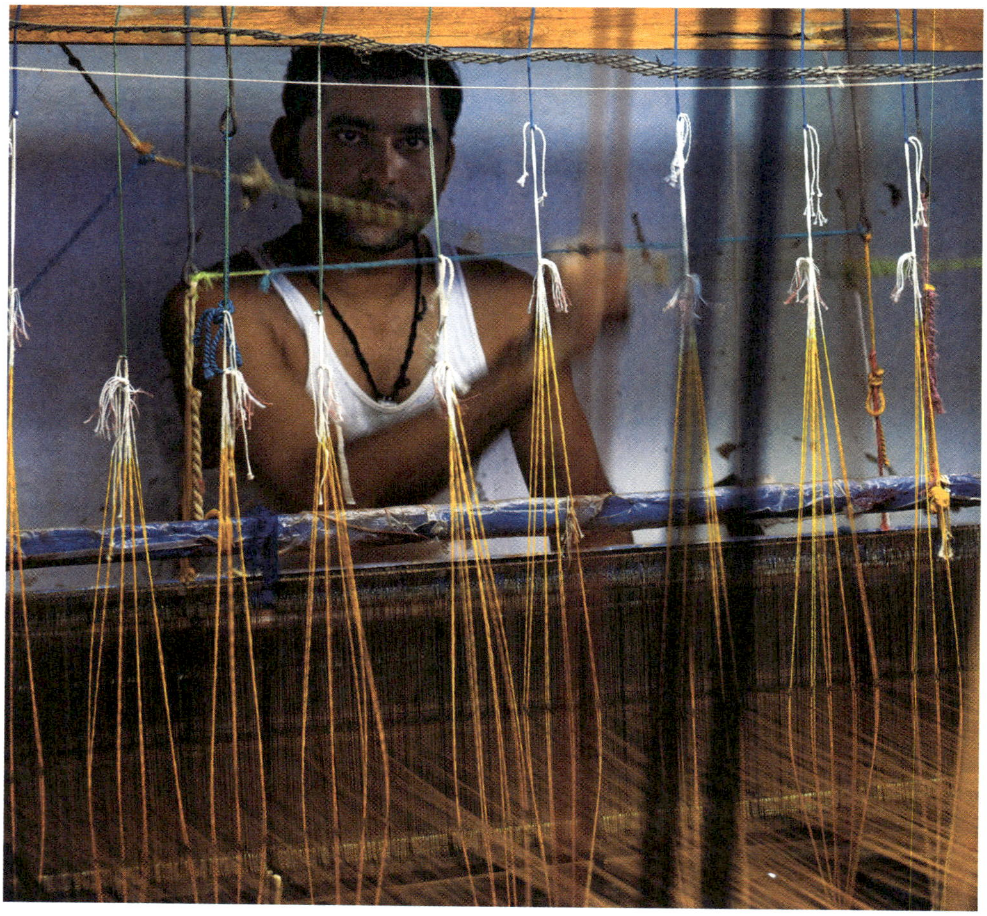

Worker weaving a sari in a traditional workshop, Maheshwar, Madhya Pradesh, India.

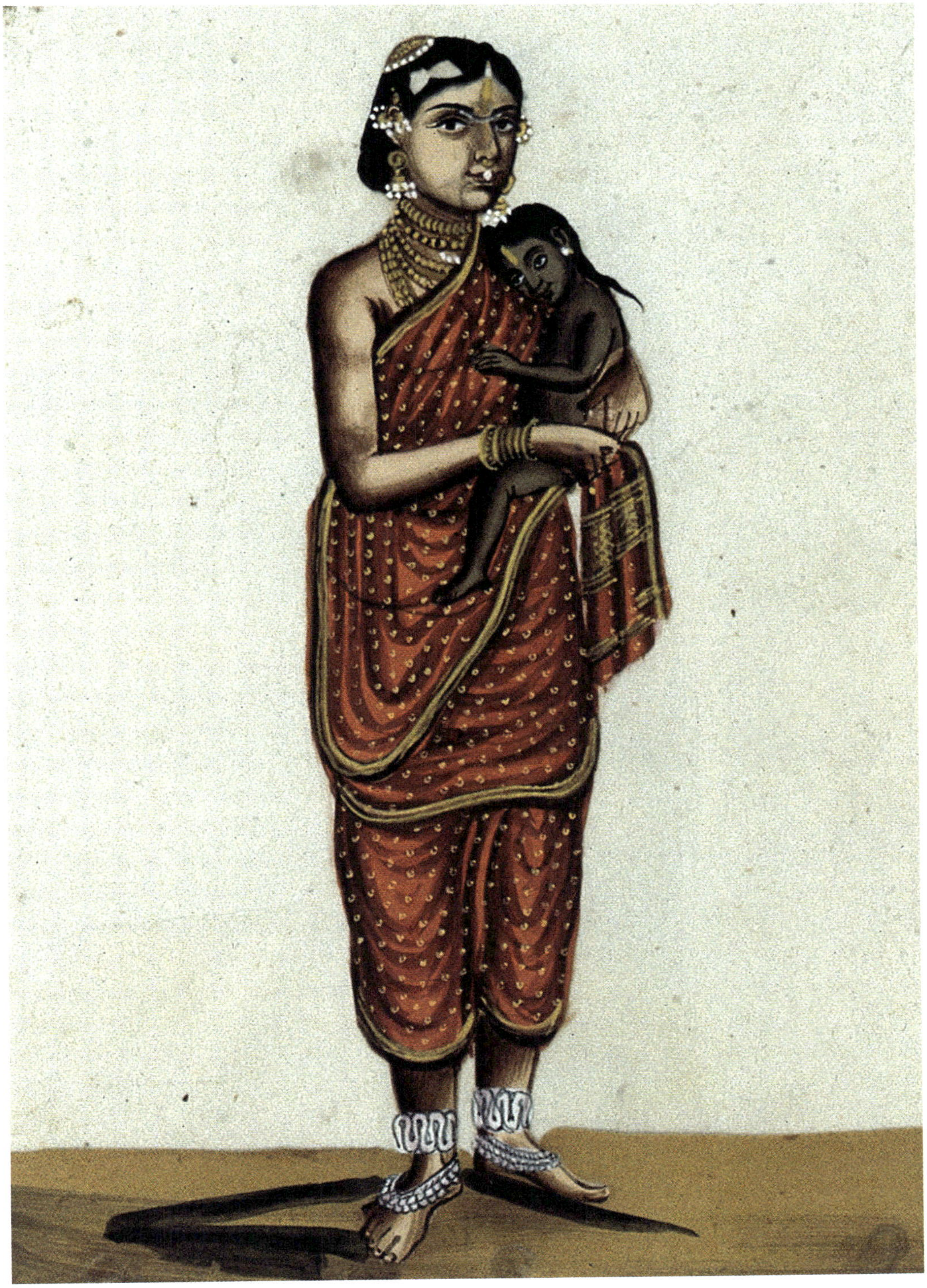

A Brahmin's wife holding her child, gouache painting on mica, 19th century.

Indian saris. The variety reflects the diversity of regional textile traditions across India.

through the afternoon. Into the dye pits where colour clings to cotton and silk. Into the state-specific traditions where a weave or motif is not merely decoration, but a signature of identity.

This is where the next chapter begins: where history meets craft, and every sari is born.

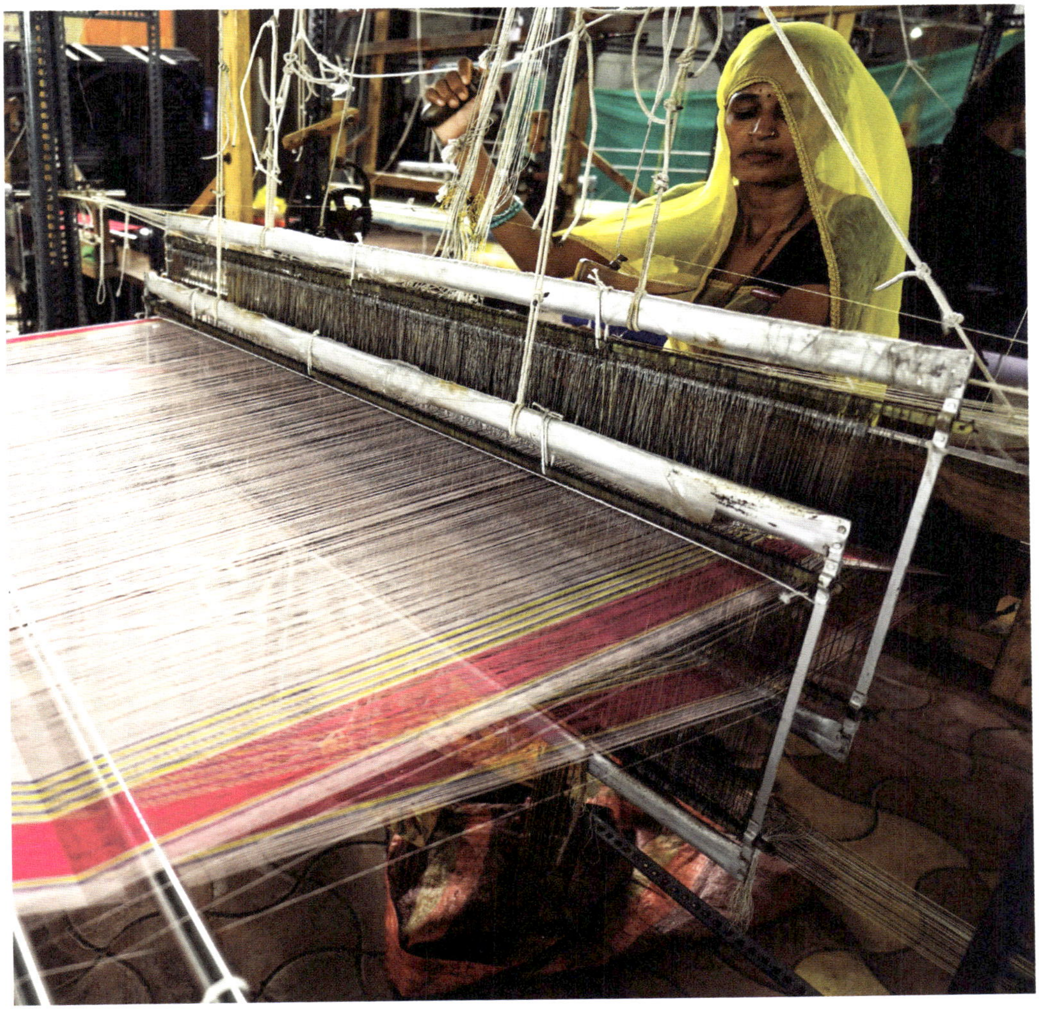

Worker weaving a Banarasi sari on a handloom in a workshop, India.

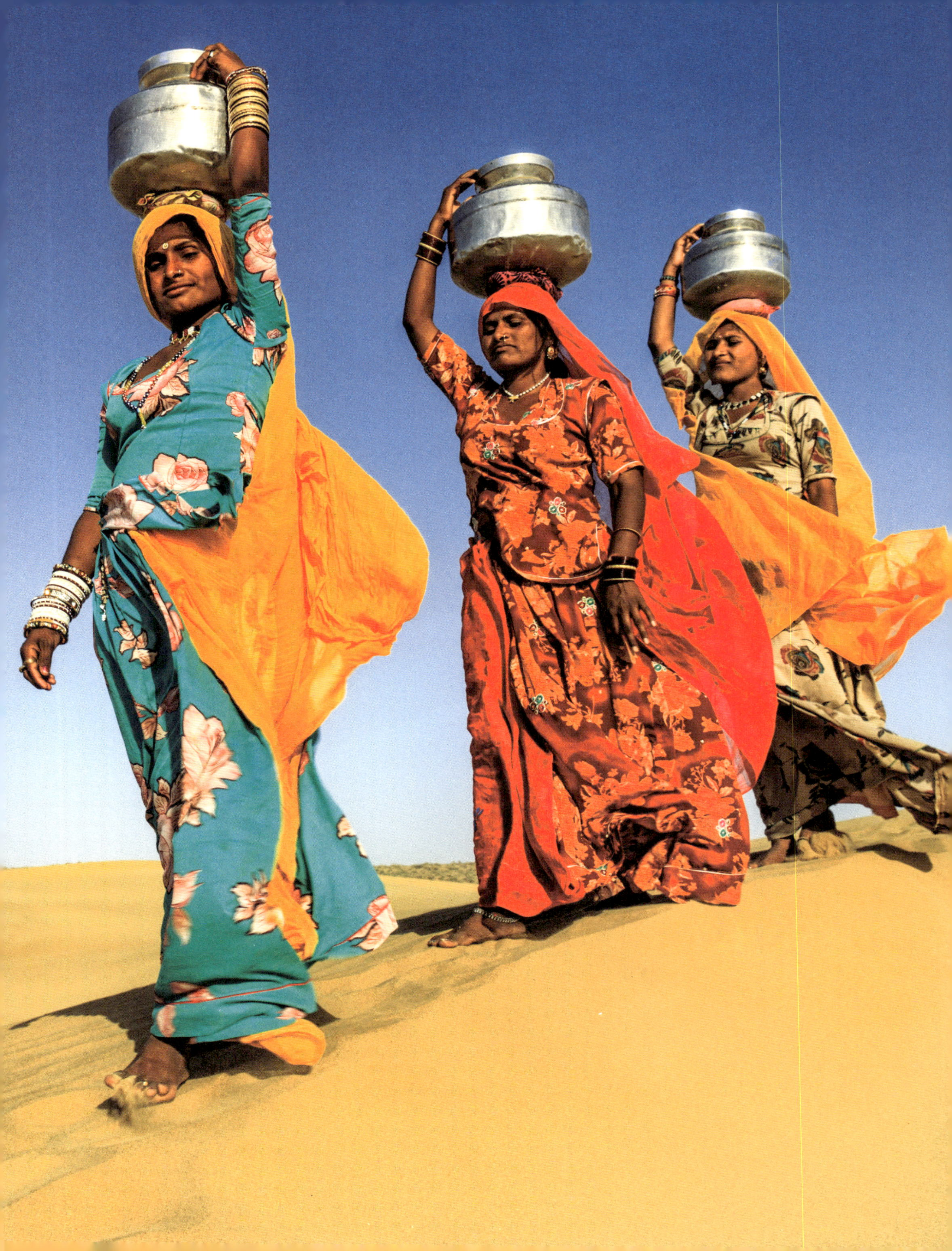

CHAPTER 2

कारीगर की आवाज़: साड़ियाँ कैसे बनती हैं

The Artisan's Voice: How Saris are Made

History shows us how the sari has survived dynasties, colonialism and reinvention. Yet survival alone does not explain its power. To truly understand the sari, we must leave the halls of history and step into smaller, humbler spaces: courtyards where yarn is sun-dried, workshops alive with looms, villages where entire families live by the rhythm of thread.

The sari may look like a simple 'six yards' of fabric, but it conceals an astonishingly complex journey. Behind every drape is a choreography of fibre, dye, loom and hand. It is here, in these artisanal processes, that the sari reveals its truest voice.

Selection and Preparation of Raw Materials

The journey of every sari begins before it reaches the loom, in the choice of raw material.

Rajasthani women crossing sand dunes carrying water pots, Thar Desert, Rajasthan, India. Carrying water over long distances is a common practice in arid regions.

Cotton

In regions like Bengal and Andhra, cotton has been cultivated for millennia. The finest long-staple cotton balls are harvested and ginned to remove seeds. The fibres are then carded and combed into soft slivers. In older traditions, rural women would sit together in courtyards spinning cotton on a *charkha*. The yarn they produced could be remarkably fine. Muslins from Bengal were once so delicate they were described as 'woven air'.

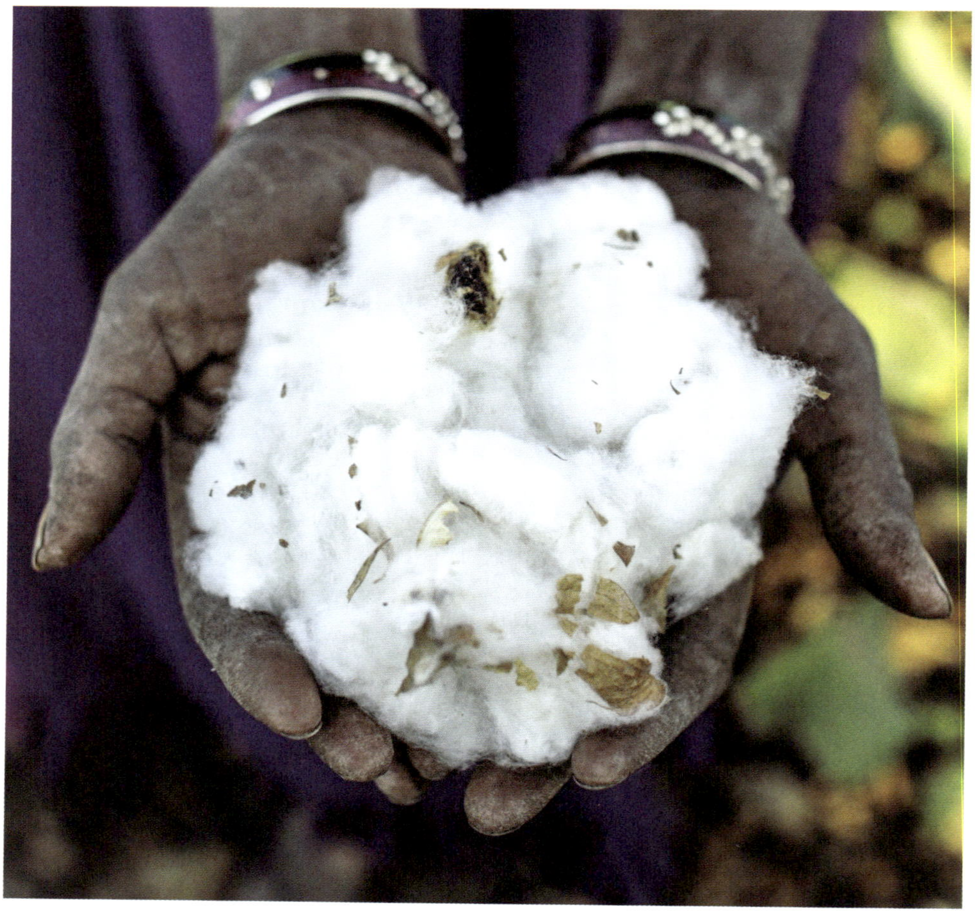

Worker displaying hand-picked cotton bolls, Wankaner, Gujarat, India. Cotton is a primary raw material in traditional sari production.

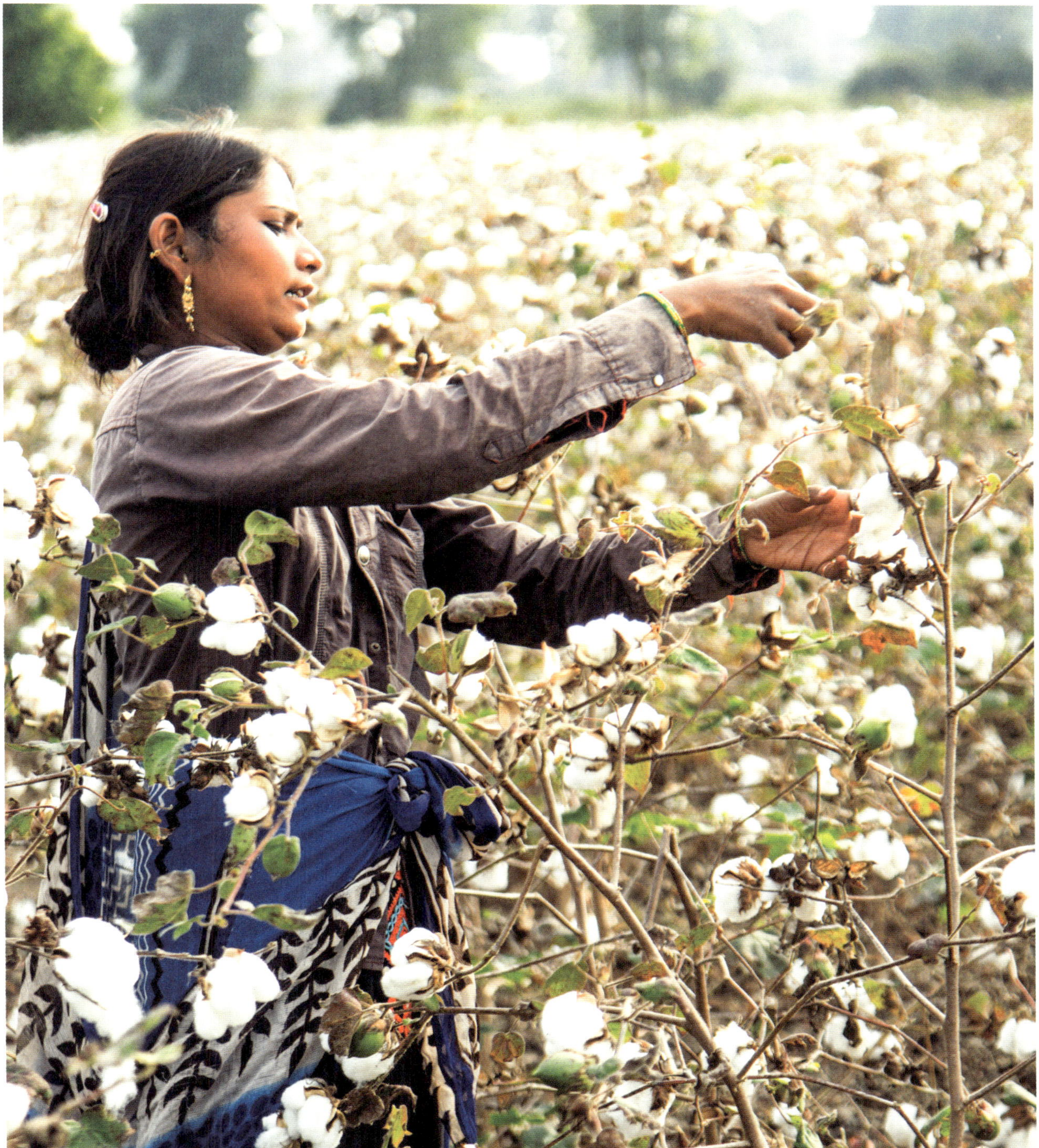

Indian woman harvesting cotton, Maharashtra, India.
Cotton farming remains a key part of India's textile economy.

Silk

In the temple towns of Tamil Nadu or the bustling lanes of Banaras, silk reigns. Extracted from cocoons of the mulberry silkworm, the filaments are reeled, boiled and degummed to remove their sticky coating, revealing lustrous, smooth strands. For saris like the Kanjeevaram, the silk is combined with *zari* threads of fine silver or gold wrapped around silk. Borders woven with *zari* shimmer not only with beauty, but with ritual significance.

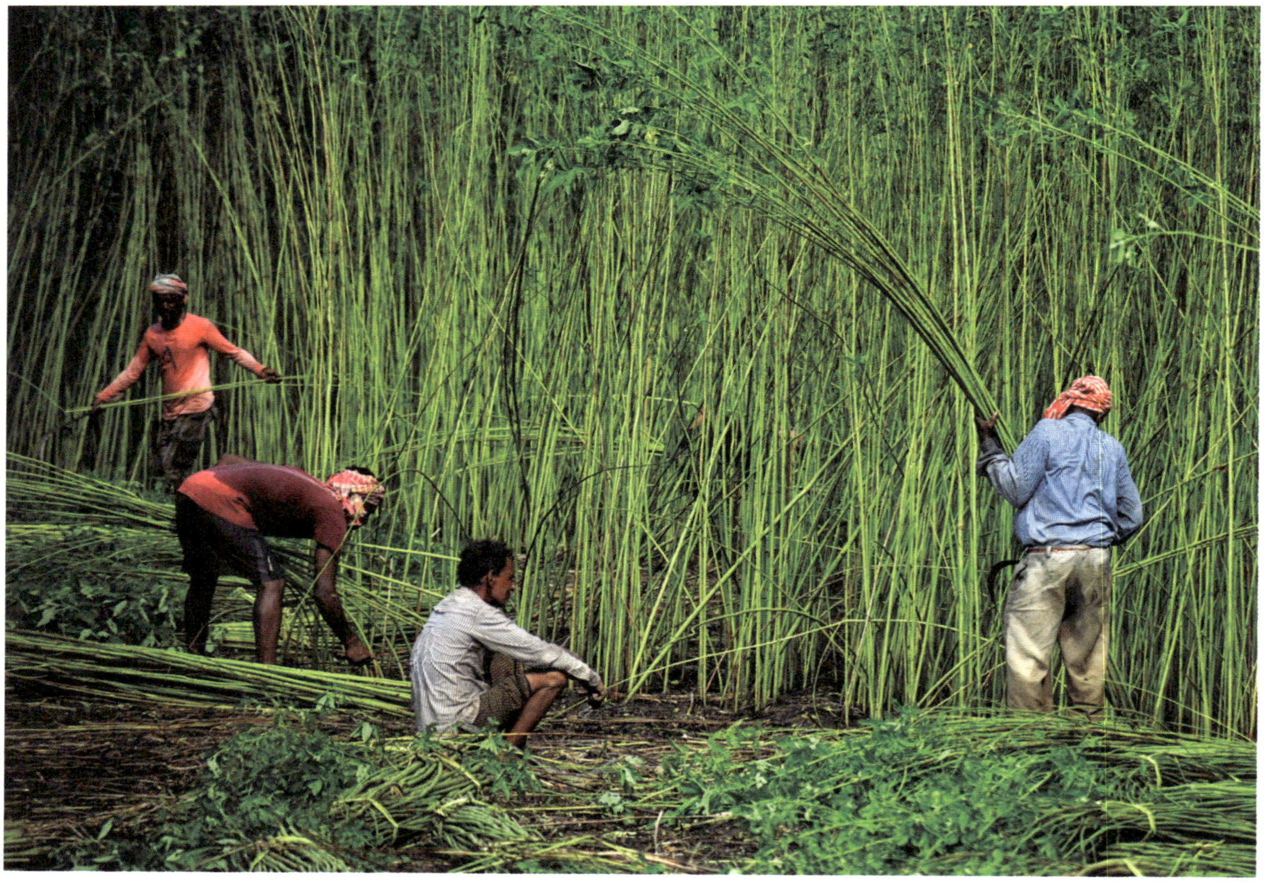

Farmers harvesting jute in wetlands, West Bengal, India.
Jute fibers are commonly used for coarse textiles and rope-making.

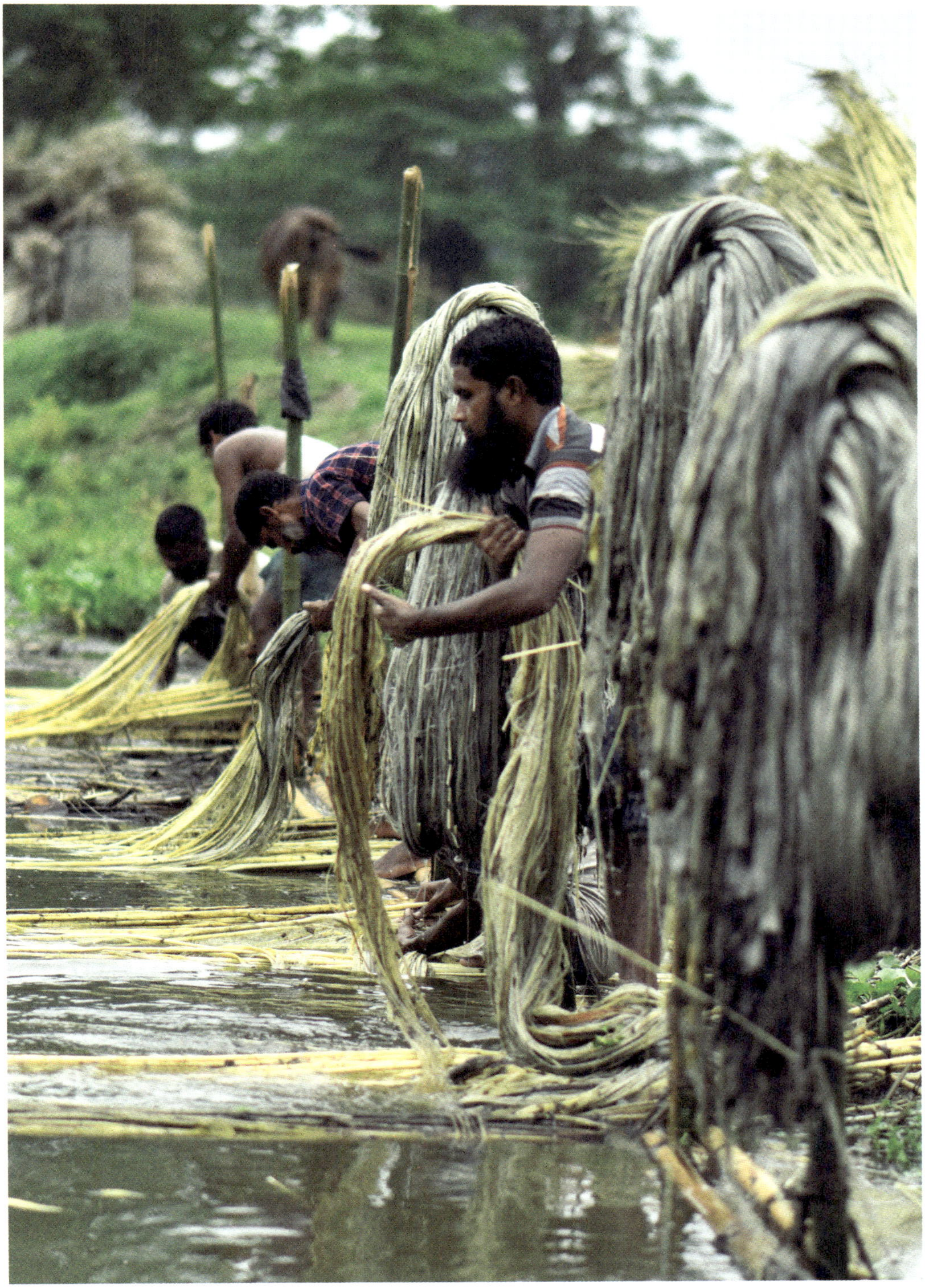

Workers extracting fibers from jute stems, Assam, India.
The process involves retting and stripping fibers from plant stalks.

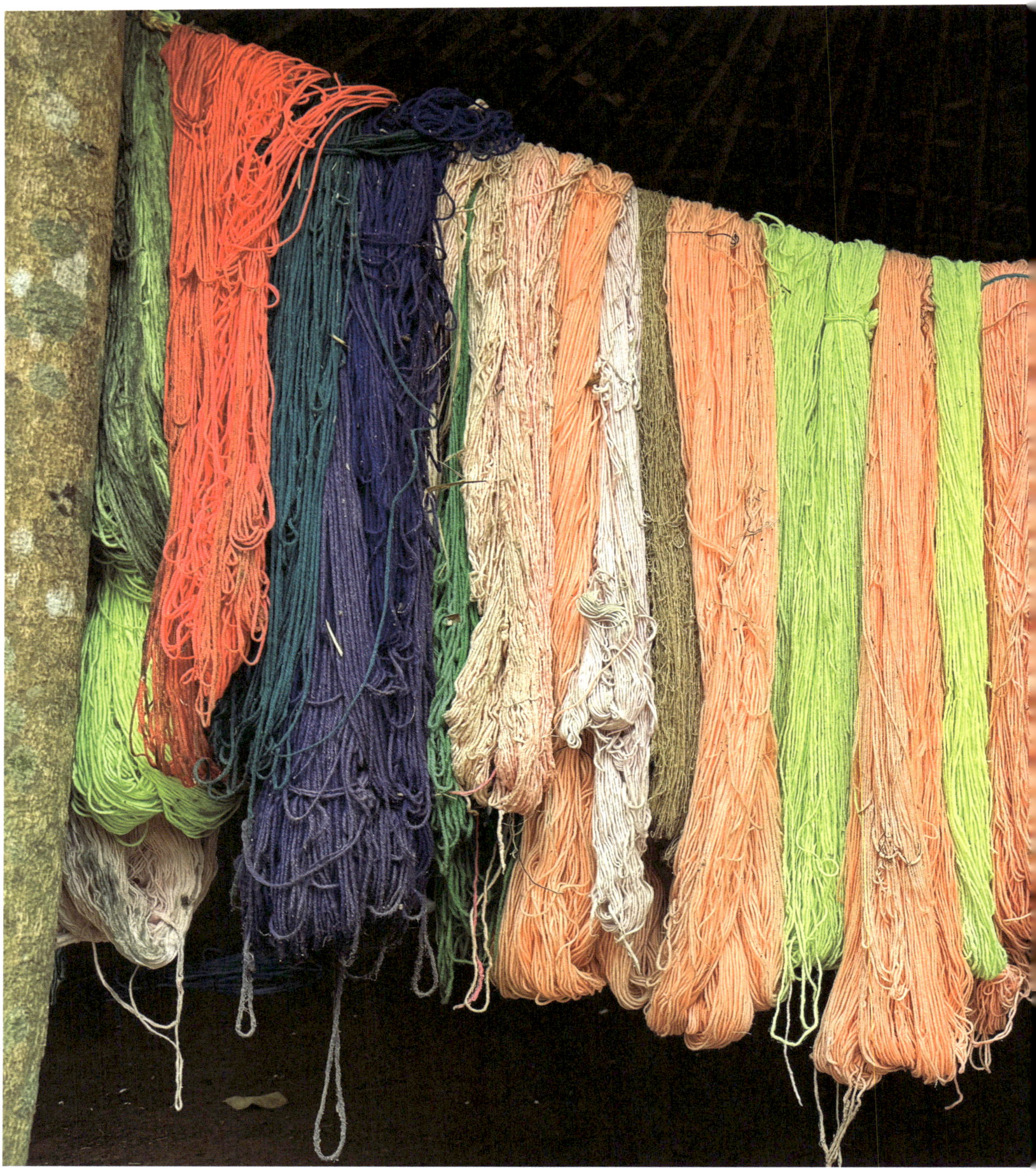

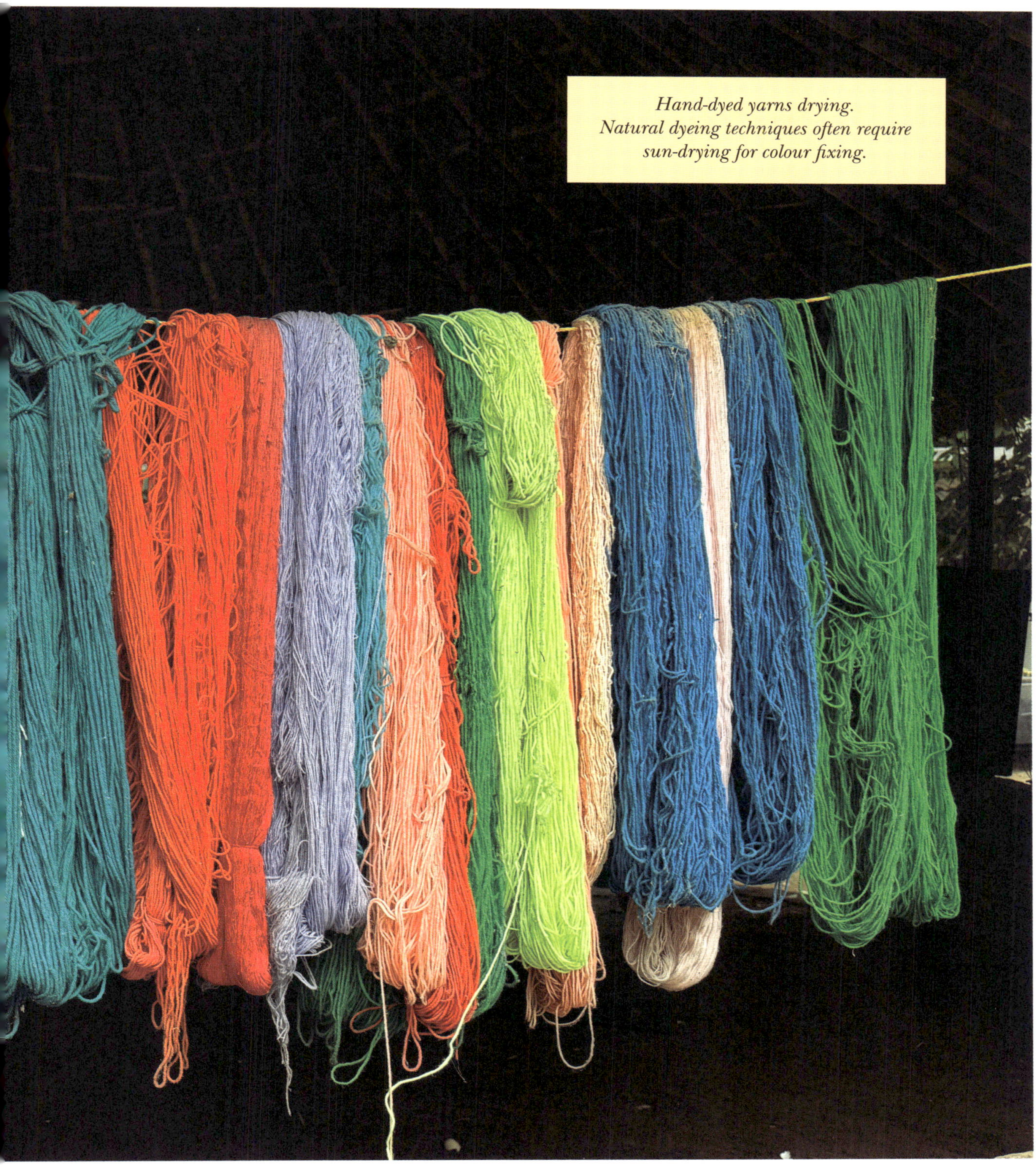

*Hand-dyed yarns drying.
Natural dyeing techniques often require sun-drying for colour fixing.*

Blends and Others

Some saris combine fibres. Chanderi, for example, uses silk in the warp and cotton in the weft, creating its translucent glow. Wool, tussar silk and plant fibres like jute also appear in regional variations.

At this stage, the destiny of the sari has already been decided: whether it will be a crisp everyday cotton or a ceremonial silk fit for a bride.

Spinning the Yarn

Once fibres are prepared, they must be spun into yarn.

In traditional hand-spinning, women used drop spindles or the *charkha*, producing yarn with slight variations in thickness. These

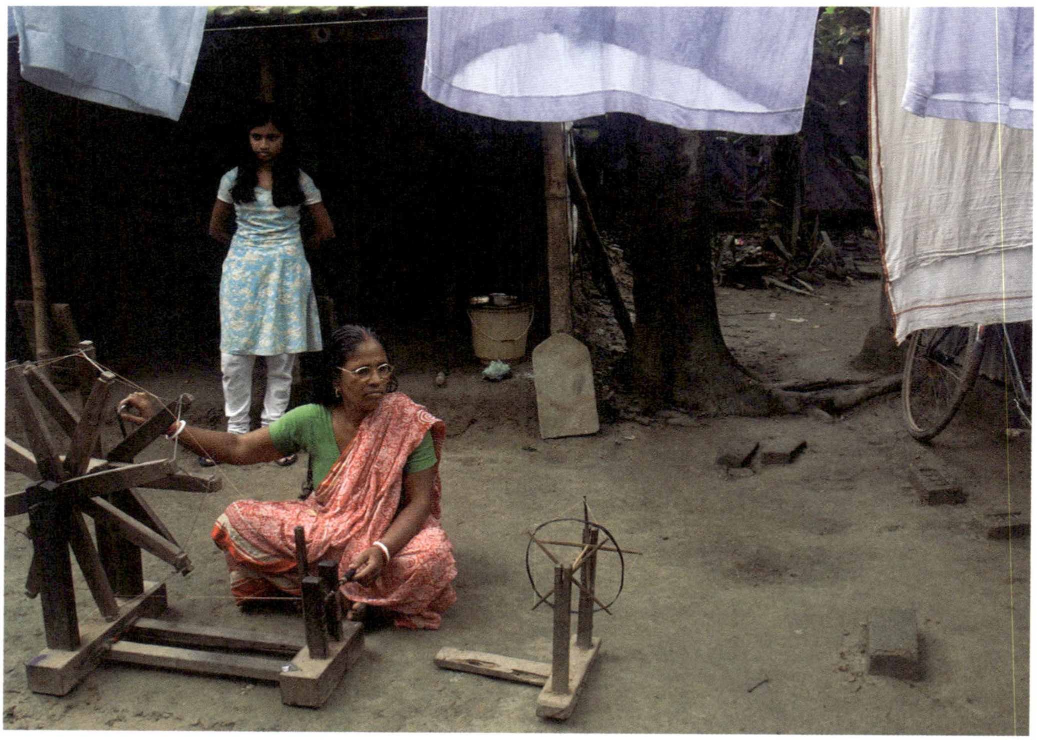

Woman spinning cotton using a spinning wheel, West Bengal, India. Spinning transforms raw fibre into thread for weaving.

irregularities gave hand-spun cloth its warmth and 'living' texture. This is the essence of khadi – cotton that is both hand-spun and hand-woven. Gandhi elevated khadi from fabric to a philosophy of self-reliance and resistance.

Today, many weavers purchase mill-spun yarns for their consistency. However, in some weaving clusters, artisans still use

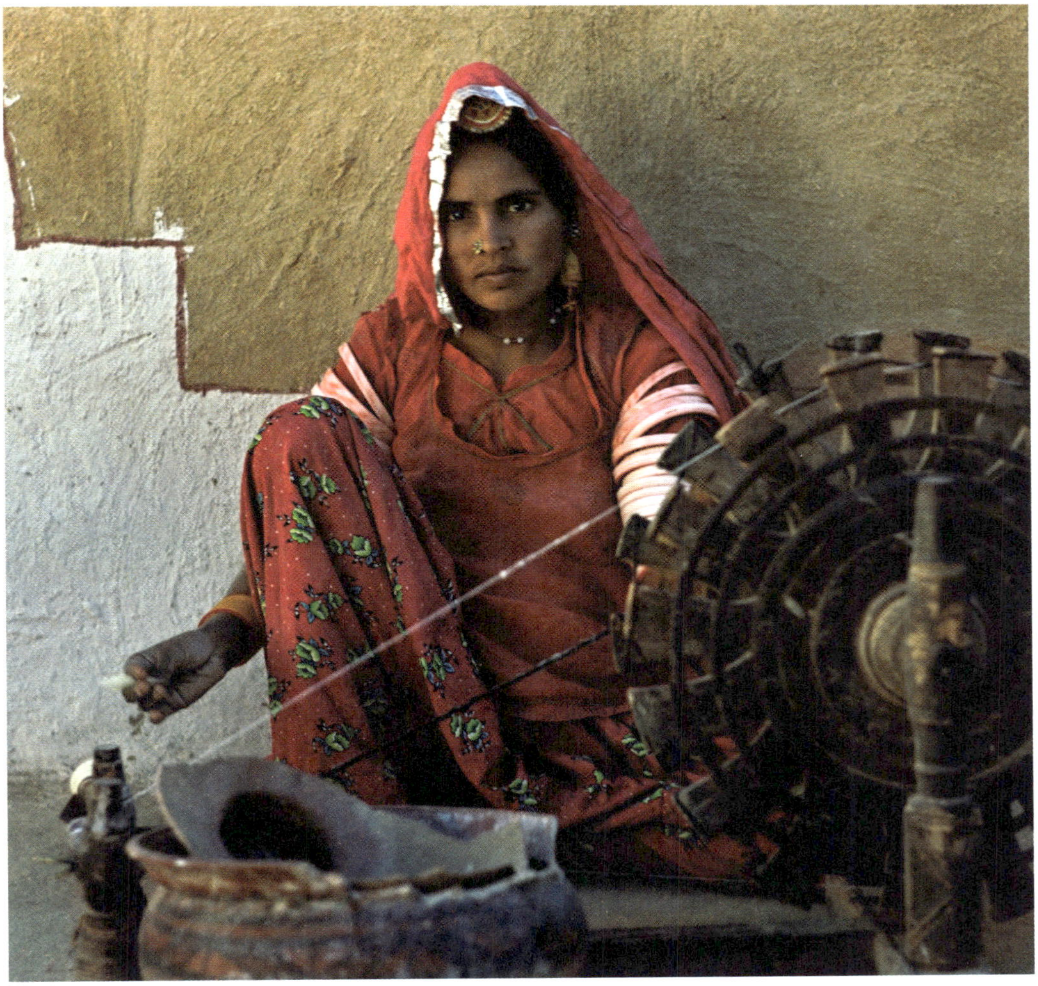

Woman with spinning wheel, Jaisalmer Fort, Rajasthan, India.
Spinning wheels have historically been associated with self-sufficient textile production.

modified charkhas like the Ambar charkha, sometimes even powered by solar energy, keeping alive the meditative rhythm of hand-spinning.

Spinning may seem like a humble step, but it is the thread's first transformation – from raw fibre into something with direction, purpose and resilience.

Dyeing the Yarn

Colour is life, and dyeing is where yarn takes on its cultural soul.

Scouring and Cleaning

Before colour, yarns are boiled with soap, ash or alkalis to strip away oils. This cleansing ensures even dye uptake.

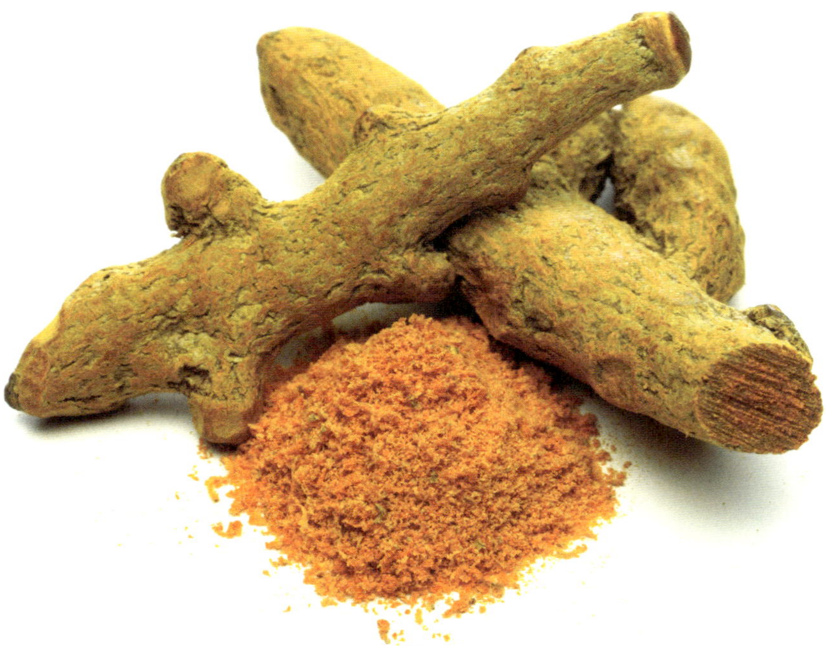

Turmeric rhizomes and powdered turmeric.
Turmeric is commonly used as a natural yellow dye.

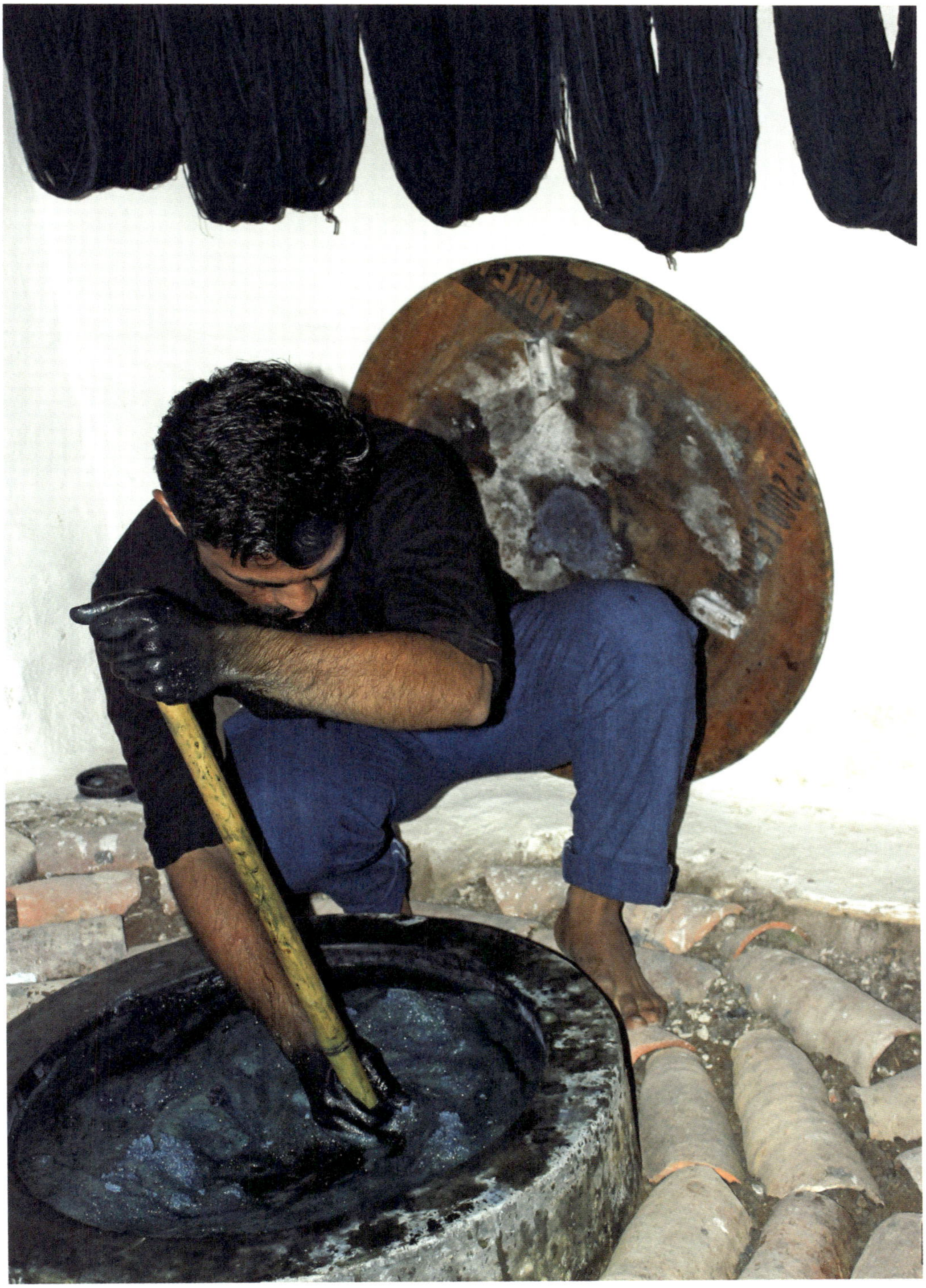

Indigo dyeing of cloth and yarn, Gujarat, India.
Indigo produces deep blue tones and has been used for centuries.

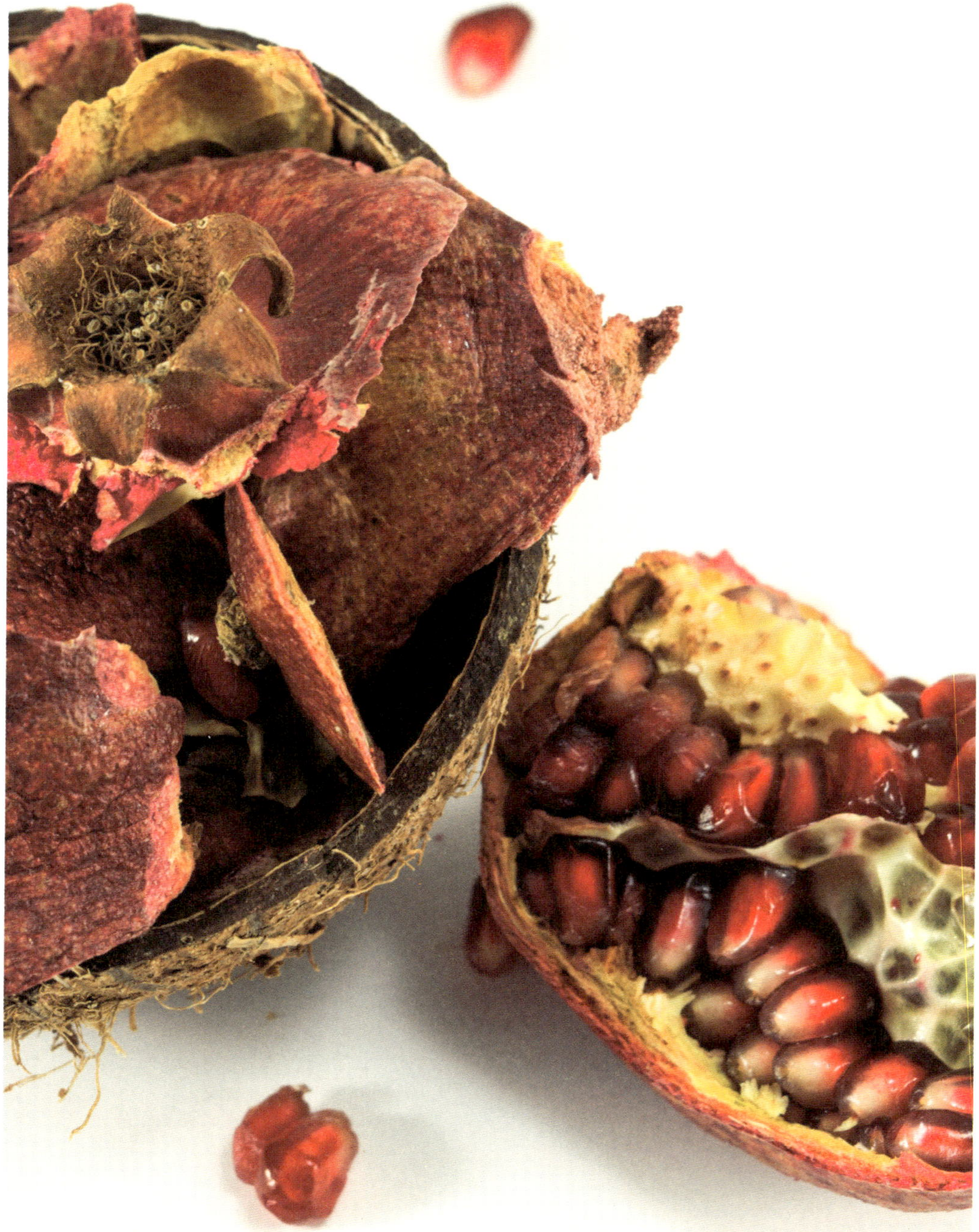

Pomegranate and dried fruit skin used for natural dye.
These materials yield earthy yellow and brown shades.

Natural Dyes

Indigo vats for deep blues. Madder root for reds. Turmeric and pomegranate for yellows. Onion skins, lac, henna and flowers for subtle shades. These recipes were often guarded within families, giving each weaving community its signature palette.

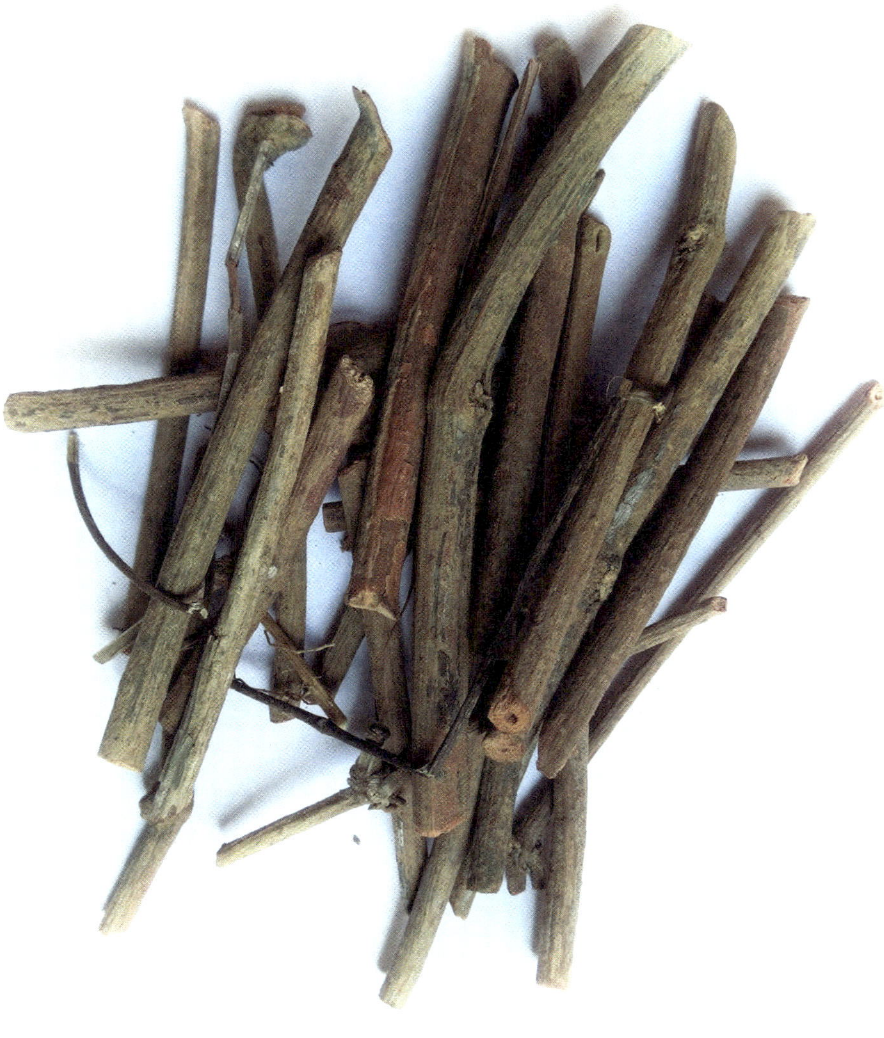

Dried madder root (Rubia tinctorum), used as a natural dye. Madder is known for producing red hues.

Synthetic Dyes

From the nineteenth century onward, chemical dyes allowed for more vivid and consistent colours. A Banarasi weaver might now demand a precise emerald, or a Chanderi weaver a delicate pastel, for modern markets.

Tie-dye & Resist

Some traditions dye the fabric itself before weaving. In Bandhani, threads are knotted tightly so that dye doesn't seep into certain areas, leaving behind patterns of dots when untied.

Beyond chemistry, colour carries meaning: red for weddings, saffron for devotion, white for mourning, green for harvest. Dyeing doesn't just change yarn, it marks a sari's destiny.

Designing the Sari Pattern

Before weaving begins, a sari must be imagined.

NATURAL DYES STILL IN USE

Many sari colours still rely on ancient dye recipes. Madder root produces reds, turmeric gives yellow, lac yields crimson and pomegranate creates soft golds. These dyes age gracefully, fading rather than cracking, which is why heirloom saris develop patina instead of wear, becoming more beautiful with time.

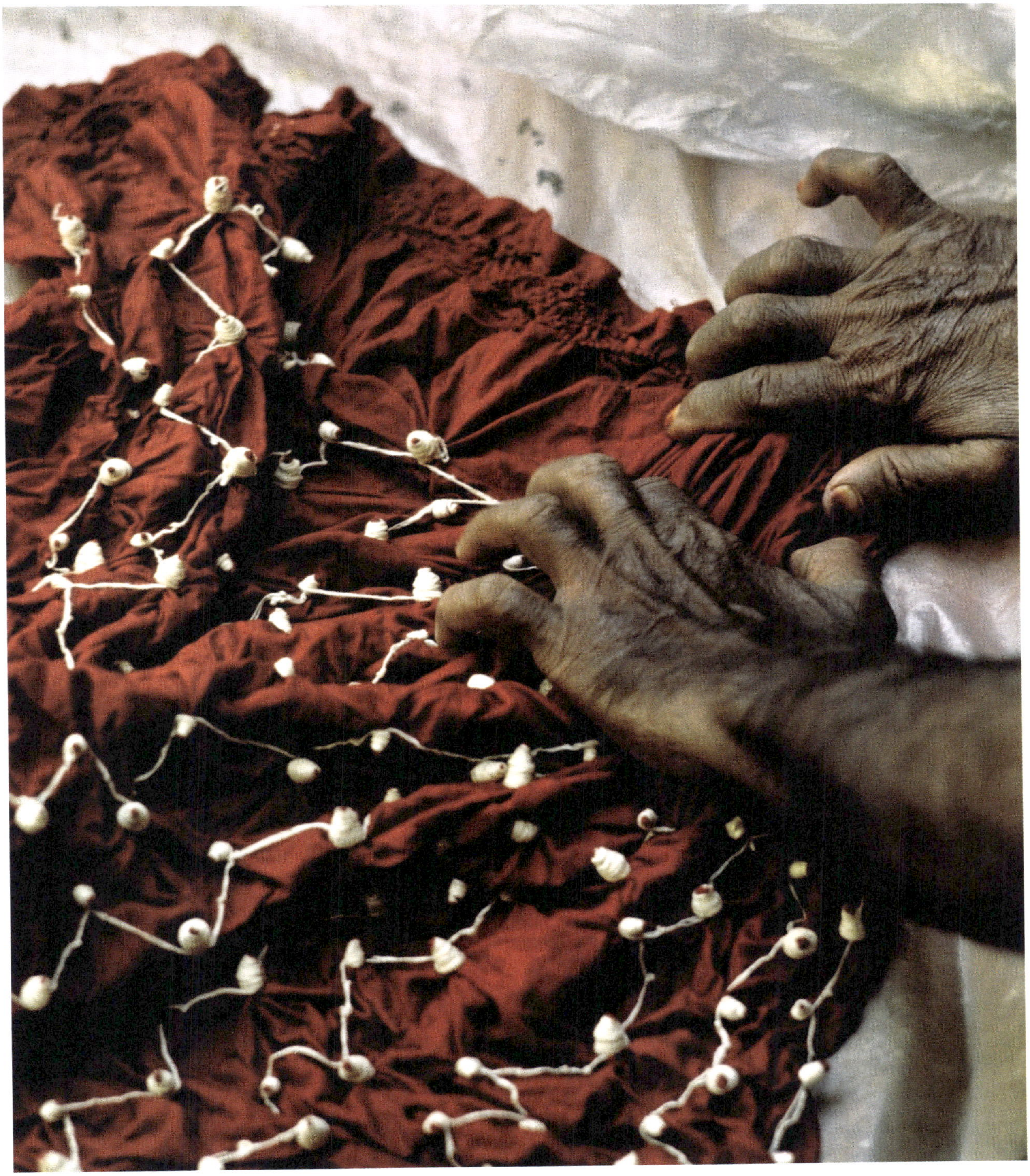

Detail of tie-and-dye (Bandhani), Gujarat, India.
Bandhani involves tying small sections of fabric before dyeing.

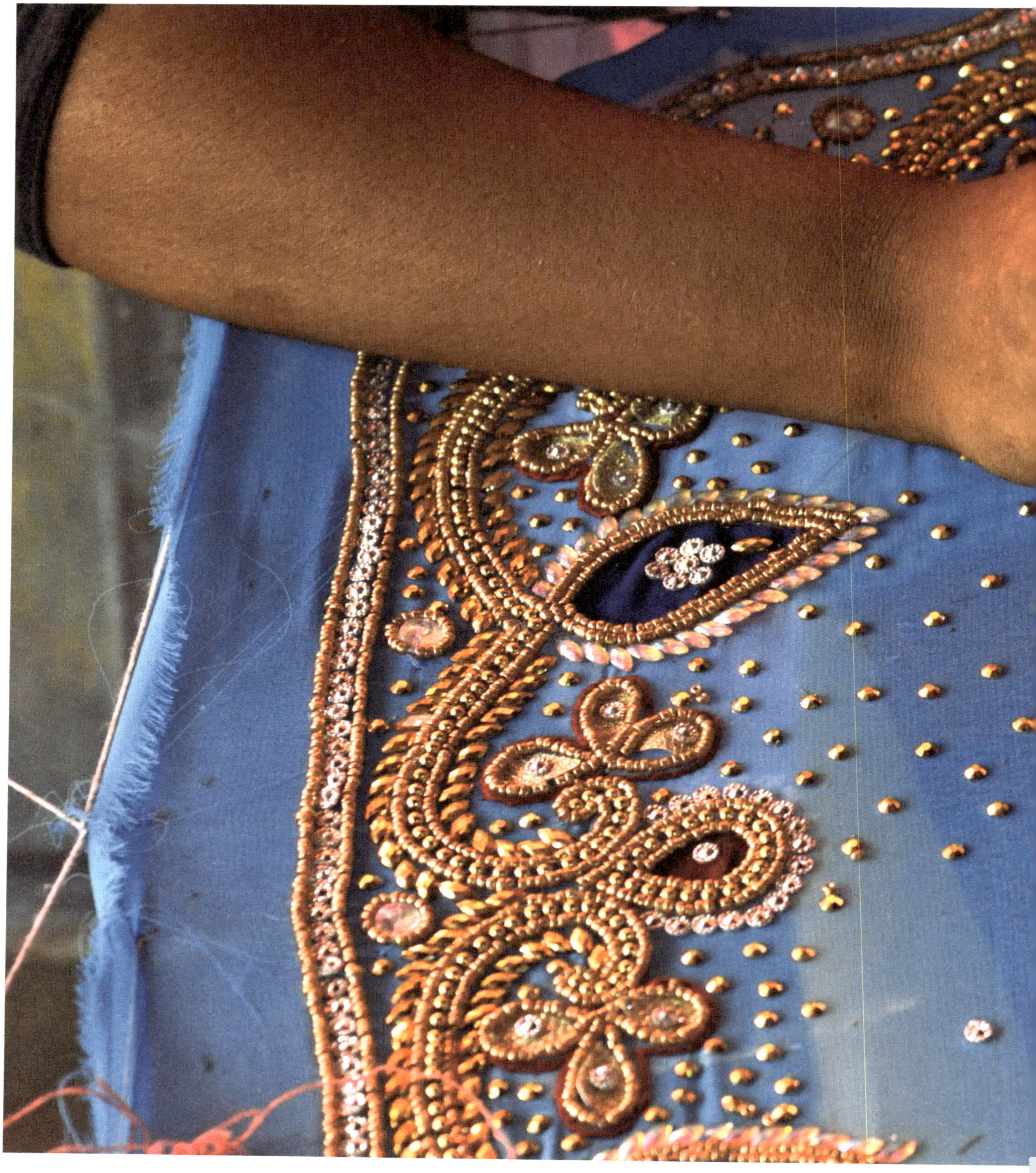

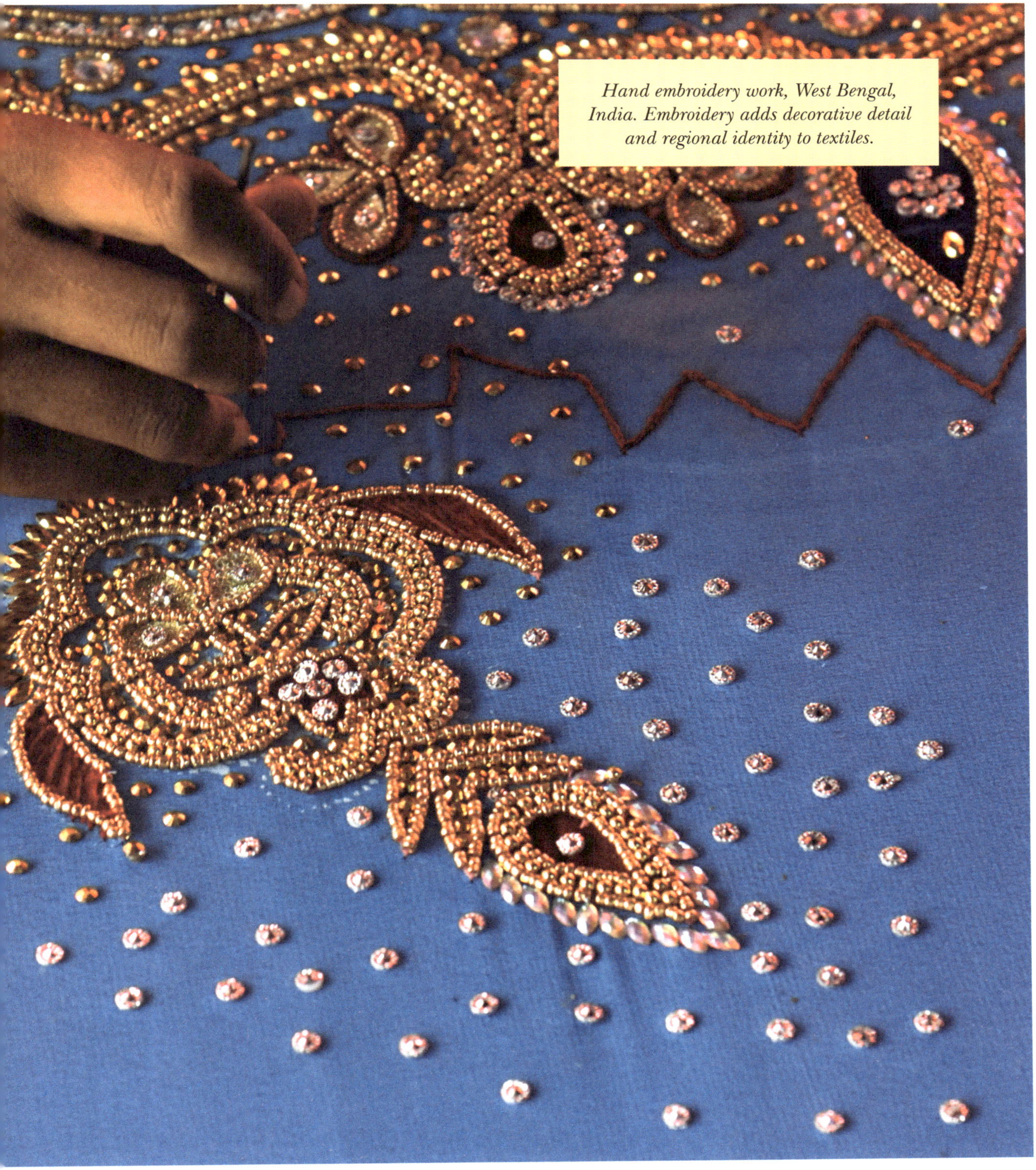

Hand embroidery work, West Bengal, India. Embroidery adds decorative detail and regional identity to textiles.

Motifs

Temple borders in Kanjeevarams, floral jaals in Banarasis, peacocks and lotuses in Paithanis or delicate buttis in Chanderis. Each motif is cultural shorthand, carrying stories of landscape, religion or community.

Blueprints

Designers (called *nakshabandhs* in Banaras) first sketch the design on graph paper. Each square represents a thread. For elaborate brocades, the design is then punched onto hundreds of Jacquard cards that guide the loom.

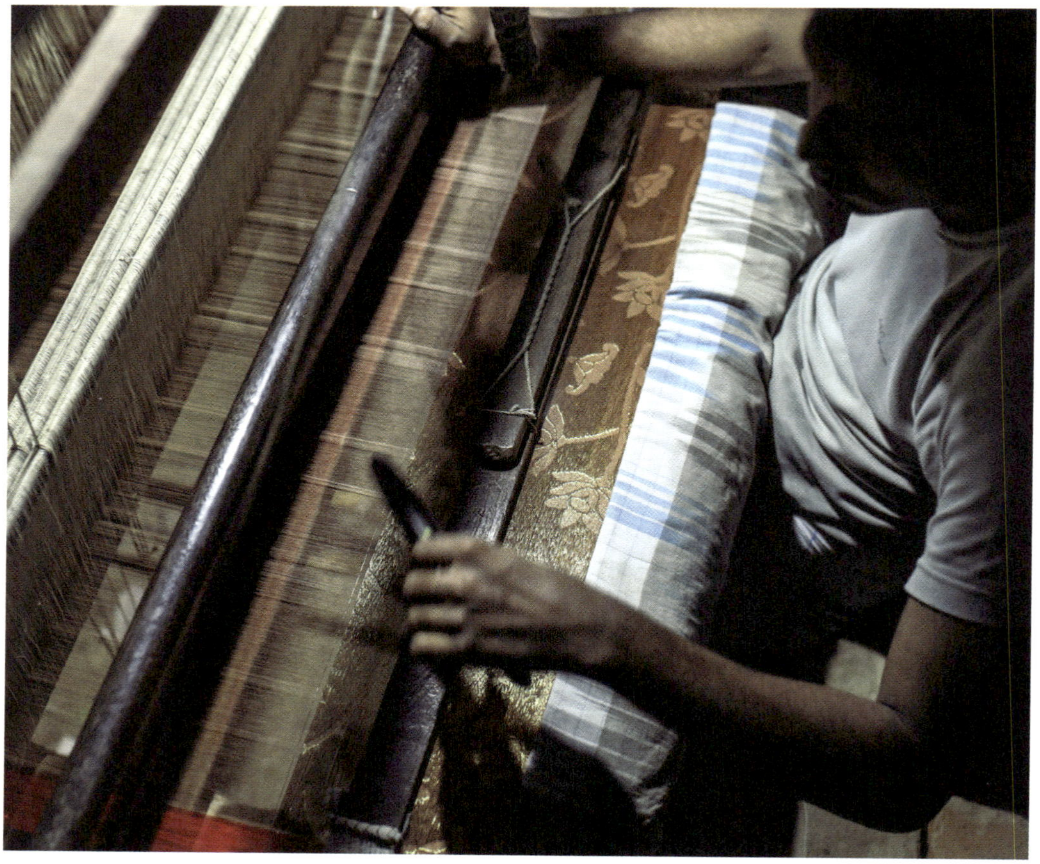

Weaver working on a silk sari using a handloom, Varanasi, India. Varanasi is renowned for its Banarasi silk weaving tradition.

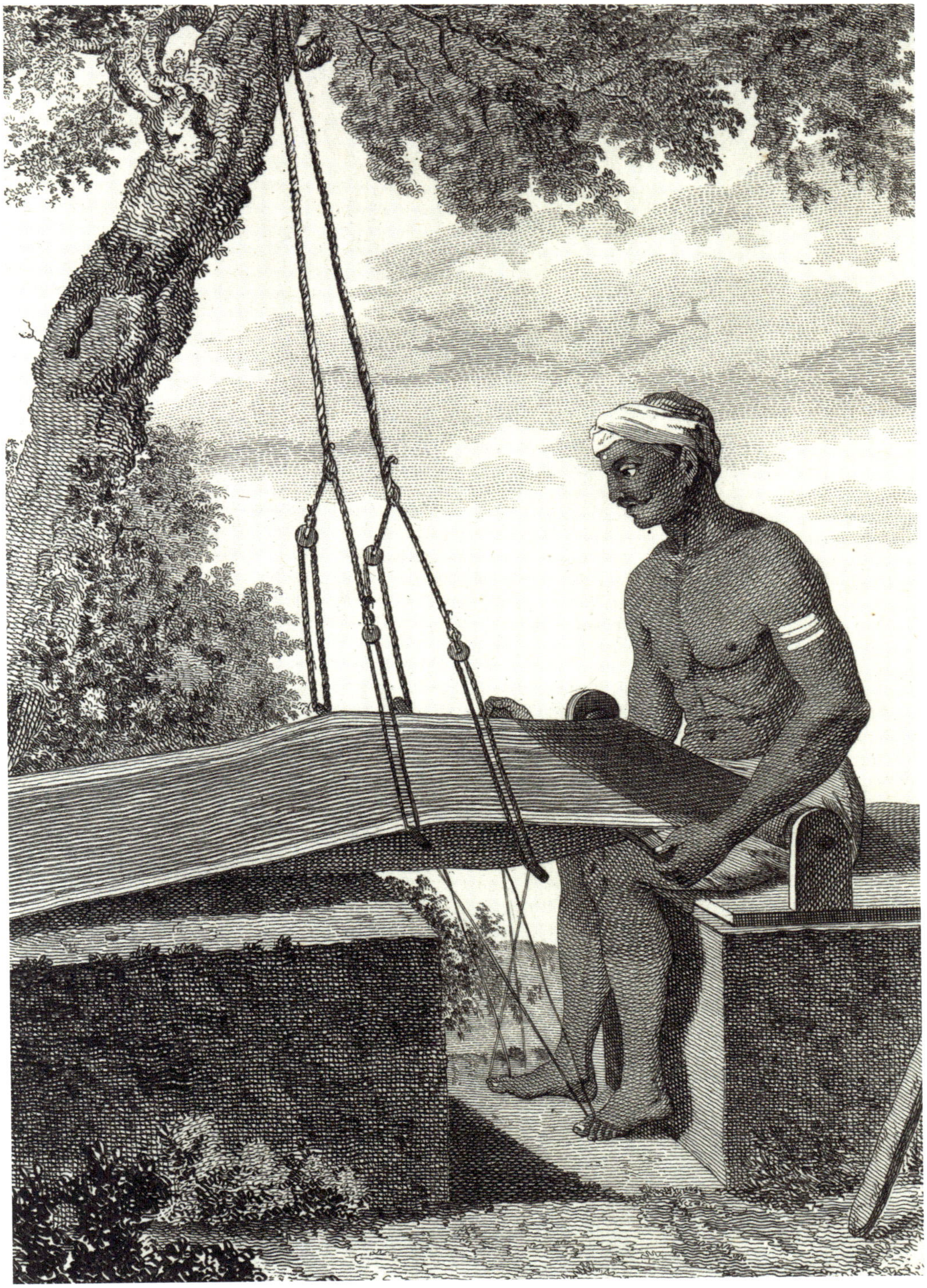

Engraving by Poisson after a painting by Sonnerat (1748-1814), of a man using a loom. He uses strings on to his feet to move the warp threads, and his hands to push the shuttle with the weft threads.

Manual Artistry

In Jamdani weaving, there are no cards. Instead, the weaver uses a needle to insert motifs by hand, one thread at a time. In Kanjeevaram weaving, the body, border and *pallu* are woven separately and joined by korvai interlocking. Designing is not just technical planning. It is the loom's language taking shape before a single thread is interlaced.

Setting Up the Loom

A loom is both a tool and altar. Preparing it is painstaking.

Hundreds (sometimes thousands) of dyed threads are stretched lengthwise onto the warp beam.

Each warp thread is drawn through heddles and reeds, ensuring exact order and tension. A single misplacement can ruin the entire sari.

The weft is wound onto bobbins and placed inside wooden shuttles.

ZARI: GOLD WOVEN INTO CLOTH

Traditional *zari* is made by wrapping pure silver threads with gold leaf. Historically produced in Surat and Banaras, *zari* transformed saris into ceremonial objects. Though modern *zari* often uses copper or synthetic cores, heritage *zari* remains prized for weddings, rituals and temple offerings across South India and North India.

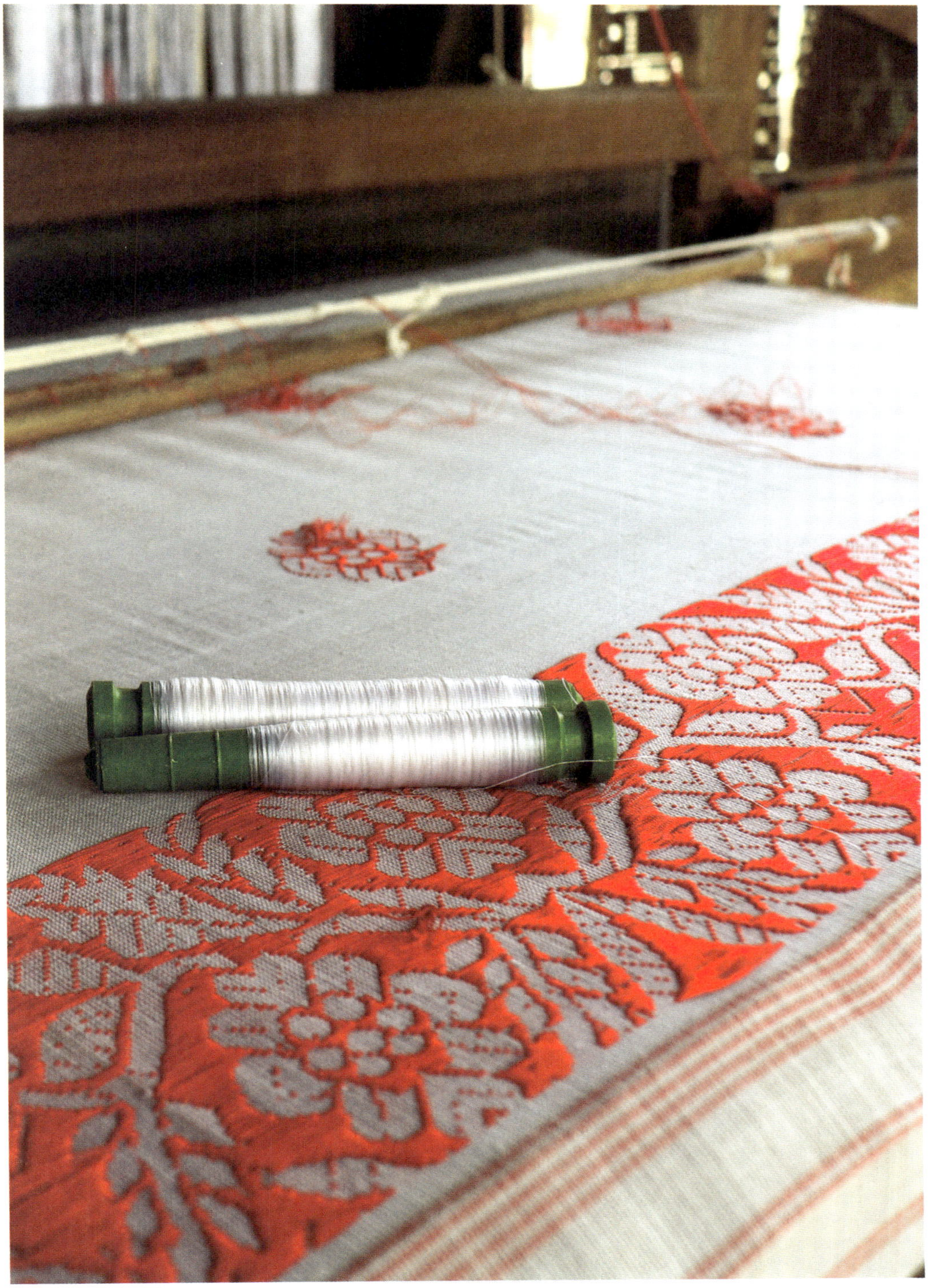

Close-up views of a traditional Indian handloom. Handlooms allow for intricate and controlled weaving patterns.

For Jacquard looms, the punched card chain is suspended above, ready to dictate the rise and fall of threads.

This setup can take days – all before a single line of fabric is woven.

Weaving the Sari

Weaving is the sari's true birth. The shuttle flies back and forth, carrying the weft through the warp. The reed beats down, locking threads into place. Treadles or levers lift and lower sets of threads, creating space for the shuttle. The rhythm is hypnotic: clack, swoosh, beat.

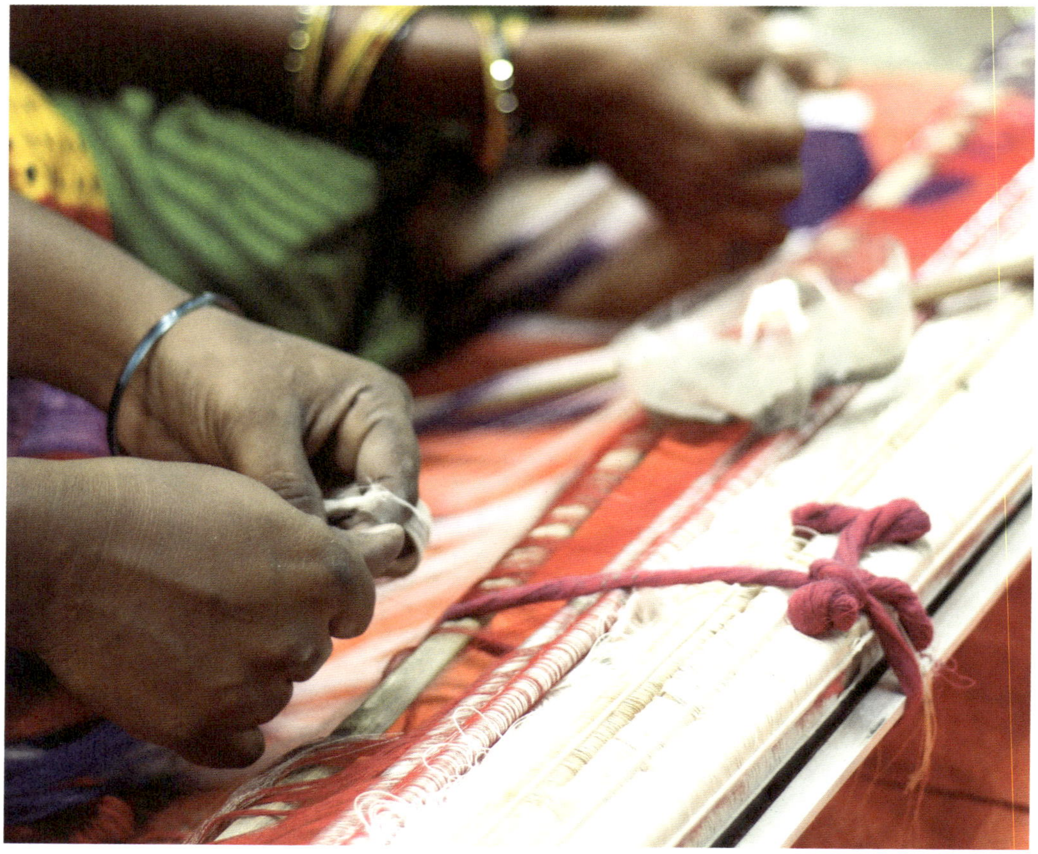

Stages in the sari-making process, India.
The process includes spinning, dyeing, weaving, and finishing.

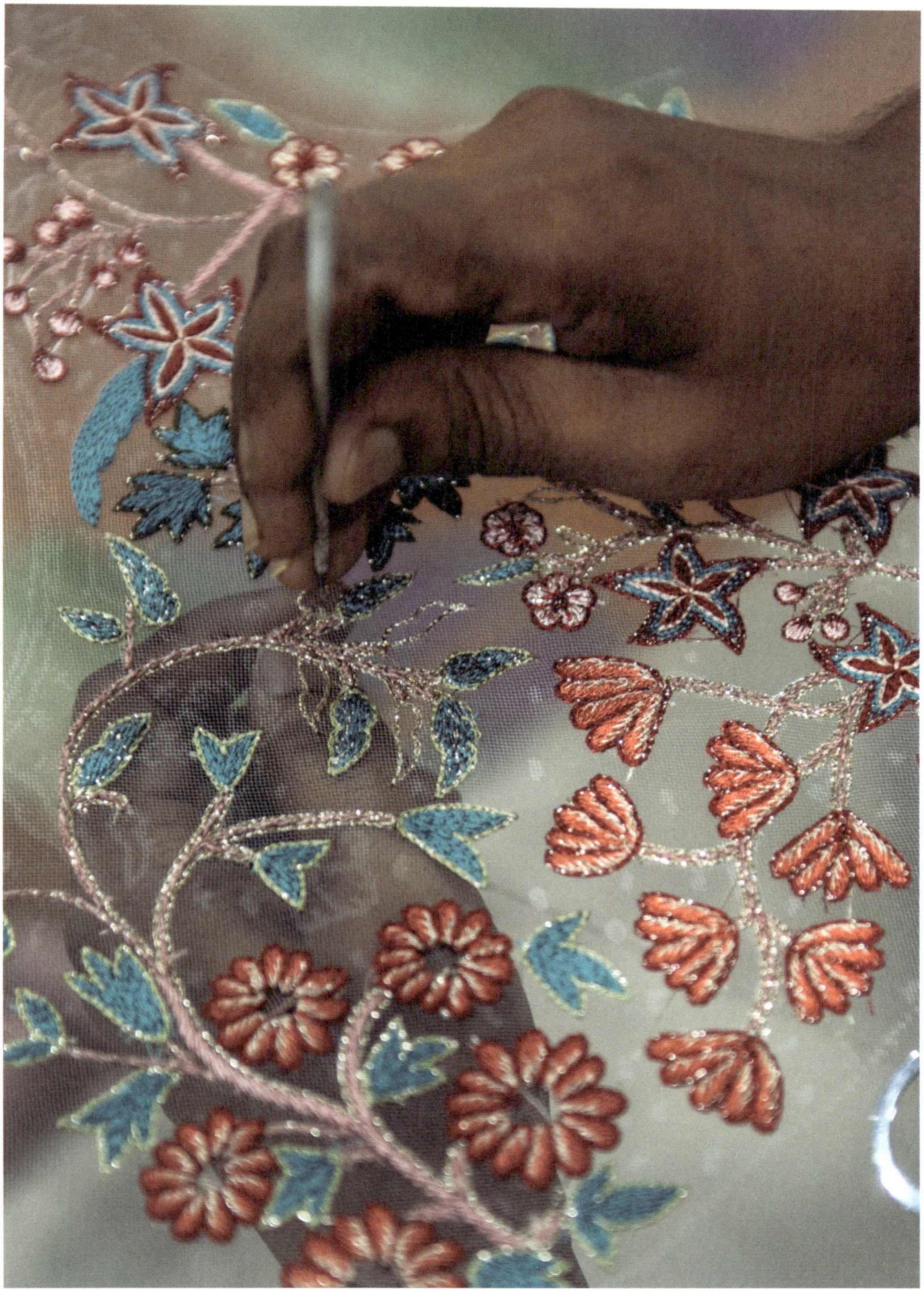

Close-up of zari embroidery by an artisan.
Zari work uses metallic threads to create ornate patterns.

Banarasi Weaves

For intricate brocades, *zari* and silk threads intertwine to form gardens of motifs. Some saris require thousands of cards and months of labour.

Kanjeevaram Weaves

Contrasting body and borders join seamlessly in these weaves featuring heavy silks, temple motifs and bold colours.

Chanderi Weaves

Silk warps and cotton wefts, producing fabric so light it seems translucent.

Jamdani Weaves

Here, motifs are hand-inserted, floating on sheer muslin like embroidery in the loom itself.

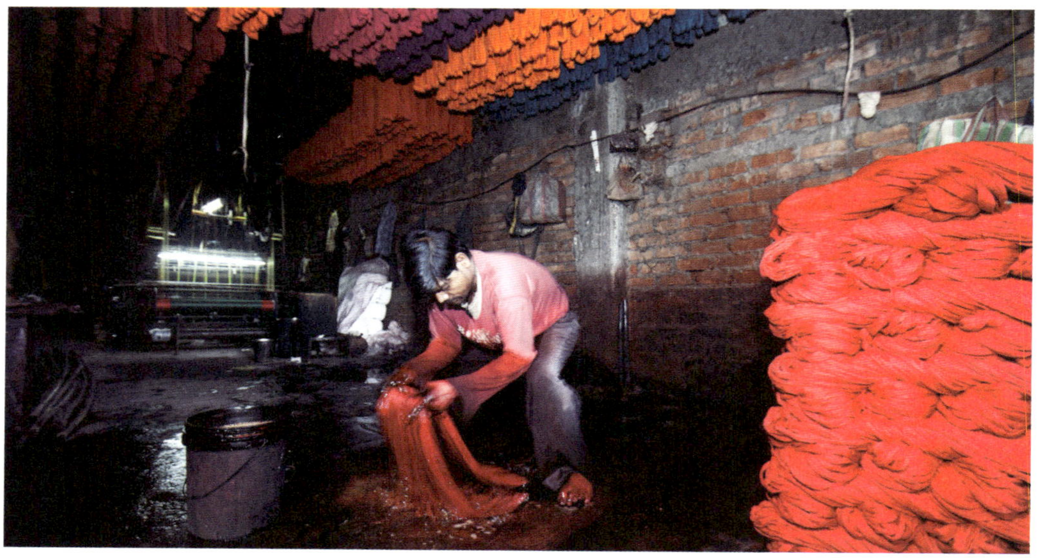

Artisan dyeing silk using traditional methods.
Dyeing techniques vary across regions and materials.

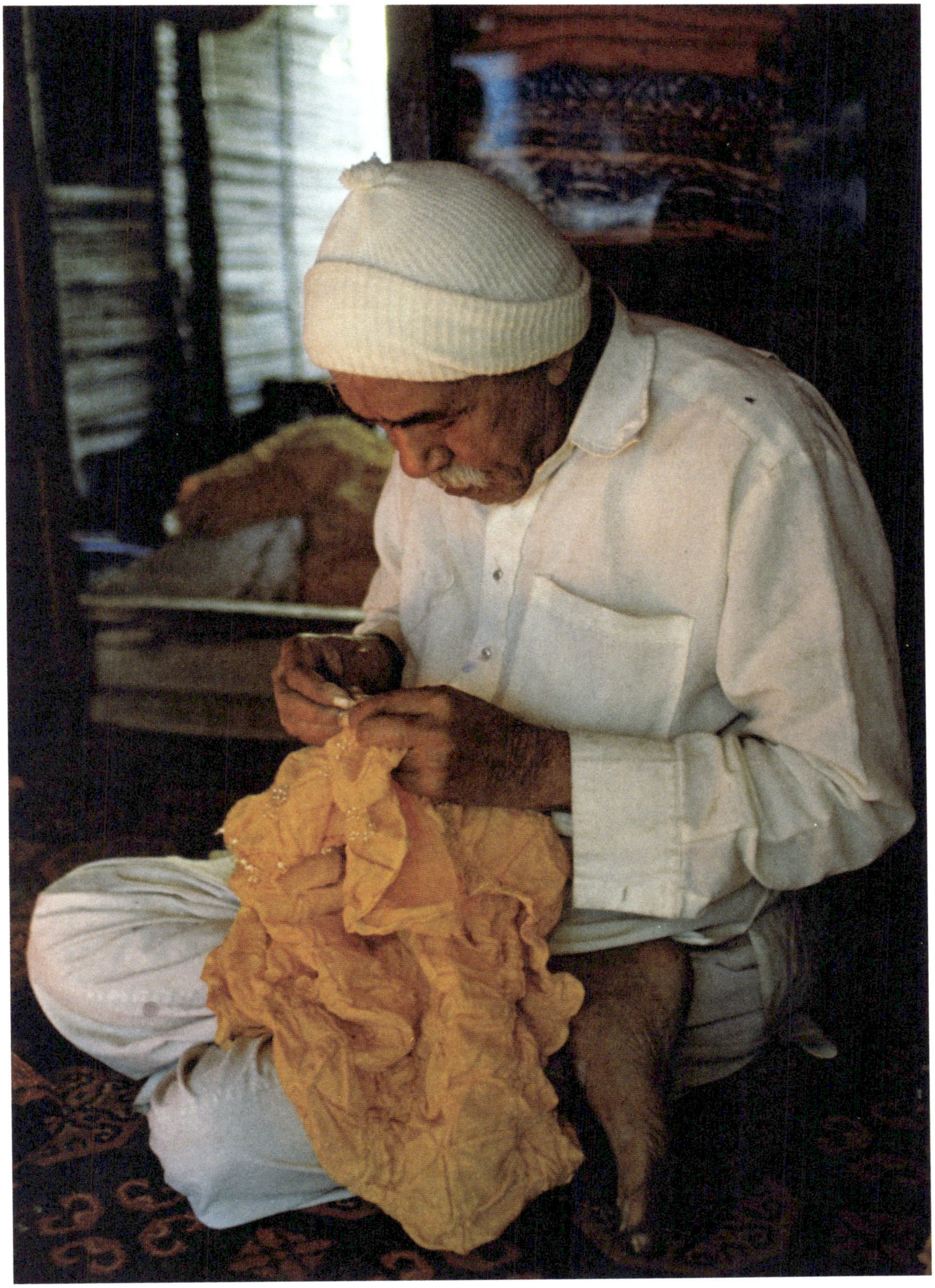

Craftsman knotting fabric using tie-dye technique, Gujarat, India.
Precise knotting determines the final pattern after dyeing.

Weaving speed varies. A simple cotton sari may take a few days. A Banarasi masterpiece can take six months. The weaver's body becomes part of the loom, each muscle remembering generations of motion.

Finishing Processes

A sari is still unfinished when it leaves the loom. It must be perfected.

Washing and starching removes excess dye and strengthens the fabric. Chanderi weavers traditionally used wild onion starch instead of rice.

Ironing and stretching smooths the weave and brings out lustre.

Polishing

Silk saris are rubbed with velvet to make them shine.

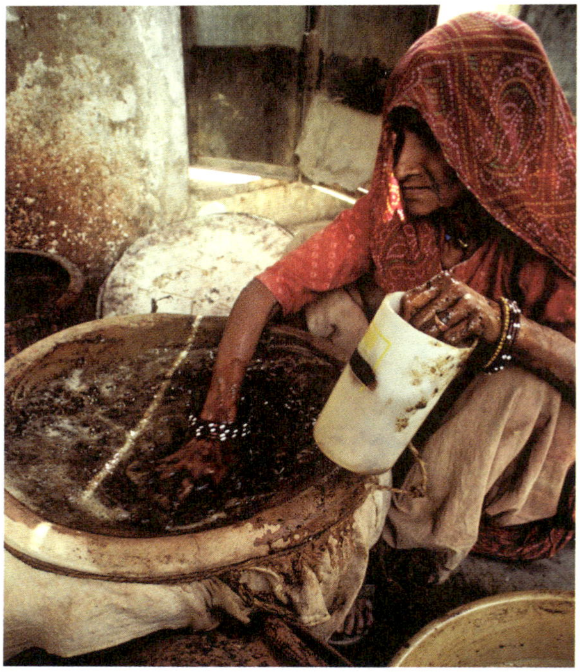

Woman mixing traditional dyes.
Colour preparation is a crucial step in textile production.

Trimming

Loose threads are clipped by hand, especially in cutwork Banarasis.

Folding and packaging

Borders aligned, *pallus* displayed. Some are wrapped in muslin or tissue, others boxed with a certificate of authenticity.

Only then is the sari ready for market – or for ritual.

The Hands Behind the Cloth

Behind every sari, there are many artisans: the spinner, the dyer, the designer, the loom-setter, the weaver and the finisher. Entire families, sometimes entire villages, sustain themselves on this cycle. Yet their names are rarely known.

The sari is celebrated on brides, on film stars and in parliaments. But it begins in the calloused hands of people whose labour is both craft and survival. Without them, there would be no fabric to carry history, no threads to weave memory.

The making of a sari is universal in rhythm yet endlessly diverse in detail. Bengal's Jamdani does not resemble Tamil Nadu's Kanjeevaram; Chanderi is not Banaras; Paithani is not Bandhani. Each region has its own fibres, dyes and motifs – its own style and traditions.

To appreciate the full richness of the sari, we must travel. Across states, across borders and across traditions. The loom's hum continues, but everywhere, it speaks a different language. That is where we go next.

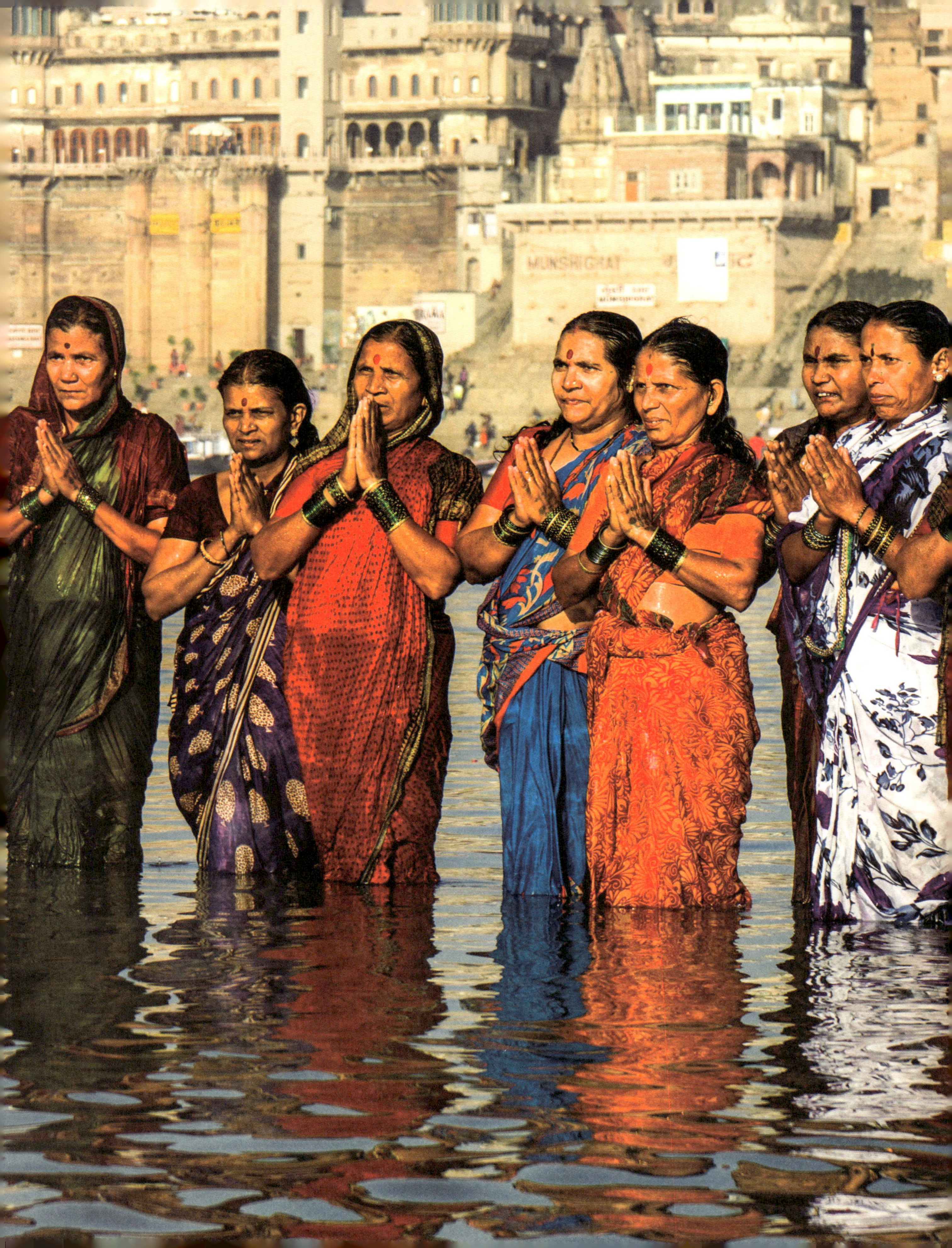
MUNSHI GHAT

CHAPTER 3

ववििधिता में लपिटी: राज्यों की यात्रा

Draped in Diversity: A Journey Through the States

The sari does not speak in one language. Its dialects change with rivers and mountains, with soils and skies. From the coconut groves of Kerala to the ghats of Banaras, from the dry heat of Gujarat to the lush valleys of Assam, each region threads its own story into 'six yards' of fabric. To travel across India through its saris is to encounter a nation woven in warp and weft.

South India: Temple Looms & Silk Traditions

Tamil Nadu – Kanjeevaram

Walk into Kanchipuram and the air is thick with the hum of looms, a rhythm that has pulsed here for more than 400 years. The Kanjeevaram sari begins with mulberry silk threads reeled into yarn so lustrous and

Pilgrims bathing at Dashashwamedh Ghat, Varanasi, India. The ritual is believed to purify the body and soul.

strong that a single strand can hold the weight of a necklace. Gold *zari*, real silver wrapped in gold leaf, is prepared alongside the silk thread, to be worked into the borders. When the weaver sits down, he does not weave a single piece of cloth: he weaves three. The body, the border and the *pallu* are all woven separately, then joined together with the traditional korvai technique that is so seamless that the junction often outlasts the fabric itself. The colours are striking: a body of deep emerald green bordered with molten gold; a vermilion sari whose *pallu* bursts into peacock feathers; a black sari edged with turmeric yellow and temple gopuram motifs. Patterns are pulled directly from the world surrounding the weaver: mango butis, rudraksha beads, mythological animals, and temple towers.

Hold a Kanjeevaram and it feels weighty and authoritative. Spread out its 'six yards' and it gleams like a field at harvest. Draped on a bride, it does not merely adorn her, it armours her. Every pleat is stiff with dignity, every border alive with devotion. Tamil women typically drape the Kanjeevaram in the classic Nivi style – pleats neatly aligned at the waist, with the *pallu* thrown over the shoulder – so that the heavy borders and *pallu* are on full display. In Brahmin families, the more elaborate Madisar drape (a nine-yard variation) is often reserved for rituals, bringing even more ceremony to the garment. This is why in Tamil Nadu, the Kanjeevaram is not simply worn: it is inherited, worshipped and consecrated.

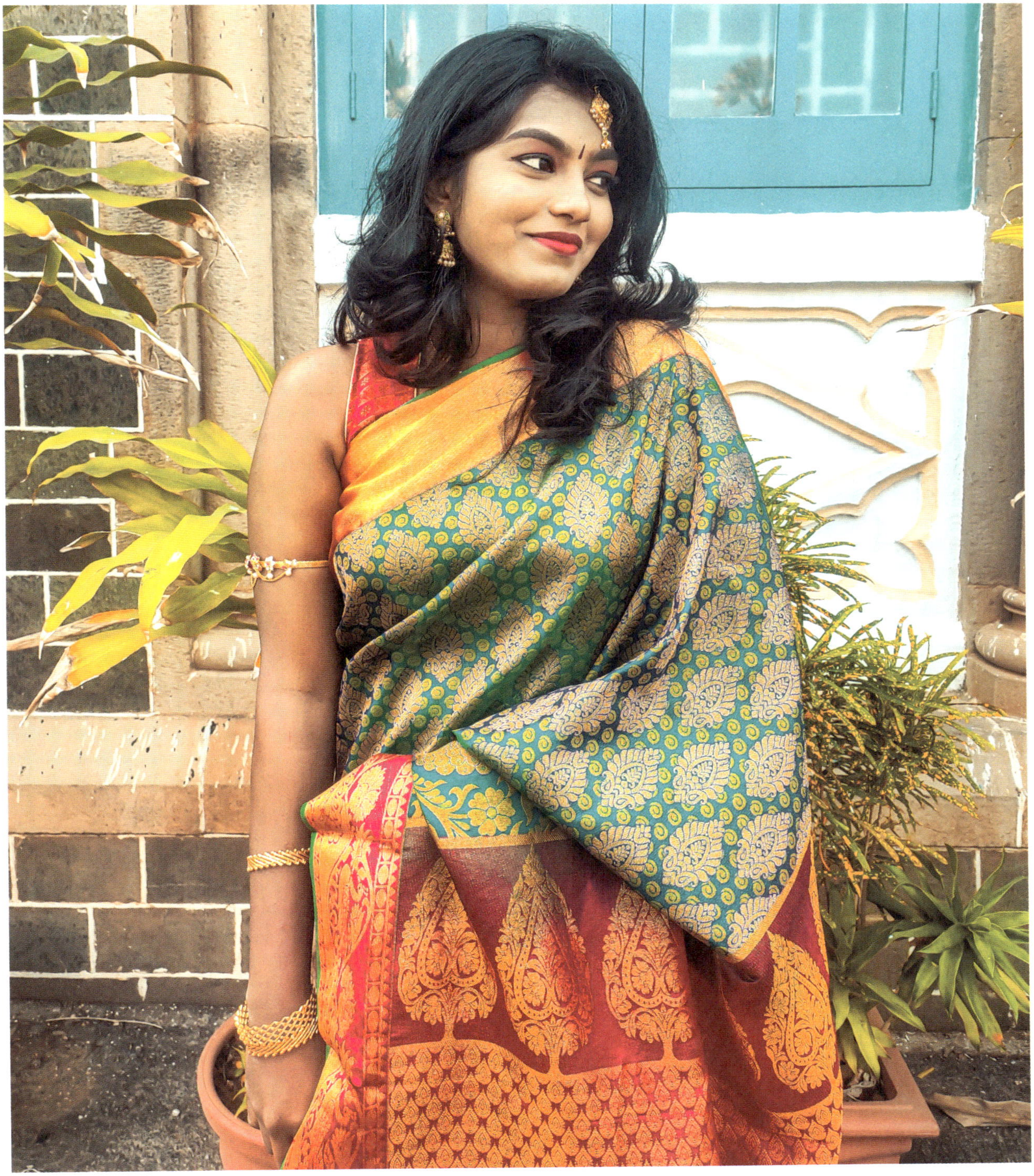

South Indian woman wearing a red and green Kanchipuram sari. Kanchipuram saris are known for their rich silk and contrasting borders.

Kerala – Kasavu & Mundum Neriyathum

If Tamil Nadu's Kanjeevaram is fire, Kerala's Kasavu is moonlight. Walk into a festival morning in Kerala and you'll see a sea of cream and gold. The Kasavu sari, woven in unbleached cotton with a gleaming gold border, is simplicity distilled. No loud colours, no heavy motifs – just a pale body edged with radiance. The gold itself (traditionally real, now often copper or synthetic *zari*) is woven into borders of varying widths. Some saris are edged with a slim line of gold, others with broad swathes almost 0.15m (0.5ft) deep. Occasionally, borders are coloured – temple reds, peacock greens – but the soul of a Kasavu remains its restraint. The Kasavu sari is not ornate, nor is it loud. Its beauty lies in restraint

ANTARIYA TO SARI

The sari evolved from the *antariya* – an ancient pleated lower garment worn with separate cloths. Over centuries, these pieces merged into one continuous length of fabric. This evolution allowed infinite draping styles without tailoring, making the sari adaptable across regions, climates and social customs without losing its core identity.

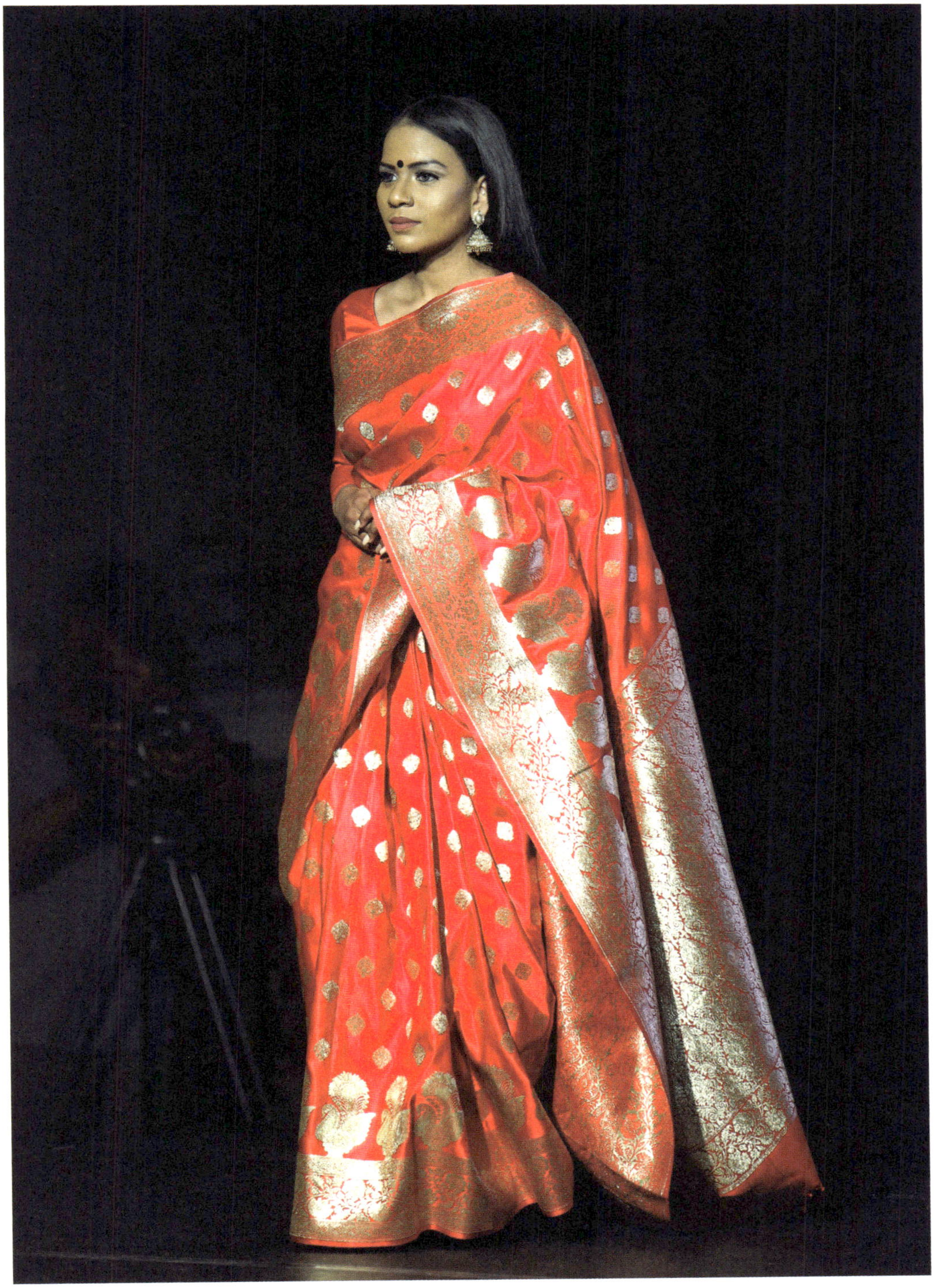

Model showcasing a Kanchipuram sari at a bridal fashion show, Ontario, Canada, 2020. The event reflects the global presence of traditional Indian textiles.

– a plain ivory body with a shimmering gold border, often woven from real *zari* in earlier times. During Onam, Kerala's harvest festival, entire streets turn into rivers of cream and gold as women dress in Kasavu saris, their hair adorned with fresh strands of jasmine, and their fragrance mingling with the scent of sambar and coconut oil.

Originally, the Kasavu came as a two-piece outfit made up of the *mundu* (lower cloth) and the *neriyathum* (upper cloth). The *mundu* is wrapped around the waist, while the *neriyathum* is draped over the shoulder like a graceful shawl. On festival days, many women still wear the Kasavu in this traditional Mundum Neriyathum style, the extra

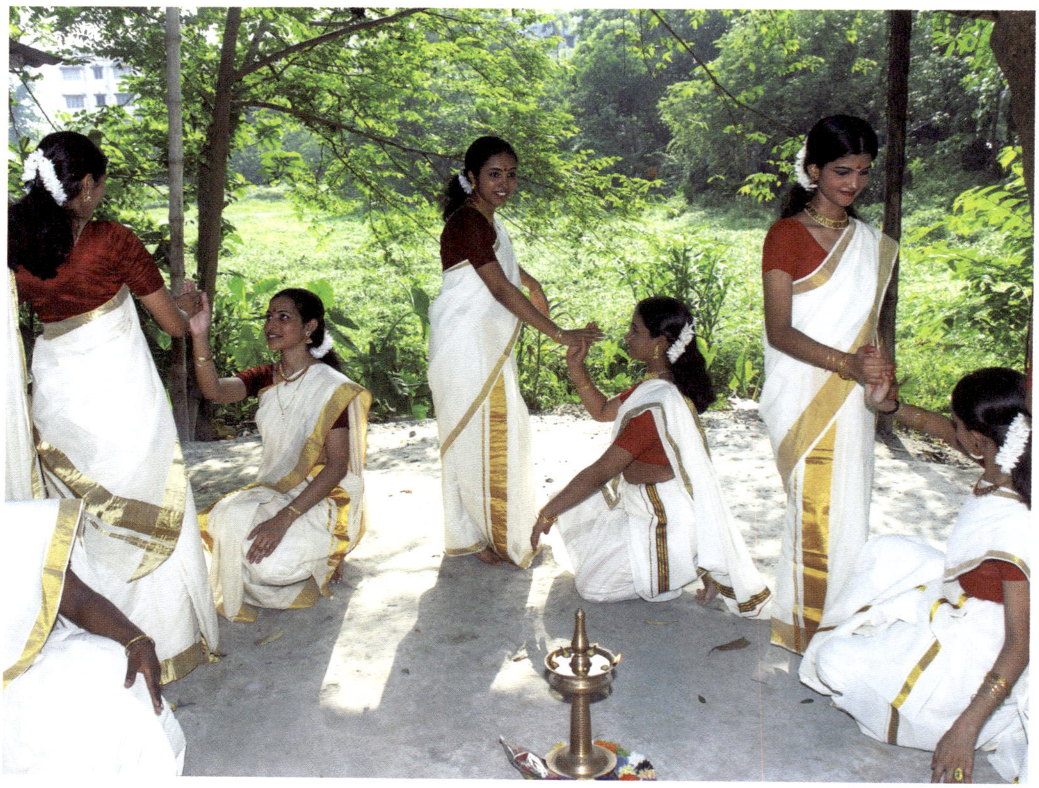

Women celebrating Onam festival, Kerala, India.
Onam marks the harvest season and is celebrated with traditional attire.

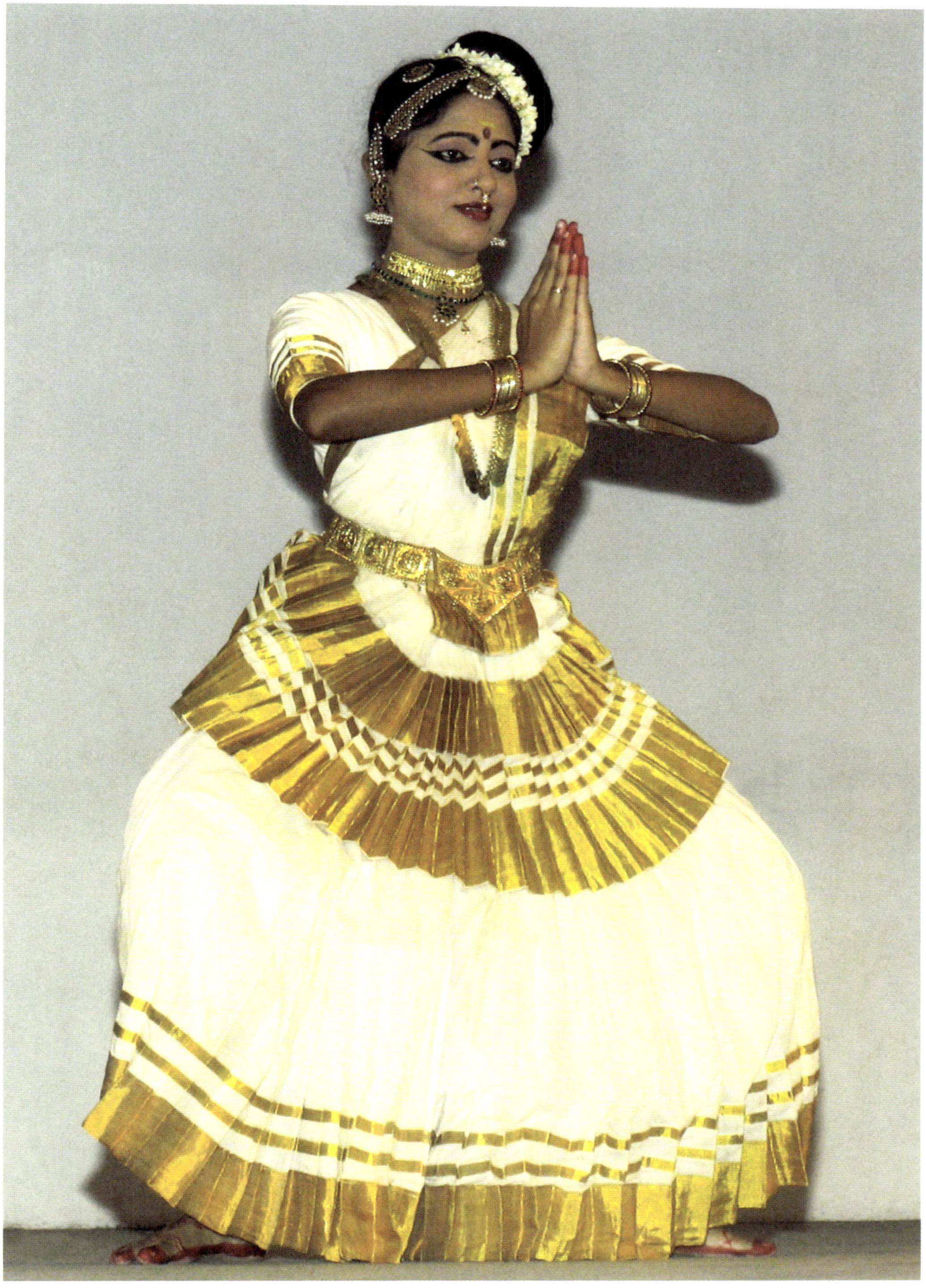

Bharatanatyam performer during Onam festival, Kerala, India.
Bharatanatyam is a classical dance form rooted in temple traditions, originating in Tamil Nadu.

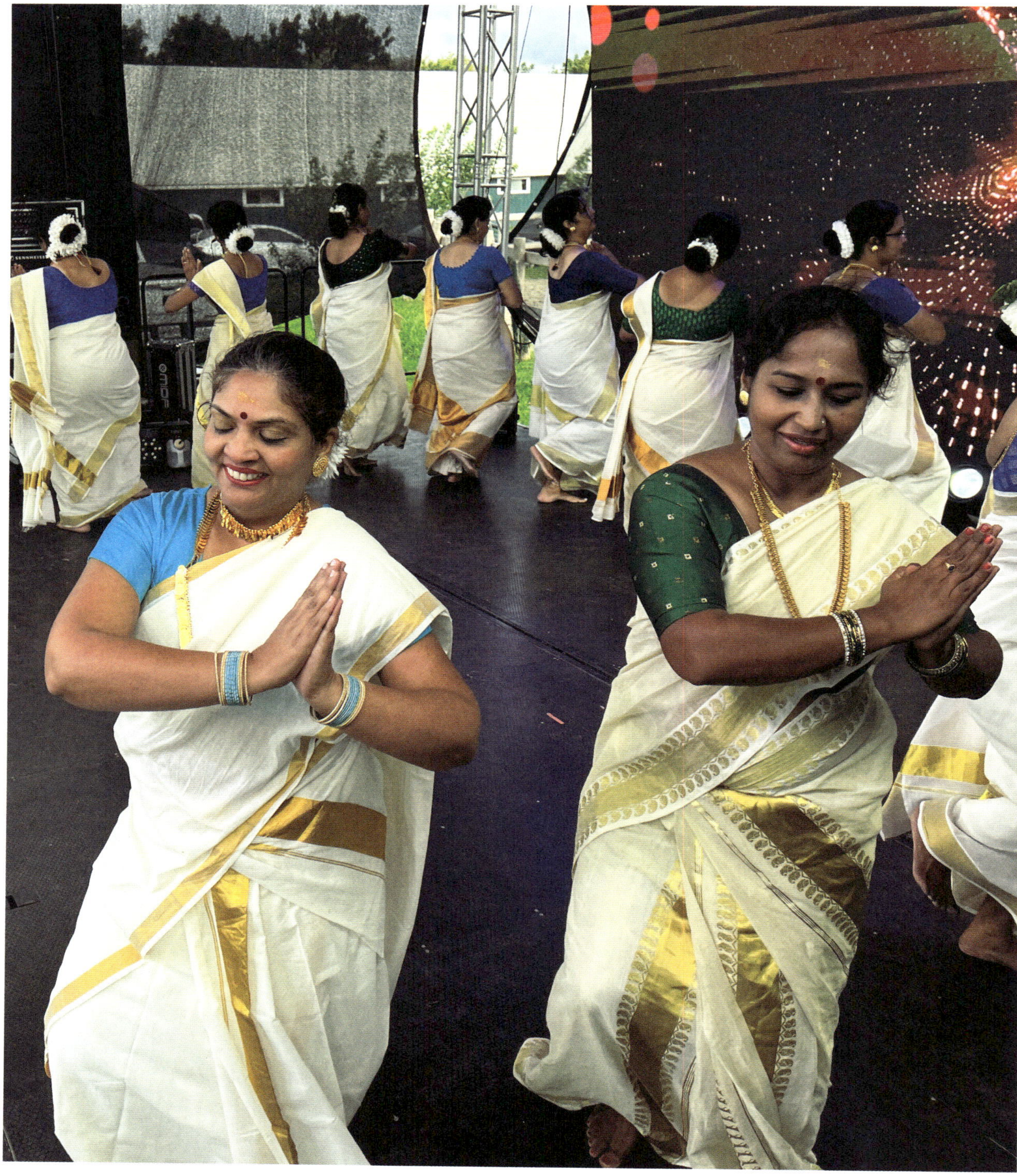

Women performing Thiruvathirakkali dance in Kasavu saris during Onam. Kasavu saris are characterized by their white fabric and gold borders.

cloth held over the shoulder or tucked at the waist. In modern times, it's often stitched as a single sari, but the drape remains elegant and functional – pleated at the waist, and with the gold-edged *pallu* carried over one shoulder. There is a poetry to simplicity: white for purity, gold for prosperity and jasmine for grace. Together, they create an image as timeless as Kerala's own backwaters – serene, luminous, unforgettable.

Andhra Pradesh & Telangana – Pochampally *Ikat* & Gadwal

In Pochampally, near Hyderabad, the roads are lined with *ikat*-dyed yarns hanging out to dry – streaks of red, black, yellow and indigo fluttering in the breeze. The *ikat* technique here is legendary: threads are tie-

KANJEEVARAM'S TEMPLE BORDERS

Kanjeevaram sari borders draw directly from South Indian temple architecture. Gopurams, chariots, bells and sacred animals are woven as visual prayers. The korvai technique – joining body and border separately – ensures durability, allowing these heavy silk saris to be passed down across generations without fraying.

dyed before they are woven, so the final sari blooms with blurred-edge diamonds, checks and geometric patterns that seem to shimmer as the fabric moves. A Pochampally sari resembles a kaleidoscope: precise yet dreamlike, mathematical yet alive. The Gadwal sari, by comparison, is a study in contrast and craft. Its hallmark is the interlocking of a cotton body with silk borders and *pallu*, woven so finely that legend says the entire 'six yards' can be folded into a matchbox. Imagine a body of earthy brown cotton edged with blazing maroon silk and topped with golden

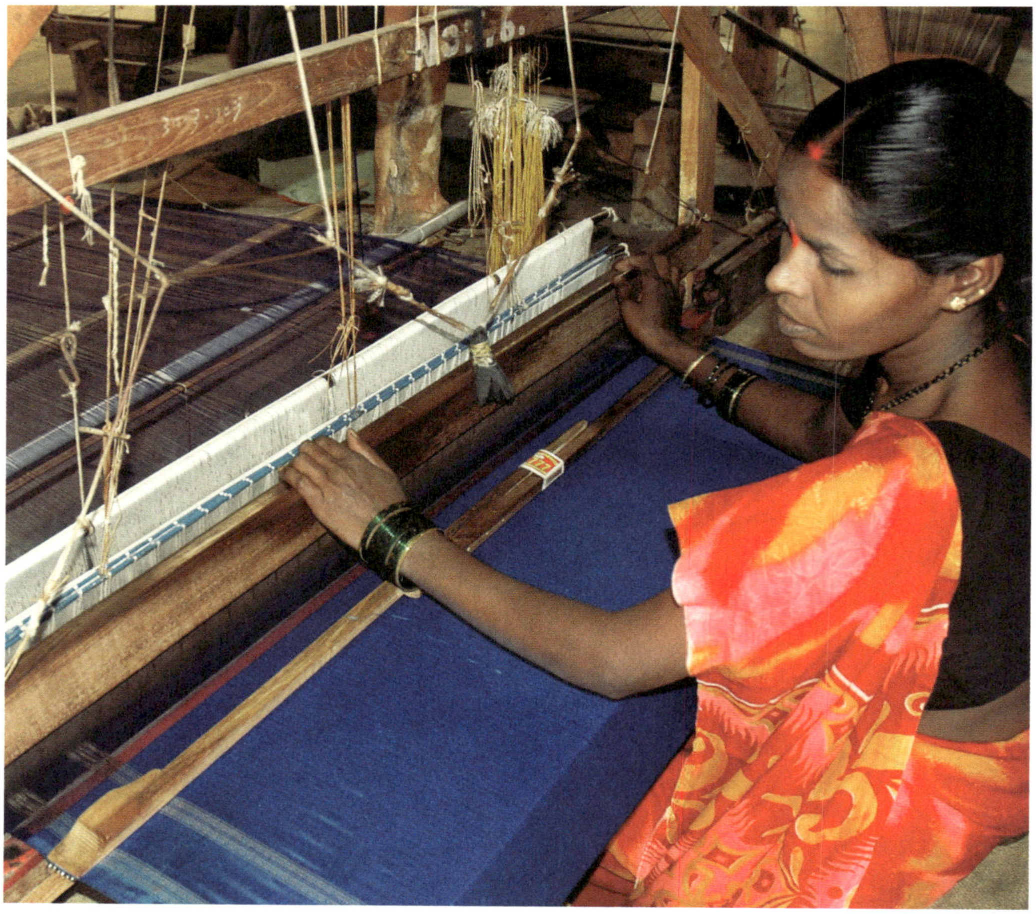

Weaver working on a sari, Pochampalli, Telangana, India. Pochampally is known for its ikat weaving tradition.

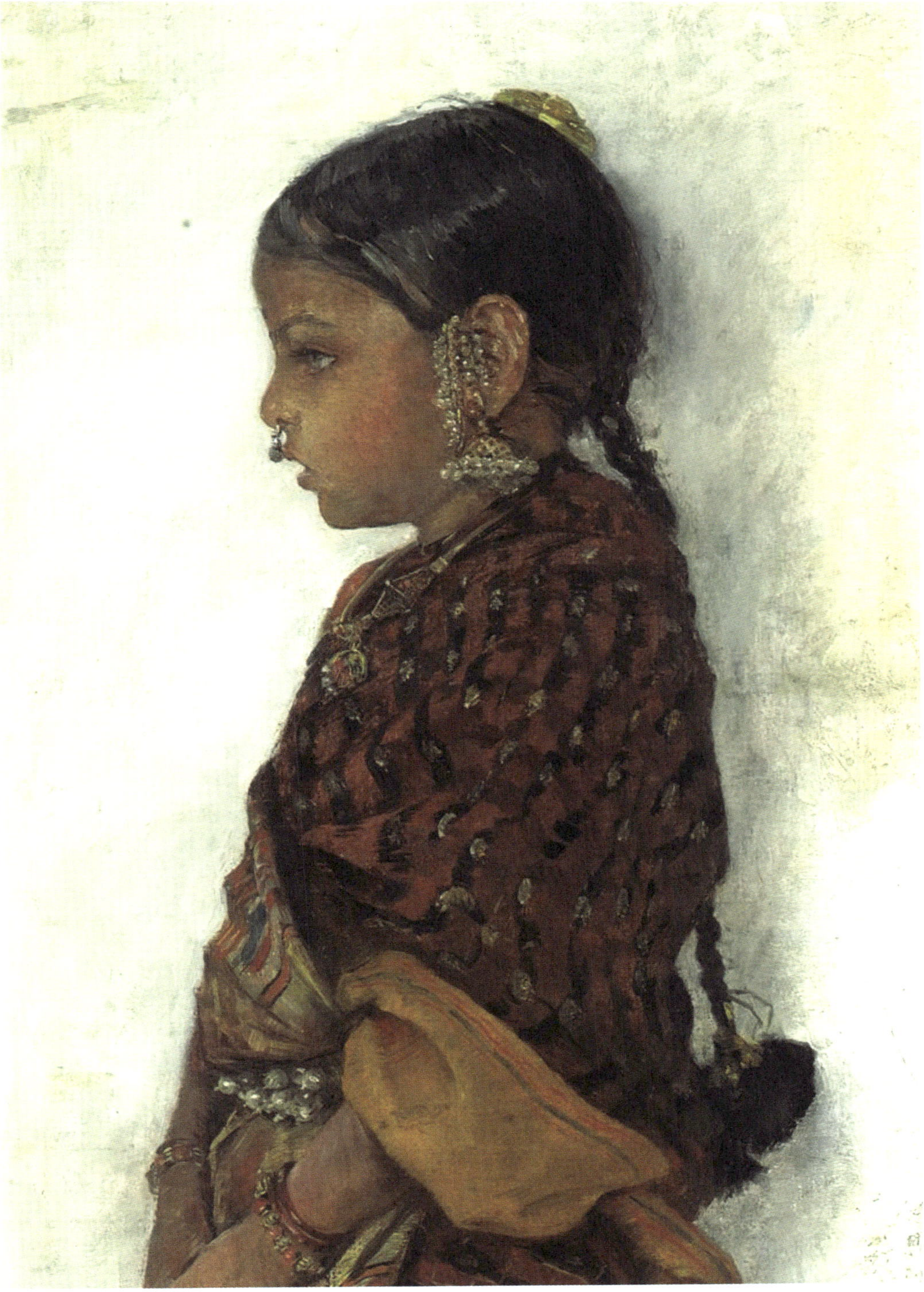

*Girl standing in a veranda wearing a Pochampalli sari, c. 1895.
Such garments reflect regional textile identities.*

zari peacocks dancing across the *pallu*. It's a garment born of necessity – cool cotton for the Deccan heat, regal silk for temple and festival. Mangalgiri saris, woven in the eponymous town, are quiet, understated cousins. They are defined by their plain bodies and Nizam borders, which are wide bands of gold or threadwork that create balance. The weave is so fine and tight that the fabric never needs starching. Worn, a Mangalgiri falls like a second skin, dignified and minimal.

Women in Andhra and Telangana drape these saris in graceful, practical styles. The Pochampally and Gadwal are usually worn in the familiar Nivi style, with the pleats tucked at the waist and the *pallu* draped over the shoulder. In some Telugu households, a variation is seen: after tucking the sari and pleating the *pallu*, the loose end is

JAMDANI: MOTIFS WITHOUT MACHINES

Jamdani weaving uses no graphs, no cards, no automation. Motifs are inserted by hand, thread by thread, using extra weft. This makes each sari subtly unique. Recognized by UNESCO, Jamdani is as much mental labour as physical – requiring memory, rhythm and mathematical precision.

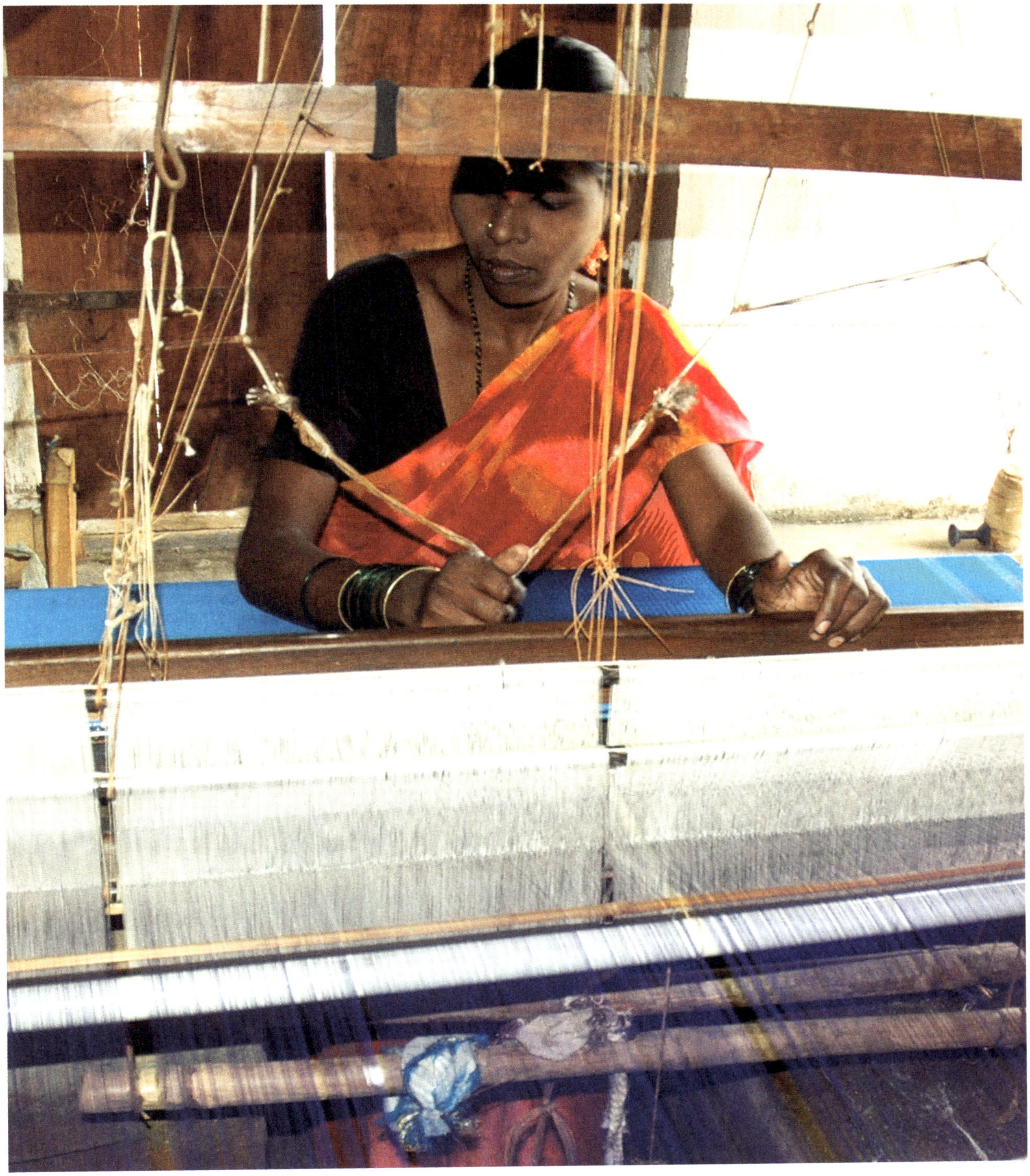

Weaver working on a loom, Pochampalli, Telangana, India.
Handloom weaving requires coordination of multiple threads and tools.

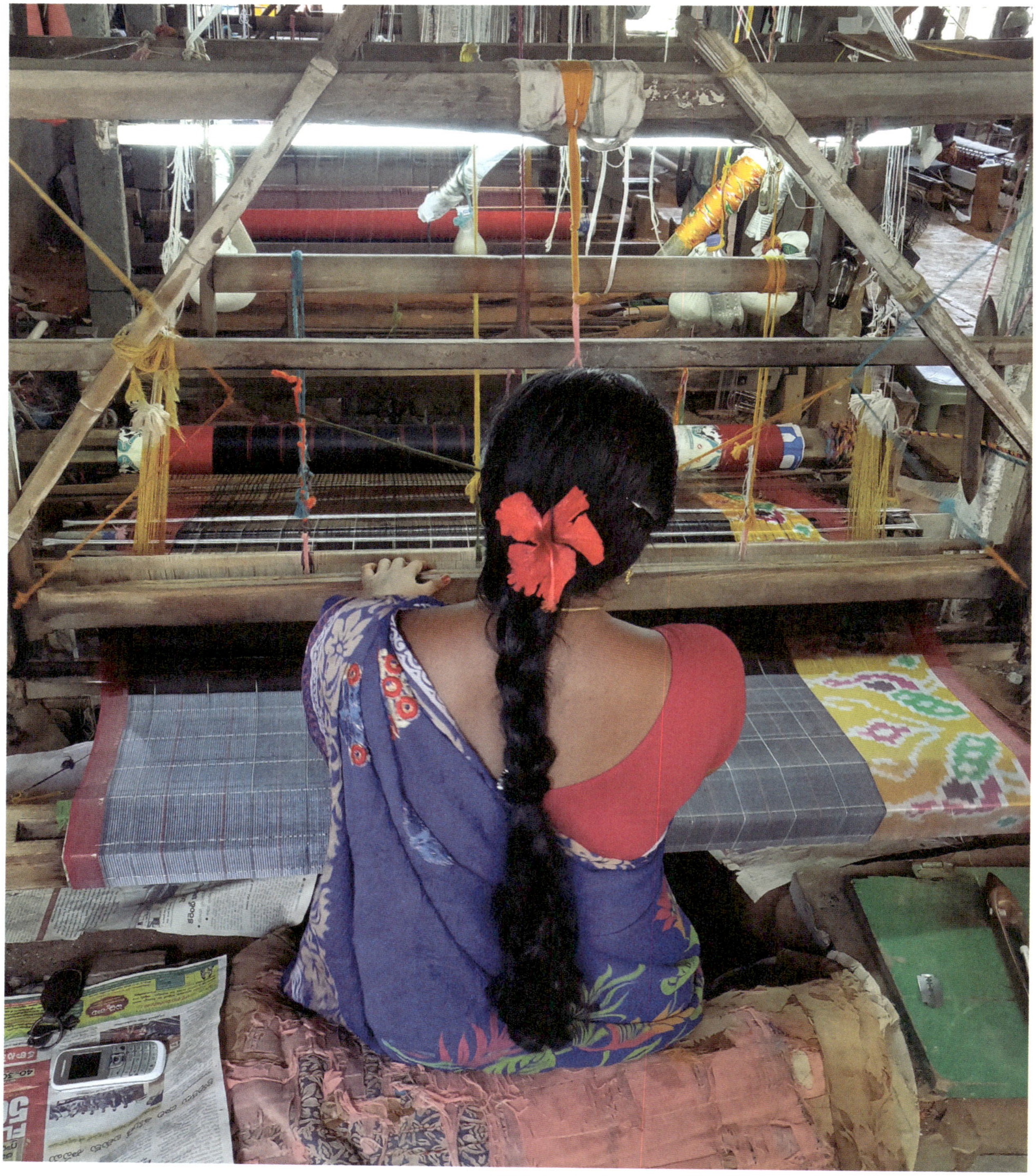

Woman weaving a sari in Mangalagiri, Andhra Pradesh, India.
Mangalagiri saris are known for their fine cotton and simple borders.

brought around from the back to the front and thrown over the right shoulder in what is known as the Andhra or Telugu style drape. This adapts well to the climate and is often seen in daily wear. Whether pleated at the front or gathered at the back, the emphasis is on letting the rich colours and patterns of the fabric flow freely. A Gadwal's cotton-silk drape or a Pochampally's blurred *ikat* design takes on life as it moves with the wearer – each style honouring the weaver's balance of art and utility.

Karnataka – Ilkal and Molakalmuru

In Karnataka, silk is not just fabric – it is legacy. Mysore silk, originating in the royal patronage of the Wodeyars, still has a regal simplicity. Unlike the heavy brocades of Kanchipuram, Mysore silks are sleek, featherlight and drenched in jewel tones. Think sapphire blue, ruby red, emerald green, each sari shimmering with a liquid gloss that comes from mulberry silk reared locally in Karnataka's sericulture belts. Borders are minimal but edged with pure gold *zari*, creating an understated luxury. Wearing a Mysore silk feels like slipping into water – fluid, cool, and effortless. Travel north to the weaving town of Ilkal, and the mood shifts. Here, looms beat out saris that are sturdy, practical, yet stunning. The weavers use cotton for the body and silk for the *pallu*, joining them together with the ingenious tope teni technique which is a kind of knot that never unravels. The *pallu* comes alive with bright red, peacock green and mustard yellow, often patterned with bold stripes or temple motifs. Unlike the grandeur of Mysore silks, Ilkal saris feel rustic, and are meant for farmers' wives, schoolteachers, ordinary women – yet are no less resplendent.

Karnataka women wear these saris in simple elegance. The Mysore silk is typically draped in the classic Nivi style, letting its lightweight body fall in neat pleats and the *pallu* trail gently over the shoulder. In Ilkal, because the cotton-silk join is so durable, the sari can also be draped firmly – the *pallu* often thrown over the left shoulder, and sometimes tucked at the back – reflecting the no-nonsense practicality of the weave. Whether cascading like water or knotted securely, the drape accentuates the sari's strength. To wear these is to feel both the legacy of royal courts and the grounded pride of the Deccan.

BANDHANI'S THOUSAND KNOTS

Bandhani saris are created by tying thousands of minute knots before dyeing. Each dot is tied by hand, often by women artisans. The placement of dots follows symbolic patterns – fertility, prosperity, protection – making Bandhani a sari traditionally worn for weddings, childbirth and festivals across Gujarat and Rajasthan.

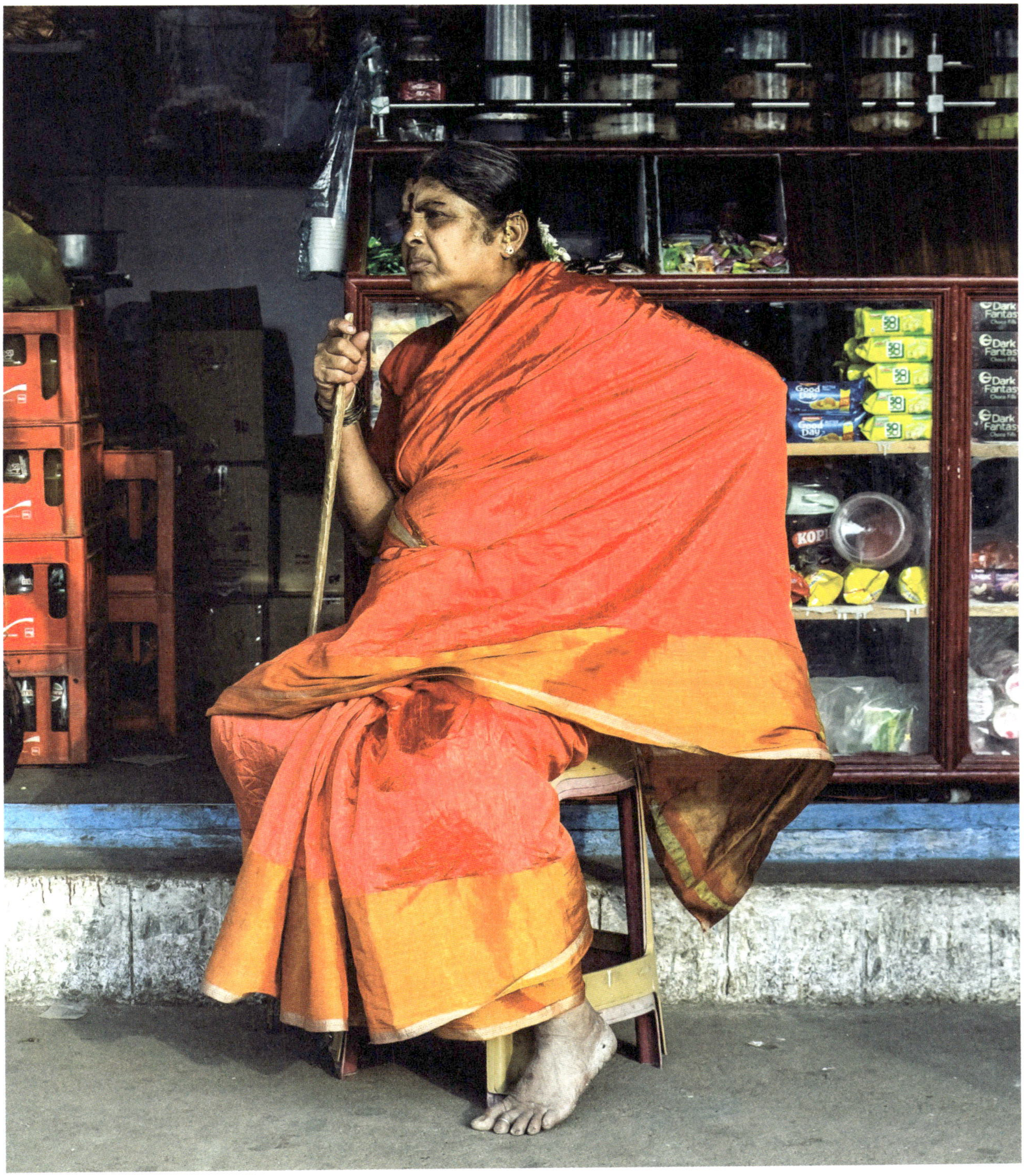

Woman sitting outside a grocery shop, Mysuru, Karnataka, India.
Everyday life scenes often reflect regional clothing practices.

East India

West Bengal – Jamdani, Tant and Baluchari

In Bengal, the sari is not simply attire – it is poetry draped in 'six yards'. The Jamdani, descended from the legendary muslins of Dhaka, is woven so finely it is known as woven air. Picture a gossamer fabric, light as a whisper, scattered with motifs of lotuses, fish or paisleys, each added painstakingly by hand using the extra-weft technique. A Jamdani does not shout but shimmers softly, like moonlight on water. Draped, it feels weightless, as though you are wrapped in nothing but pattern and breath. Then comes the Tant, the everyday sari of the Bengali woman. Woven from crisp cotton, its charm lies in its practicality – starched, airy, perfect for Bengal's humidity. Look closer, however, and you'll see the magic:

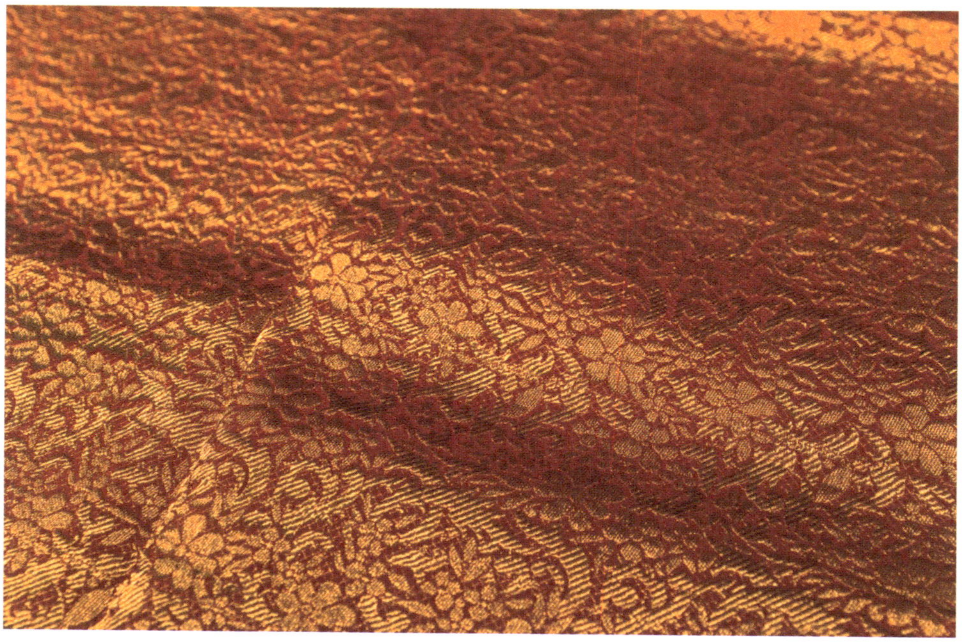

Machine-woven Mysore silk fabric. Mysore silk, also known as mulberry silk, is renowned for its smooth texture and durability.

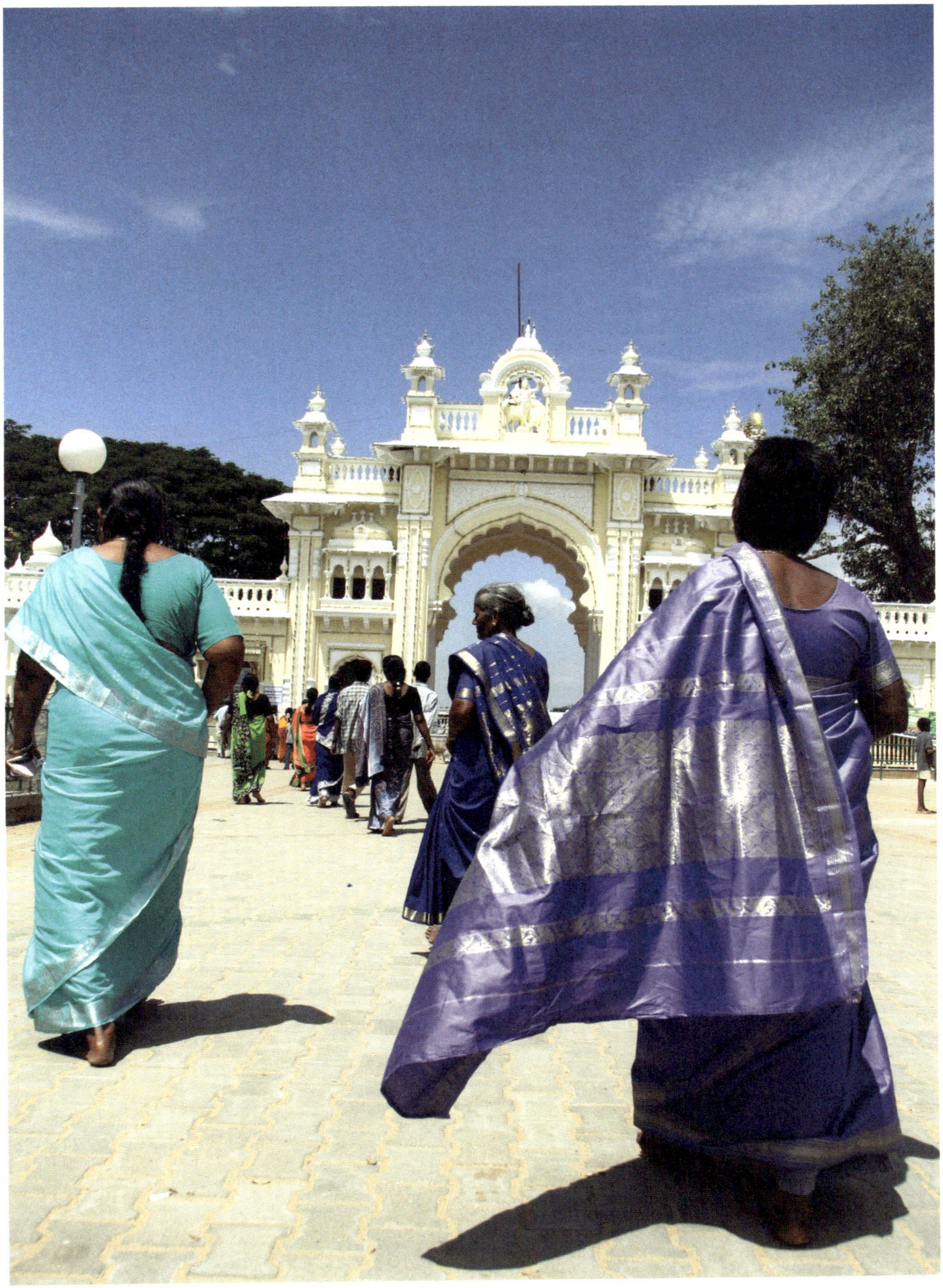

Women entering Mysore Palace, Karnataka, India. Mysore Palace, also known as Amba Vilas Palace, is a historical palace and a royal residence. Designed by Henry Irwin, an English architect, the style is that of Indo-Saracenic architecture.

red borders framing white bodies, fine stripes, and floral butis. During the Hindu festival of Durga Puja, the image of women in white-and-red Tant saris, vermilion on their foreheads, is etched into memory itself. The Baluchari, by contrast, is a storyteller. Woven in Murshidabad, its silk expanse carries elaborate narratives on the *pallu* – episodes from the epic poem *Ramayana*, Krishna's flirtations, and Nawabi court scenes. Each sari is like a scroll unfurling, history and myth entwined in thread. Holding a Baluchari is like holding an illustrated manuscript, and draping it is to wear a story on your body.

Bengali women have a distinctive style of draping these treasures. The Tant and Jamdani are often worn in the traditional Bengali style: pleats

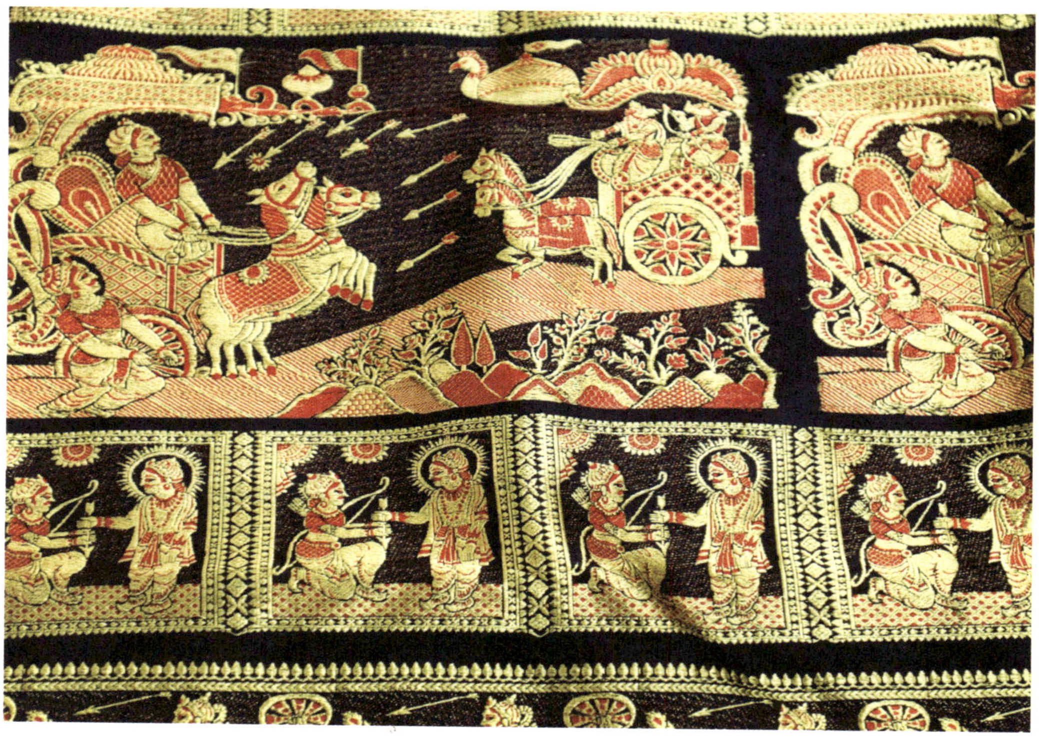

Baluchari silk handloom sari, Bishnupur, West Bengal, India.
Baluchari saris often feature mythological scenes woven into the fabric.

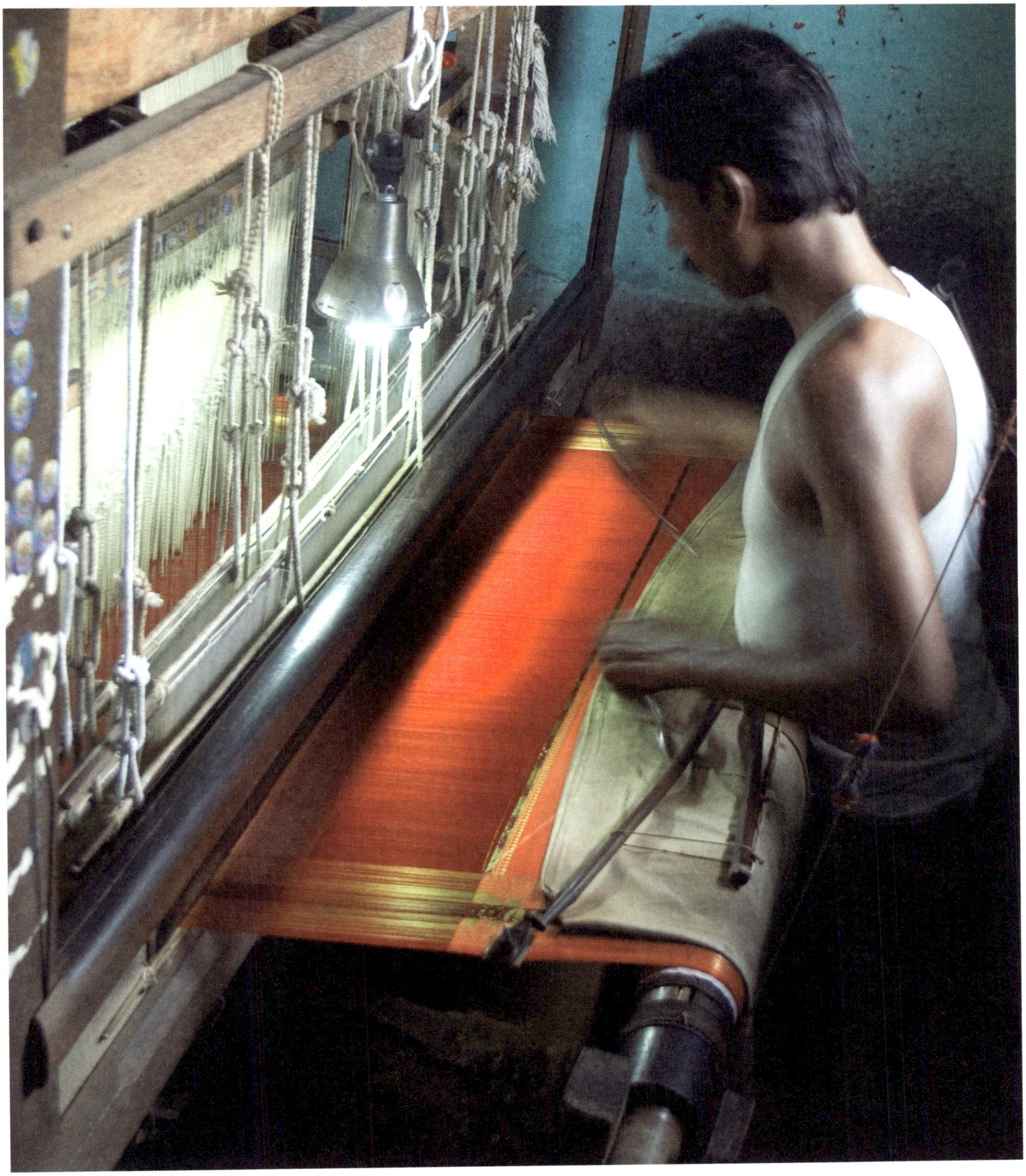

Handloom cotton-silk sari, Bishnupur, West Bengal, India.
Blended fibres combine durability with softness.

at the waist and a long *pallu* that comes from the back and is laid over the left shoulder (sometimes covering the left arm) so that the ornate *pallu* or border is seen hanging in front. During Durga Puja, the 'seedha *pallu*' drape is iconic – the *pallu* brought from behind and thrown over the right shoulder to fall boldly across the front, with its red border bright against white. Even the Baluchari's elaborate *pallu* is arranged similarly so that its pictorial scenes can be admired head on. Whether it's the daily crispness of a Tant or the fine filigree of a Jamdani, the drape is graceful and unhurried, a reflection of Bengal's own languid rhythms.

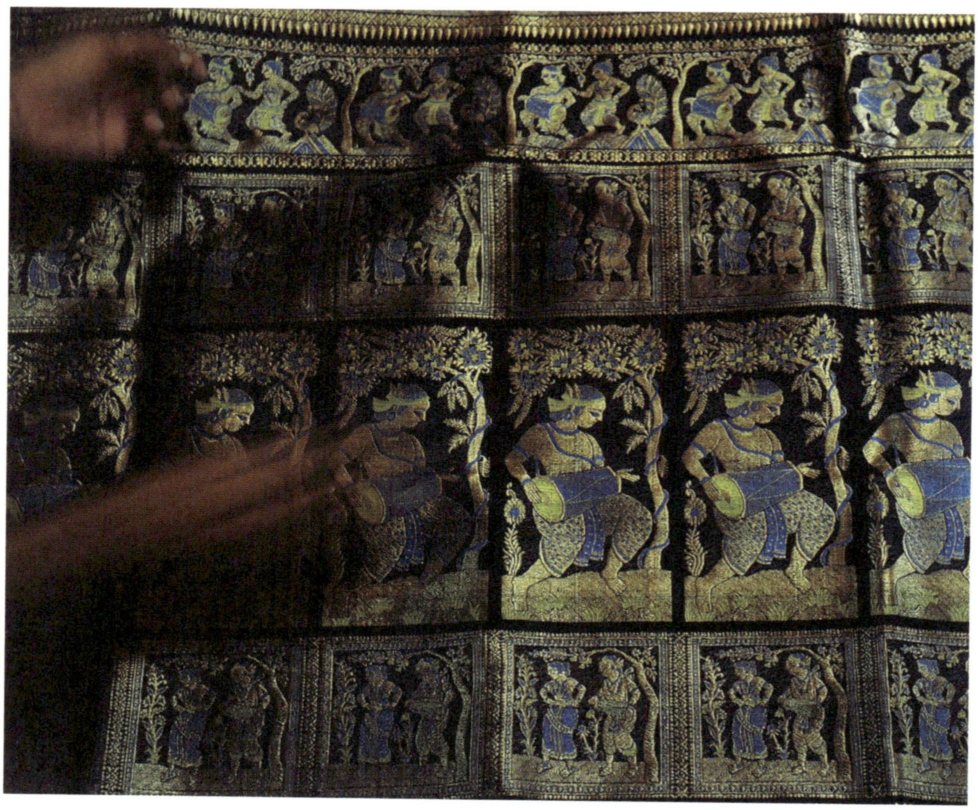

Weaver inspecting a Baluchari sari, Bishnupur, West Bengal, India. Inspection ensures quality and accuracy of woven motifs.

Assam – Muga, Eri & *Mekhela Chador*

In Assam, weaving is less a profession and more a rhythm of life. Most households own a loom, and the click of shuttle against warp is as common as birdsong. Here, the sari is not just attire – it is inheritance, identity and ritual.

The crown jewel of Assamese textiles is Muga silk, a fabric so rare it is called the 'golden thread'. Unique to Assam, Muga is woven from the cocoons of the Antheraea assamensis silkworm, which thrives only in the Brahmaputra valley. The silk emerges naturally golden – no dye needed – and it gleams with a luster that only grows richer with age. Unlike other silks, a Muga does not fade; grandmothers hand down saris that shine as brightly as the day they were woven. Draped, a Muga feels almost alive: crisp, cool, heavy with dignity.

PATOLA: DOUBLE *IKAT* MASTERY

Patola saris are woven using double *ikat*, where both warp and weft threads are resist-dyed before weaving. Patterns must align perfectly, leaving no room for error. One mistake can ruin months of work. Historically worn by royalty, Patolas are still considered auspicious heirlooms.

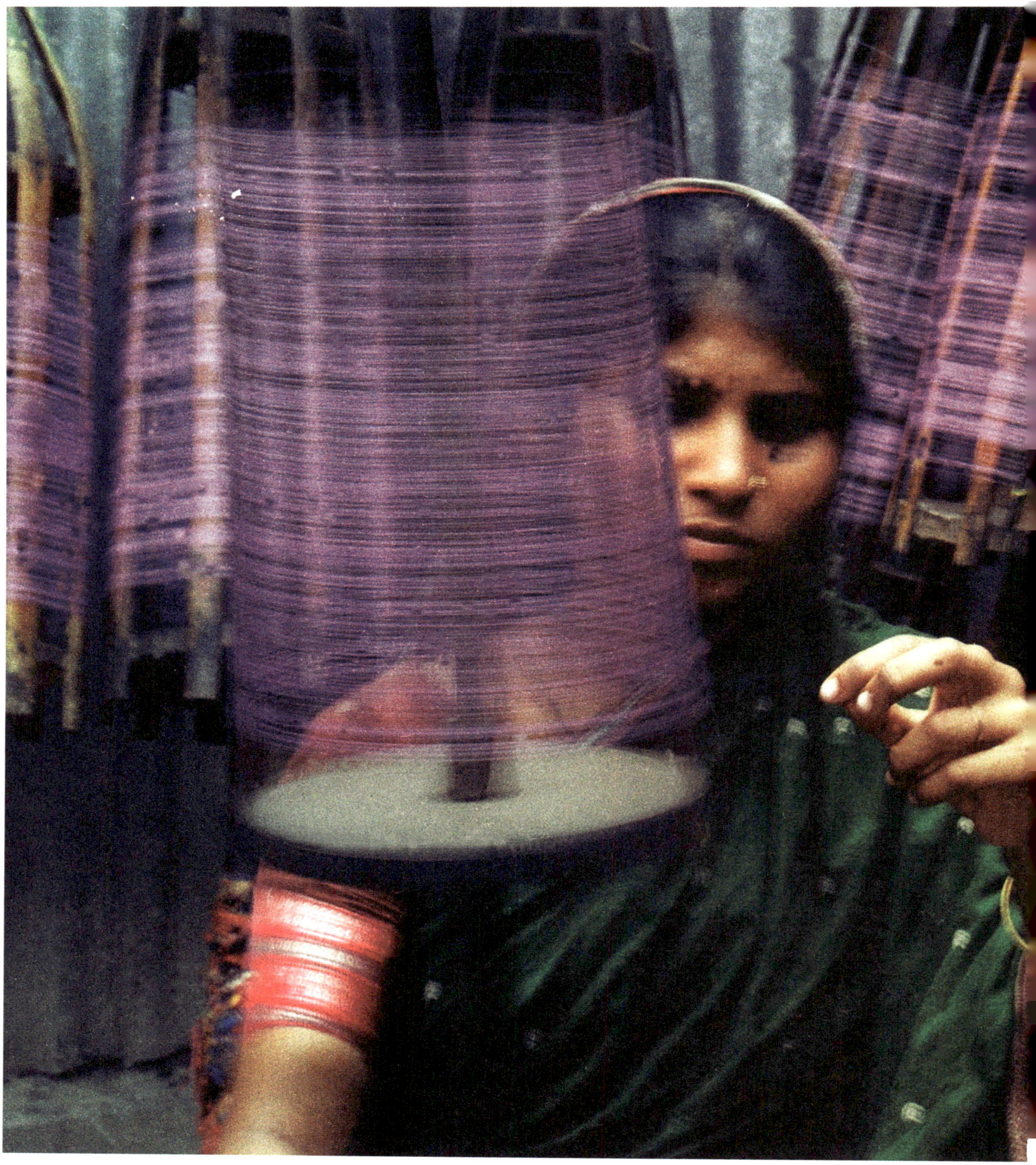

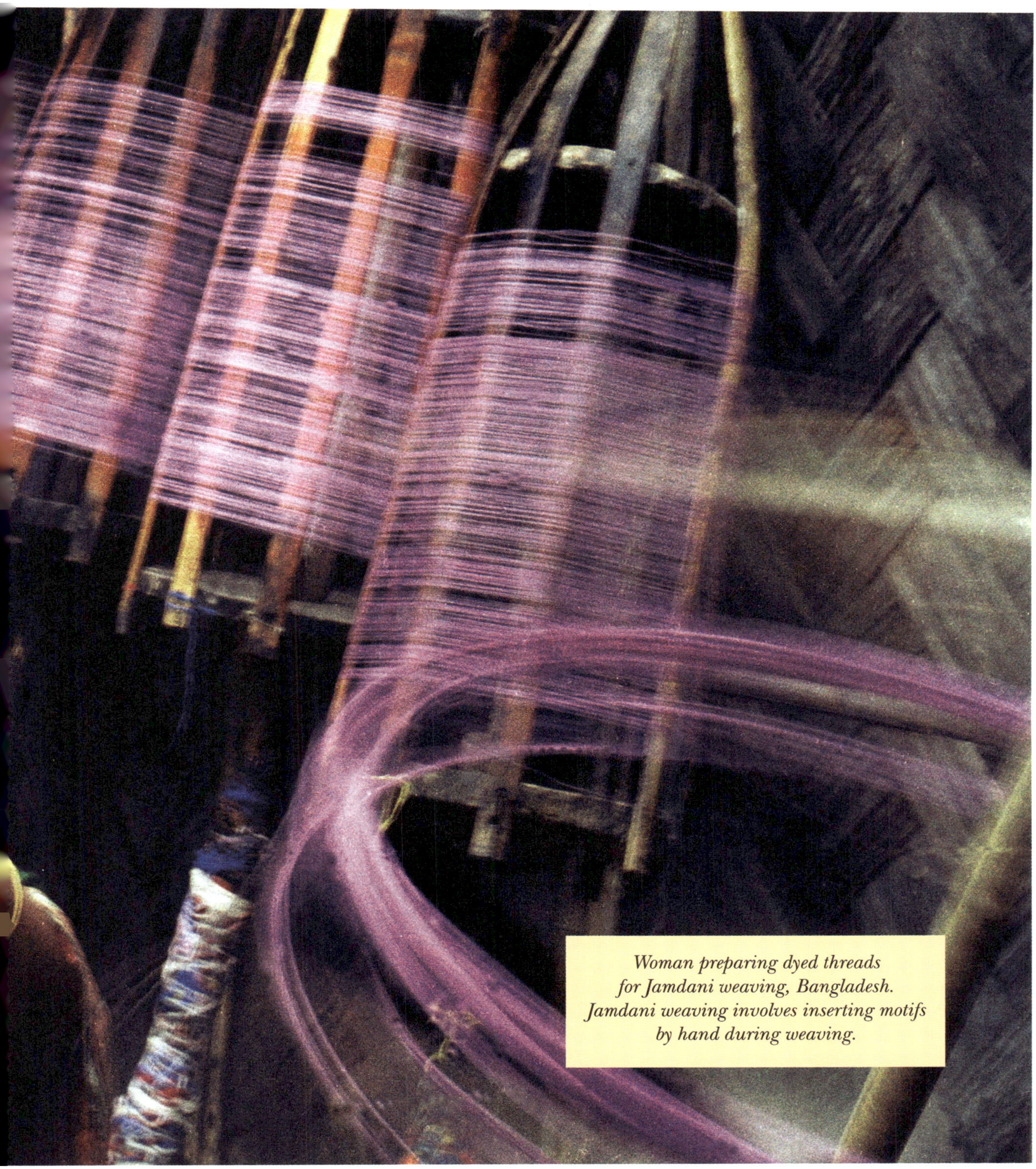

Woman preparing dyed threads for Jamdani weaving, Bangladesh. Jamdani weaving involves inserting motifs by hand during weaving.

Then there is eri silk, also called 'ahimsa silk' because the silkworms are not killed in its making. Eri is soft, warm, and almost woolly in texture, perfect for Assam's cooler winters. Woven into saris, it creates folds that are less lustrous than Muga yet deeply comforting, a gentle fabric, often dyed with natural colours from plants and roots.

The Assamese sari is more than just fabric: it is form. Unlike the 'six yard' drape of much of India, Assam's women traditionally wear the *mekhela chador*: a two-piece garment consisting of the *mekhela* (a cylindrical lower garment) and the *chador* (a length of cloth draped around the torso). The *mekhela* is pleated into soft folds at the waist, while the *chador* is draped gracefully across the shoulder – a style that is both practical and elegant.

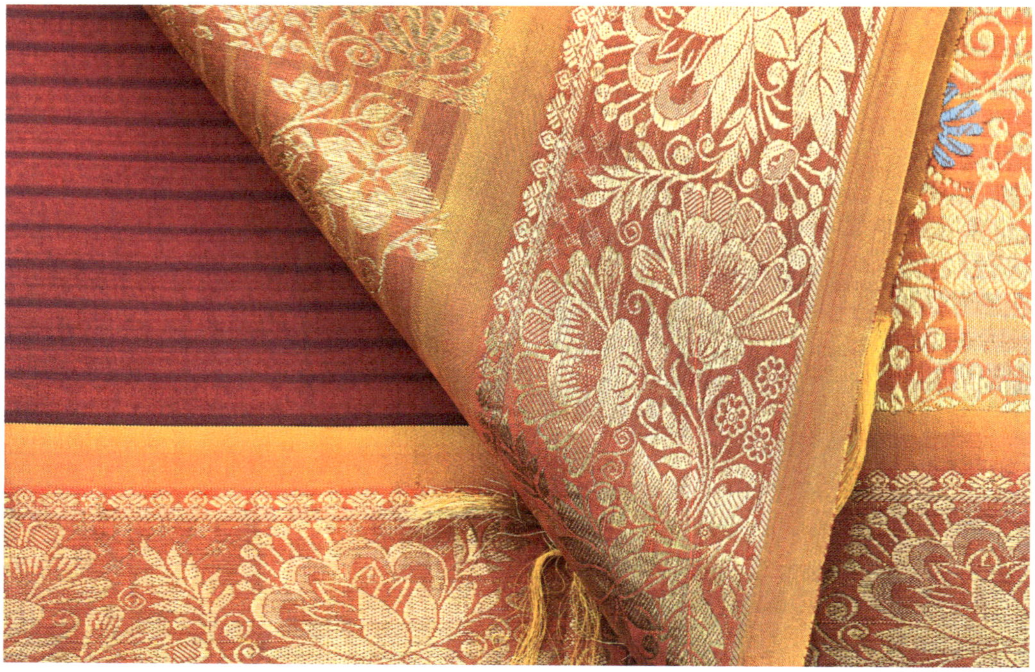

Silk sari with gold border.
Gold borders are often associated with ceremonial attire.

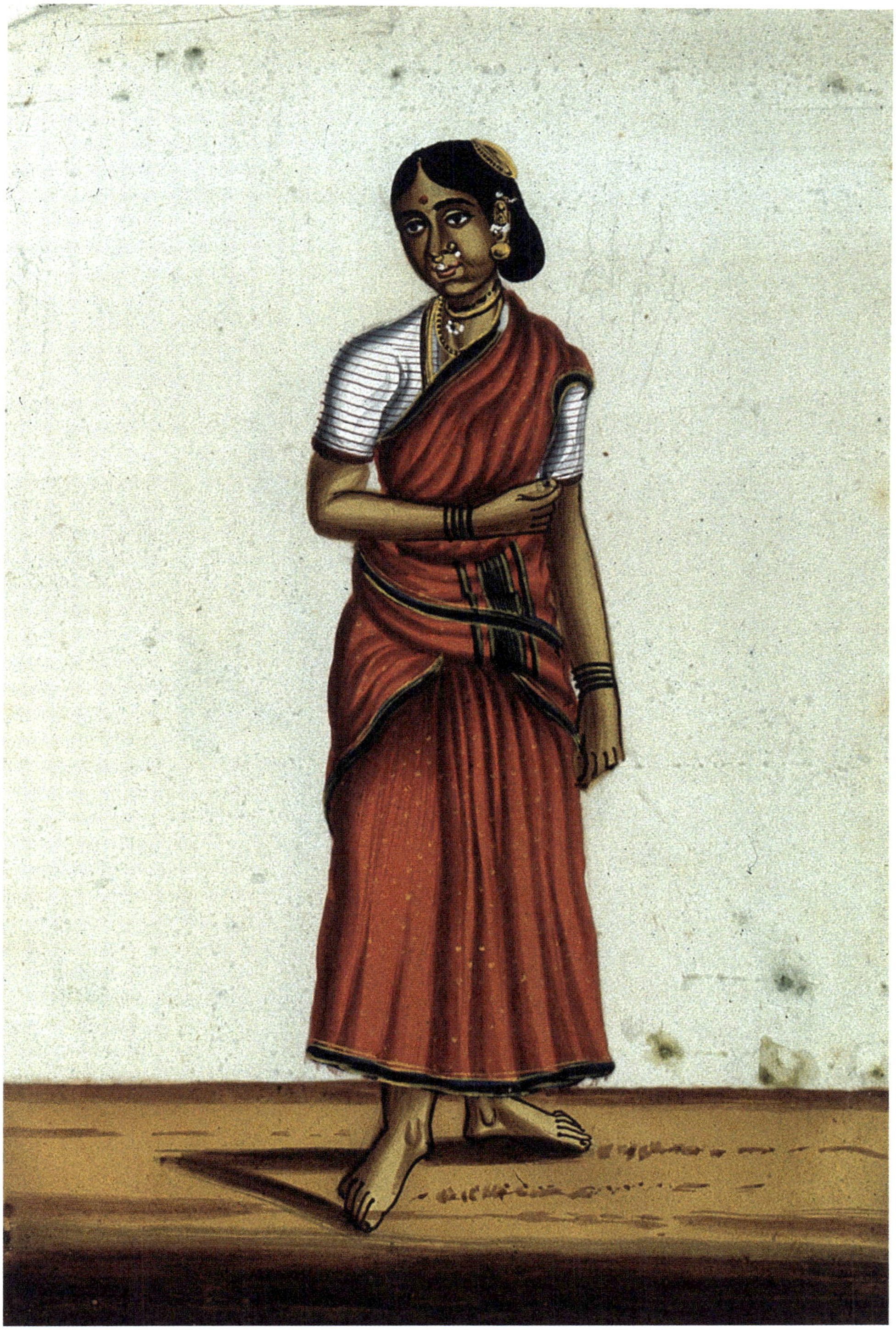

Woman wearing a red sari, gouache painting on mica.
Mica paintings were popular for their translucent surface.

Patterns are woven in motifs called butis: stylized flowers, birds, creepers and the famous *jaapi* (the traditional Assamese hat). Each motif is tiny but exact, created in supplementary weft, where extra threads are inserted into the base weave by hand. The borders and *pallus* often blaze with red, green and black against the golden or cream body, simple yet striking.

A festival morning in Assam is incomplete without the sight of women in crisp white Muga *mekhela chadors* with bright red borders, carrying plates of flowers to temples during Bihu or Durga Puja. A bride in Assam glows in her wedding Muga, the fabric itself blessing her with longevity.

To hold an Assamese sari is to hold a piece of the land – the golden floodplains of the Brahmaputra, the green of tea gardens, the red of betel nut stains. No other weave captures its geography so completely. A Muga sari is not just worn for a lifetime. It outlives its wearer, carrying memory forward in threads that never fade.

Odisha – Sambalpuri & Bomkai

In the looms of Odisha, colour and geometry meet in dazzling symmetry. The Sambalpuri *ikat* is instantly recognizable: bold, sharp-edged motifs like conch shells, wheels, elephants, fish – all created by resist-dyeing the threads before they're woven. The result is a sari where patterns line up with mathematical precision, as if woven by destiny. Draped, it carries the energy of tribal drums, temple dances and river festivals. The Bomkai, also called the Sonepuri, is a subtler cousin. Its base is often deep, earthy tones like rust, black, indigo, with borders and *pallus* woven in stark, contrasting colours. Motifs are drawn from folklore: rudraksha seeds, fish scales, tribal totems. The weave is rougher, heavier, carrying the texture of village life. A Bomkai does not dazzle at first glance – but wear it, and it grows on you, its earthy dignity wrapping around you like a fireside tale.

Odisha's women usually drape their saris in the straightforward Nivi style: pleating the sari at the waist and letting the patterned *pallu* fall from the shoulder. In some rural areas, a variation known as the 'giri-gas' style is seen, where pleats are tied at the waist and a smaller portion is thrown over the shoulder. Whether in a simple Nivi drape or a local style, the focus is on balance – the sharp-edged Sambalpuri designs or the tribal Bomkai motifs are always on full display in front. Each drape, simple as it is, allows the bold Odisha geometry to emerge unhidden, tying the wearer to her land and lore.

TUSSAR: SILK FROM THE FOREST

Tussar silk comes from wild silkworms that feed on forest leaves. Unlike mulberry silk, it retains a matte, uneven texture. Bhagalpur in Bihar remains a major Tussar centre. Its earthy sheen and strength make it suitable for both ritual wear and everyday elegance.

Bihar – Tussar and Bhagalpuri

In Bihar, forests hum with the rustle of silkworms – this is the land of Tussar silk. Unlike the gleaming smoothness of mulberry silk, Tussar has a matte, textured finish, its natural colour a warm honey-gold. Dyers in Bhagalpur take this wild silk and flood it with colour – crimson, deep green, or indigo – while keeping its uneven, organic sheen intact. The result is a fabric that feels alive, less polished, and more rooted. A Bhagalpuri sari, often striped or patterned with checks, is simple yet striking. It drapes with a slight stiffness, holding its shape in dignified

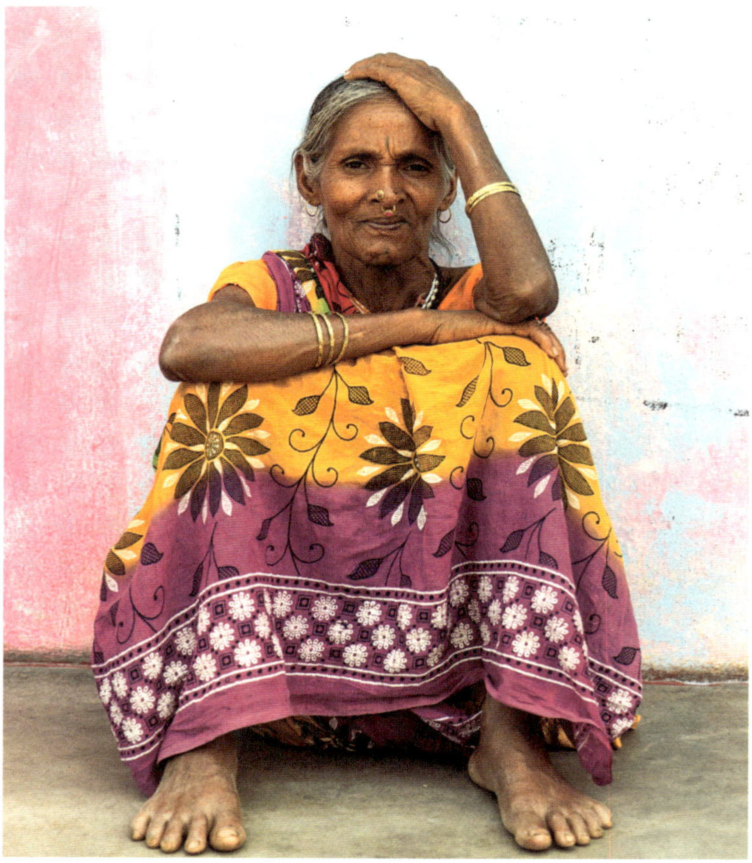

Woman in a sari seated against a painted wall, Odisha, India.

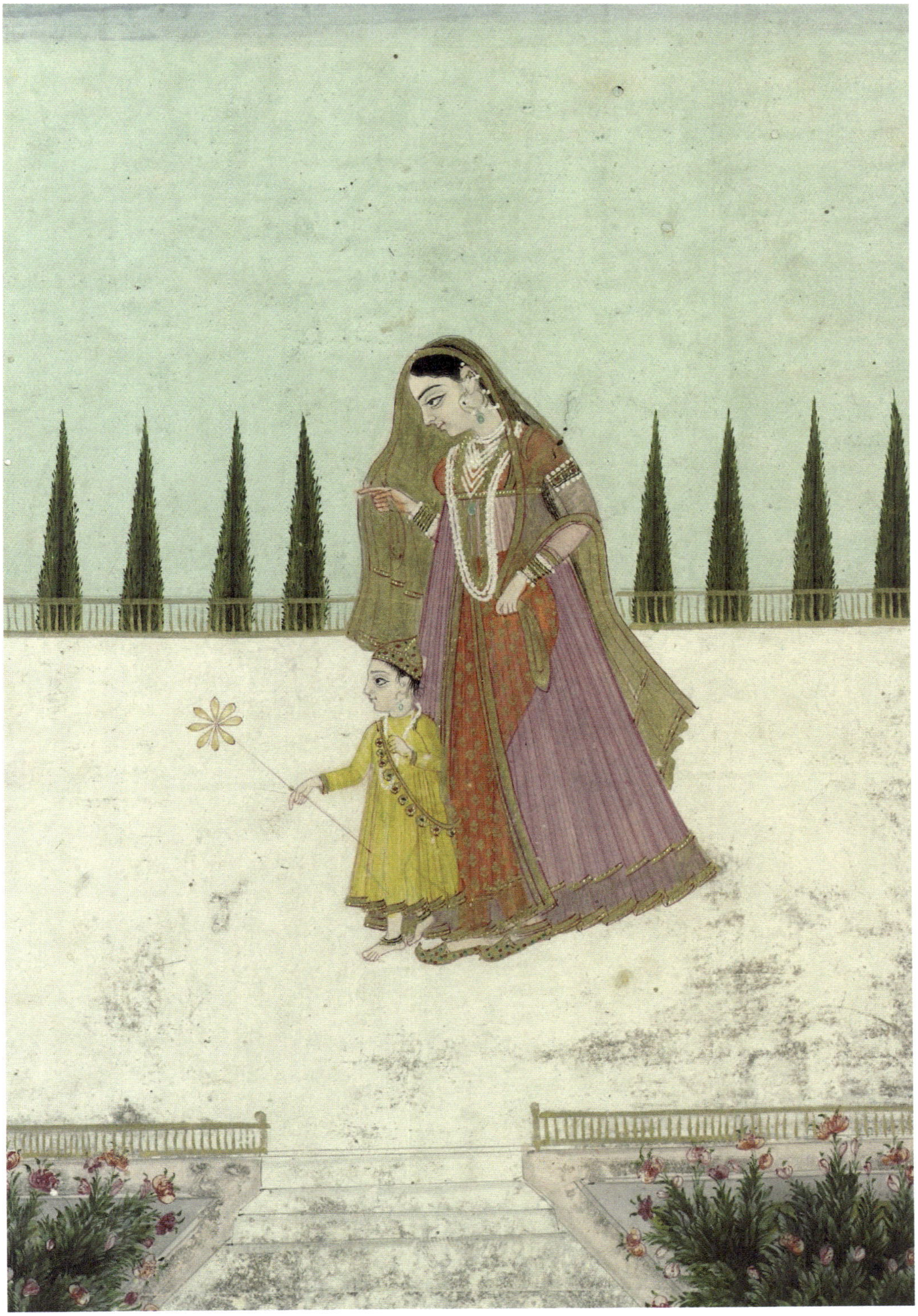

Woman with child, Indian miniature painting, c. 1770–1790.
Such works often depict domestic and maternal themes.

folds. When the sun catches it, the surface glows, not with the flash of gold, but with the warmth of amber. For centuries, the Tussar sari has been worn by villagers, queens and monks, its versatility unmatched. In Bihar, to gift a Tussar is to gift a piece of the forest itself.

In rural Bihar, the Tussar sari is usually worn in the familiar Nivi drape, the sturdy fabric folded into pleats and the *pallu* carried over the

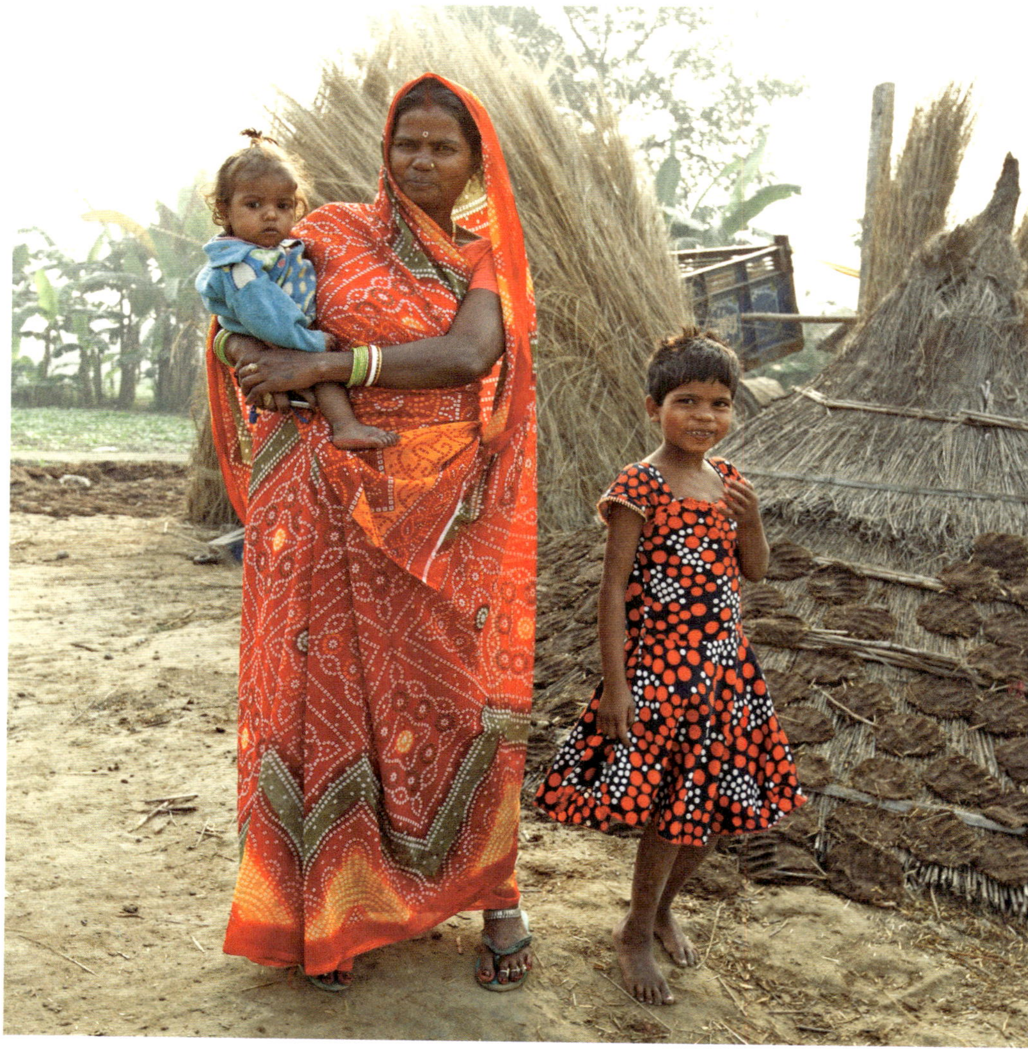

Mother and children in a rural village, Bihar, India.
Family life is often reflected in everyday clothing practices.

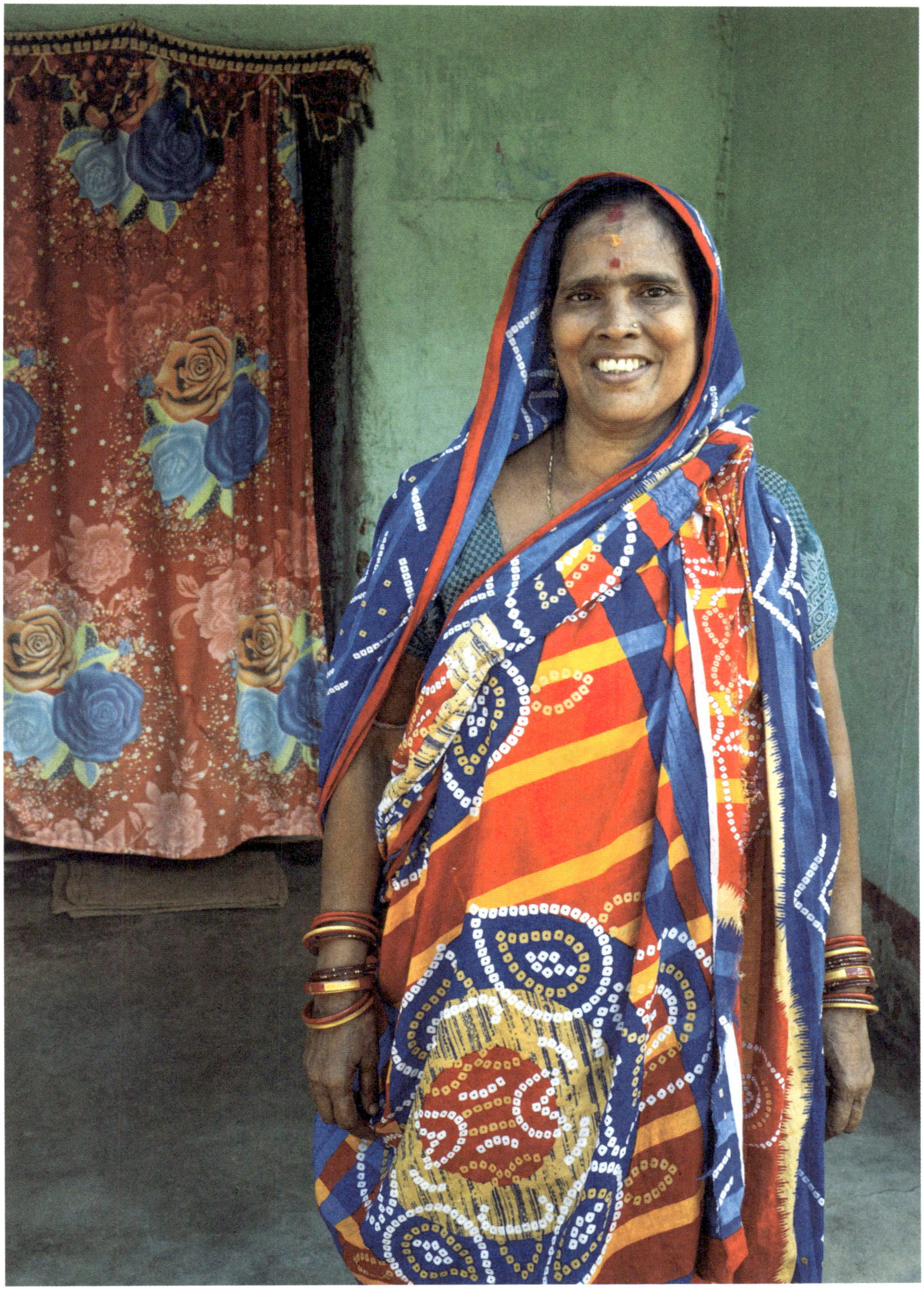

Textile worker with handwoven ikat cloth, Odisha, India.
Ikat textiles are created using resist-dyeing techniques.

shoulder. This uncomplicated style lets the coarse sheen take centre stage. Occasionally, one might see a simpler drape without front pleats, especially among elders, but mostly the emphasis is on comfort and modesty. The sari's own character – its colours and texture – is the star, flowing in gentle folds. Each fold of a Bhagalpuri holds the rustic elegance of the wilderness from which it came.

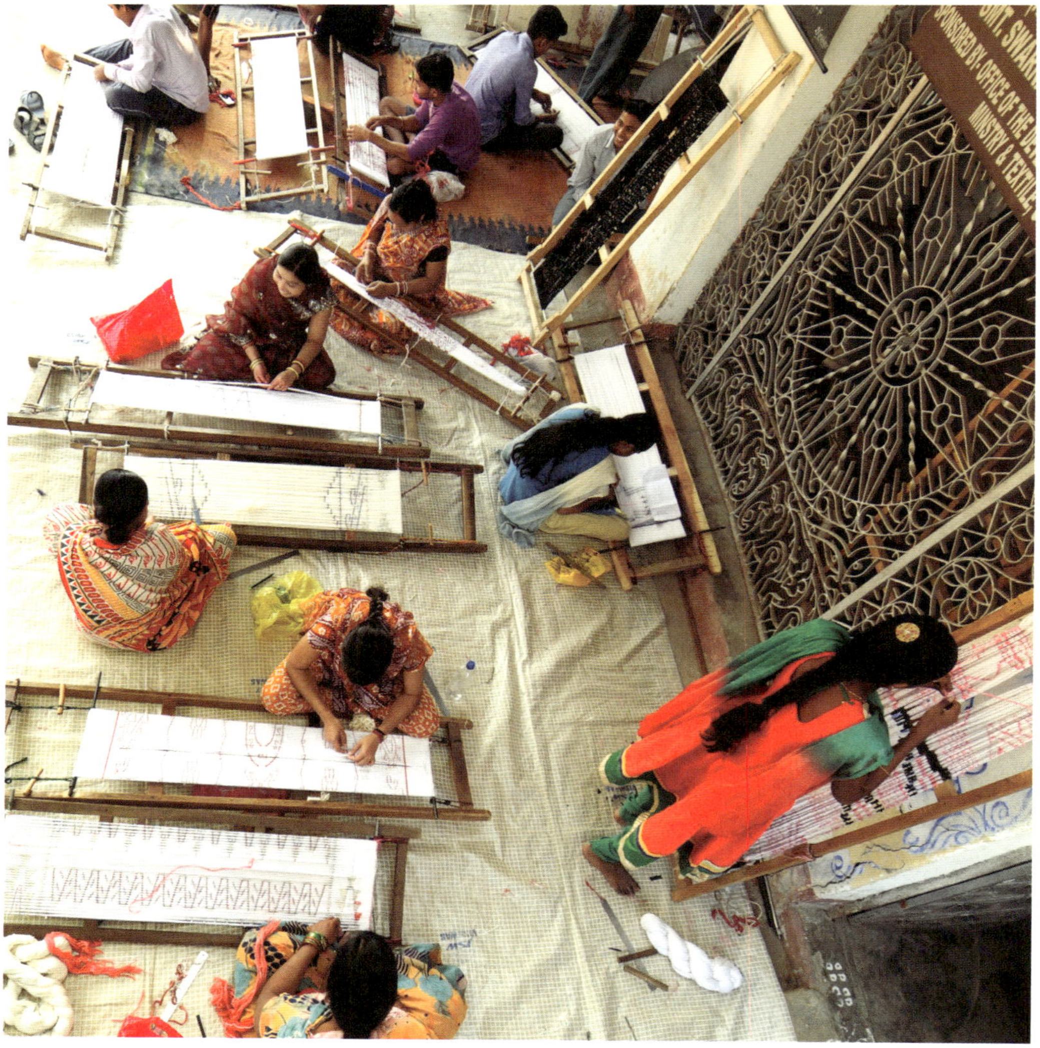

Traditional handloom weaving workshop.

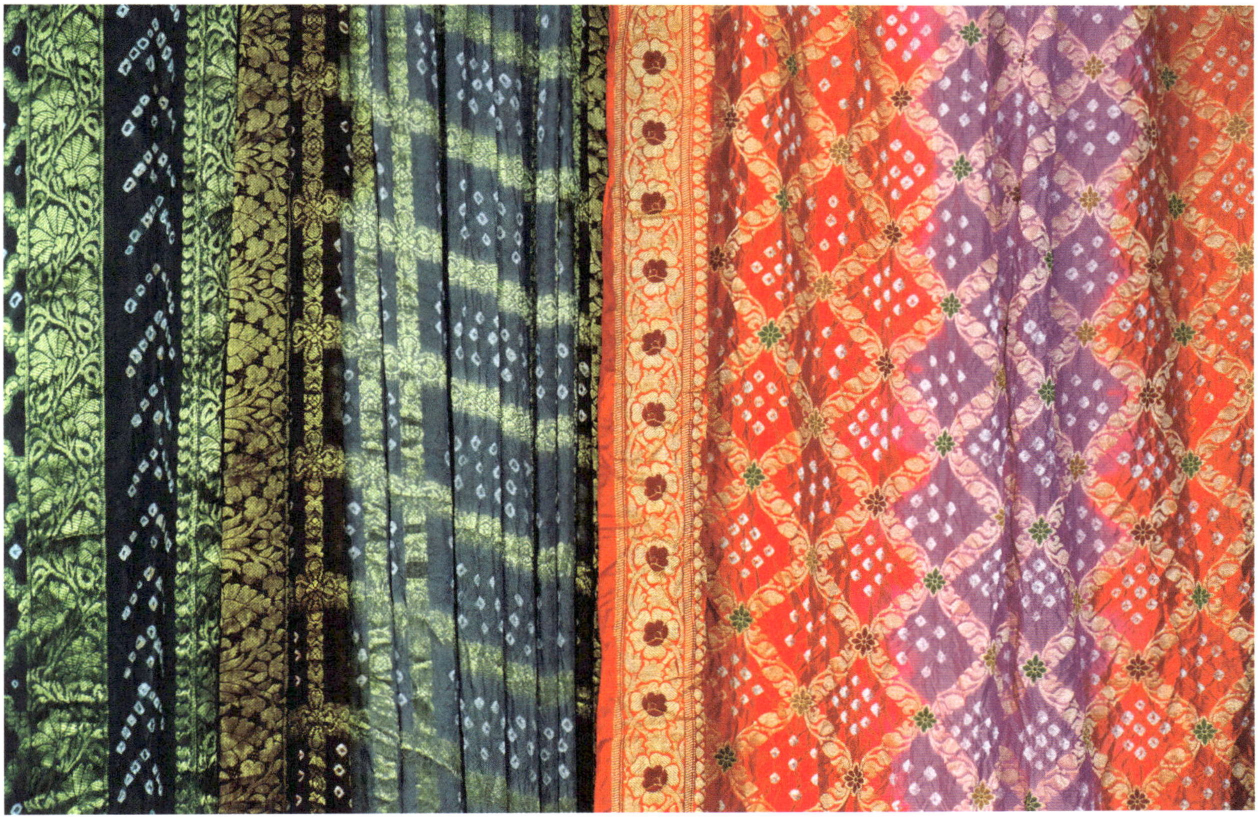

Colourful Bandhani (Bandhej) saris displaying tie-dye patterns arranged in geometric and dotted motifs. Originating from Gujarat and Rajasthan, this technique involves carefully tying sections of fabric before dyeing to create detailed designs.

West India

Gujarat – Patola and Bandhani

In Patan, Gujarat, the Patola sari is regarded less as cloth and more as crown jewel. It is made using the double *ikat*, where both warp and weft threads are tie-dyed before weaving, aligned so precisely that when woven the patterns emerge with razor-sharp clarity. Elephants, parrots, dancing women, and flowers – all come alive in symmetry. No blurring, no hesitation. A Patola can take six months to a year to weave, and it shows: the colours – crimson, emerald, and indigo – remain unfaded

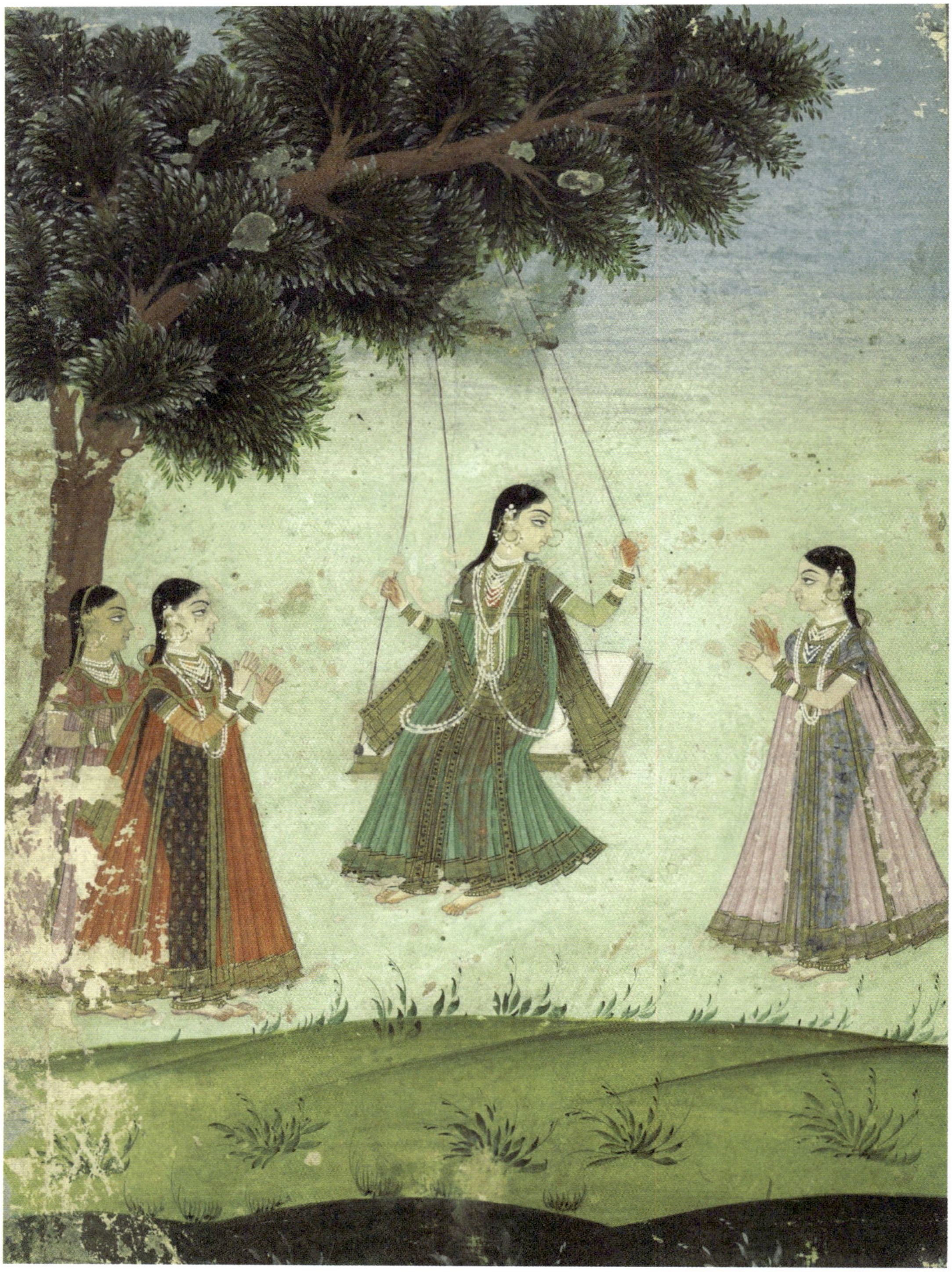

'Swinging Lady', creator unknown, 1740-1760. Such scenes often represent monsoon leisure and courtly life, celebrating themes of beauty, romance, and seasonal change.

for generations, glowing with an almost eternal fire. Draping one feels like draping geometry itself, exact and regal. Then there is Bandhani, the art of dots. In towns like Jamnagar and Bhuj, women sit for hours tying thousands of tiny knots on plain fabric, each with a fingernail-sized thread. When dyed, these knots resist colour, creating constellations of white against fields of red, yellow, black or green. The fabric opens like the night sky, every dot a star, every fold a galaxy. Bandhani saris carry a celebratory spirit and are worn at weddings, births and festivals. To wear one is to carry joy in motion, fabric dancing with dotted light.

Gujarat has its own flair for draping: the Gujarati style (Seedha *Pallu*). Women typically wrap the sari around the waist and bring the *pallu* from the back to the front, draping it over the right shoulder so that the ornamented end is displayed at the front. Thus, a Patola's precise pattern

MUGA: SILK THAT NEVER FADES

Muga silk, unique to Assam, naturally emerges golden – without dye. Remarkably, it grows more lustrous with age. A Muga sari can last decades, even centuries, and is often passed down as family wealth. No other silk carries longevity, geography and prestige so visibly.

or a Bandhani's clustered dots are always visible. The boldness of this style matches the sari's energy: the rich Patola patterns or playful Bandhani dots swirl down the body like a flourishing tapestry. Even when worn simply, these saris make a statement. A Gujarati bride in a red Bandhani, the *pallu* pulled forward, is a portrait of festivity and tradition.

Maharashtra – Paithani and Nauvari

In Paithan, near the banks of the Godavari, weavers craft the Paithani, a sari so resplendent it was once traded for its weight in gold. Woven from fine silk,

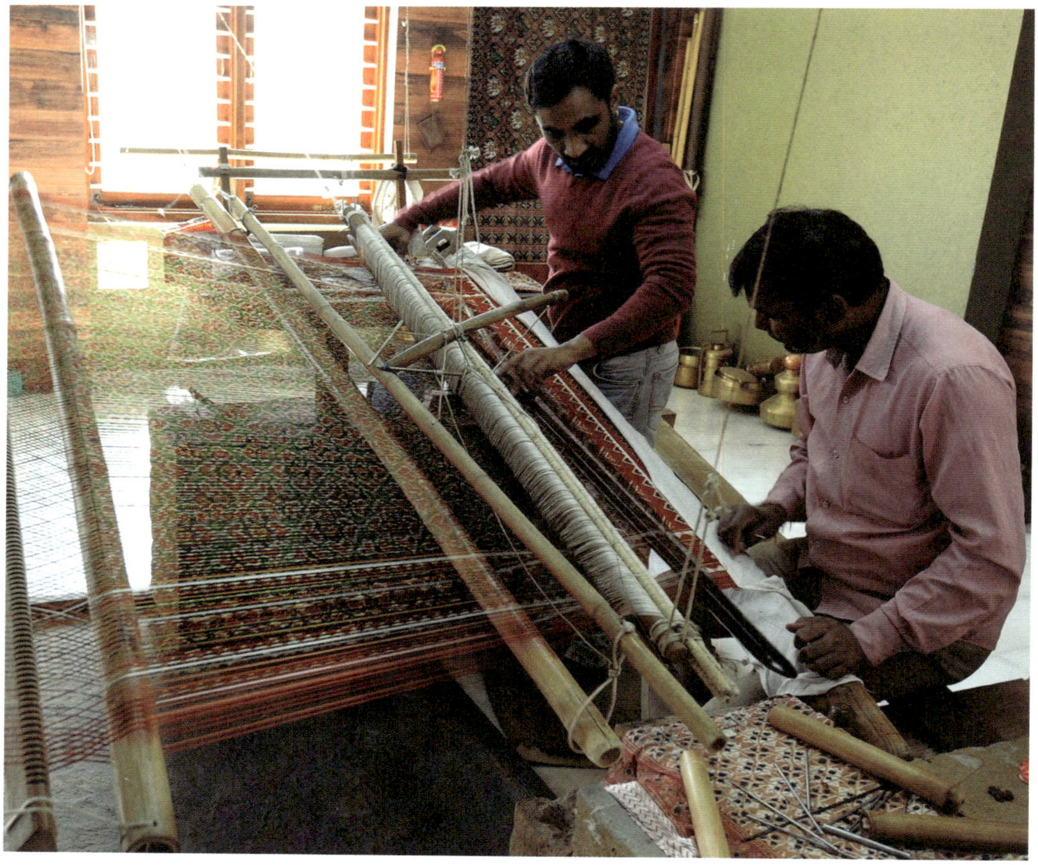

Patan, Gujrat, two weavers working to weave a double ikat Patola sari using a harness loom slanted to one side.

its hallmark is the *pallu* – a panel of intricate motifs, including peacocks with spread tails, lotuses, and vines, all woven in *zari* so rich it gleams like molten metal. The body often features plain colours such as magenta, parrot green, or royal blue, allowing the border and *pallu* to dazzle like framed paintings. Hold a Paithani up to the light and you'll see it change shades. This is because the weavers use a special dyeing technique that creates a play of colour – green turning into yellow, purple into red. A Paithani is not simply worn; it is unveiled like a treasure. And then, there is the Nauvari, Maharashtra's warrior drape. Nine yards (8.2m) long, and tucked at the back like a dhoti, it leaves the legs free for movement. Once worn by women who fought battles alongside the Maratha armies, today it is still worn for dances, wedding rituals and festivals. A Nauvari in bold red or green cotton, its gold border glinting, is more than a sari – it is an expression of strength. When draped, it transforms its wearer into both goddess and warrior, practical yet commanding.

Paithani saris are usually worn in the classic Nivi style by Maharashtrian women, with pleats at the waist and the *pallu* looped over the shoulder so as to highlight the elaborate border. In contrast, the Nauvari is draped uniquely: the nine-yard (8.2m) length is first tucked in at the back to free the legs, then wrapped around like a dhoti, while the *pallu* is finally passed over the shoulder. This Peshwai style creates a striking look – the Paithani's shining *pallu* or a Nauvari's sunburst pattern will billow over the wearer's arm as she moves. Whether gently folded in pleats or tied for activity, both drapes showcase the richness of colour and weave that is quintessentially Maharashtrian.

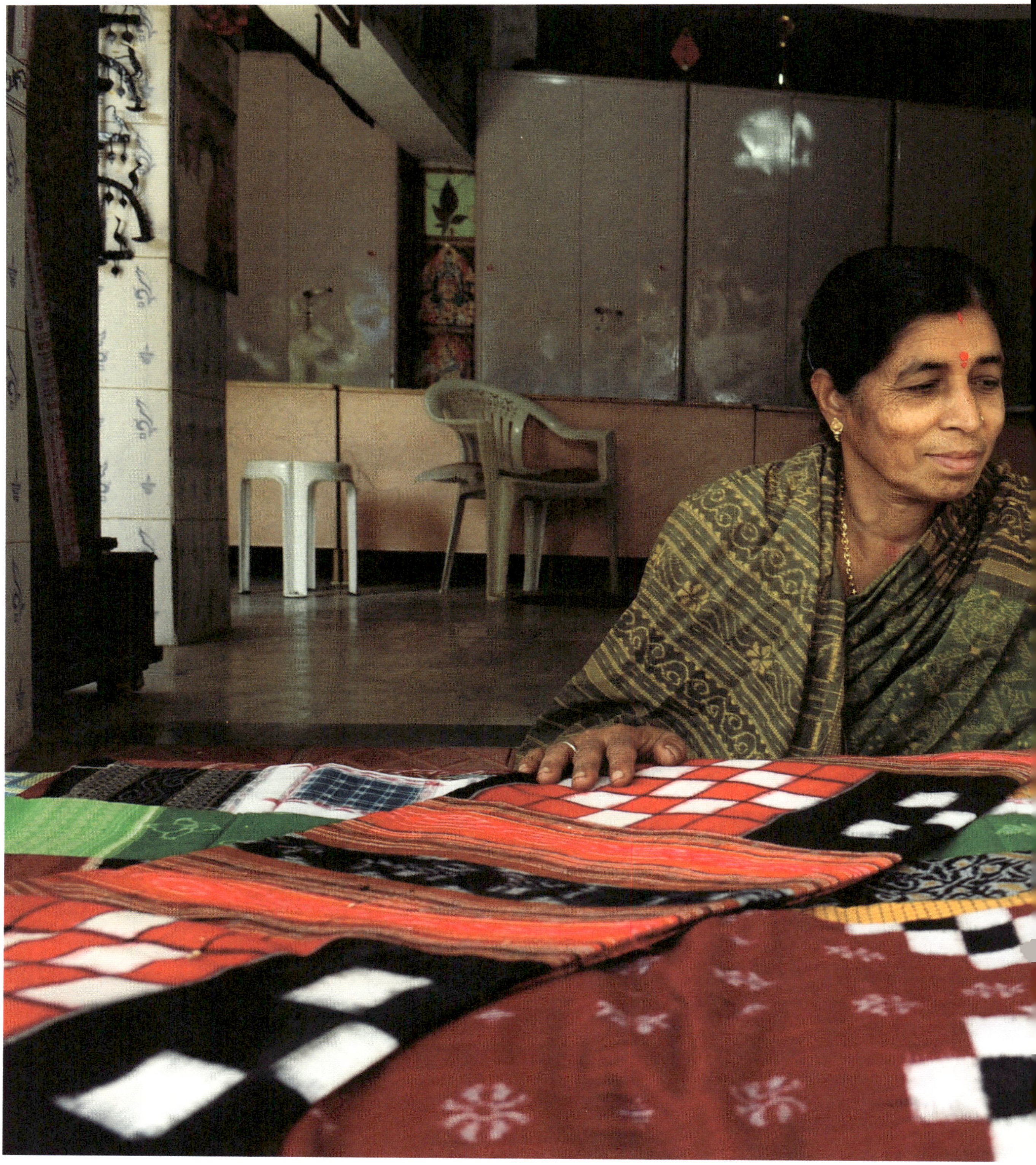

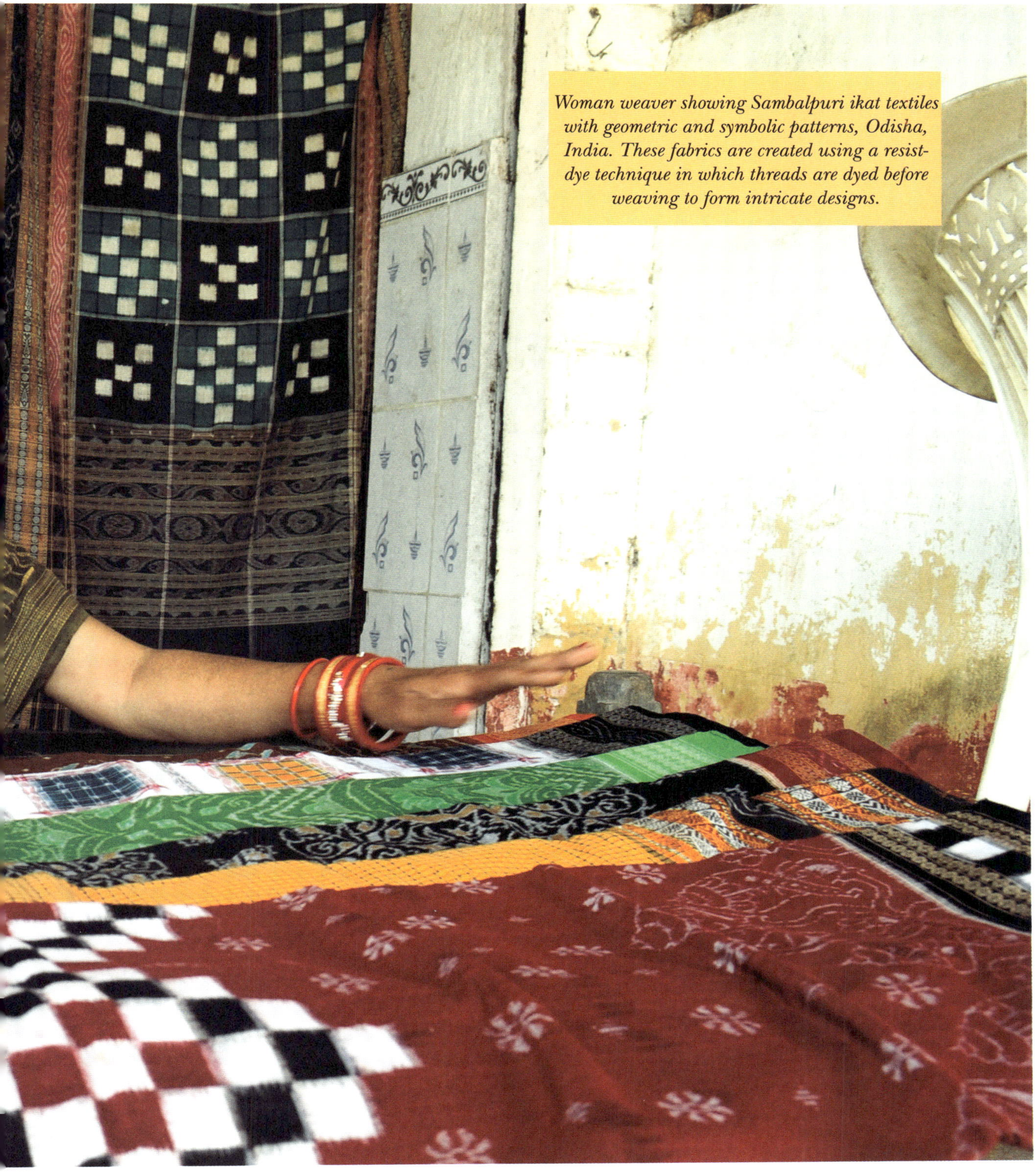

Woman weaver showing Sambalpuri ikat textiles with geometric and symbolic patterns, Odisha, India. These fabrics are created using a resist-dye technique in which threads are dyed before weaving to form intricate designs.

Rajasthan – Leheriya and Kota Doria

In Rajasthan, colour represents resistance – a rebellion against the endless beige of the desert. Women here wear the landscape transformed, desert sand turned into rainbows. Leheriya, whose name comes from *leher* (wave), is the sari of monsoon dreams. Imagine a plain cotton or silk cloth folded diagonally, tied at intervals, then dipped repeatedly into vats of colour. When it is opened, the cloth reveals undulating waves – blues rippling into pinks and yellows dissolving into reds, like rainwater coursing over sand dunes. No two Leheriyas are ever the same. Draped, they seem to be alive, the fabric undulating as if catching a breeze. Once worn during Sawan and Teej, festivals that celebrate rain and fertility, Leheriya saris convey an unmistakable joy, as if the desert itself has broken into song. Yet Rajasthan also offers us the Bandhej, kin to Gujarat's Bandhani but with its own distinct character. Thousands of tiny knots create not only dots, but spirals, lattices and suns. Picture a deep crimson sari scattered with white dots that swirl into mandalas across the *pallu* like an entire sky of stars stitched only cloth. These are worn by brides, mothers and dancers alike, each knot a blessing, each dot a prayer. Then there is Kota Doria, from the small town of Kota. Unlike the exuberance of Leheriya and Bandhej, Kota implies quiet elegance. Woven with a cotton-silk blend, it forms delicate square checks known as khat. Hold it to the light and it seems to vanish. A summer staple, it is often dotted with tiny *zari* flowers, like dew drops on a spider's web. Draped, it clings with a crisp coolness, the perfect counterpoint to Rajasthan's heat.

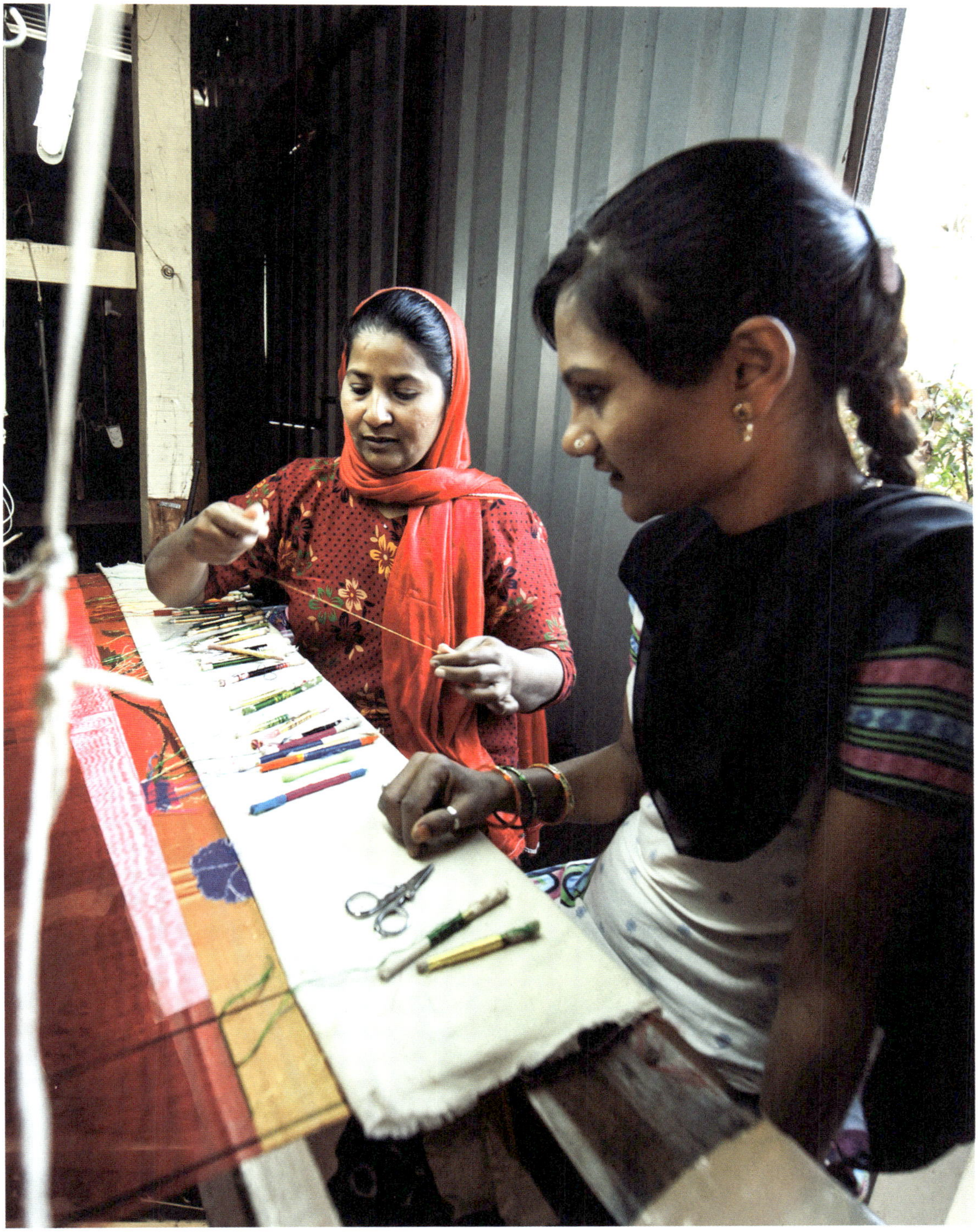

Women engaged in hand embroidery, adding decorative threadwork to textile fabric. The process involves stitching coloured threads onto the surface to create detailed patterns and embellishments.

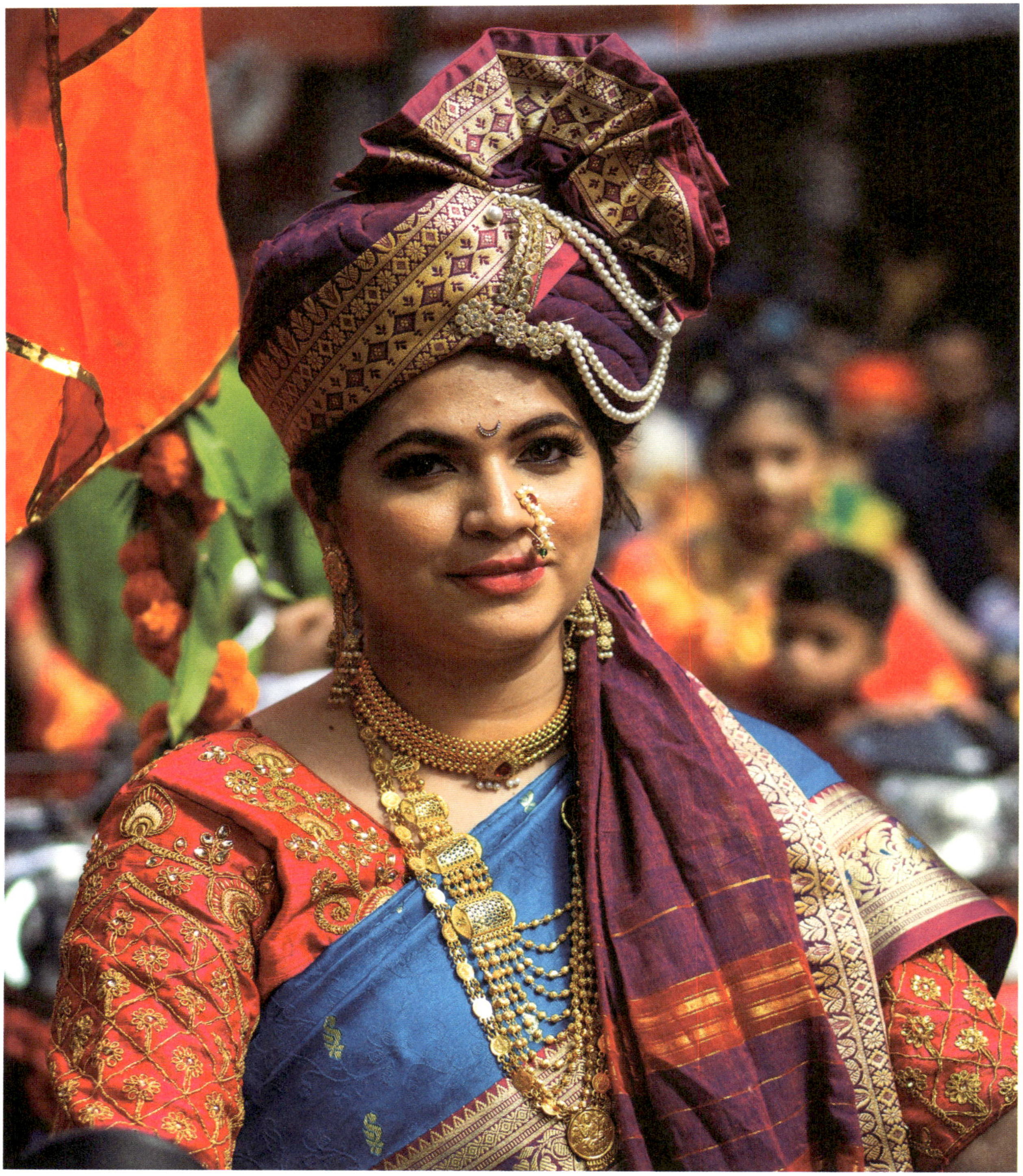

Woman dressed in traditional Maharashtrian attire wearing a Paithani silk sari with ornate gold jewellery. Paithani saris are known for their rich silk, vibrant colours, and intricate zari borders woven in Maharashtra.

To walk through Rajasthan during a festival is to see this spectrum unfold: women in swirling Leheriyas that look like rolling rainbows, brides shimmering in red Bandhej heavy with auspicious knots, and others radiating elegance in whisper-light Kota Dorias. Together, they are proof that even in the driest desert, colour and craft bloom endlessly.

Rajasthani saris have their own distinctive drape. Women often tuck one end at the waist, wrap the sari around and throw the *pallu* over the left shoulder; the *pallu* is frequently used as a *ghoonghat* (veil) to cover

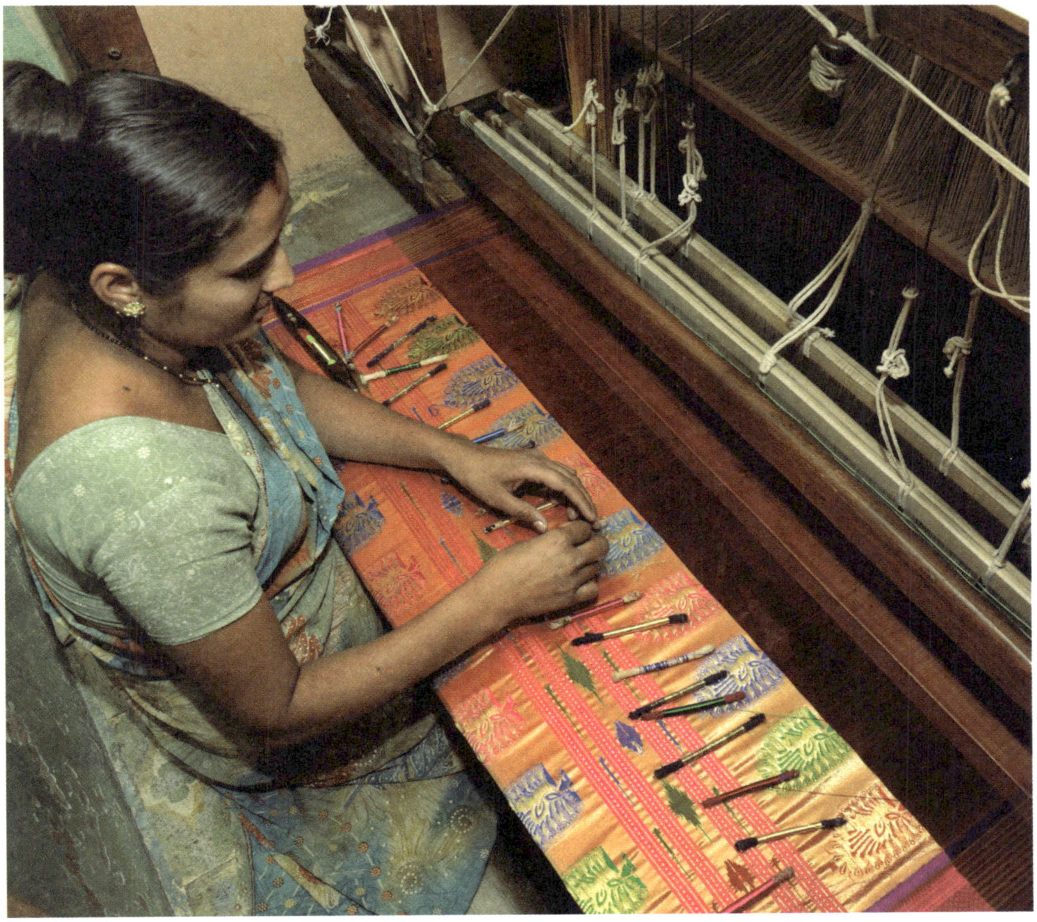

Artisan weaving a Paithani sari on a handloom using the tapestry technique to create intricate motifs. This traditional weaving method from Maharashtra involves manually interlocking coloured weft threads to form detailed designs.

the head or pinned across the chest for modesty. Some use a Gujarati-style drape (*pallu* from back to front), but typically the heavy Leheriya and Kota *pallus* fall freely from the shoulder, each twist of colour on display. The pleats may be neatly at the centre or swept slightly to the side, but always the vibrant borders and patterns take the limelight. The effect is majestic: a whirl of colour set against the sand with each drape like a walking festival. Even the simplest tucked sari, when made of Leheriya or Kota, expresses the joy of Rajasthani rain or the cool breeze of Kota's lakes in its very folds.

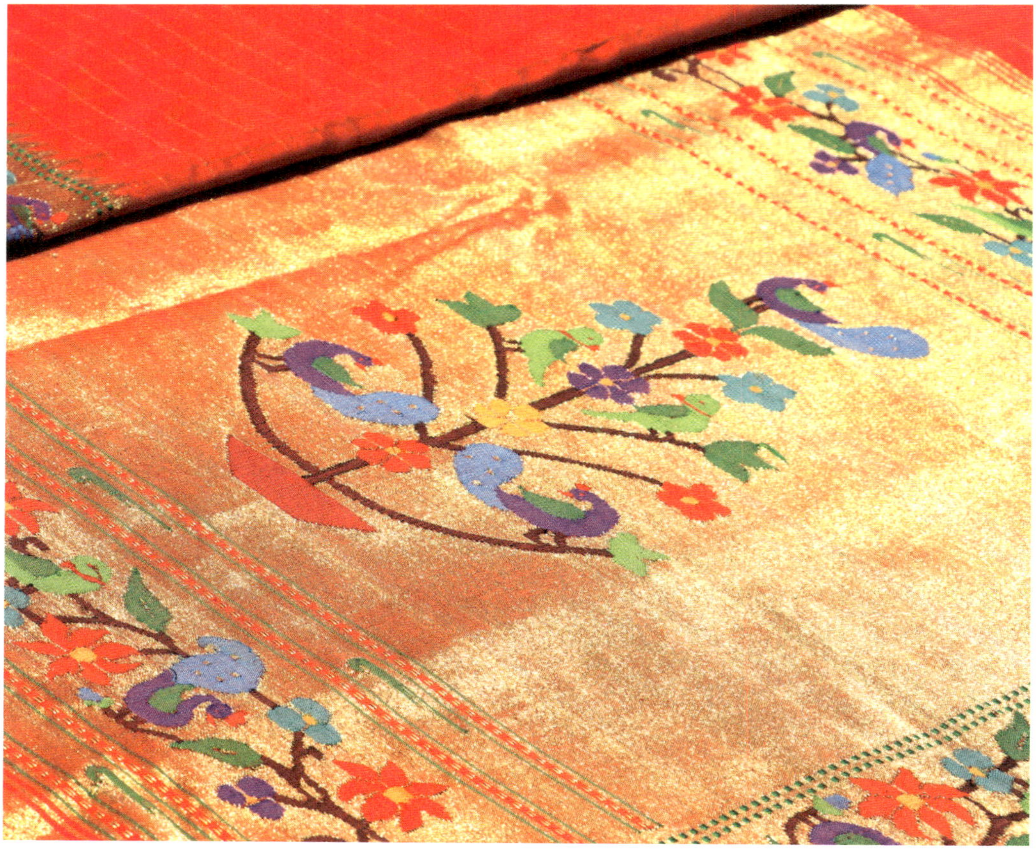

Close-up of a Paithani silk sari pallu featuring peacock motifs woven in multicoloured silk on a gold zari ground.

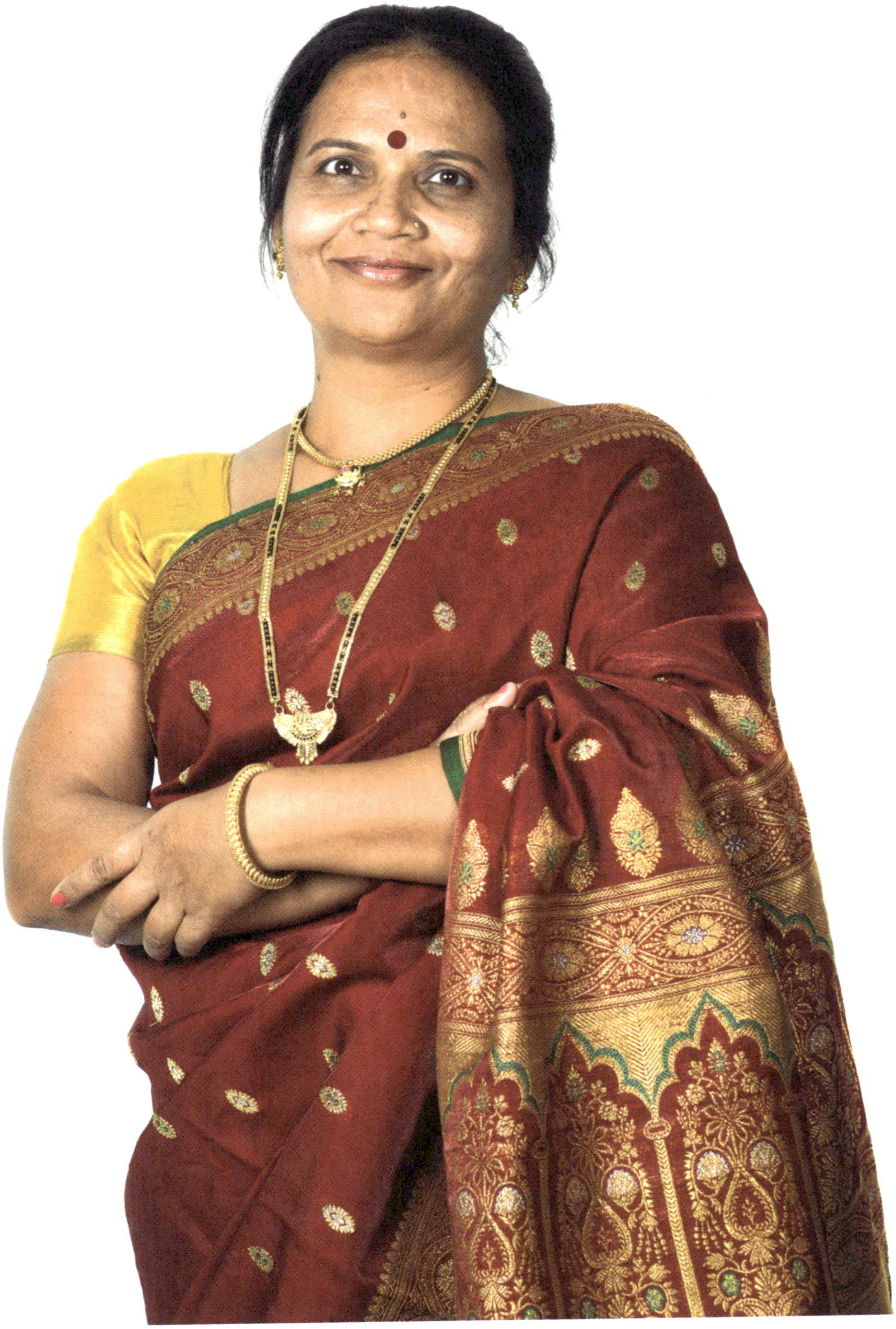

Woman wearing a traditional Paithani silk sari with a richly woven zari border, Maharashtra, India.

North India

Uttar Pradesh – Banarasi

To step into Varanasi is to encounter a city where faith and fabric are deeply intertwined. The *ghats* (steps to the water) smell of incense and ghee lamps, the River Ganges flows with chants and just a street away, the rhythmic clack of looms spills out from shadowy homes. Here, in these bylanes, the Banarasi sari has been born and reborn for centuries.

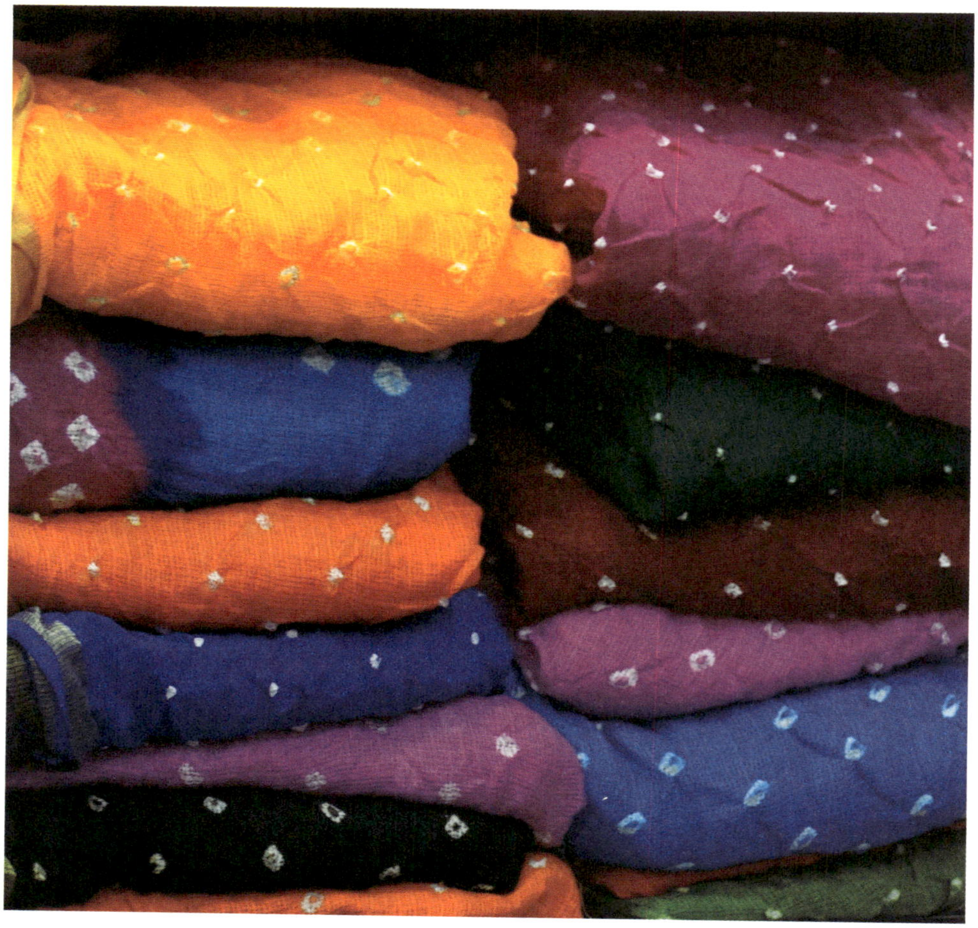

Stacks of colourful Bandhani textiles featuring characteristic dotted tie-dye patterns, India.

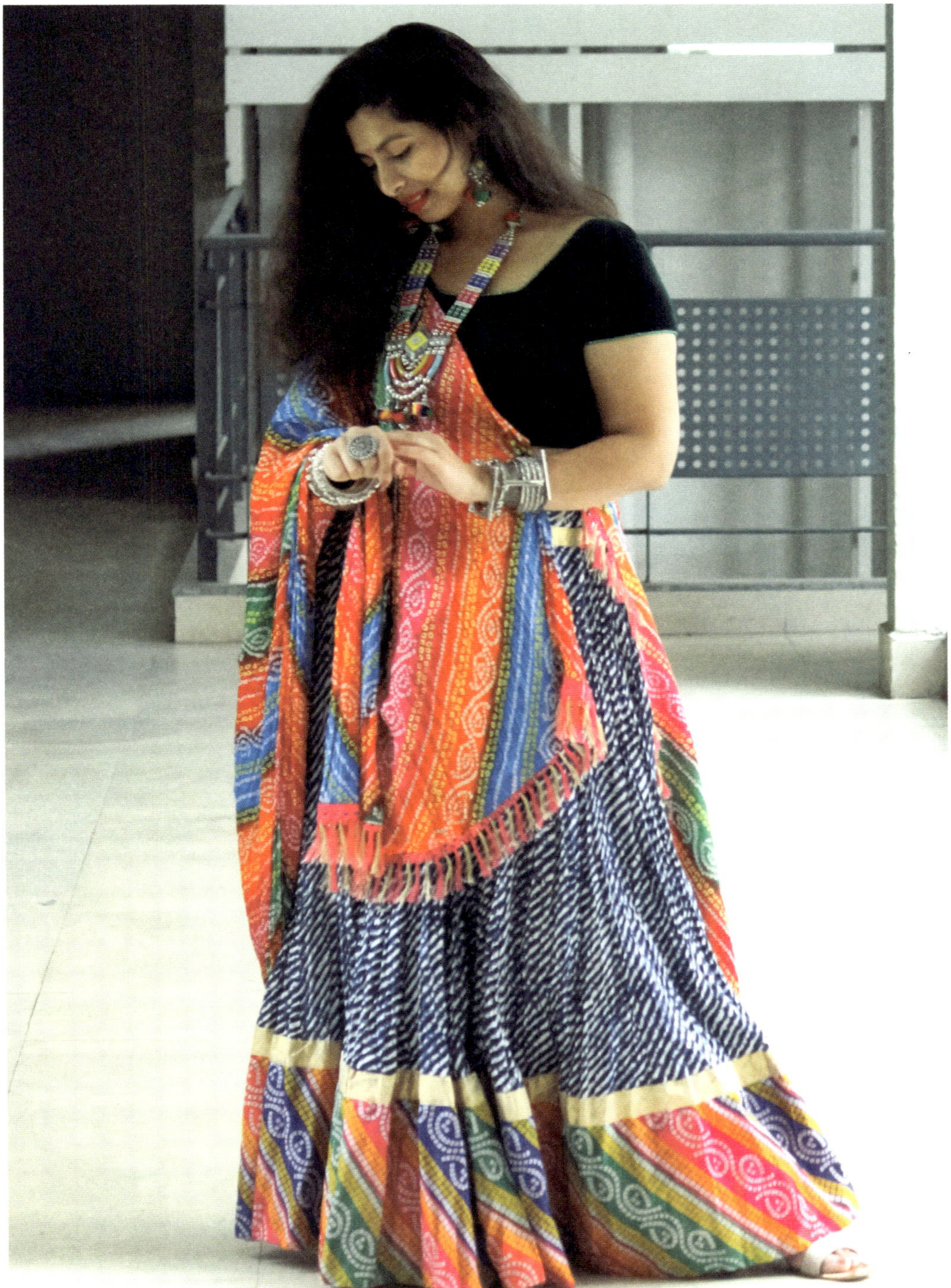

Woman wearing a contemporary outfit featuring Leheriya tie-dye patterns with vibrant diagonal stripes. Leheriya textiles from Rajasthan are created through resist dyeing and are traditionally associated with festive wear.

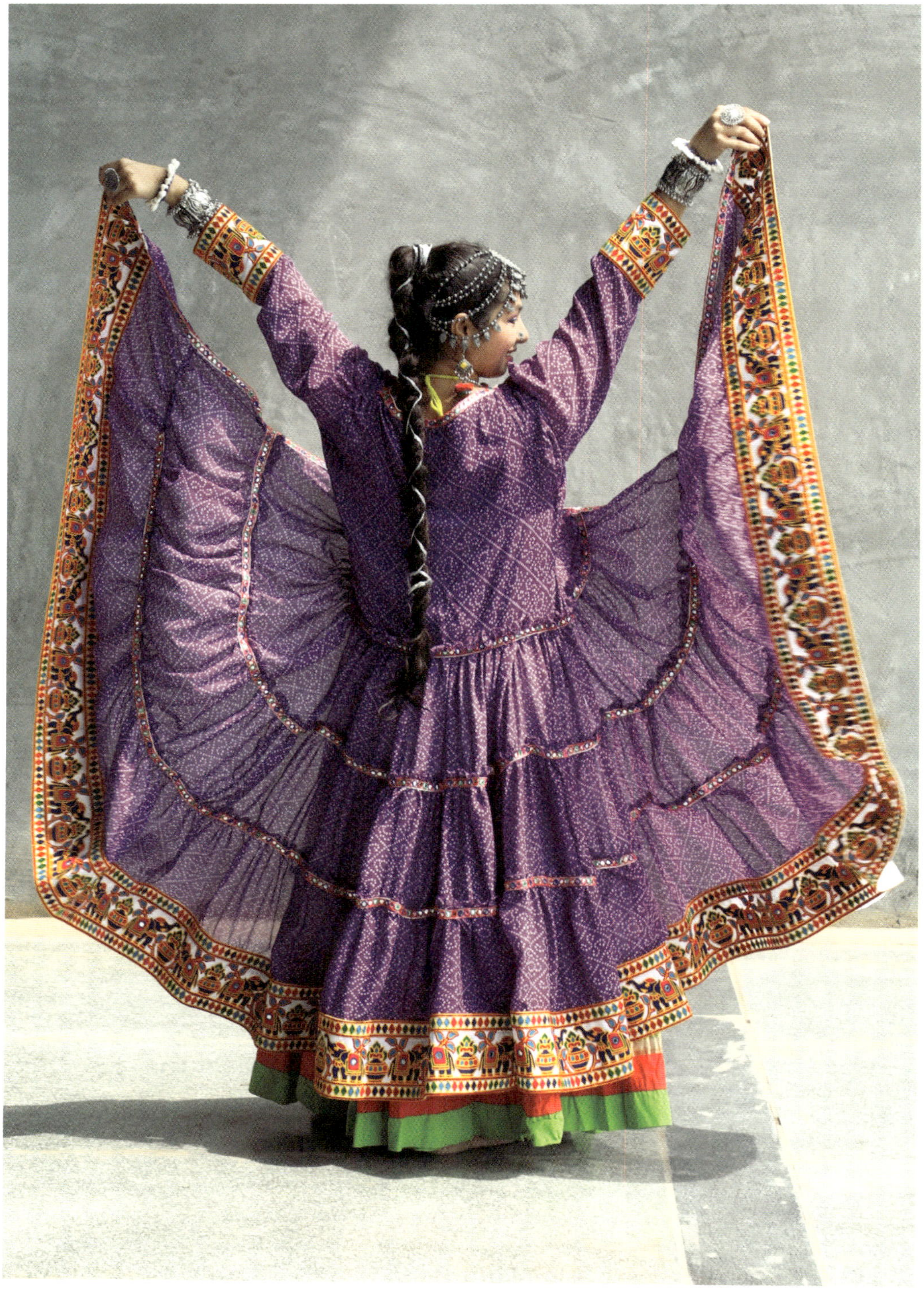

Woman wearing traditional Gujarati/Rajasthani attire, including a flared ghagra with a decorated dupatta.

Its history is multilayered. Some say Mughal emperors brought Persian weavers here in the 14th century, who introduced floral motifs and *zari* work into Indian weaving looms. Others believe the craft predates that era and is tied instead to Buddhist and Hindu temple rituals. Whatever its origin, the Banarasi was already legendary by the Mughal period, when it was prized for courtly splendour. Worn by queens and *begums* (high-ranking Muslim women), its motifs mirrored

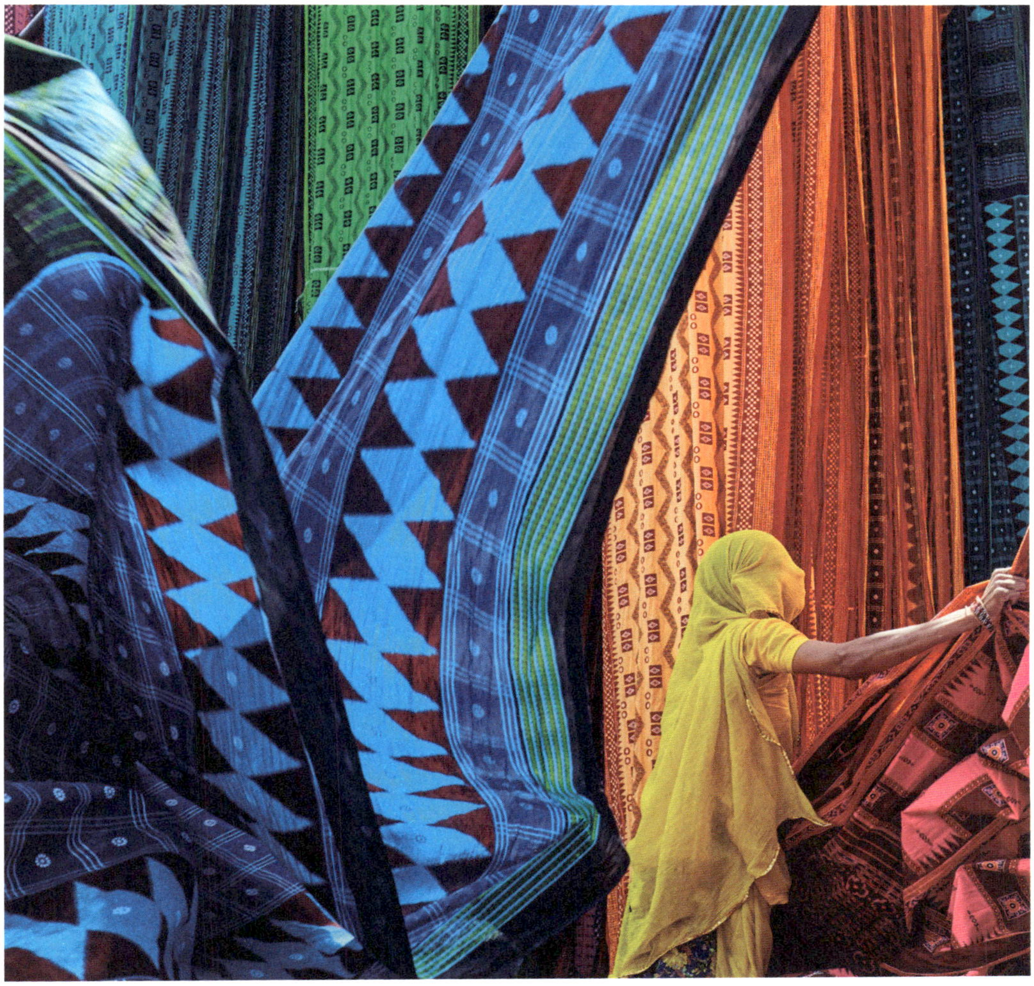

Ikat weaving, practiced in regions such as Odisha and Telangana.
Display of colourful ikat textiles featuring geometric patterns created through resist-dyeing of yarns.

Mughal gardens: curling vines (*bel*), stylized flowers (*butis*) and sprawling lattice-like *jaal* pattern. Persian aesthetics mingled with Indian geometry, producing a textile as hybrid as the city itself – sacred yet worldly.

The weaving is meticulous. The *kadhua* technique, in which each motif is woven separately rather than repeated across the fabric, ensures that every buti stands proud on its field of silk. No floating threads, no weak backs – only dense, enduring embroidery woven into the sari itself. This labour is immense: a small border can take days, a grand jaal months. In some houses, entire families sit together at one loom, father and son passing shuttles in perfect rhythm, while women wind the bobbins and prepare the threads.

Banarasis are drenched in colour – the deep maroon of sindoor, emerald green like river weeds, or midnight blue echoing the Ganga at dusk. Against these hues, *zari* glitters like trapped sunlight. Borders carry temple spires, zigzag chevrons, or the delicate *jhallar* fringe of small leaves, while the *pallus* unfurl into lavish storytelling panels.

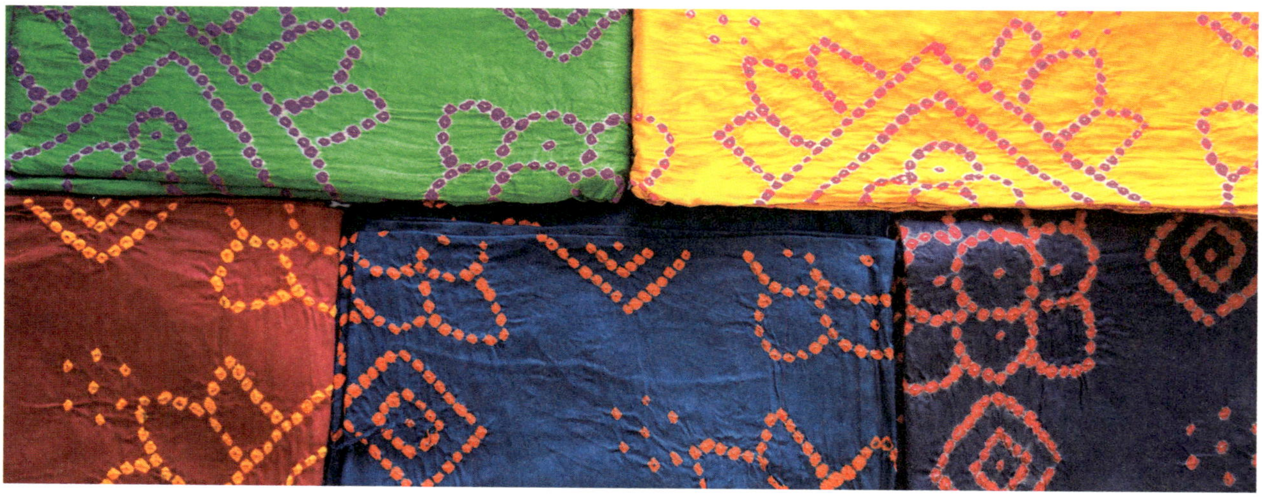

Colourful Bandhani textiles displaying intricate dotted patterns created through tie-dye techniques, India. This resist-dye method involves tying sections of fabric before dyeing to produce detailed geometric and floral designs.

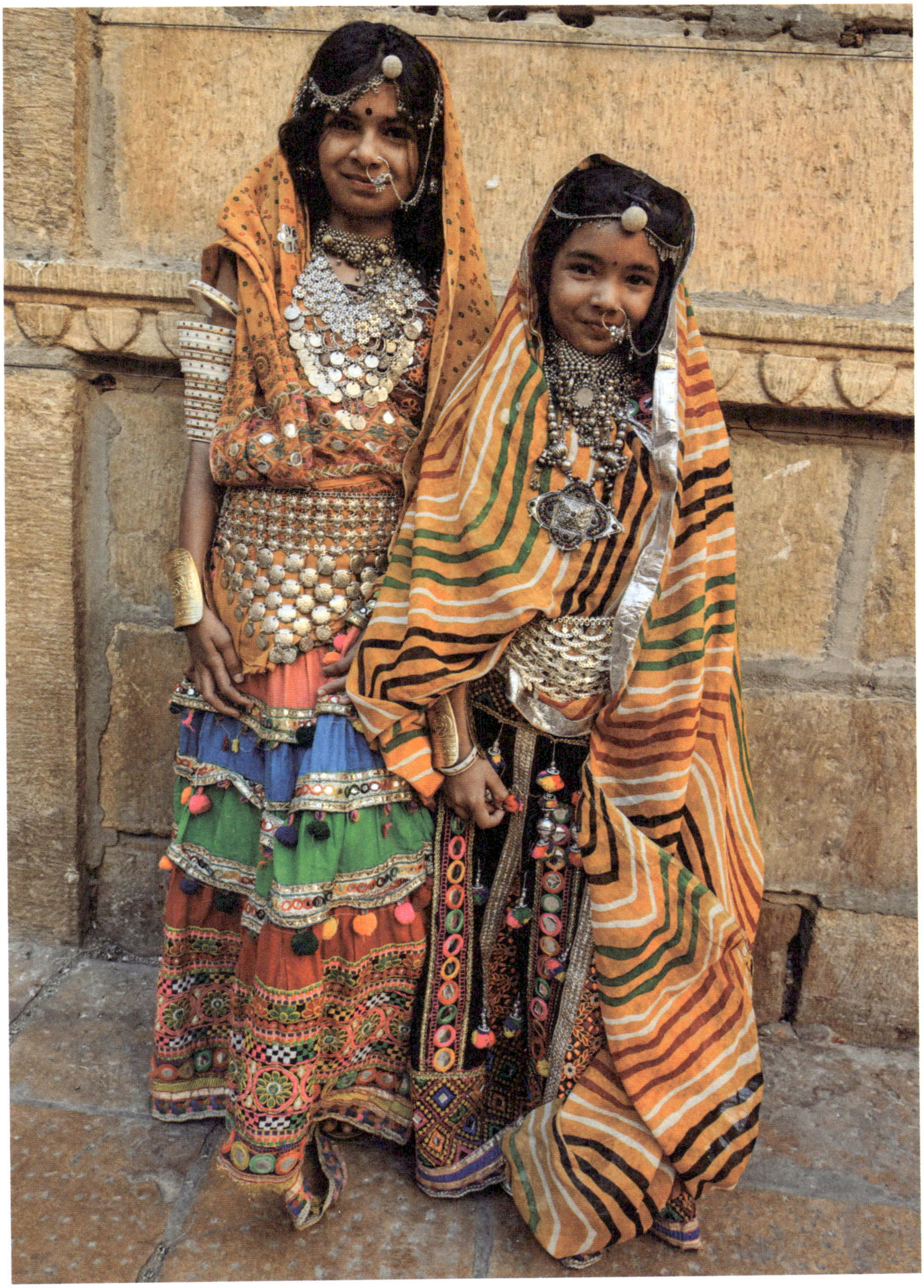

Young girls wearing traditional Rajasthani attire featuring brightly coloured ghagra-choli and patterned odhnis. These garments often incorporate Bandhani and Leheriya tie-dye techniques.

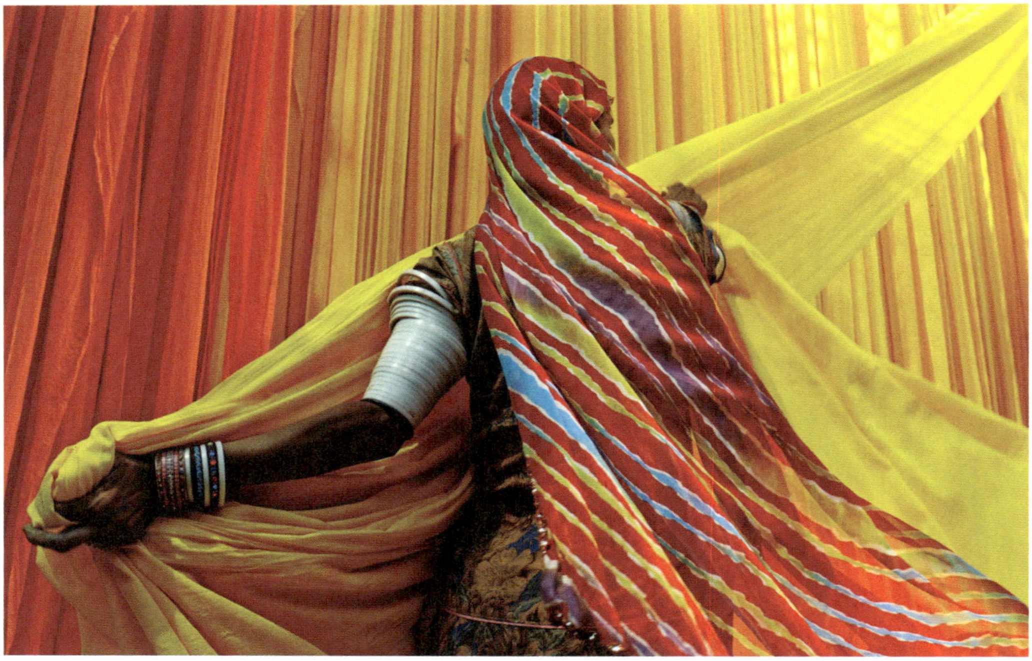

Woman draped in vibrant Leheriya tie-dye textile with flowing diagonal stripe patterns, Rajasthan, India.

For a bride, the Banarasi is less a choice, more destiny. Generations of women across North India have been married wearing its folds, red silk heavy with gold, each pleat gleaming against the wedding fire. Even today, when machine-made saris flood the markets, the hand-woven Banarasi remains untouchable for prestige.

To drape one is to convey Varanasi itself – the river's weight, the city's chaos, its spirituality, and endurance. Every Banarasi is not simply woven; it is chanted into being, like a prayer in silk.

Madhya Pradesh – Chanderi and Maheshwari

Walk into the historic town of Chanderi, perched between forests and lakes, and you'll hear the soft thrum of pit looms echoing through courtyards. The Chanderi sari is born from a marriage of silk in the warp and cotton in the weft – two threads intertwining until they create a fabric so sheer it is often called 'woven air'. Lift one against the light and it glows translucently, catching the sun like ripples of water. The motifs shimmer in fine gold and silver *zari* – coins, peacocks, and celestial lotuses. These are not printed or embroidered, but woven directly into the cloth by extra weft threads, so delicate that they appear suspended in space. The touch is featherlight, yet the drape carries a dignified uprightness, perfect for temple visits, royal courts or contemporary celebrations. A woman in Chanderi seems to float, her sari a veil of light and heritage. A few hours away, on the ghats of the Narmada in Maheshwar, another story unfolds.

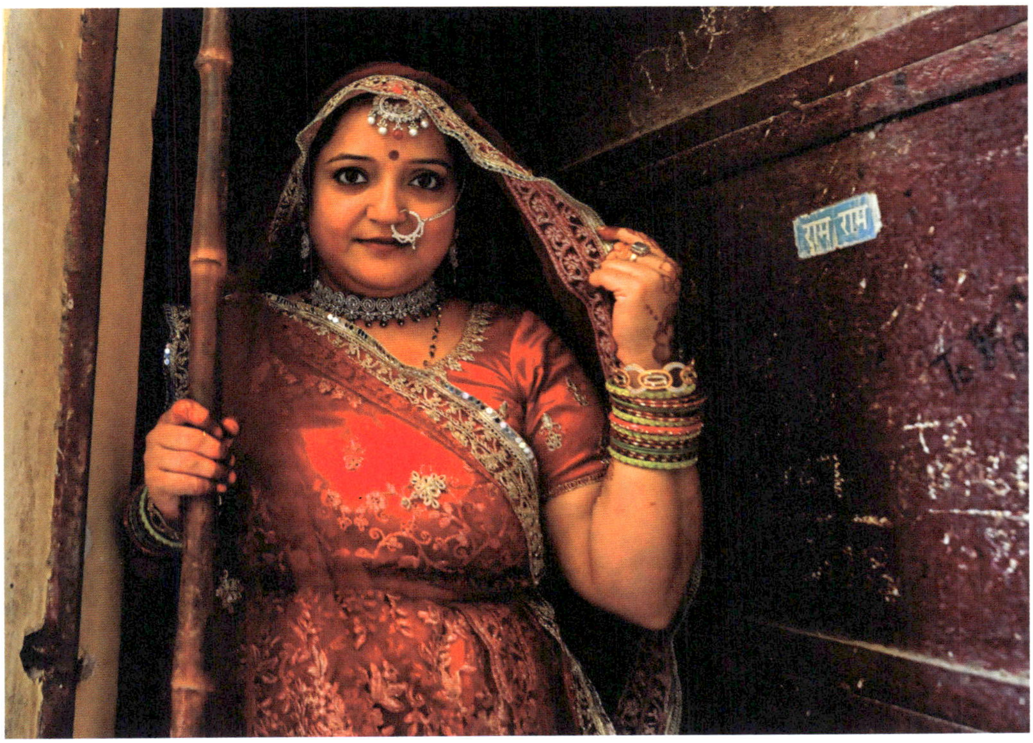

Woman wearing a red Banarasi silk sari adorned with intricate gold zari work, Varanasi, India. Banarasi saris are renowned for their opulent brocade weaving.

Here, the Maheshwari sari was first commissioned by Queen Ahilyabai Holkar in the eighteenth century. Legend says she invited artisans from across India to create a weave that could rival that of Banaras but convey the spirit of her land, Indore. They produced was a textile of striking geometry – stripes, checks and reversible borders, all achieved through a unique weaving technique. Maheshwaris are light, airy and suitabled for daily wear in central India's heat, yet their elegance also makes them fit for queens. The borders are often inspired by local architecture: temple spires, palace steps, and river currents. Run your fingers along one and

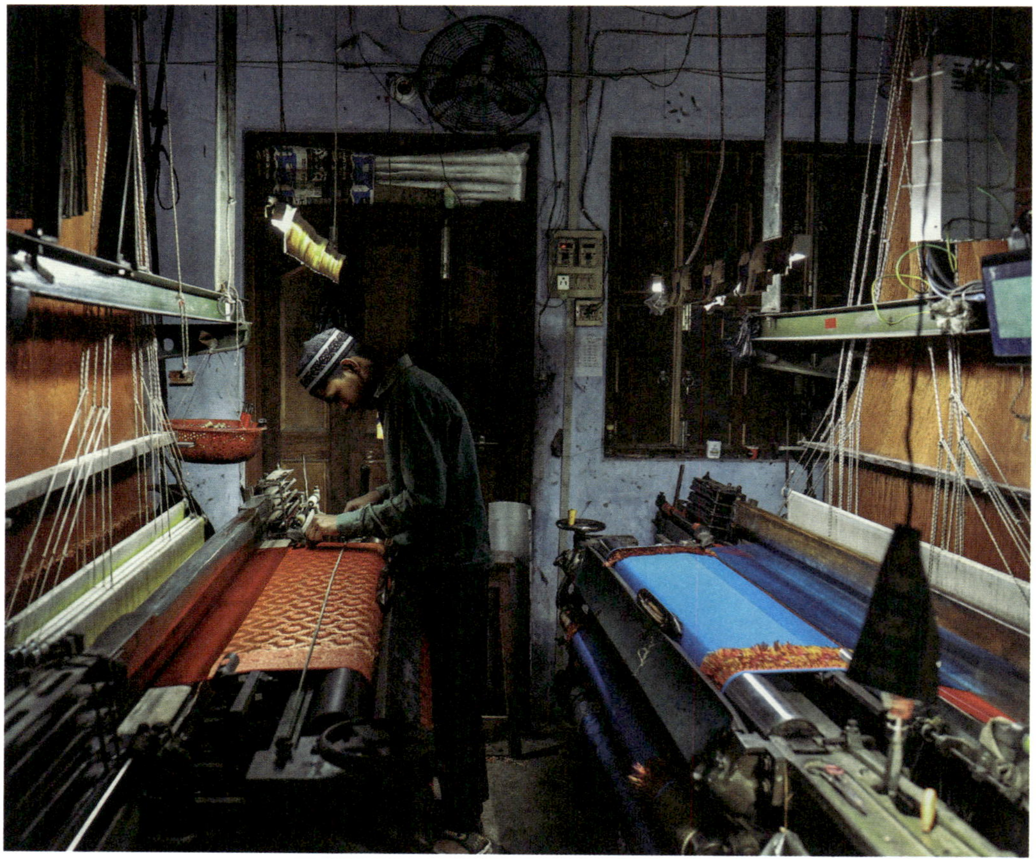

Weaver producing a Banarasi silk sari on a handloom using supplementary weft brocade techniques, Varanasi, India. This intricate process incorporates zari threads to create dense floral and ornamental patterns characteristic of Banarasi textiles.

you can almost trace the majestic sandstone carvings of Ahilya Fort. Unlike the glowing translucence of Chanderi, Maheshwaris are slightly crisper, their cotton-silk blend giving them body without weight. Spread a Maheshwari *pallu* out and you'll see contrasting shades like indigo meeting gold, parrot green against deep maroon, sometimes even the famous Ganga–Jamuna border, where two colours flow side by side like twin rivers. The drape is practical, breathable, yet undeniably regal.

Chanderi and Maheshwari saris are usually draped simply, each pleat aligned at the waist and the *pallu* tossed over the shoulder. The lightweight weave of Chanderi allows the sari to float around the legs,

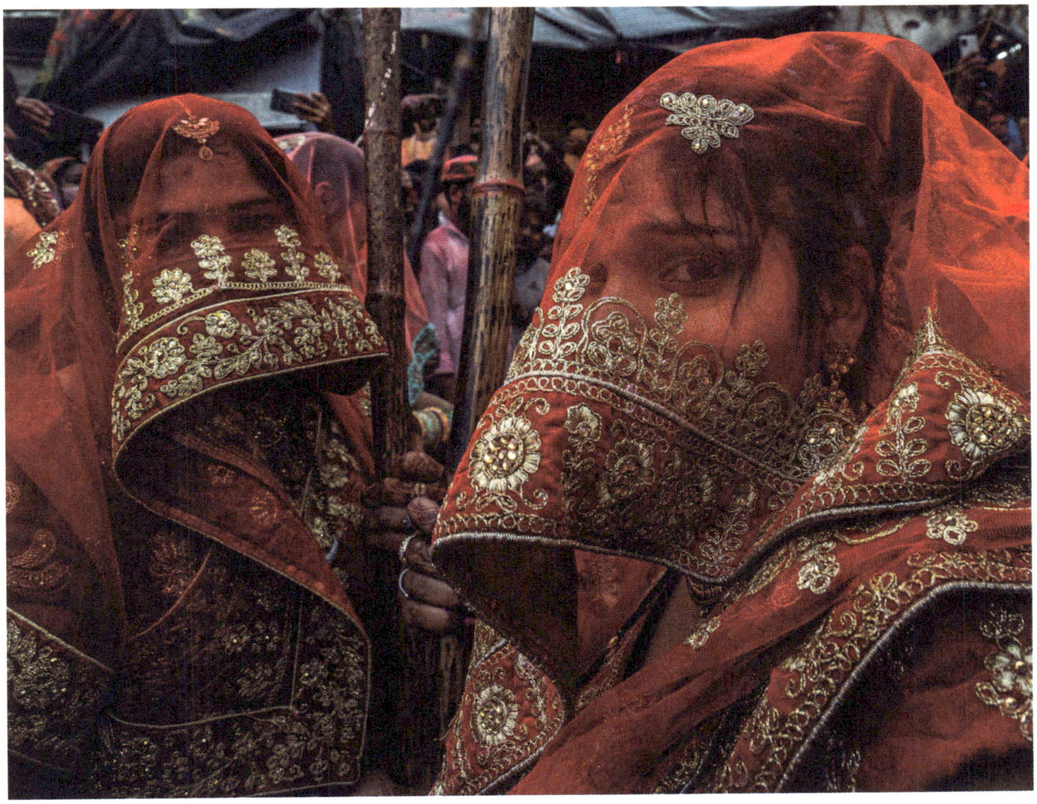

Women wearing red Banarasi bridal saris with ornate gold zari work, traditionally used in wedding ceremonies, symbolizing prosperity and auspiciousness.

almost clinging, so women often let the fabric flare naturally with movement. Maheshwaris also follow the Nivi style, but sometimes the two-colour border is displayed: after pleating the sari, women might fold part of the *pallu* from back to front to show both hues, a subtle nod to the Ganga–Jamuna theme. Every sari here carries the memory of a queen who wove her celebrated reign not just in stone and policy, but also in thread and loom. To hold a Chanderi is to hold a whisper of light. To wear a Maheshwari is to embody balance – geometry and grace, tradition and everyday ease. Together, they represent the twin

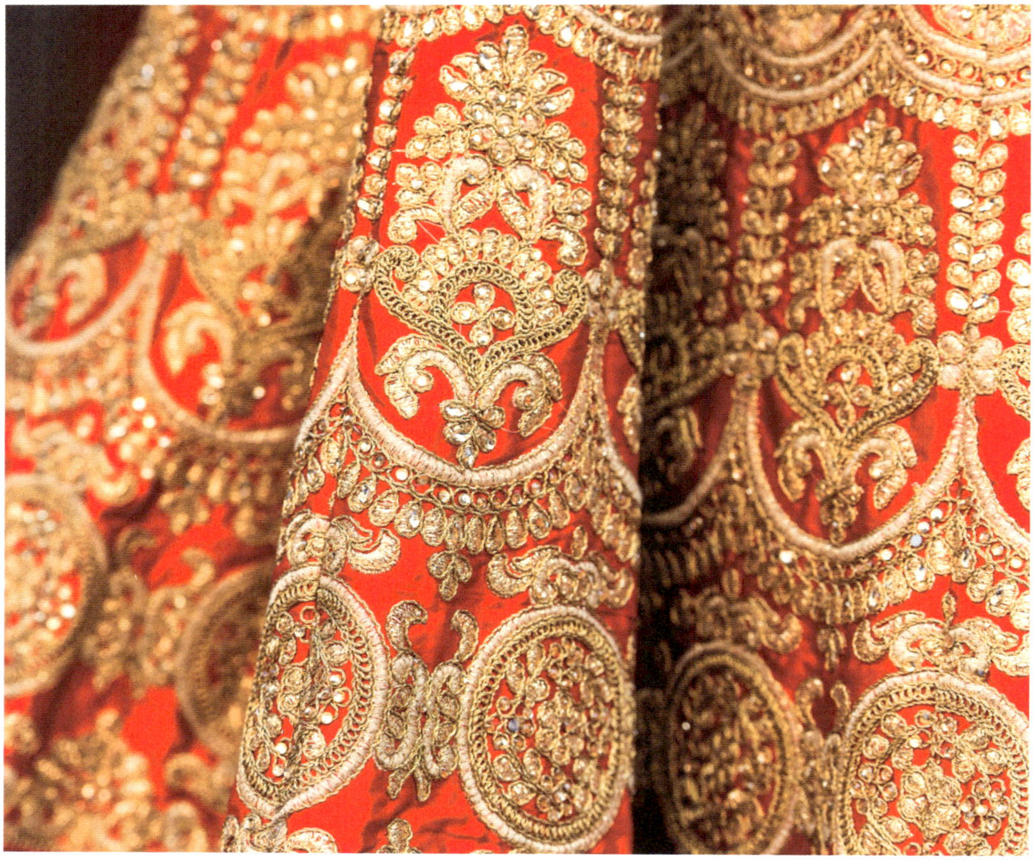

Close-up of a Banarasi silk sari featuring intricate gold zari brocade motifs on a red ground. These patterns are created using supplementary weft weaving.

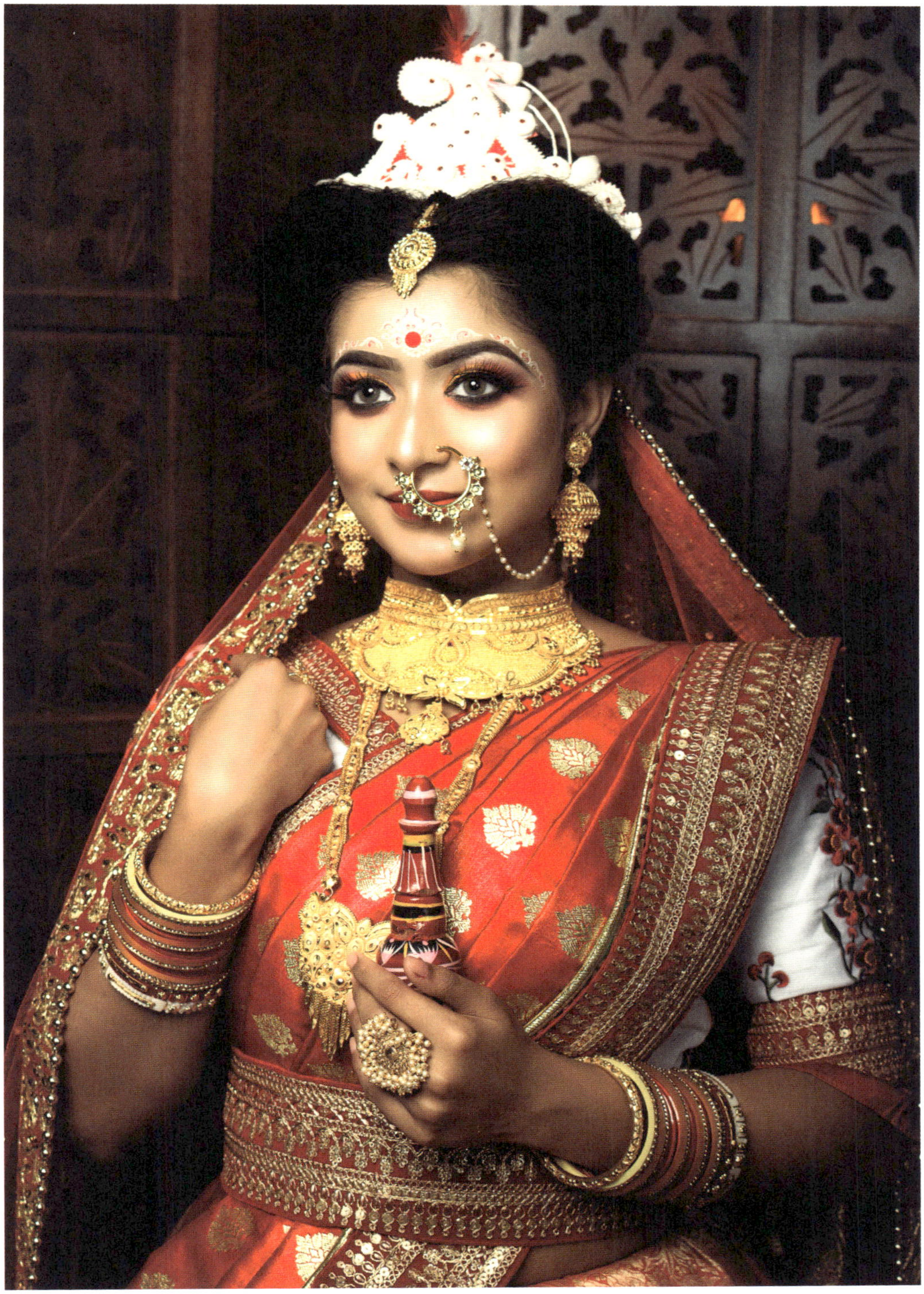

Bride wearing a red Banarasi silk sari adorned with intricate gold zari motifs and traditional jewellery. Banarasi saris are widely associated with weddings and are valued for their rich silk and elaborate brocade weaving.

souls of Madhya Pradesh, weaving royalty into cloth that still breathes with the rhythm of rivers and looms.

Kashmir – Kashida and Pashmina

In Kashmir, where winters blanket the valley in snow, looms punctuate the silence with the quiet click of the 'kani'. Unlike the Banarasi or Kanjeevaram, the Kani weave is not made with shuttles, but with tiny wooden sticks called 'tujis', each wrapped with coloured yarn. The weaver, following a coded graph, patiently places one stick at a time, building the pattern like an artist painting stroke by stroke. The result is a sari dense with detail – Mughal gardens, almond blossoms, chinar

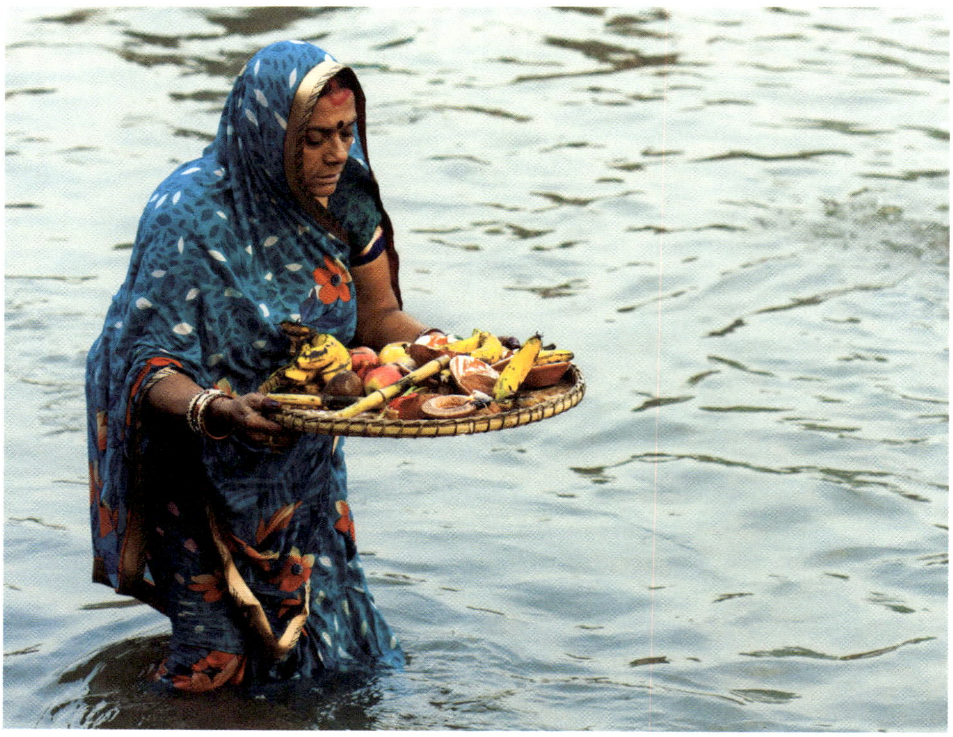

Woman performing a ritual offering while standing in a river, holding a Pooja tray with fruits and offerings, India. Such practices are part of traditional Hindu ceremonies where water bodies are considered sacred.

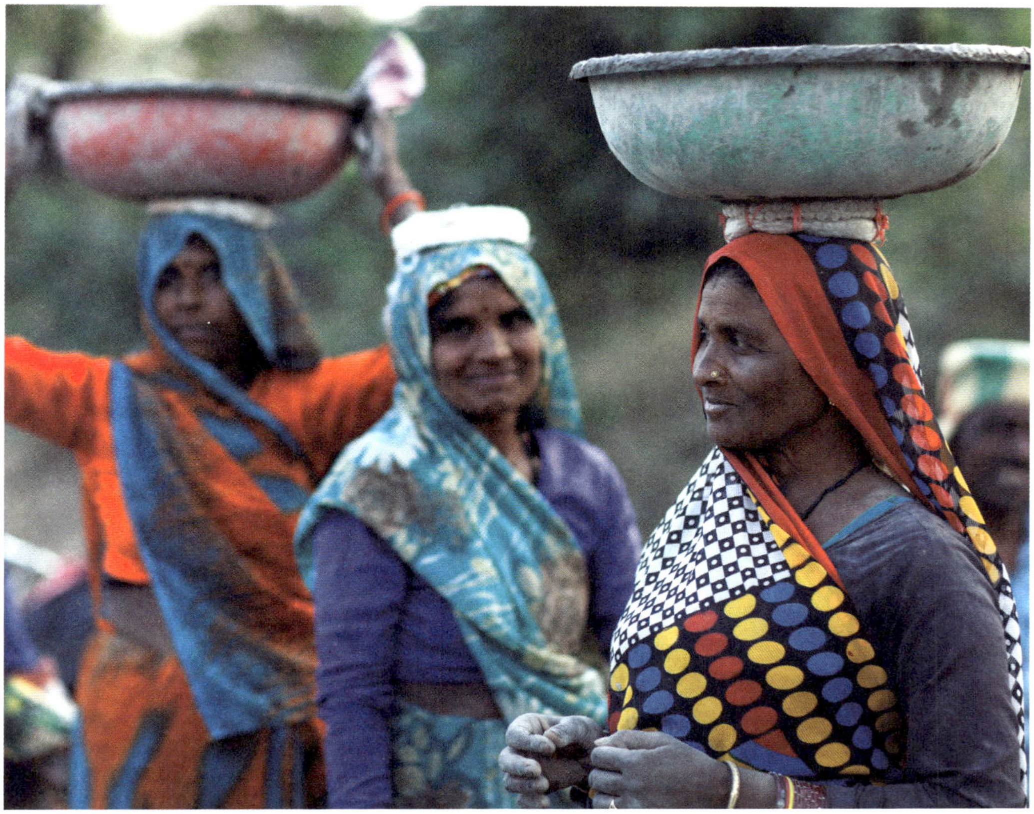

Women carrying baskets on their heads in a rural setting, Madhya Pradesh State, India.

trees, and curling vines. Colours are soft yet vivid: pomegranate reds, almond pinks, and twilight blues. Each piece may take months, even years. Then there is Tilla embroidery, in which threads of gold and silver are hand-stitched into flowing paisleys, arabesques and floral sprays. Draped, a Kashmiri sari feels like a shawl of poetry – warm, regal, and filled with the melancholy and majesty of the valley itself. More than saris to wear, these are heirlooms to treasure. Kashmiri women traditionally emphasize the shawl, but when saris are worn (especially among Kashmiri Pandit brides), they follow a simple, functional drape.

Often the heavy–woven Kani or embroidered Pashmina is used as a shawl over the shoulders rather than the usual *pallu*. When a Kashmiri sari is draped, it's generally in the basic Nivi style, with an added shawl-like *pallu* wrapped securely around the torso for warmth. The rich embroidery or kani patterns are shown on the back or front as a focal point. In any case, the drape exudes comfort – the soft wool against skin, the warmth embraced, like the valley's hospitality itself.

Punjab and Haryana – Phulkari

In Punjab, fields of mustard sway yellow under the sun, and the same vibrancy spills into its textile: Phulkari, 'flower work'. Traditionally embroidered on coarse cotton or khaddar, Phulkari saris are less

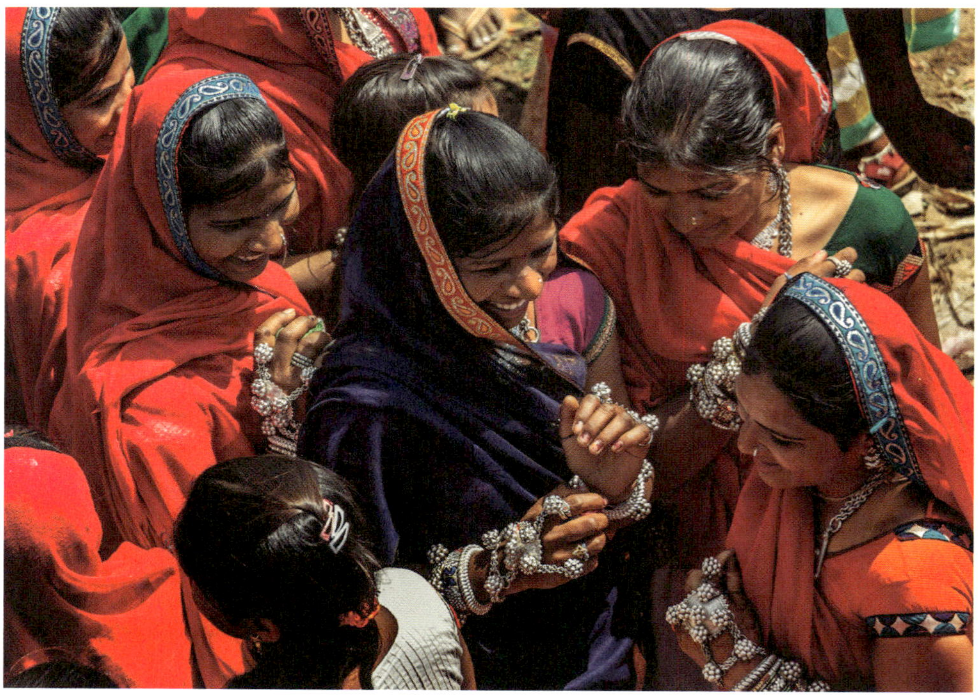

Women gathered together in traditional attire with colourful odhanis and jewellery, India.

about the base and more about the riot of stitches that cover them. Picture a dull maroon soil bursting with sunflower yellows, flaming oranges, and peacock blues. Each motif is worked in long and short darn stitches using untwisted silk floss. Patterns include bold, stylized flowers, diamonds, and chevrons. Draped, a Phulkari is less sari and more tapestry, radiating abundance. Traditionally used as dowry cloths and festive wear, Phulkaris were stitched by mothers and grandmothers for their daughters. To wear one is to carry an entire household's love

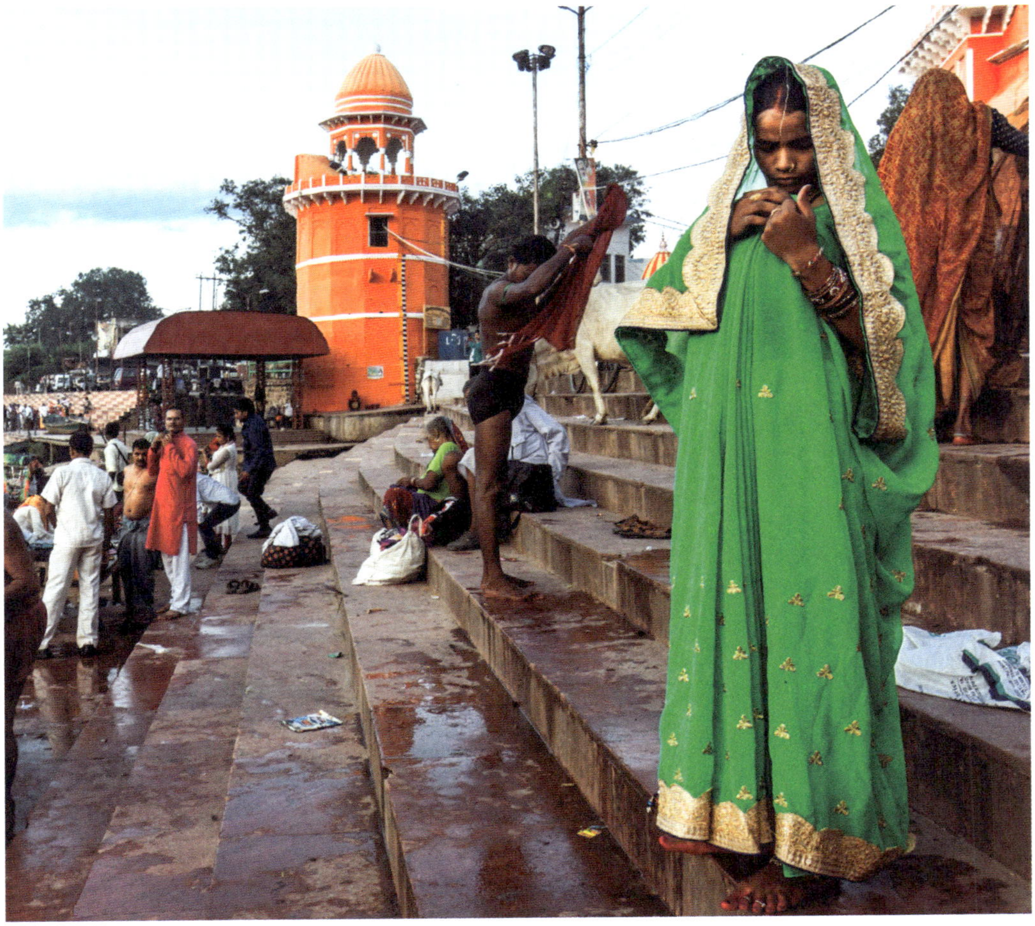

Woman in a green sari standing at a river ghat, a site of ritual bathing and daily activity, India. Ghats serve as important cultural and religious spaces where everyday life and spiritual practices intersect.

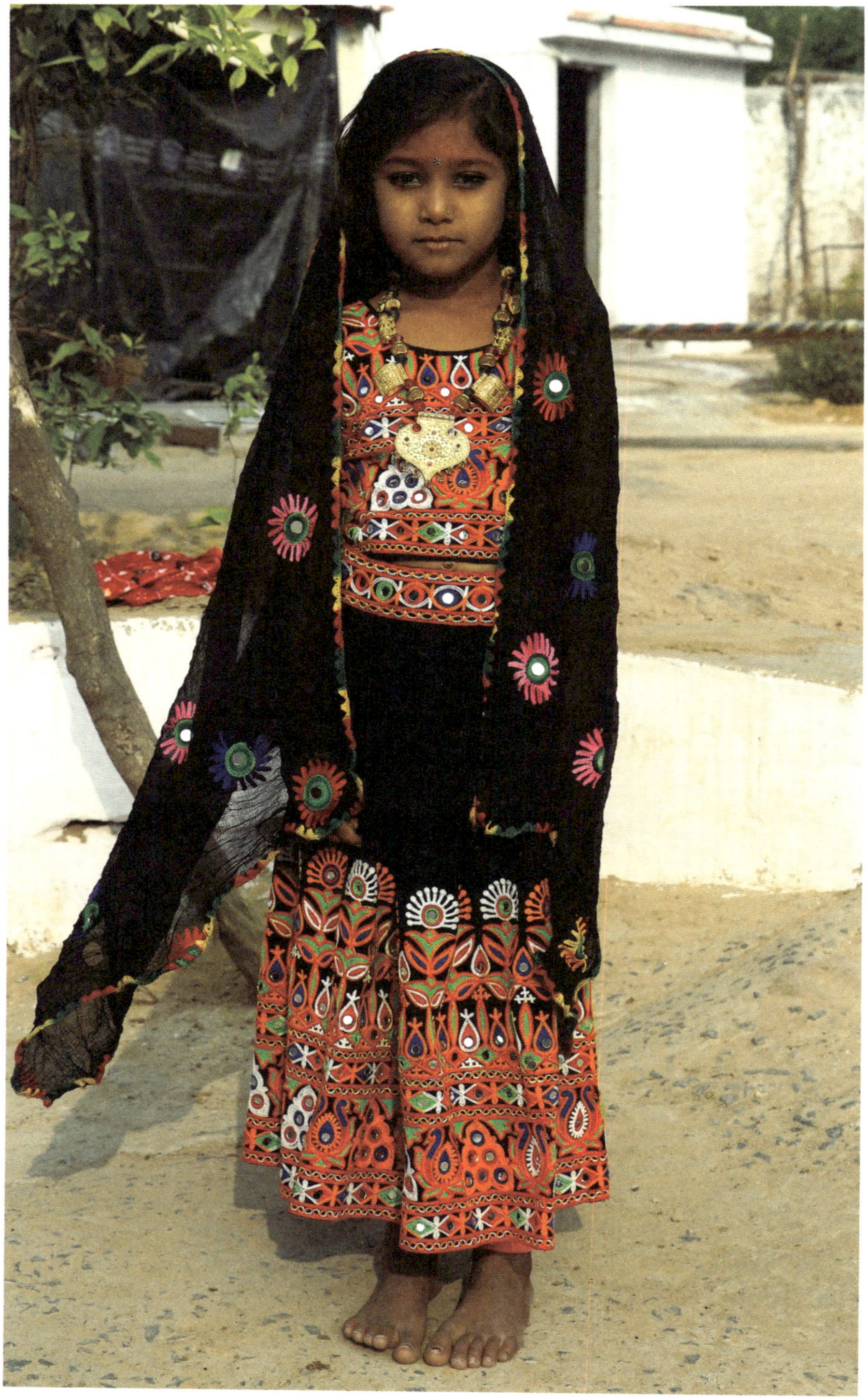

Young girl wearing traditional Punjabi attire adorned with Phulkari embroidery, featuring dense geometric and floral patterns. Phulkari is created using darning stitches worked from the reverse side, forming textured surfaces.

embroidered into cloth. Today, adapted into saris, they retain their exuberance, and their unapologetic embrace of colour and life.

Punjabi women typically drape saris in the common Nivi style, but often with the phulkari *pallu* spread prominently over the shoulder like a richly embroidered panel. The *pallu* may be allowed to hang long and loose or pleated neatly, but it usually covers much of the body, as if carrying the embroidery like a second skin. In some cases, the Phulkari is worn more like a *dupatta* (scarf) over a suit, but when made as a sari, it follows tradition. The bright motifs practically dance down the drape, with each fold revealing new bursts of colour. A bride in Punjab might even use the Phulkari as a veil over her head before draping it over her shoulders, blending the local

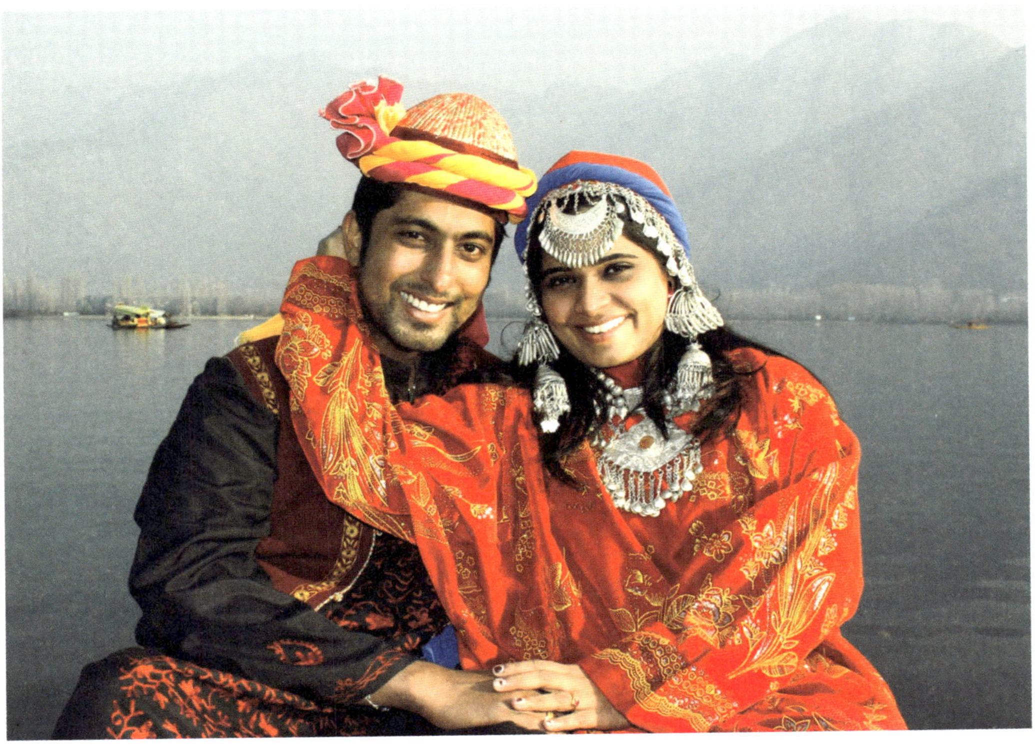

Newly-wed couple dressed in traditional attire featuring Phulkari-embroidered textiles, Punjab region.

embroidery craft into the sari's worn form. The overall effect is a riot of colour with every swish, a sari that becomes a wearable festival of Punjabi joy.

Himachal Pradesh – Kullu Weaves

High in the Kullu Valley, wool and cotton keep bodies warm, but it is the bright bands of colour that bring warmth to the eye. Kullu saris, though less famous than Banarasi or Kanjeevaram, have a distinct identity. The base is usually plain – muted grey, black or cream – but along the borders runs a carnival of colour: reds, greens, yellows, and blues, all in bold geometric patterns. The motifs are drawn from local flora and fauna: stylized flowers, stars and tribal shapes. The wool makes the sari heavier than its silk cousins but also warmer as it is meant for

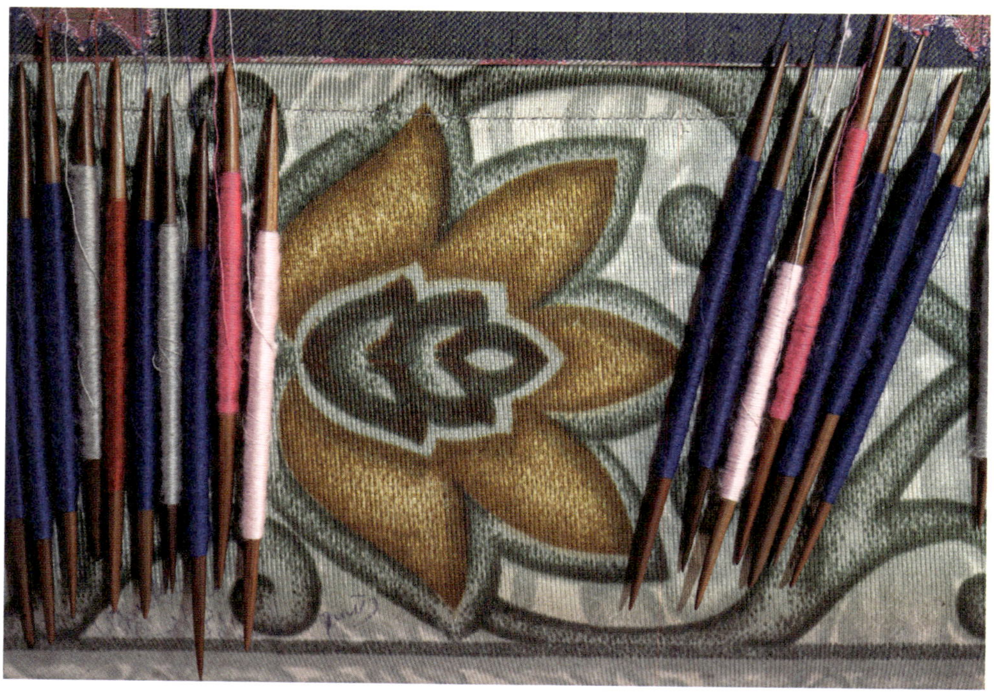

Kani weaving tools (tujis) used to create intricate patterns by interlacing coloured yarns, Kashmir, India. This technique involves manually inserting small sticks of thread to build complex designs without the use of a shuttle.

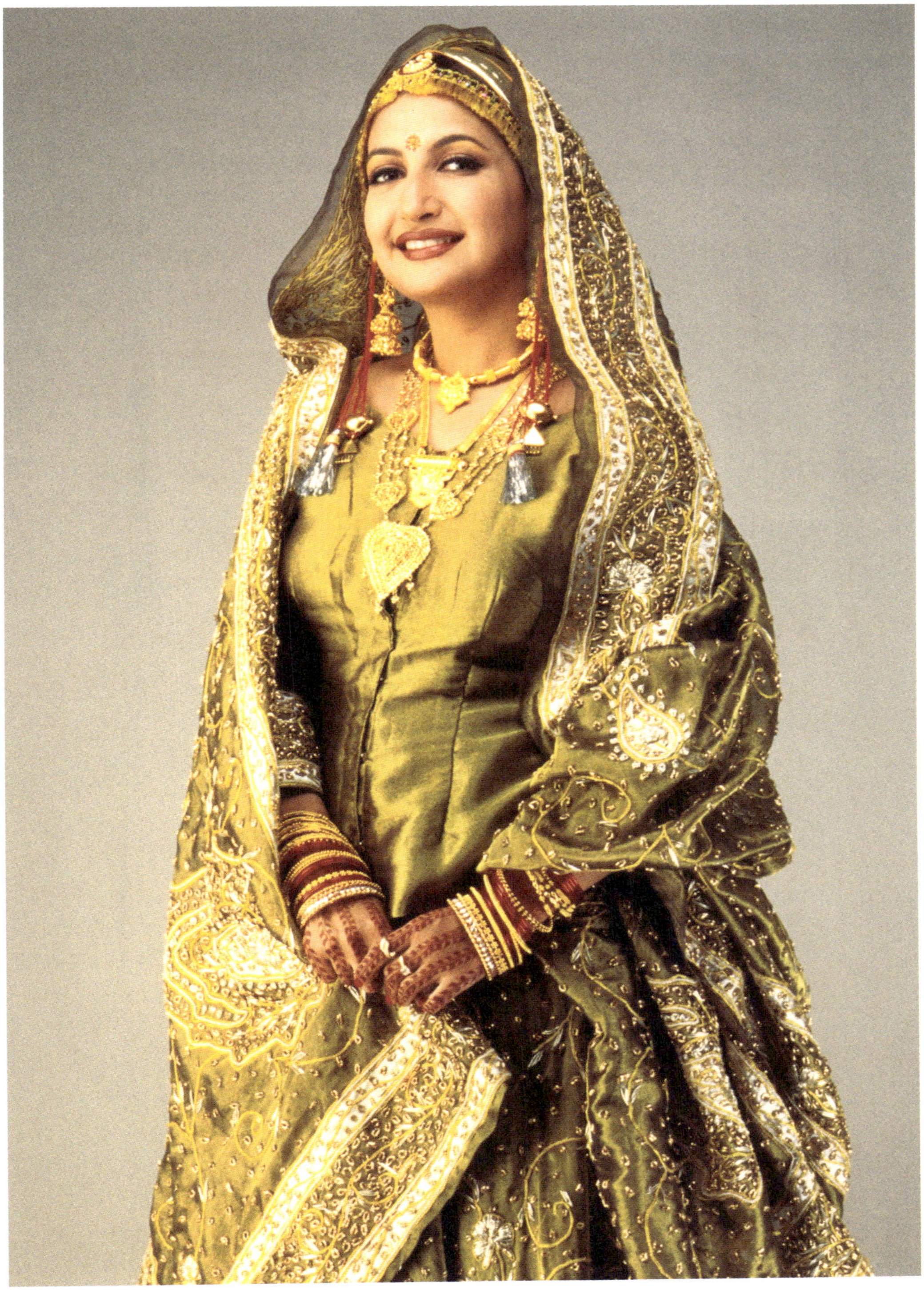

Woman dressed in an ornate traditional bridal outfit featuring rich embroidery and jewellery.

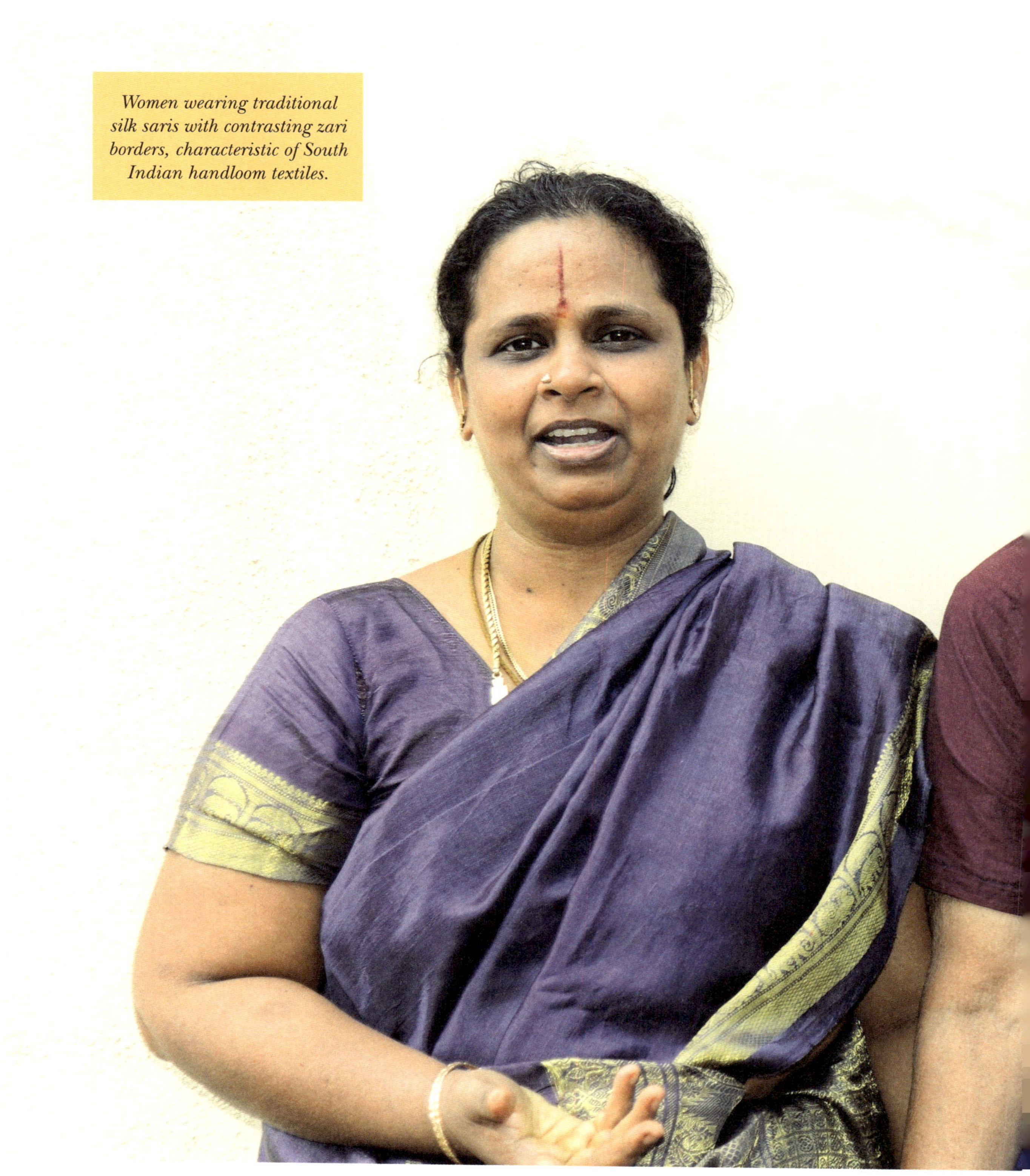

Women wearing traditional silk saris with contrasting zari borders, characteristic of South Indian handloom textiles.

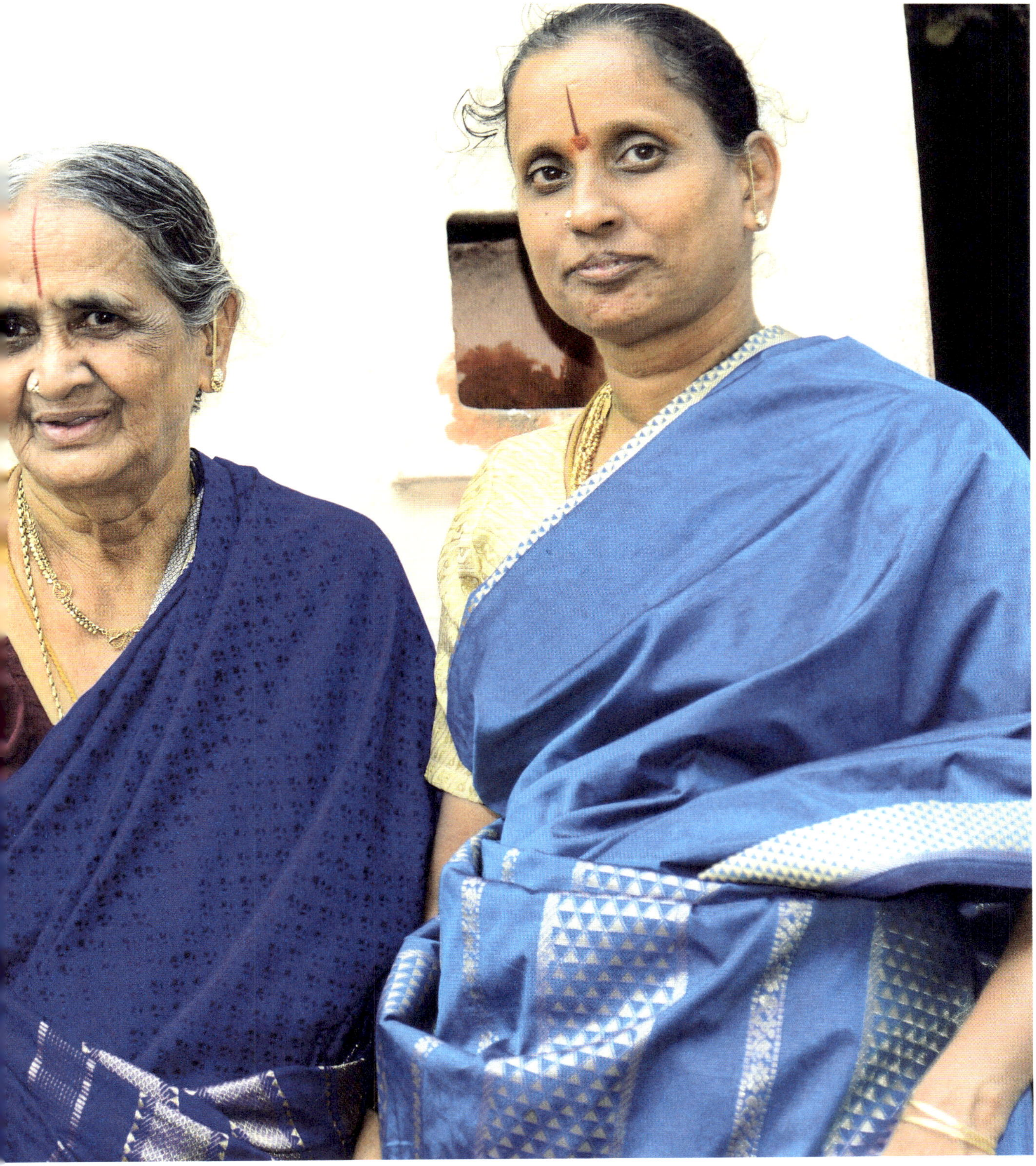

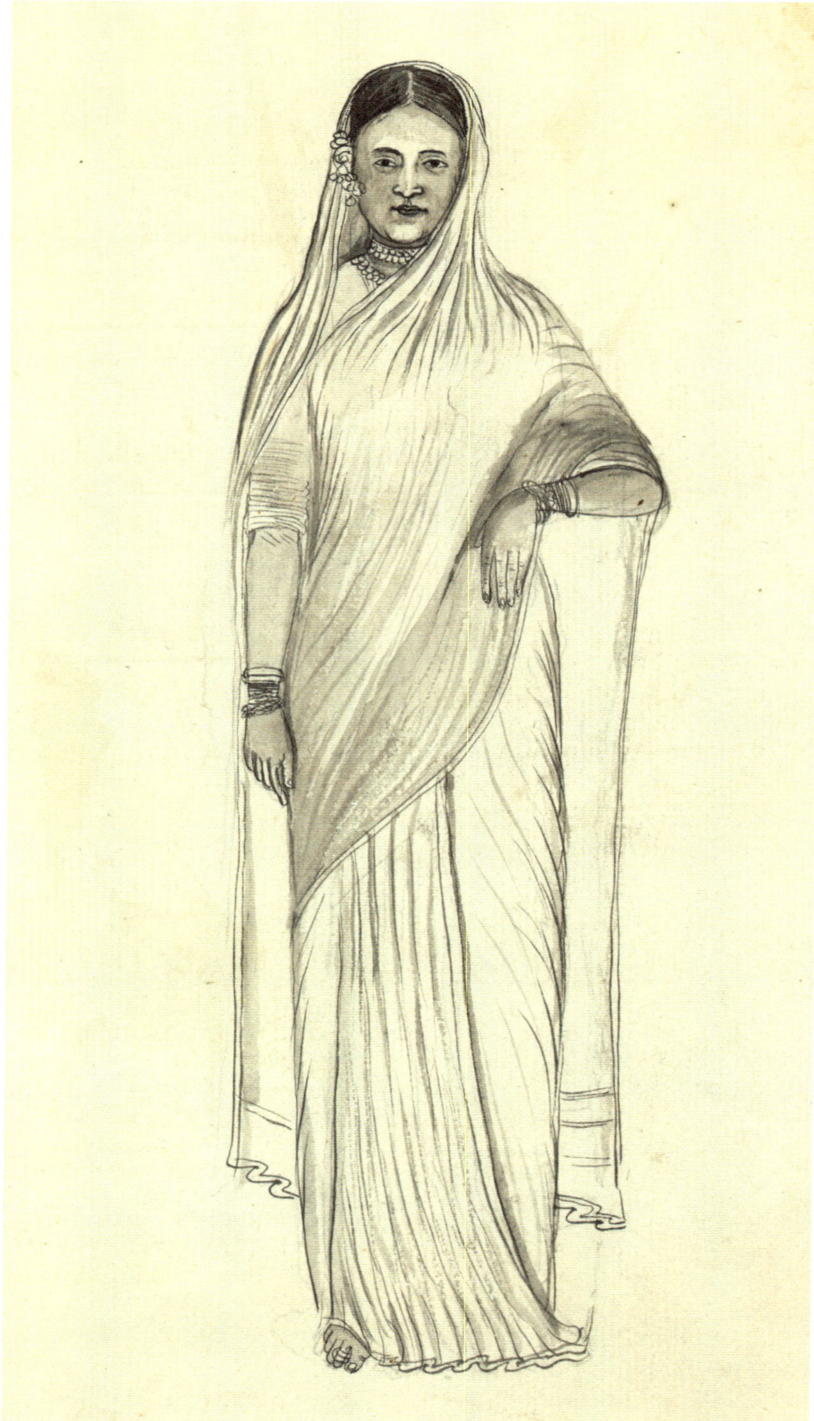

Illustration of a woman wearing a sari in the Nivi drape style, shown through a line drawing.

the mountain climate. Draped, a Kullu sari looks rustic yet striking, like a mountain landscape suddenly interrupted by wildflowers. In Himachal, these saris are often gifted at during weddings and festivals, a reminder of home woven into celebratory threads. Each border tells a story of the valley's hills, rivers and resilient people.

Women in Kullu traditionally wrap their saris snugly. The Kullu sari is usually draped in the Nivi fashion, with extra pins securing the heavier woollen *pallu* in place so it won't slide in the brisk wind. Sometimes the *pallu* is pulled over the shoulder and brought around the back and front again, as if adding an extra layer of shawl. Because the fabric is thick, the folds stay put without starch, and the bright border patterns remain visible. A Kullu sari wrapped around the wearer, with its vibrant stripes hugging the hem and shoulder,

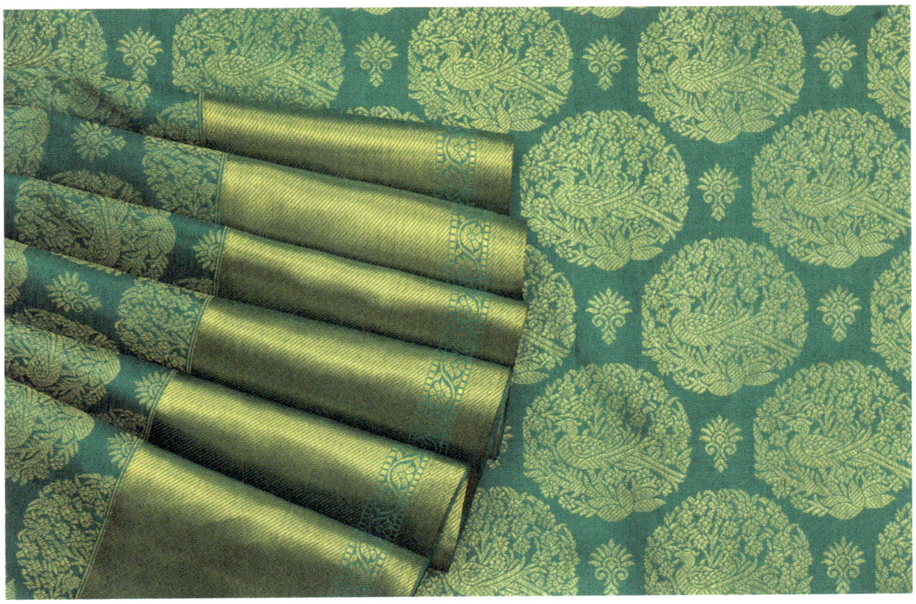

Silk sari with gold zari motifs arranged in repeating floral patterns, characteristic of South Indian brocade textiles.

becomes a living map of the mountains themselves – vivid against the mists, comfortable in the cold.

Despite the dizzying variety of saris across India, one thread unites them all: they are mirrors of the land, the people and the times. Each state has carved a distinct style, yet none exist in isolation. Trade routes, migrations, royal patronage and cross-cultural encounters have allowed motifs, techniques and colours to flow across regions, creating a rich weave of mutual influence. The Kanjeevaram's bold temple motifs echo in the geometric precision of Ilkal borders; the shimmering simplicity of Kasavu finds whispers in the understated elegance of Chanderi; and the vibrant Bandhani dots of Gujarat ripple into Rajasthan's Leheriya waves.

Geography and climate play their part too. Assam's golden Muga silk thrives in the Brahmaputra floodplains, while Karnataka's Mysore silk reflects the jewel tones of the Deccan. The desert heat of Rajasthan and Gujarat demands airy cotton weaves, whereas Kashmir's chill births the dense embroidery and warm Pashmina blends. Rituals, festivals and

KHADI AS RESISTANCE

Khadi saris became political symbols during India's freedom struggle. Hand-spun and hand-woven, khadi rejected British mill cloth. Women wearing plain khadi saris entered protests and public life, turning clothing into quiet defiance. Even today, khadi represents self-reliance, ethics and indigenous production.

political history further shape the saris – Onam mornings, Durga Puja processions, royal courts and dowry traditions all leave their mark on fabric and design.

In essence, the sari is not merely cloth – it is a living record. It carries the whispers of rivers, the colours of soils, the rhythms of looms and the stories of generations. Each six-yard (5.4m) drape is simultaneously local and universal, rooted in place yet in conversation with the whole subcontinent. Through saris, India weaves itself, showing that diversity and dialogue, heritage and adaptation, are inseparable threads in the nation's enduring fabric.

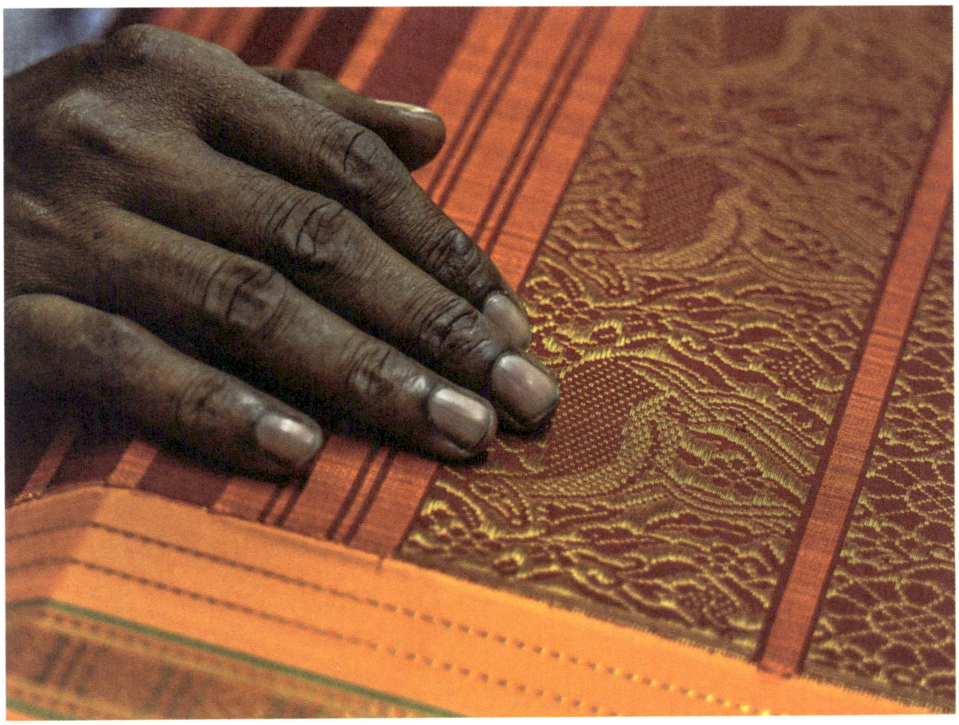

Close-up of a Kanjivaram silk sari highlighting its richly woven zari border with intricate motifs. These saris from Tamil Nadu are known for their contrasting borders and durable silk.

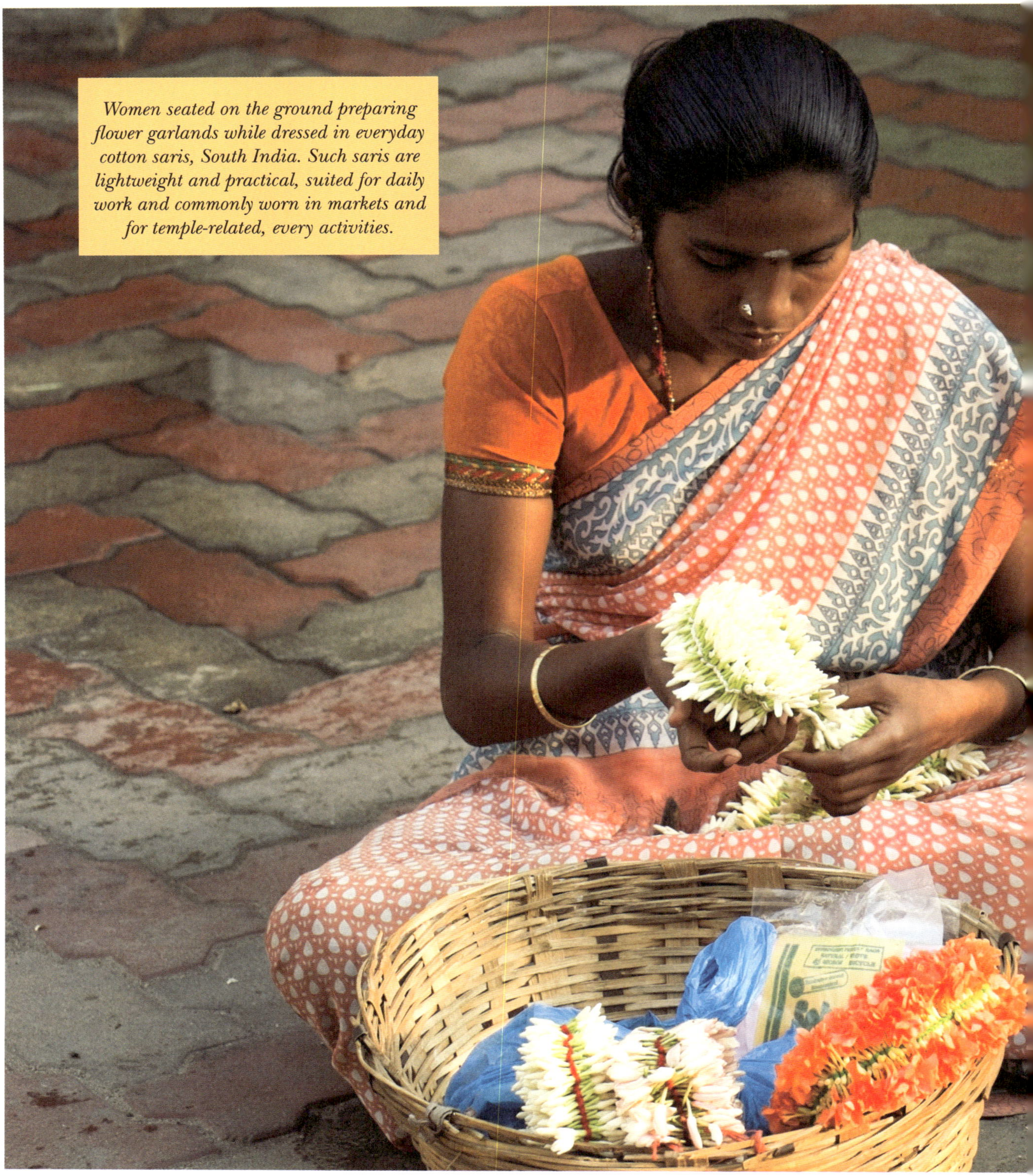

Women seated on the ground preparing flower garlands while dressed in everyday cotton saris, South India. Such saris are lightweight and practical, suited for daily work and commonly worn in markets and for temple-related, every activities.

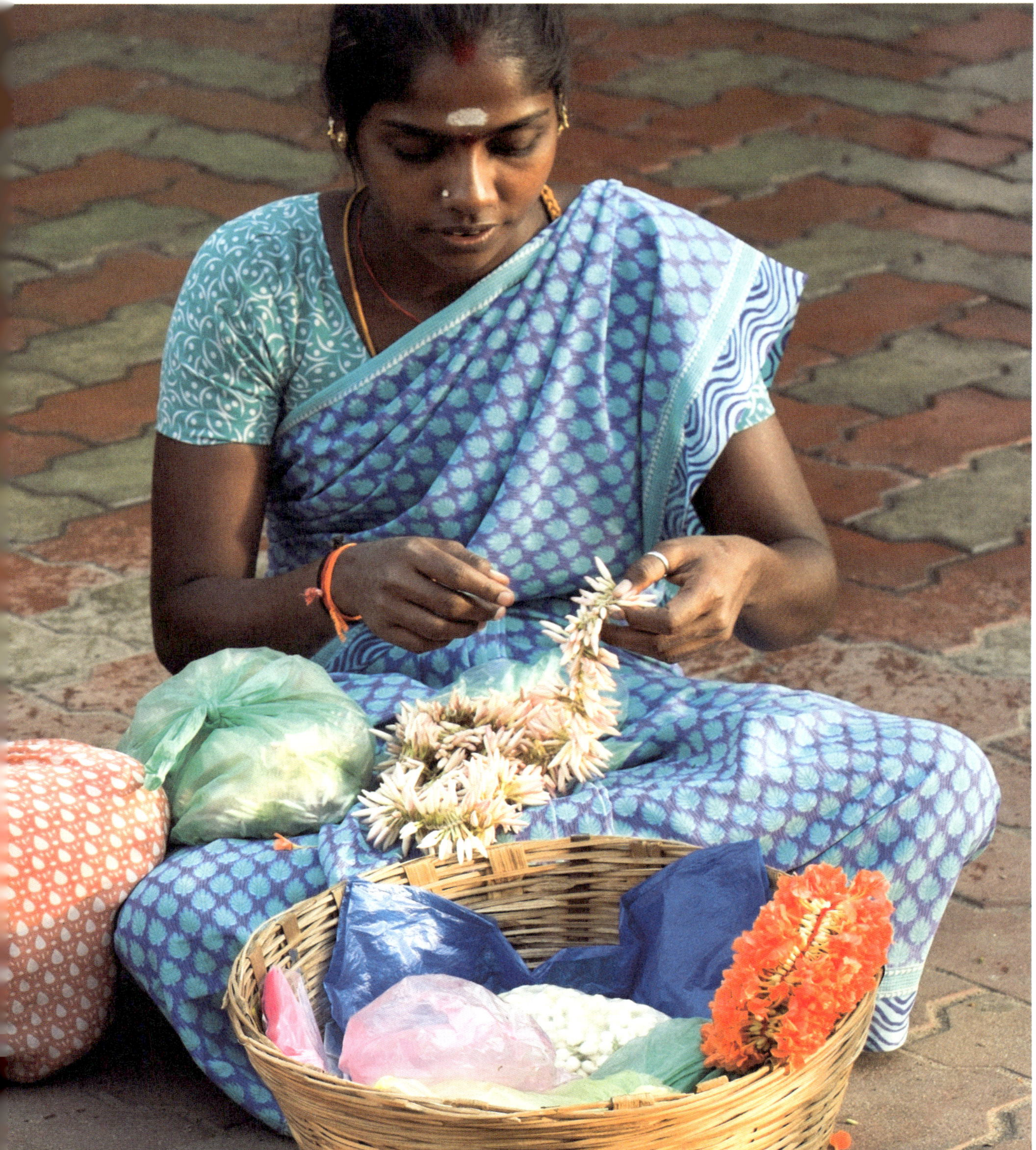

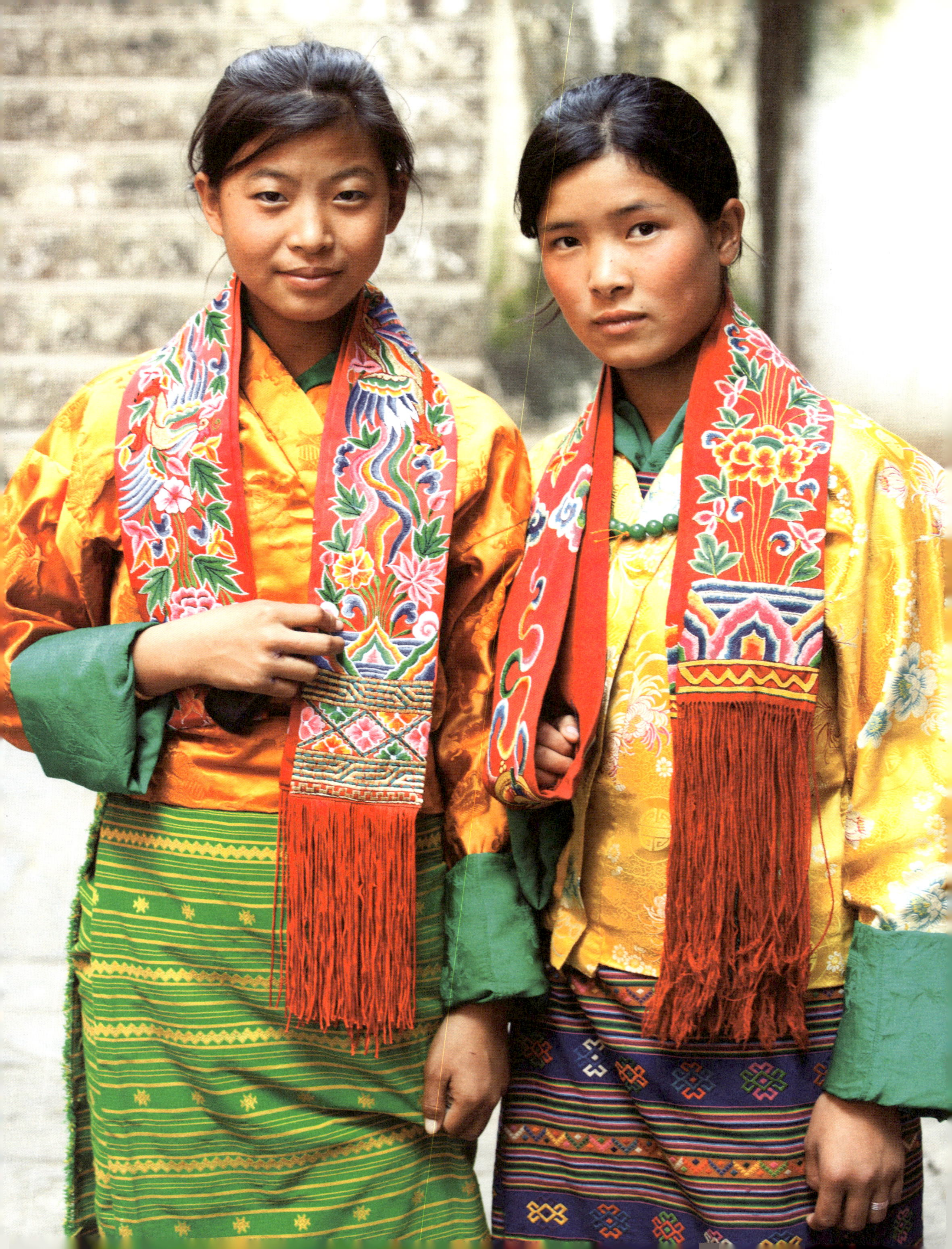

CHAPTER 4

सीमाओं के पार: दक्षिण एशिया में साड़ी

Beyond Borders: The Sari Across South Asia

The sari is not constrained by India's borders. Like rivers that ignore lines on maps, its 'six-yard' drape flows through the lives of millions across South Asia. In Bangladesh, it clings to the humid air of Dhaka and the floodplains of the Padma. In Sri Lanka, it adapts to island rhythms, bridging Sinhala and Tamil traditions. In Pakistan, though contested and reshaped, it remains a quiet thread linking memory with modern identity. In Nepal, it folds into both plains and mountains, merging with unique local garments to create a story of its own. Across these lands, the sari continues to be more than attire – it embodies inheritance, intimacy and resilience.

Two young women in traditional dress, Wangdue Phodrang (Wangdi), Bhutan.

Bangladesh – The River's Loom

In Bangladesh, the fabled Dhakai muslin, once spun so finely it could pass through a signet ring, was the pride of Bengal and the envy of neighbouring empires. According to legend Mughal queens draped themselves in nine yards (8.2m) so sheer it was called *rawan,* meaning 'flowing water'. This muslin, spun along the humid banks of the Meghna Riverand dyed with indigo and madder, took Bengal's craftsmanship to courts across the world.

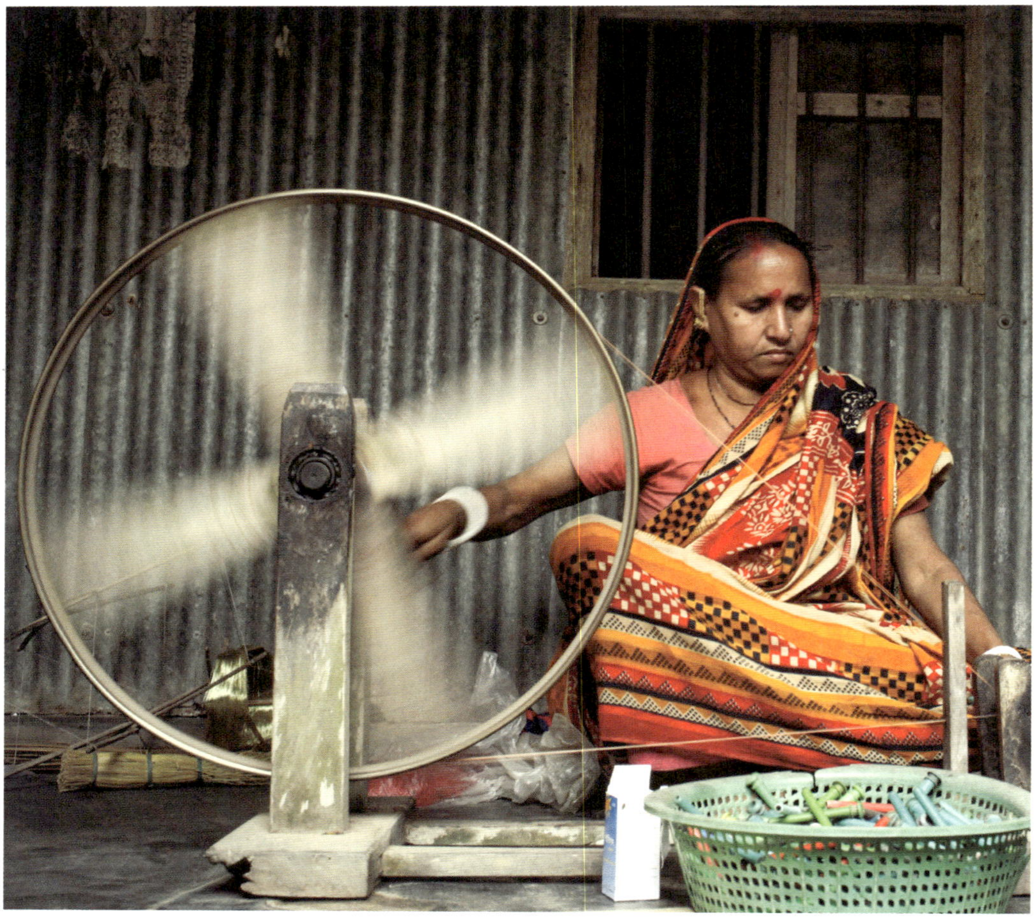

Weaver working on traditional sari weaving at Tangail Tantipara (weavers' village), Bangladesh. Tangail is renowned for its fine cotton saris, especially Jamdani-inspired designs.

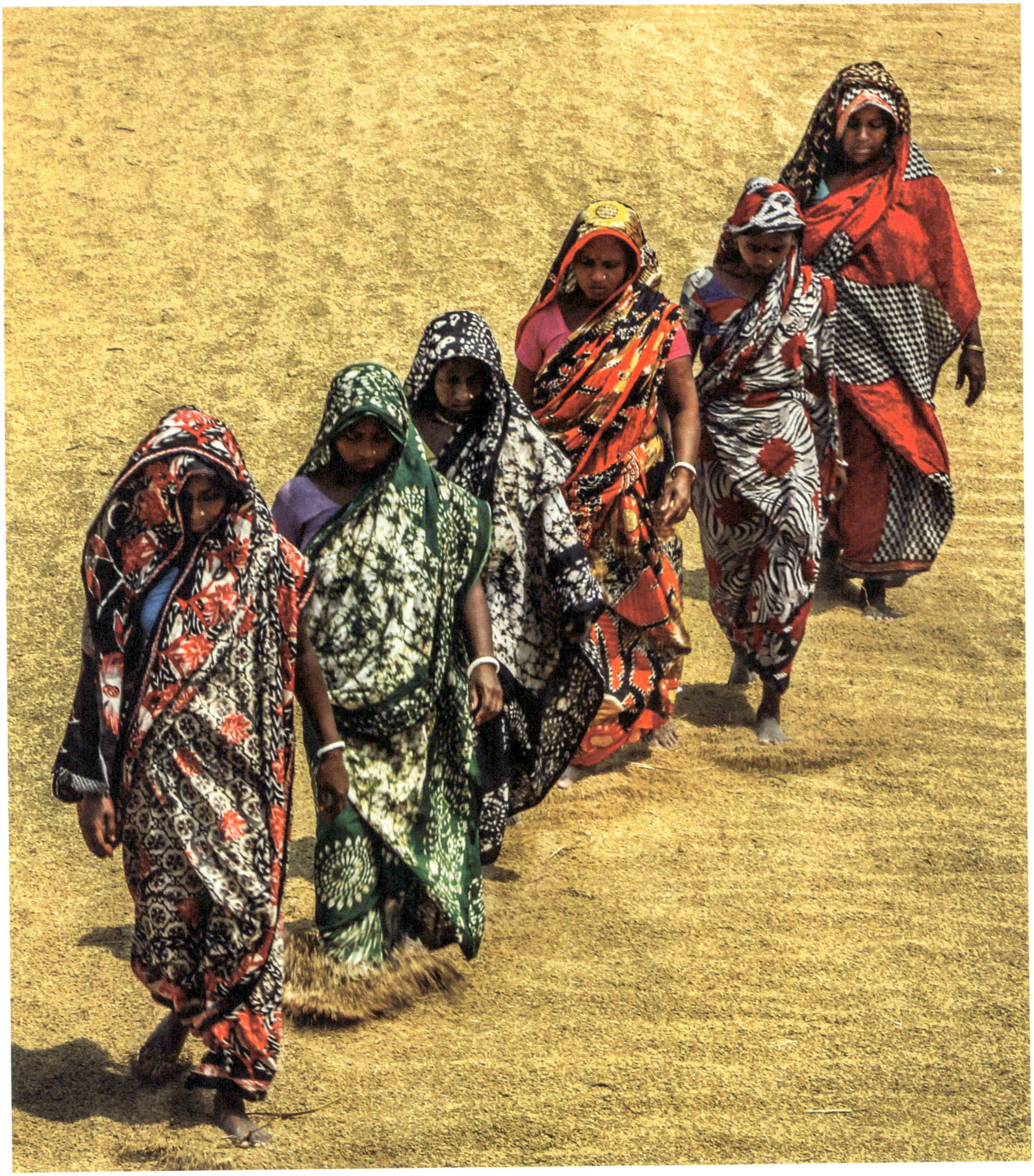

Women workers carrying agricultural produce across fields, Bangladesh.
Women have always played a significant role in rural agricultural labour across the region.

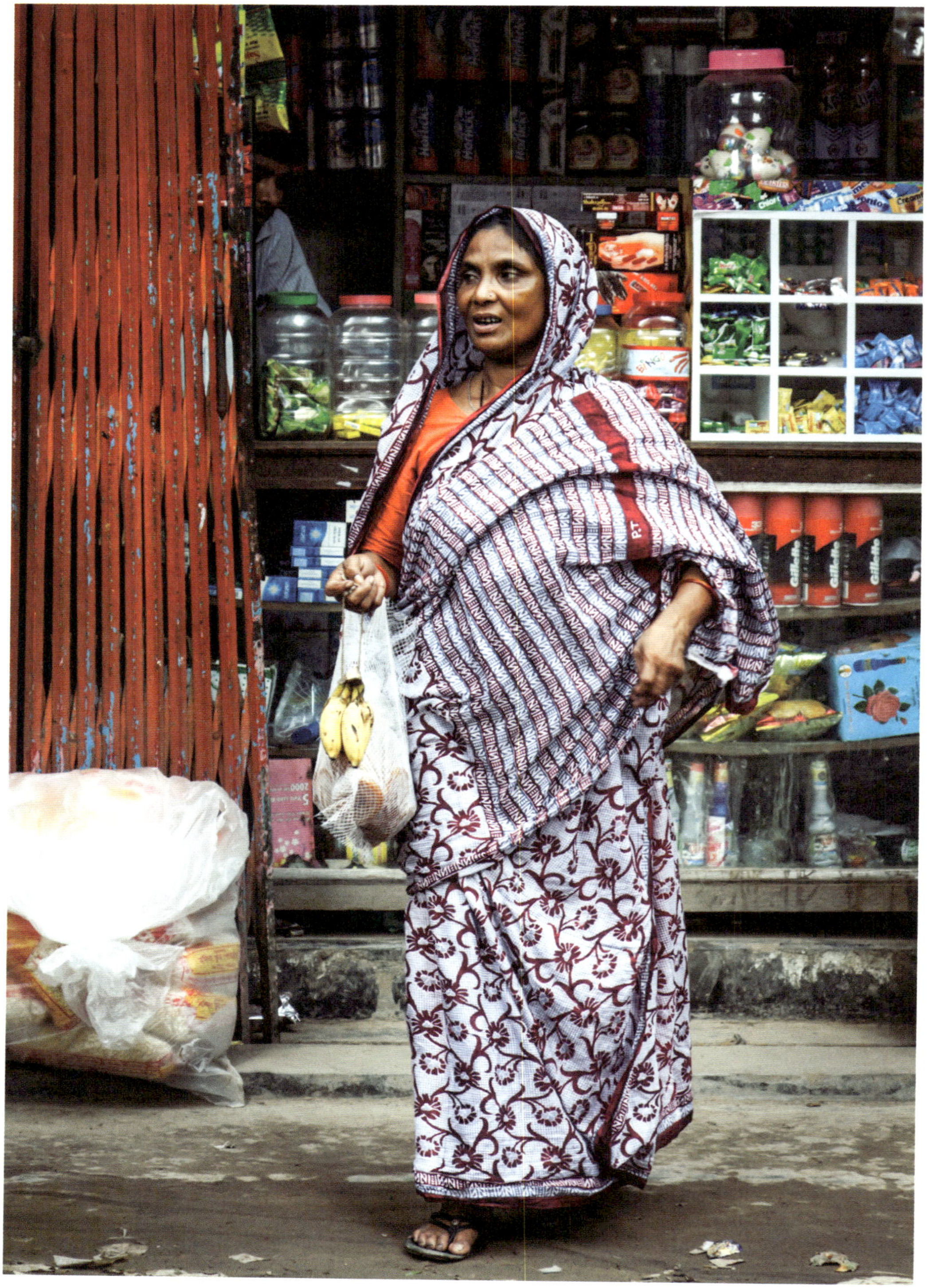

Woman shopping in a local market wearing a sari, Bangladesh.
The sari remains a widely worn everyday garment suited to the country's humid climate.

Today, the Jamdani – a descendant of that muslin – is Bangladesh's national textile. Its motifs are added painstakingly by hand: lotus blossoms, fish scales, paisleys. Draped in a Jamdani, a Bangladeshi bride carries the river's shimmer, the loom's patience and the weaver's prayer. Beyond Jamdani, the country thrives on regional saris too: the coarse, hand-spun Tangail cottons, striped and airy; the rich Rajshahi silks in jewel tones; the vibrant Khadi saris that once symbolized resistance during nationalist movements.

For Bangladeshi women, the sari is not only a celebration, but it is an everyday identity. In markets, universities and weddings, it clings light against the humid air, practical yet poetic. To wear one is to belong to a tradition that has survived colonizers who taxed muslin into extinction, floods that washed away fields and a partition that split Bengal in two. The sari remains, whispering resilience in every pleat.

CHANDERI'S TRANSLUCENCE

Chanderi saris combine silk warp with cotton weft, creating a fabric that appears almost transparent. Originating in Madhya Pradesh, Chanderi was once patronized by royalty. Its lightweight nature makes it ideal for heat, while delicate motifs lend it ceremonial refinement without heaviness.

Sri Lanka – Drapes of the Island

On the island of Sri Lanka, the sari is called the *osariya* among Sinhala women, and its drape takes on a distinctive style. Unlike the pleated *pallu* of India, the *osariya*'s drape is neatly tucked at the waist, creating a form This is both graceful and practical for island life. Its fitted blouse, often with short sleeves and a modest neckline, reflects colonial-era influences but has become part of the island's own tradition.

Among Tamil women of Jaffna, the sari remains closer to the South Indian drape, with temple silks and cottons bridging cultural ties across the Palk Strait. Wedding saris here often gleam with Koorai silk, richly brocaded in gold, while everyday cottons are dyed in the vibrant hues of the tropics – turmeric yellows, hibiscus reds, and sea-greens evoking the Indian Ocean.

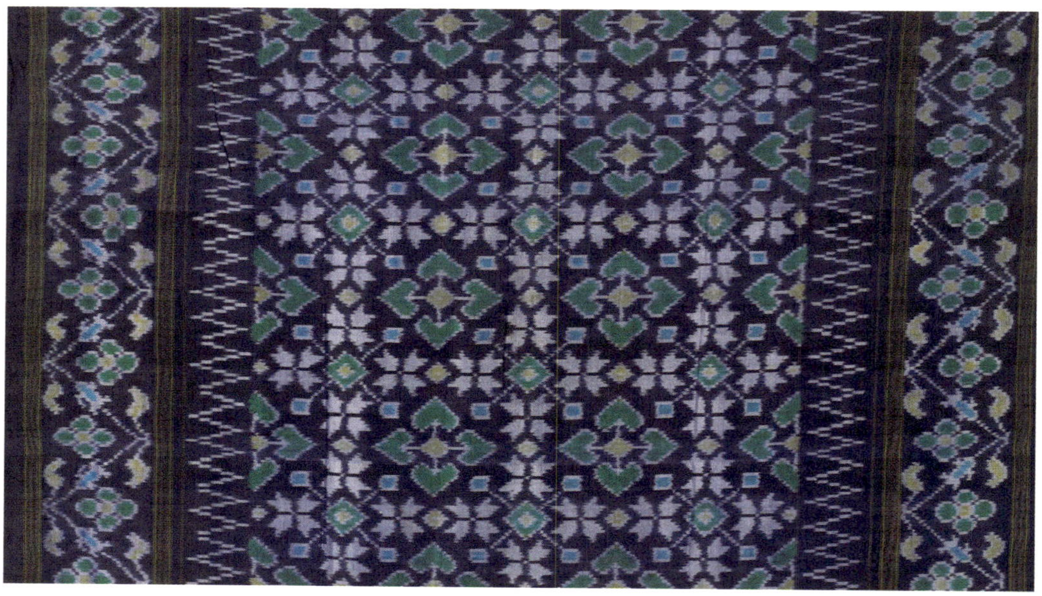

Silk sari; weft ikat, India, 20th century.
Ikat weaving involves resist-dyeing yarns before weaving to create patterned textiles.

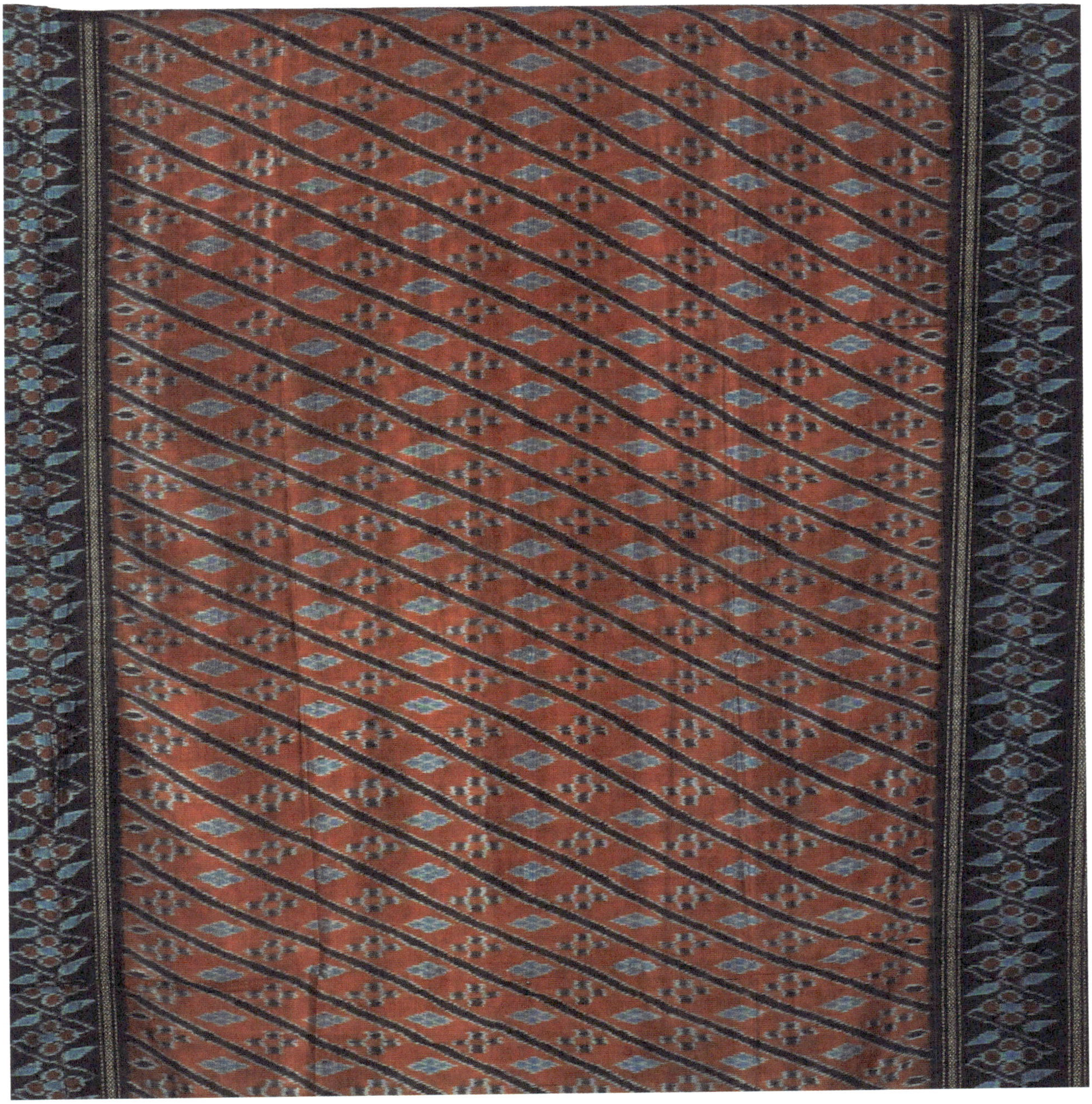

Silk sari; weft ikat, India, 20th century. This technique produces characteristic blurred motifs, a hallmark of ikat textiles.

Sri Lanka's saris also tell stories through print. The *batik* saris, born of Indonesian influence, bloom with wax-resist florals and geometric motifs, each piece hand-painted like a canvas. During festivals like Sinhala and Tamil New Year, streets brighten with saris in coral, orange and ocean blue, embodying the island's lush palette.

To wear a sari in Sri Lanka is to hold multiple inheritances: colonial overlays, South Indian continuities and island innovations. Each *osariya* pleat is a negotiation between tradition and adaptation, marking the sari as an emblem of both continuity and change.

RETAIL THEN AND NOW

Historically, saris were sold directly from weavers or through temple towns and royal courts. Today, retail has shifted to urban boutiques and exhibitions. However, clusters like Banaras, Kanchipuram and Ilkal still rely on local cooperatives to protect artisans from exploitative middlemen.

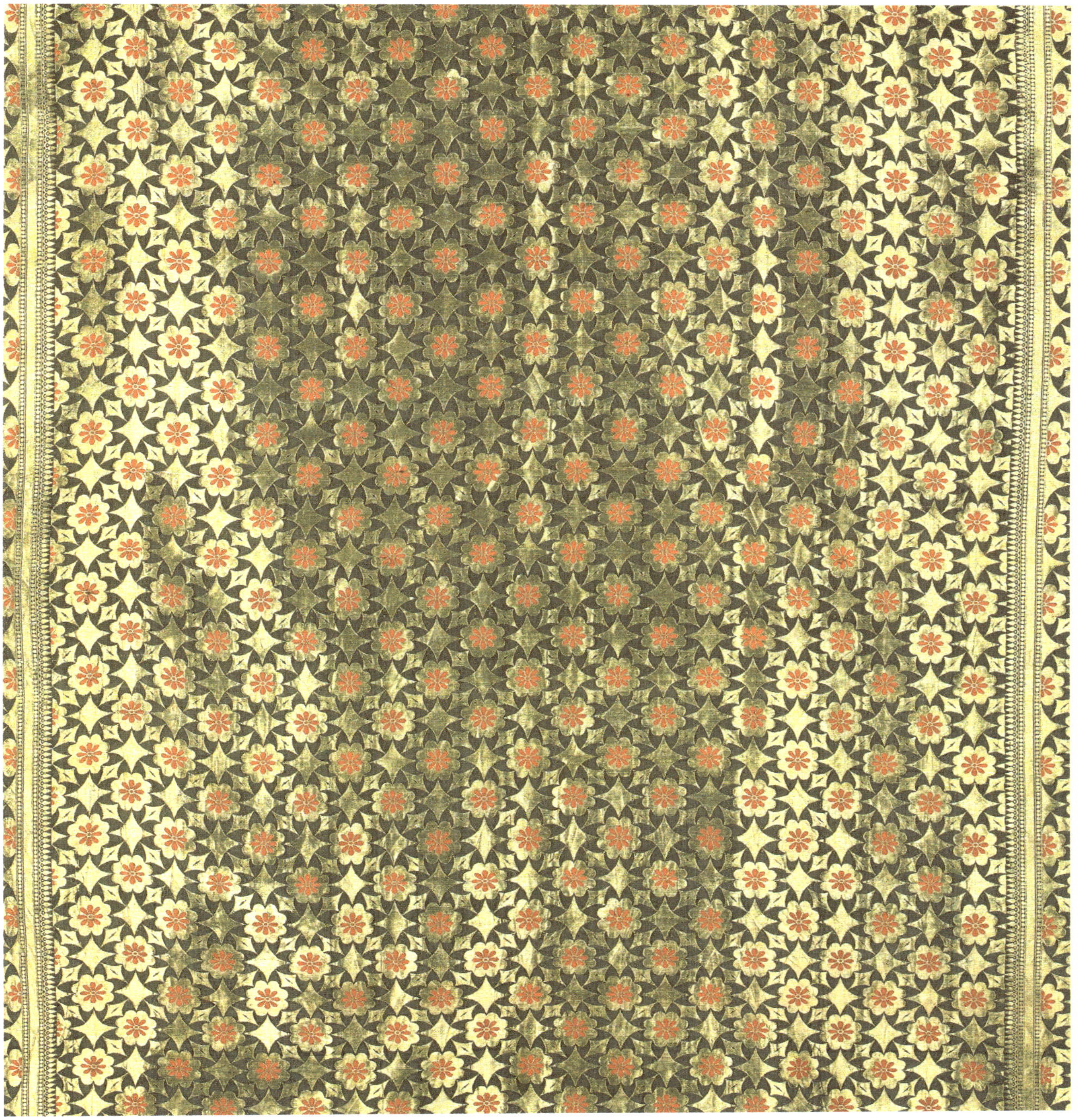

Sari with floral and geometric metallic gold brocade pattern, India, 20th century. Such brocades are often woven using zari threads, traditionally made with fine metal-wrapped yarn.

Pakistan – Threads of Memory

In Pakistan, the sari carries a more complicated story. Once a shared garment across undivided Punjab, Sindh and Bengal, the sari after Partition slowly receded from public life, replaced in many urban spaces by the *shalwar kameez*. Yet it never disappeared. In Karachi and Lahore, in Sindhi and Bengali households, the sari remained tucked in cupboards, emerging for weddings, cultural gatherings and intimate family rituals.

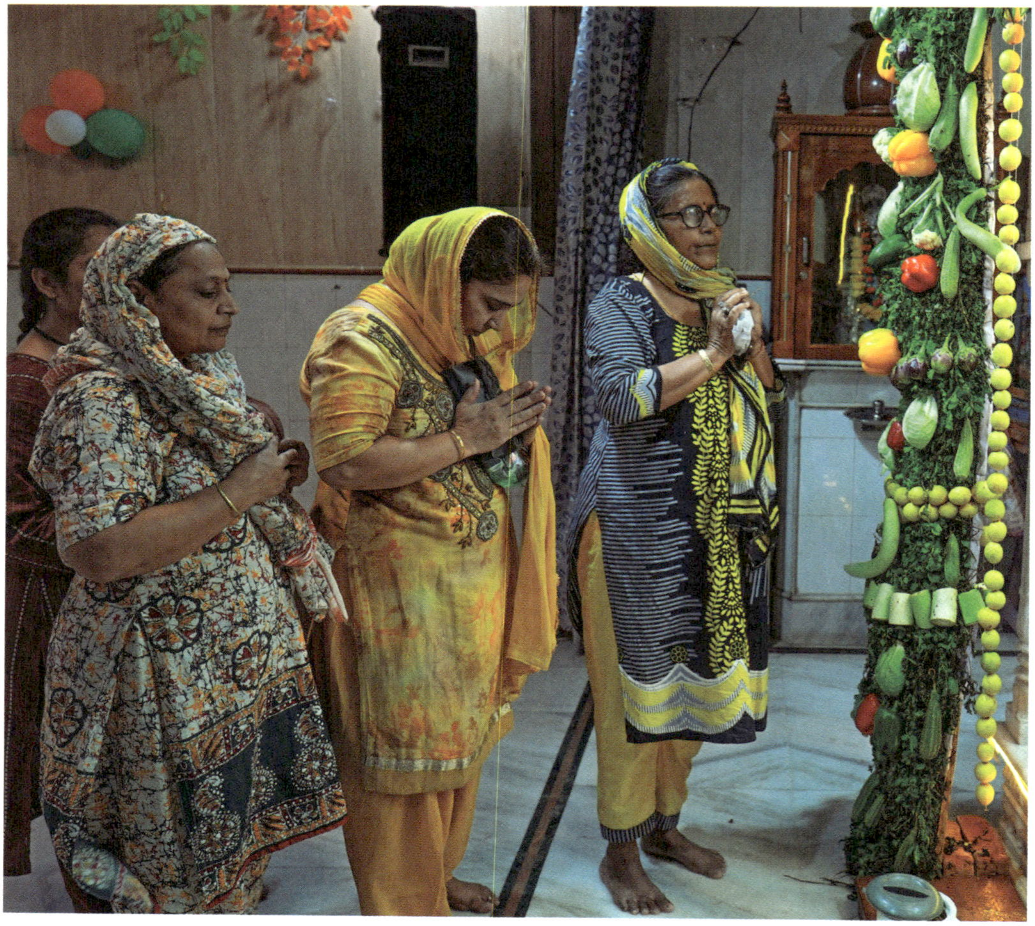

Sindhi women offering prayers during the Chaliho festival at Jhulelal temple, India. Jhulelal is revered as a patron saint of Sindhi communities, symbolizing unity and devotion.

In rural Sindh, handloom traditions like the *Ajrak* – deep indigo and madder block-prints with geometric stars and borders – are sometimes adapted into saris. Ajrak carries both identity and politics, worn as much for pride as for beauty. In Punjab, phulkari embroidery occasionally edges saris with its riot of colour, flowers bursting into every border. For Pakistani women of an older generation, especially those with roots in Bengal or India, the sari holds the memory of migration, of a homeland left behind. To drape one is to drape longing. For younger generations, it is slowly re-emerging, worn by artists, activists and feminists who reclaim it as part of shared South Asian heritage. Though less common in everyday wear, the sari in Pakistan survives as a symbol: of connection, nostalgia and quiet resistance against erasure.

THE WEAVER'S HOUSEHOLD

A sari is rarely made by one person alone. Spinning, dyeing, weaving and finishing are often divided across family members. In many regions, entire households work together, turning sari production into an inherited livelihood rather than an individual profession.

Nepal – Drapes Across Mountains and Plains

In Nepal, the sari flows differently, folding into both Terai lowlands and Himalayan highlands. Among women in the Terai, the sari is everyday attire: light cottons in checks and florals, practical for the humid plains. Brides, however, often gleam in Banarasi silks, imported from India but embraced as tradition, with shimmering red and gold saris symbolizing prosperity and fertility.

MOTIFS AS MAPS

Sari motifs often map geography. Fish motifs reflect river cultures, temple borders echo sacred towns, floral jaals suggest Mughal gardens. These designs are not decorative accidents – they encode where a sari comes from, who made it and what the land around them looks like.

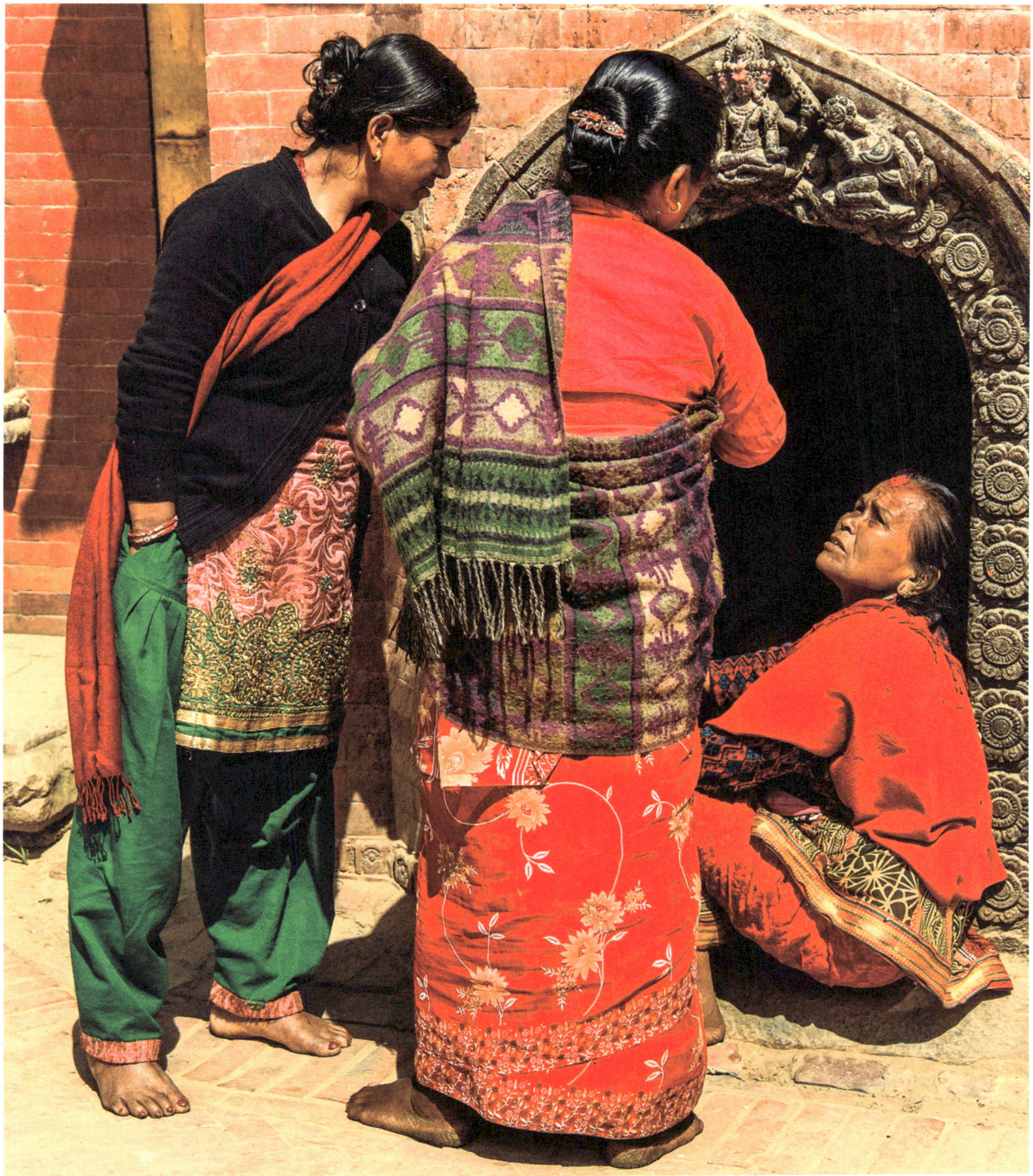

Chhetri women in traditional dress conversing, Nepal.
The Chhetri are one of the largest ethnic groups in Nepal.

Other garments unique to Nepal live alongside the sari. Among the Newar community of the Kathmandu Valley, women wear the *haku patasi*, which is a black sari with a striking red border, paired with a white blouse and shawl. Worn during festivals and rituals, it embodies both elegance and cultural pride. In other communities, the *gunyo cholo* (long shirt and blouse) marks a girl's coming of age, often gifted with a sari as part of her passage into womanhood.

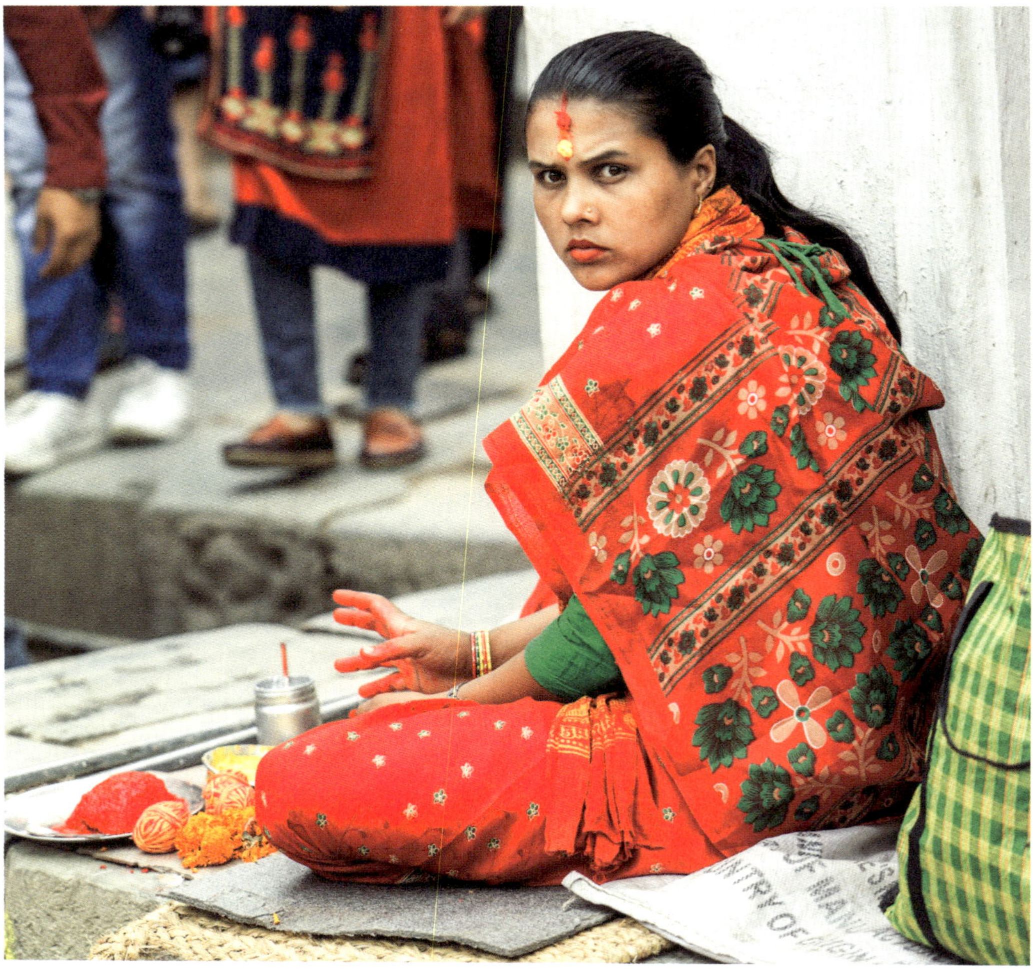

Hindu devotees celebrating Janai Purnima at Pashupatinath Temple, Kathmandu, Nepal. The festival involves tying sacred threads as a symbol of protection and renewal.

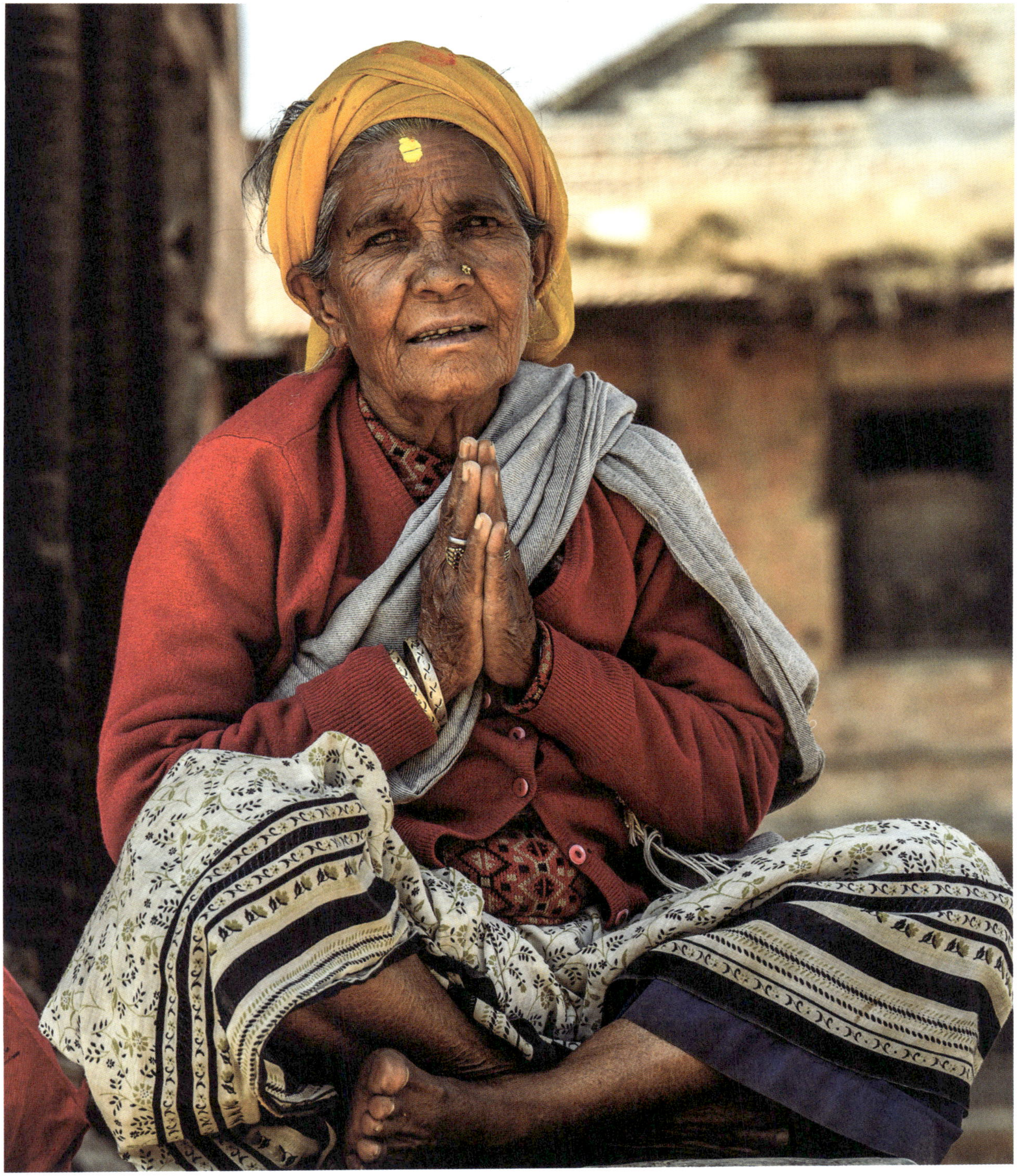

Elderly Chhetri woman in traditional attire seated in prayer, Nepal.

Consequently, the sari in Nepal exists in dialogue with multiple traditions, adapting to mountain and valley, urban and rural, ritual and everyday. It is both a shared inheritance with India and a distinctly Nepali expression – resilient, meaningful, and alive.

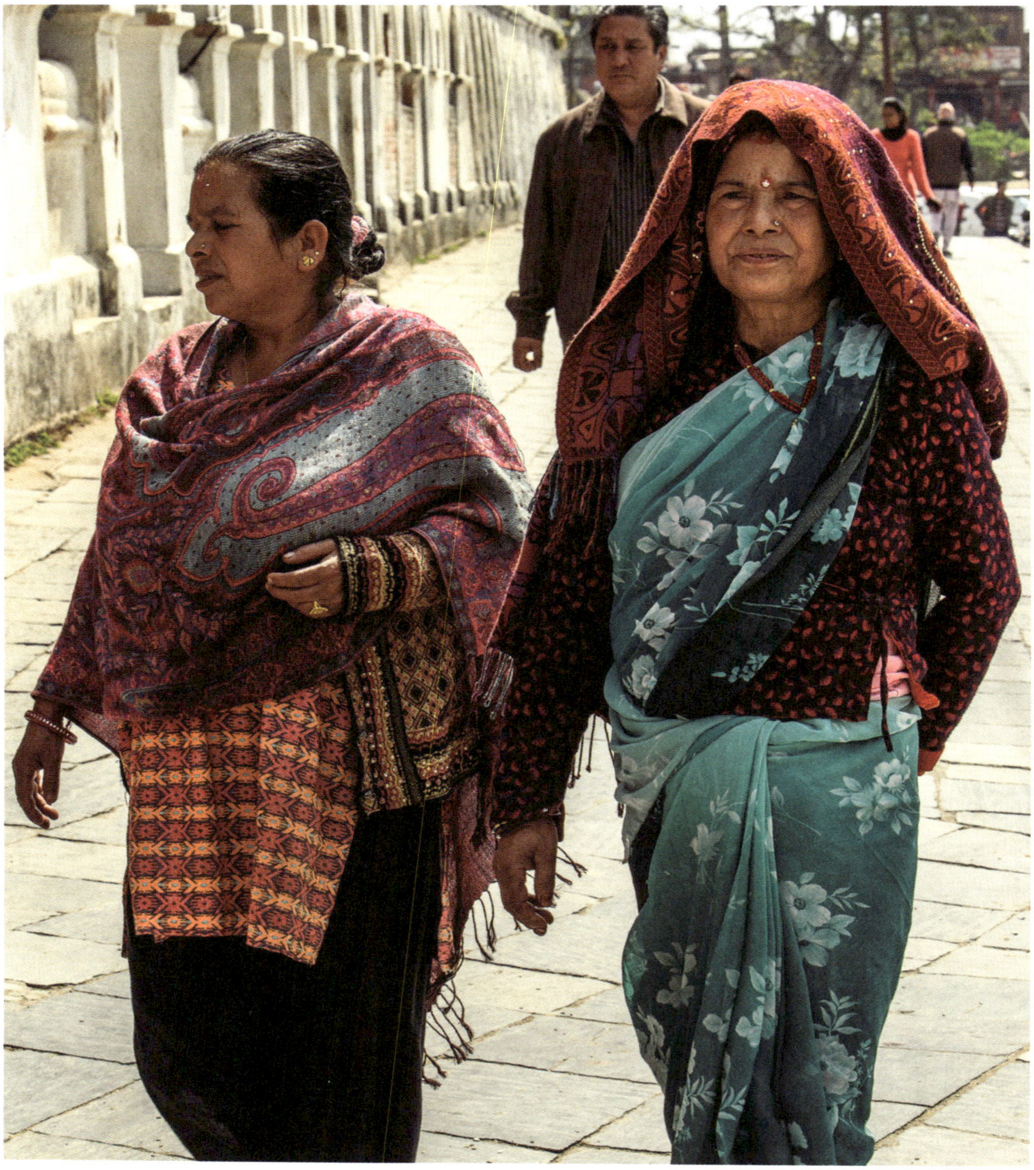

Chhetri women walking along a street in traditional dress, Nepal.
Everyday clothing reflects both cultural identity and practical adaptation to the environment.

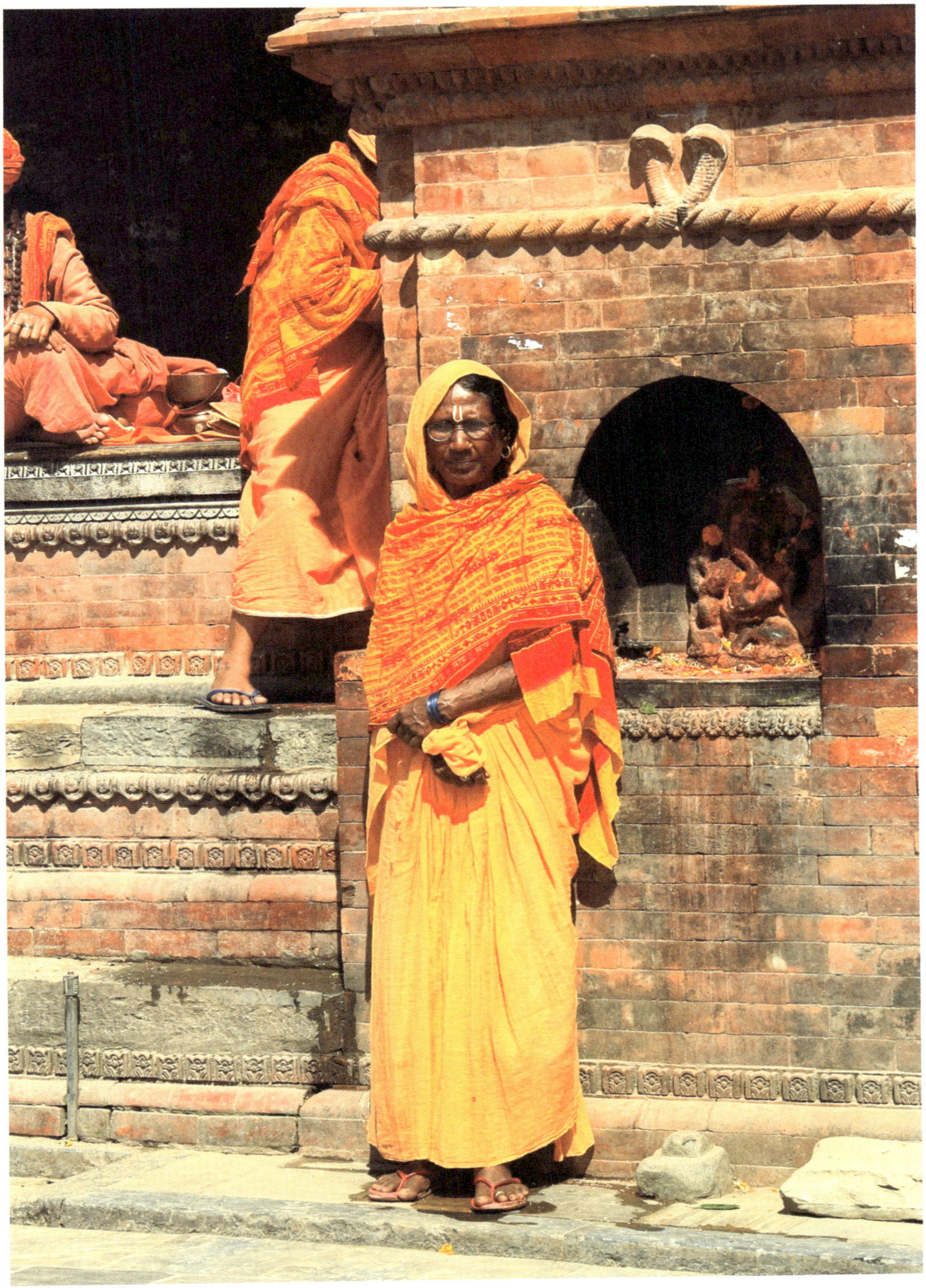

Holy woman near a shrine, Kathmandu, Nepal.
Religious figures are often seen in temple spaces central to community life.

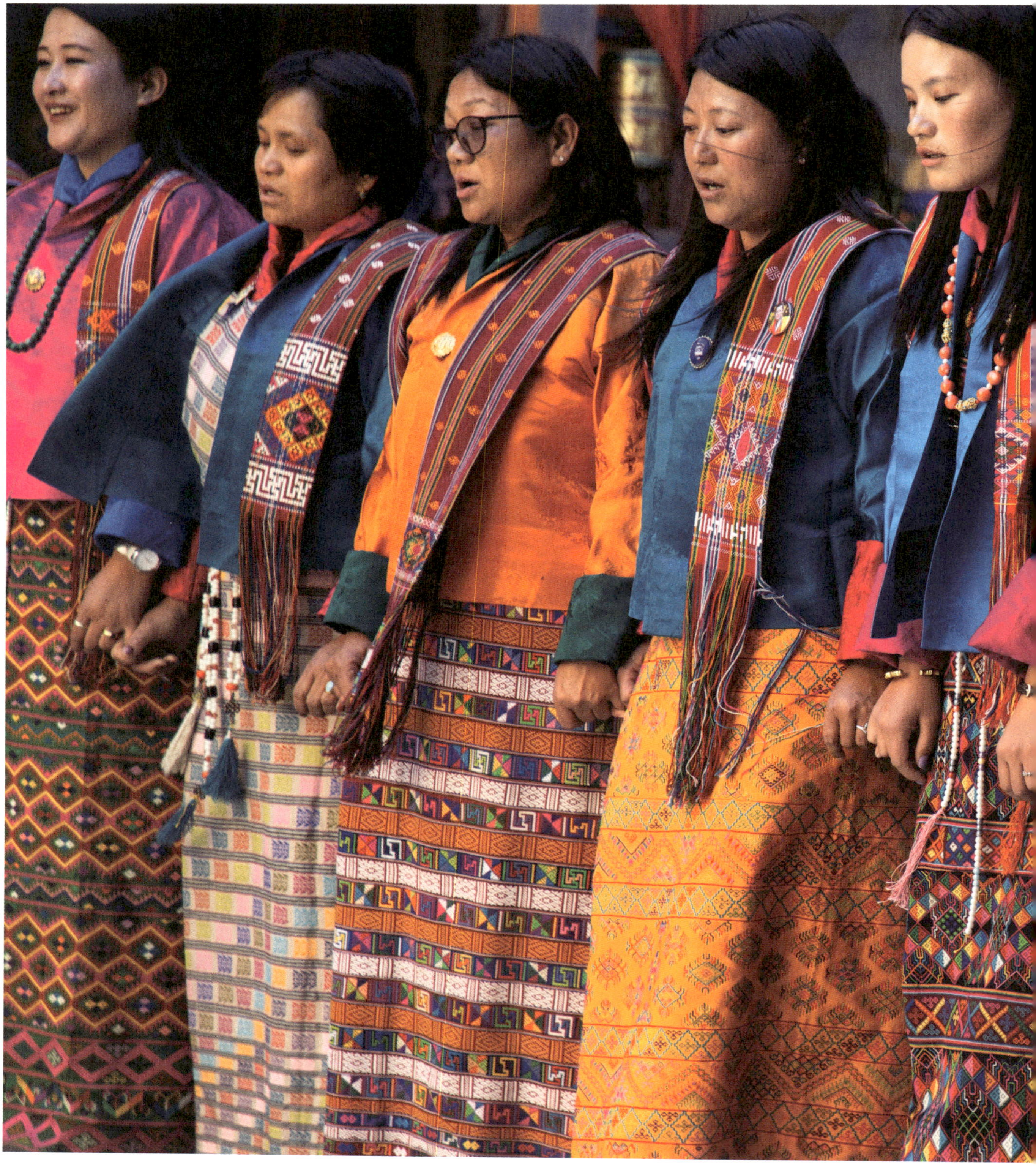

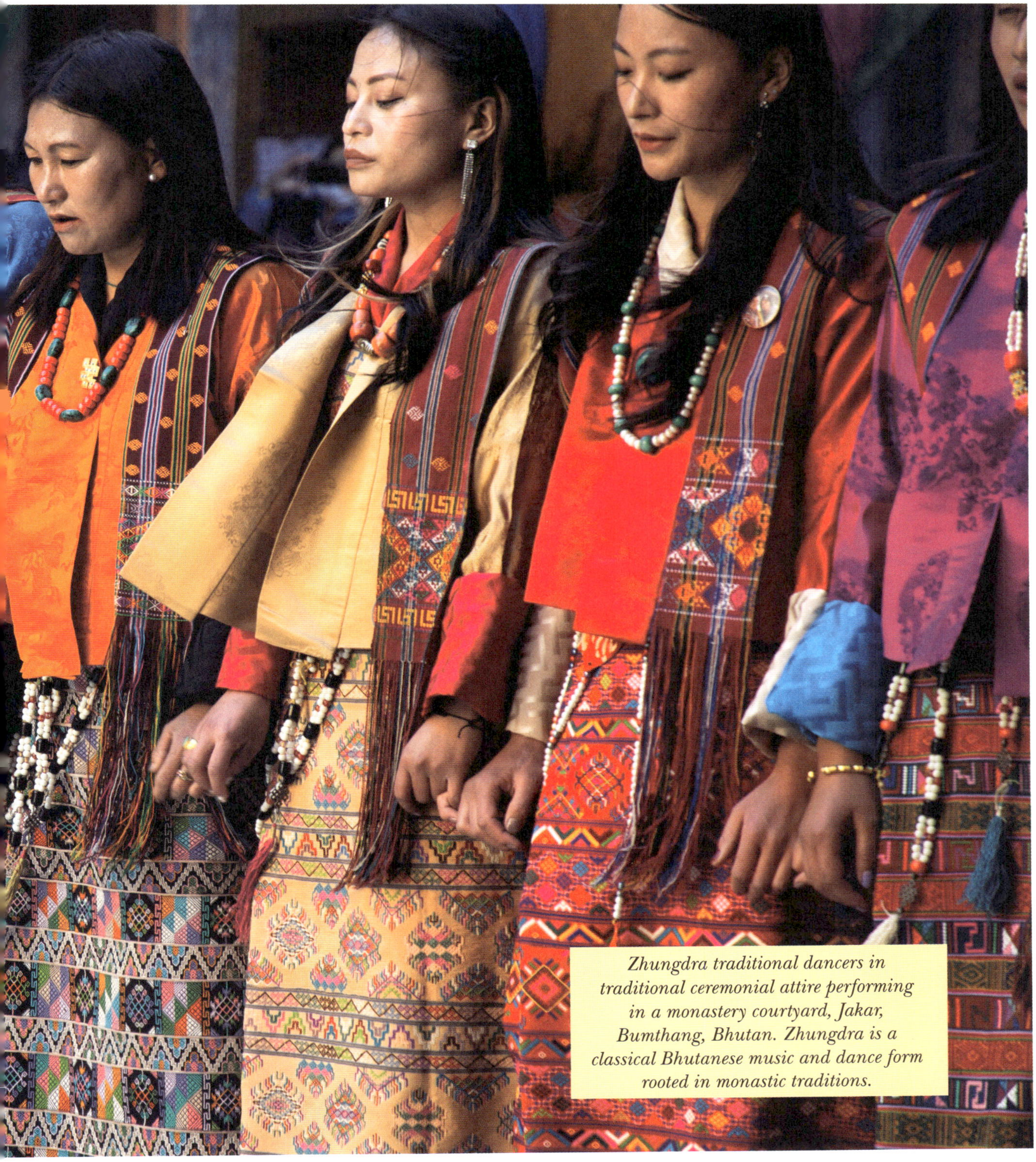

Zhungdra traditional dancers in traditional ceremonial attire performing in a monastery courtyard, Jakar, Bumthang, Bhutan. Zhungdra is a classical Bhutanese music and dance form rooted in monastic traditions.

A Shared Weave

Across Bangladesh, Sri Lanka, Pakistan and Nepal, the sari tells stories parallel to India's, yet distinctly their own. It is at once a garment of weddings, markets and festivals, and a record of survival – through colonial exploitation, partitioned borders and shifting identities. In every land, the sari adapts to climate, ritual and politics, yet its essence endures: 'six yards' that carry history, artistry and belonging.

To trace its folds across South Asia is to realize that the sari is not India's alone. It is a regional language, spoken in dialects of cotton and silk, of Jamdani and Ajrak, of *osariya* pleats and haku patasi stripes. It is proof that fabric can bind what borders divide.

URBAN REVIVAL BOUTIQUES

Modern retailers and designers have begun reintroducing handloom saris to younger audiences through storytelling and transparency. By naming weavers, clusters and techniques, these boutiques reconnect urban consumers with rural craft, bridging tradition and contemporary fashion without erasing labour.

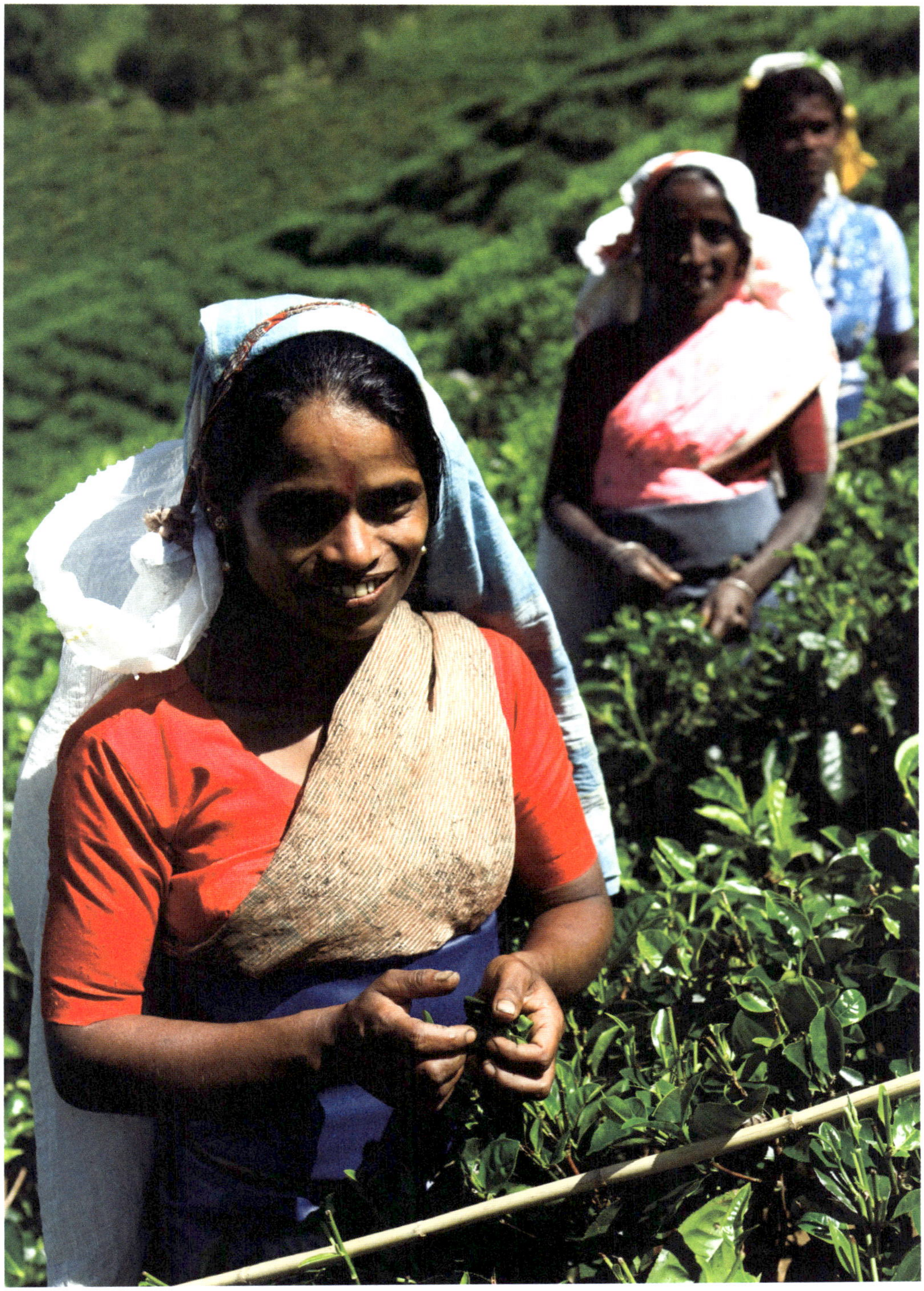

Tamil tea pluckers working in plantation fields, Nuwara Eliya, Sri Lanka.
Tea production remains a major part of Sri Lanka's economy and colonial legacy.

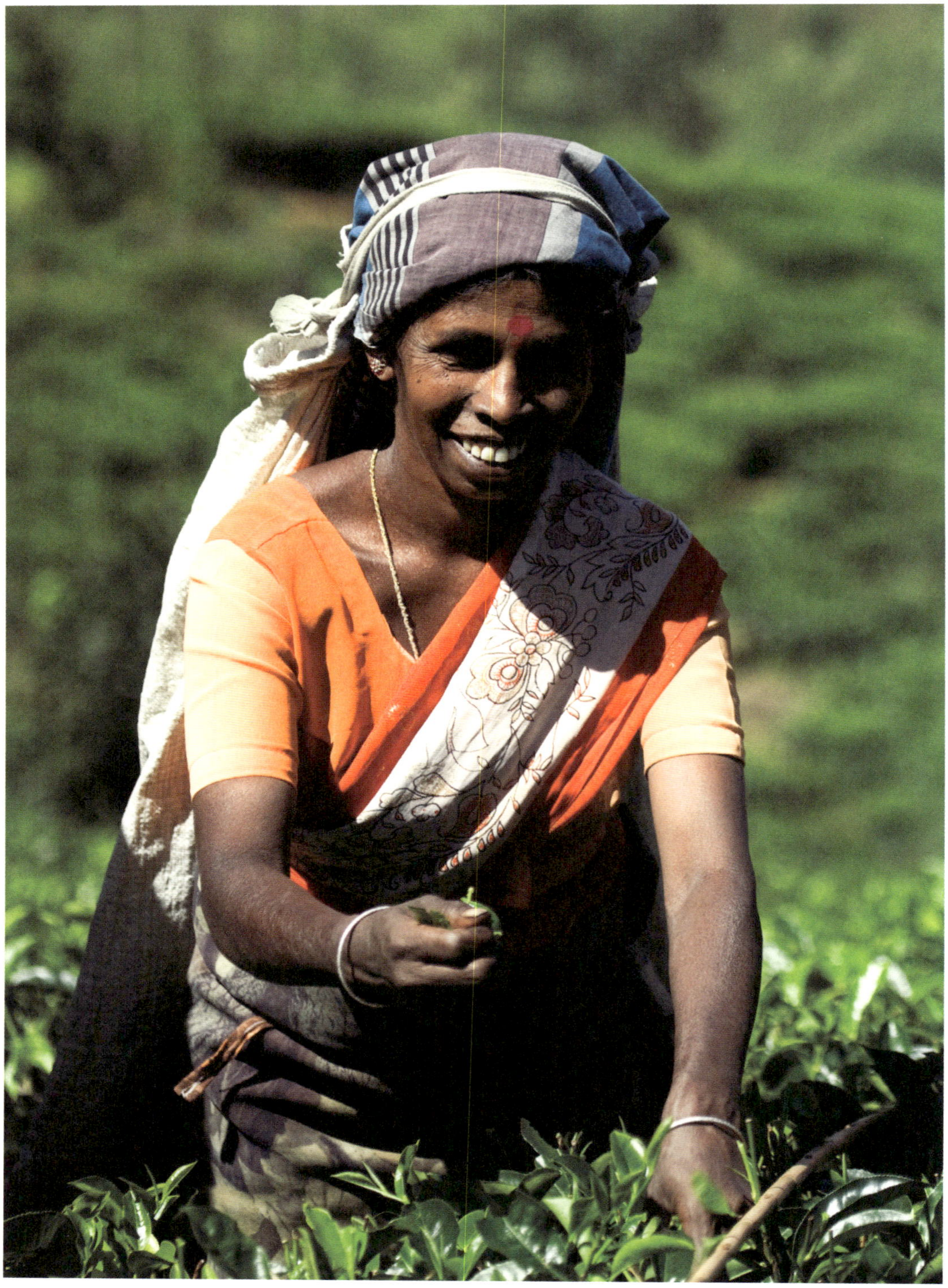

Tamil tea pluckers harvesting tea leaves, Nuwara Eliya, Sri Lanka.
Workers often follow age-old techniques of hand-plucking for quality control.

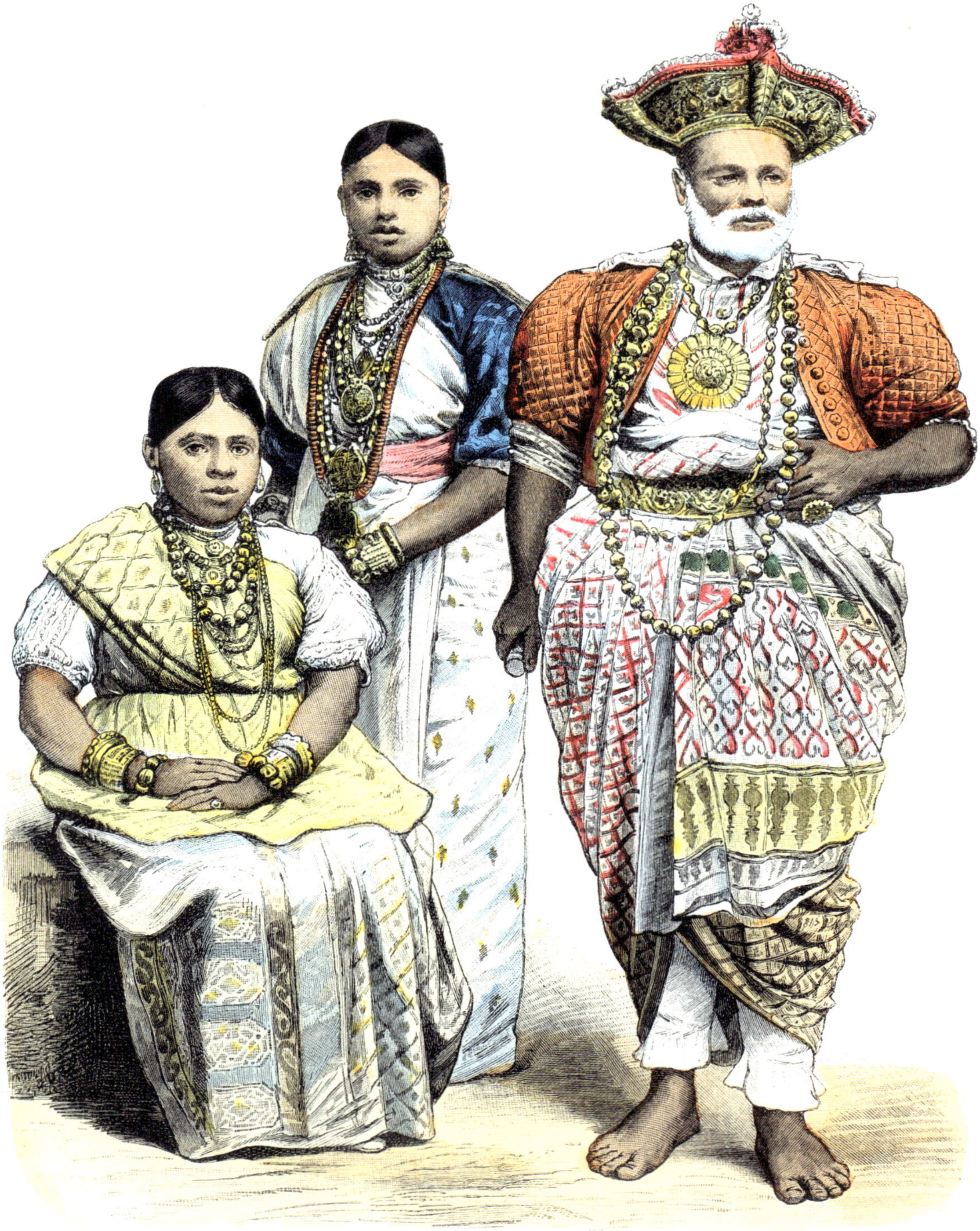

Sri Lankan middle-class costume, hand-coloured wood engraving, 19th century. Such prints were widely produced in Europe to document global dress traditions.

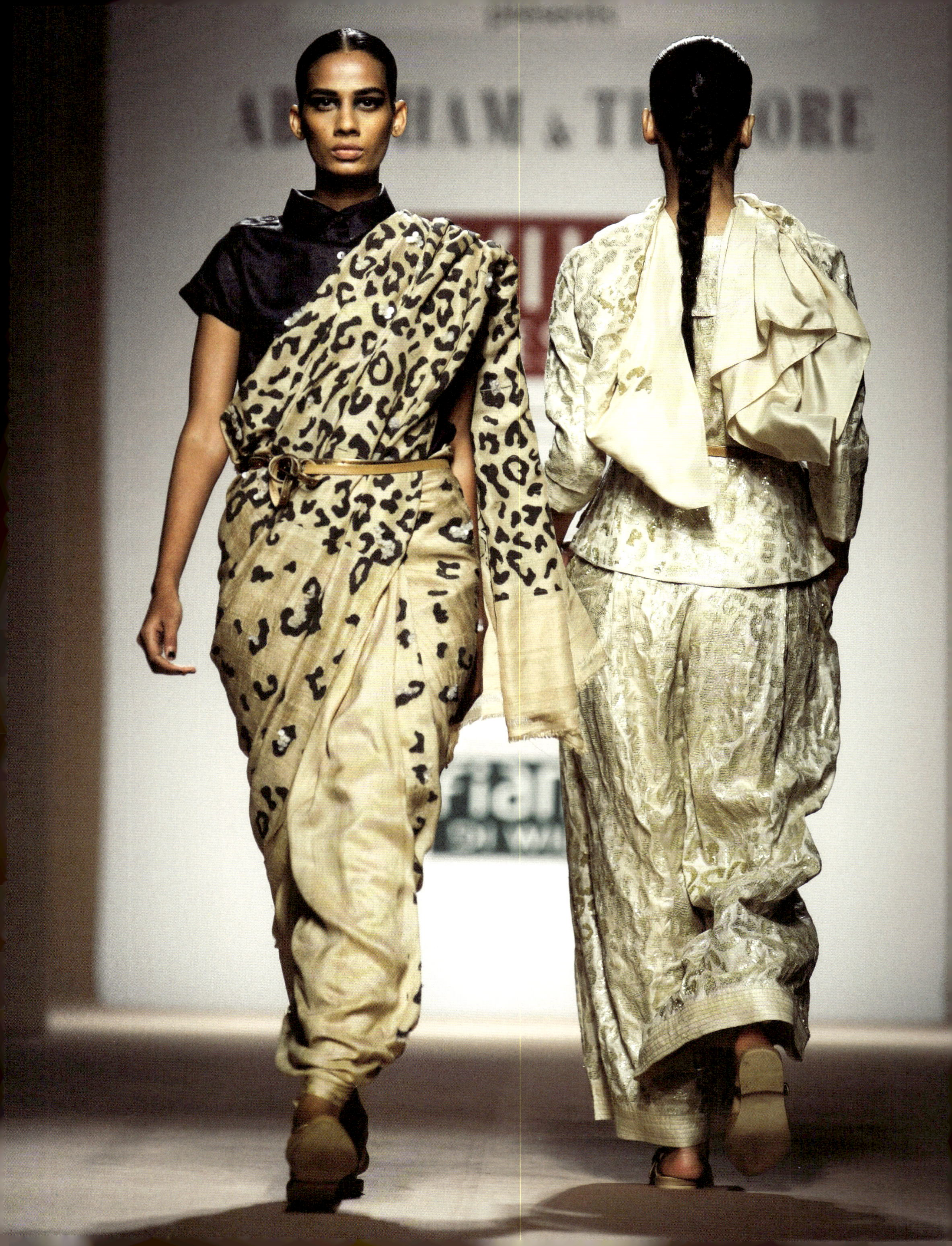

CHAPTER 5

परविर्तन का वस्त्र: आधुनकि समय में साड़ी

Fabric of Change: The Sari in Modern Times

Sustainability and Craftsmanship

Leading fashion houses and indie labels alike now treat the sari as an eco-conscious canvas. Leading Indian fashion designer Anita Dongre has 'carved a unique niche' by blending traditional craft with modern design and 'championing sustainability and ethical practices'. Her brand's Grassroot line, for example, is built entirely on hand-woven silks and organic cottons – fabrics that are renewable, biodegradable, and locally made. Similarly, Rahul Mishra infuses his sari and couture creations with environmentalism: his designs are 'rooted in sustainability and mindful creative practices,' transforming recycled materials into 'wearable art'. Other designers interpret the name of the sari literally. Anavila Misra's label is known for linen saris with

Models presenting creations by Abraham and Thakore at India Fashion Week, New Delhi, 2014. The designers are known for blending traditional textiles with contemporary design.

minimal impact: she partners with weavers in Bengal and uses natural dyes 'to reduce environmental impact while keeping craft alive'. In every case, supporting handloom communities and time-honoured techniques goes hand in hand with green values – proving that preserving the sari's heritage can itself be sustainable.

'Waste not' has become a watchword for many sari innovators. Mumbai's Dhara Upcycle Studio (Deepika Sridhar) and brands like I Was a Sari refuse to let old or damaged saris languish. Sridhar proudly declares, 'Sustainability is the primary motto, so that nothing goes to waste.' She and others cut into pre-loved saris to craft entirely new garments, or repurpose every scrap. In one collection, designer

HANDLOOM VS POWERLOOM SARIS

Handloom saris are woven on manually operated looms, where each movement of the shuttle and reed is controlled by the weaver. Powerloom saris, introduced widely in the 20th century, use mechanized looms to increase speed and lower cost. While powerlooms democratized access, handloom saris preserve regional techniques, irregular textures and artisan livelihoods that machines cannot replicate.

Stephin Lalan engineered zero-waste drapes, pin-tucking cloth from edge to edge so that no fabric is discarded. The surplus bits become pockets, cushions or quilted accents. As Lalan notes, sustainability in sari design is a holistic process – one that values mindful construction as much as the original textile. Even the very act of upcycling is seen as meaningful: one designer explains that 'upcycling a sari is both a creative act and a mindful way to connect history with the present'.

Indeed, when Stephen Lalan reworks a cherished bridal sari into, say, a modern *lehenga*, he treats it like a heritage object. He says he examines 'which is the strongest element' of the sari's brocade border and *pallu*, and then preserves it intact, sometimes keeping the original *pallu* as the new *dupatta* so 'the whole essence of the sari is still visible' in the remake. In this way, every vintage drape is given new life, and every thread of tradition is honoured.

Innovation in Draping and Design

Alongside eco-consciousness, India's youth are also reinventing how a sari is worn. Traditional drapes exist together with playful hybrids: belts, corsets, jackets, and even trousers are brought in to refresh the look. Stylist Deepika Sridhar suggests, for example, adding an Indo-Western belt or a 'cancan inskirt' beneath the sari for 'volume and grandeur' – essentially turning the sari into a *lehenga*-like silhouette without cutting it. Other designers push the sari into streetwear. Fashion educator Purushu Arie highlights a now widespread fusion: draping a half-sari over trousers. He notes that simply pleating half the sari as usual and pairing it with pants 'gives a trendy, comfortable and chic pant-sari look'. At weddings and on runways alike, saris appear with puff-sleeved blouses, jean jackets or embroidered capes, and even with trainers instead of sandals. Some couturiers have crafted pre-stitched sari gowns, while others play with pleat placement or asymmetric puckers to merge heritage with high fashion.

In short, the sari's 'six yards' have become endlessly adaptable: by combining old and new, designers prove that this traditional drape can fit or reflect any trend or personality.

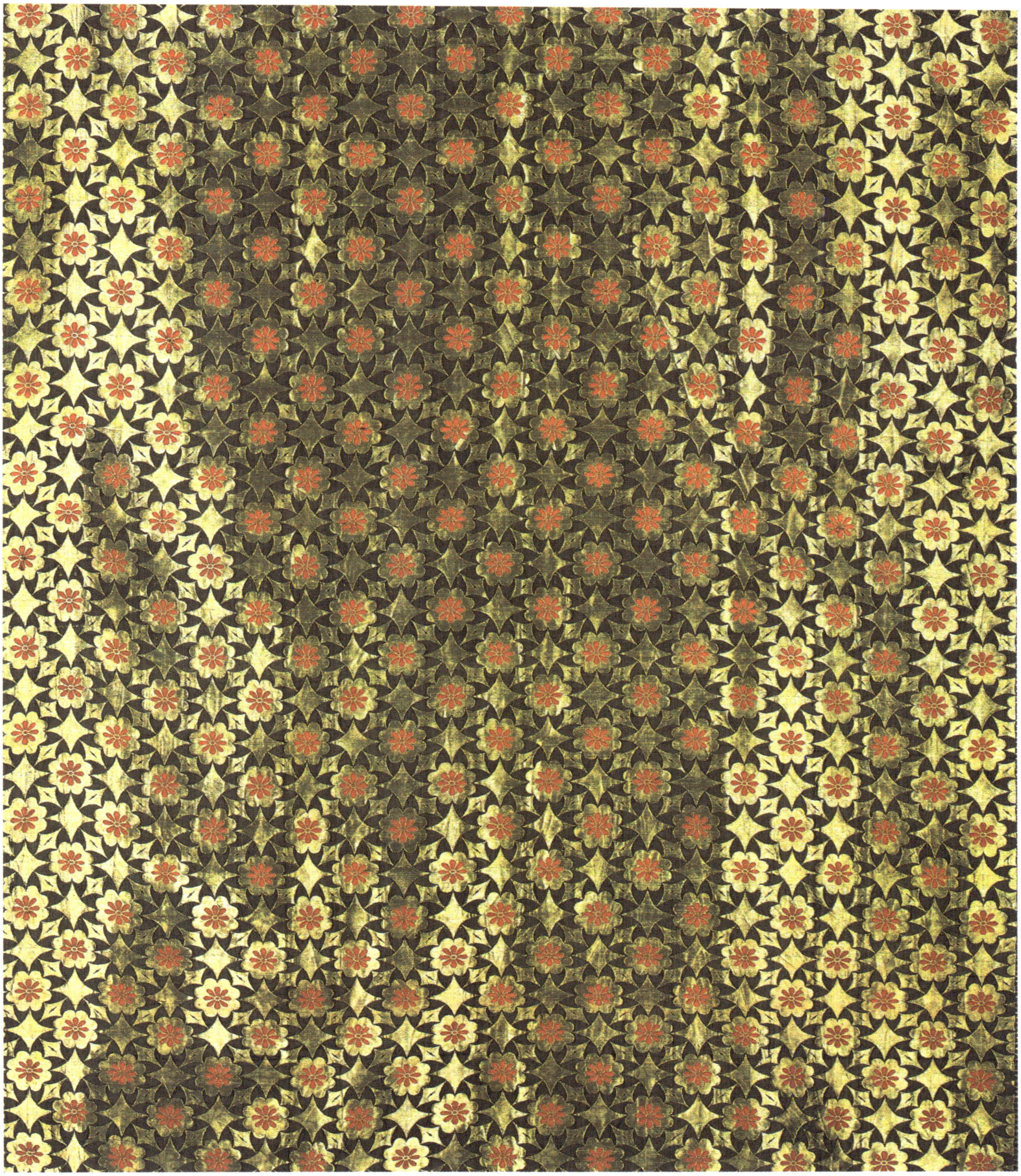

Sari, India, 20th century. Twentieth-century saris reflect a shift between handloom traditions and industrial production.

Prints of a New Generation

If older saris told stories through temple borders, floral butis and mythic figures, the modern sari reimagines them in pop art, graffiti or surrealist dreamscapes. Nowhere is this clearer than in the work of Masaba Gupta, often called the 'queen of prints'. Her saris break boldly away from convention: lipstick motifs, cow prints, candy stripes and even the outlines of cameras and telephones splash across silk and chiffon. What once might have been dismissed as irreverent is now seen as playful rebellion. A Masaba sari does not quietly evoke ancestry; it shouts personality. In her hands, the sari becomes an urban mood board – a fabric that can be as contemporary as a street mural yet as quintessentially Indian as a grandmother's wardrobe.

Earlier pioneers like Satya Paul, and later Rajesh Pratap, turned the sari into a painter's canvas long before print culture became mainstream. Their graphic saris featured watercolour-like splashes, abstract brushstrokes and even photographic imagery. In the 1990s, a Satya Paul was more than attire, it was wearable modern art – foreshadowing what the next generation would come to embrace.

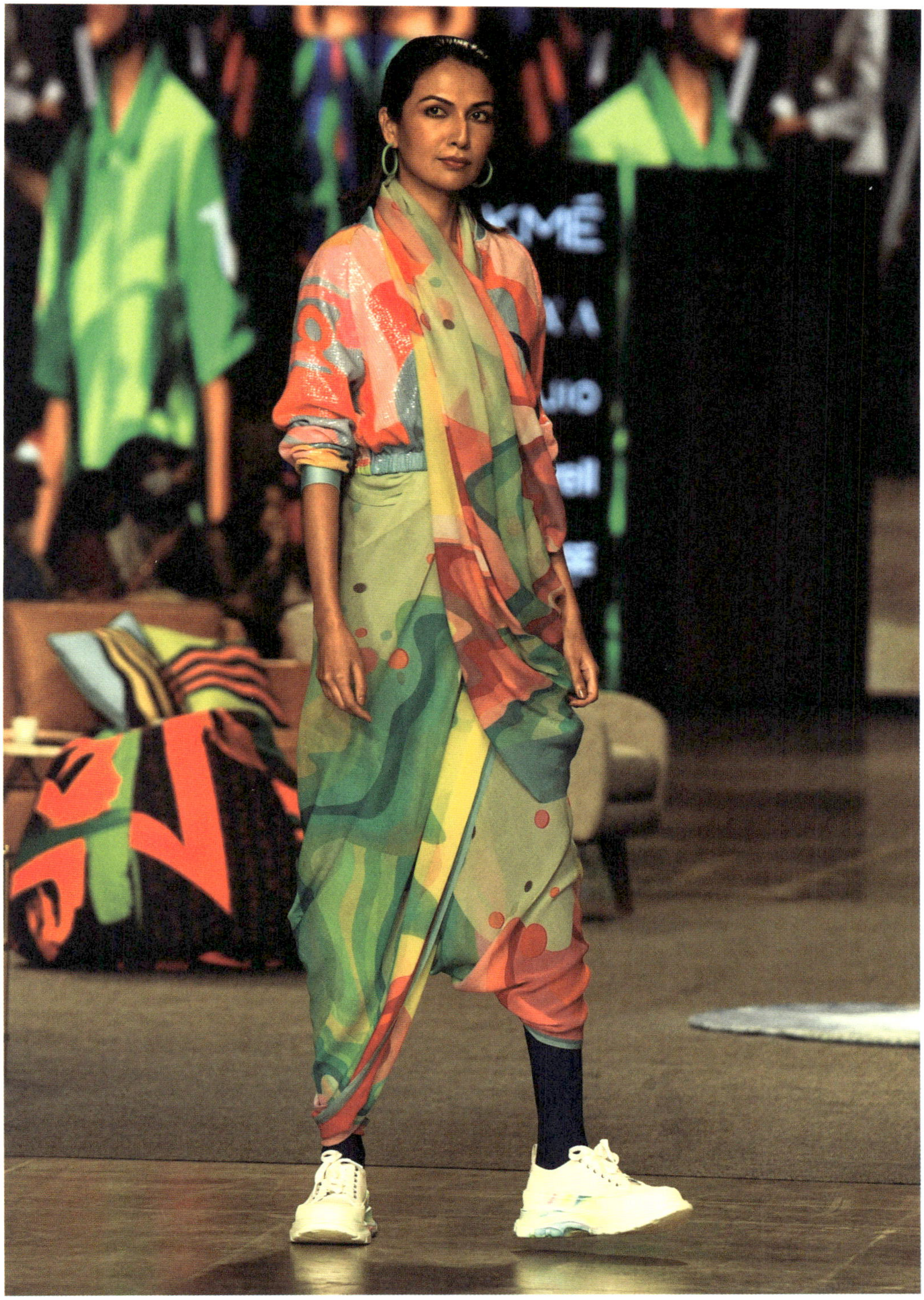

Model presenting a Satya Paul creation by Rajesh Pratap Singh at Lakmé Fashion Week, Mumbai, 2021. Satya Paul is known for bold prints and modern reinterpretations of the sari.

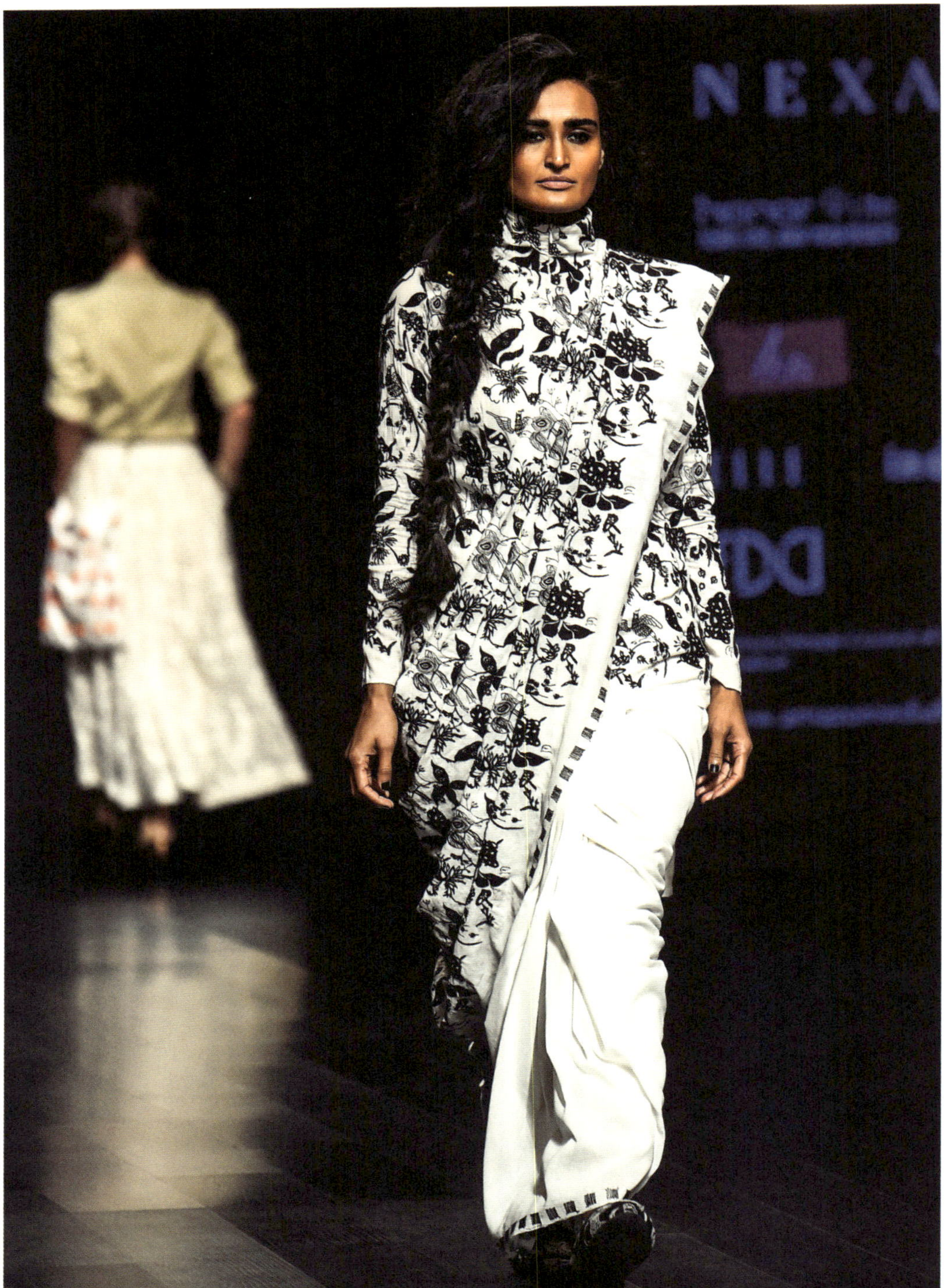

Model presenting a creation by Abraham and Thakore at India Fashion Week, New Delhi, 2018. Their work often emphasizes minimalism and craftsmanship.

Other designers treat prints as storytelling devices. Gaurav Gupta, renowned for sculptural couture, often extends his cosmic or elemental themes into sari prints – swirling galaxies, fluid smoke patterns and futuristic metallic sheens. Labels like Raw Mango or Abraham & Thakore take a subtler route, adapting block-printed checks, polka dots and hand-drawn sketches into saris that feel both minimal and edgy. Abraham & Thakore, in particular, have reimagined the sari with ikat-inspired polka dots or calligraphic typography splashed across chiffon, demonstrating that modern design can honour tradition's depth without compromise.

For younger, digital-first designers, the sari has become an Instagram-ready canvas. Bold typography, tongue-in-cheek slogans or playful reinterpretations of classic motifs – bananas, autorickshaws, postage stamps – appear on contemporary saris. Some embrace maximalism – with clashing neon hues, animal prints and sequins – while others celebrate stark monochrome and geometric minimalism.

The effect is twofold: these modern prints democratize the sari, making it approachable for new generations while also expanding its visual vocabulary. Just as a Baluchari once narrated epics in silk, today a Masaba sari might tell the story of a city's chaos or a woman's sense of humour. In this way, prints themselves become language – a dialect of the sari that is unmistakably of the present moment.

The Sari and Social Change

The sari's evolution is about more than textiles; it also serves as a banner for social movements. In terms of gender and identity, the sari has become remarkably fluid. A generation of Indian men and non-binary people are reclaiming the sari as their own. In 2006, Delhi's Himanshu Verma, dubbed 'the sari man', started wearing saris as a 'fresh landscape' with which to explore gender. For Verma and others, draping a sari is understood as a gender-neutral expression. 'It's not crossdressing, but merely appropriating the sari as a man', he says. Pushpak Sen of Kolkata became an online star when he strolled through the streets of Milan in a bold red-and-white sari and matching bindi, demonstrating that 'a piece of fabric cannot be gender specific'. And content creator Siddharth Batra has celebrated the sari's power, declaring 'Saris make you feel so powerful' while noting that such freedom is often celebrated differently in LGBTQ+ communities. In their words, the sari's fluid drape itself carries a message: as one wearer puts it, in spirit 'the sari was always gender-neutral'. The #SariNotSorry trend and viral 'men in saris' photos are the most visible symbols of this shift.

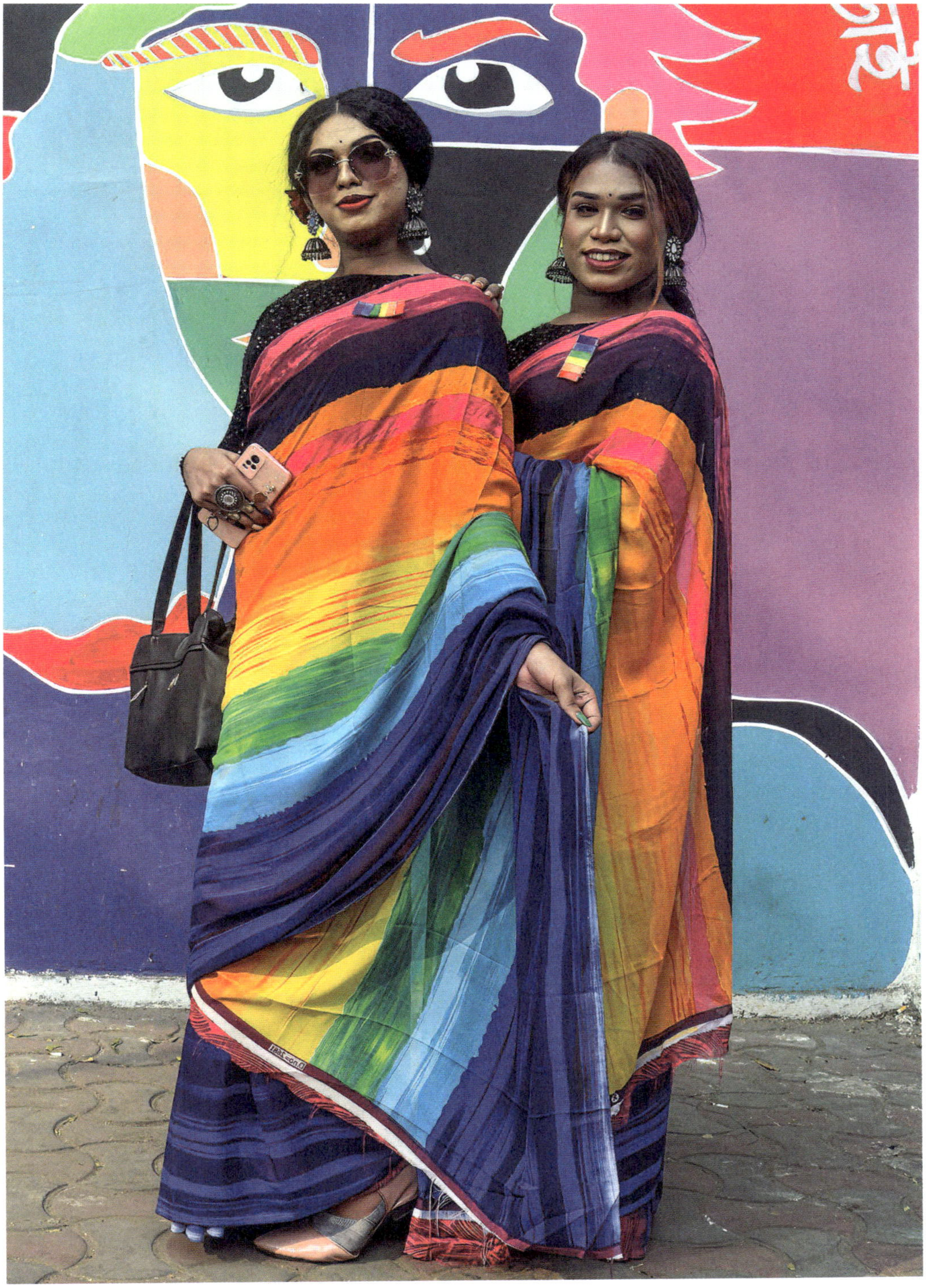

Participants at the Kolkata Rainbow Pride Walk celebrating LGBTQ+ identity and visibility. The sari has increasingly become a symbol of self-expression across gender identities.

Broader movements have also embraced the sari's legacy. In 2020, Indian activists Sindhura Kaviti and Nistula Hebbar launched World Sari Day (21 December) to honour weavers and celebrate the sari on a global scale. Their initiative – now observed by fashion communities worldwide – explicitly 'aims to honour the weaving communities and the unique art of the sari' beyond India's borders. Even in protests and pop culture, Indian women and men display the sari as a symbol of empowerment. Whether supporting rural weavers or trans and queer rights, the sari often carries a deeper message. Today it functions not only as stylish apparel but as a canvas for expressing heritage, identity, and inclusivity.

By blending its historic weave with new patterns of belief, the sari proves it is not destined for the museum, but equipped for the future. From the shore to the streets, India's sari continues to evolve. Young designers and wearers are redefining its meaning – ensuring that this 'six-yard' tradition 'lives, breathes and evolves' just as generations before have done. It's story is still being woven, with threads of history, craft, and innovation intertwining to keep the sari as vibrant and essential today as ever.

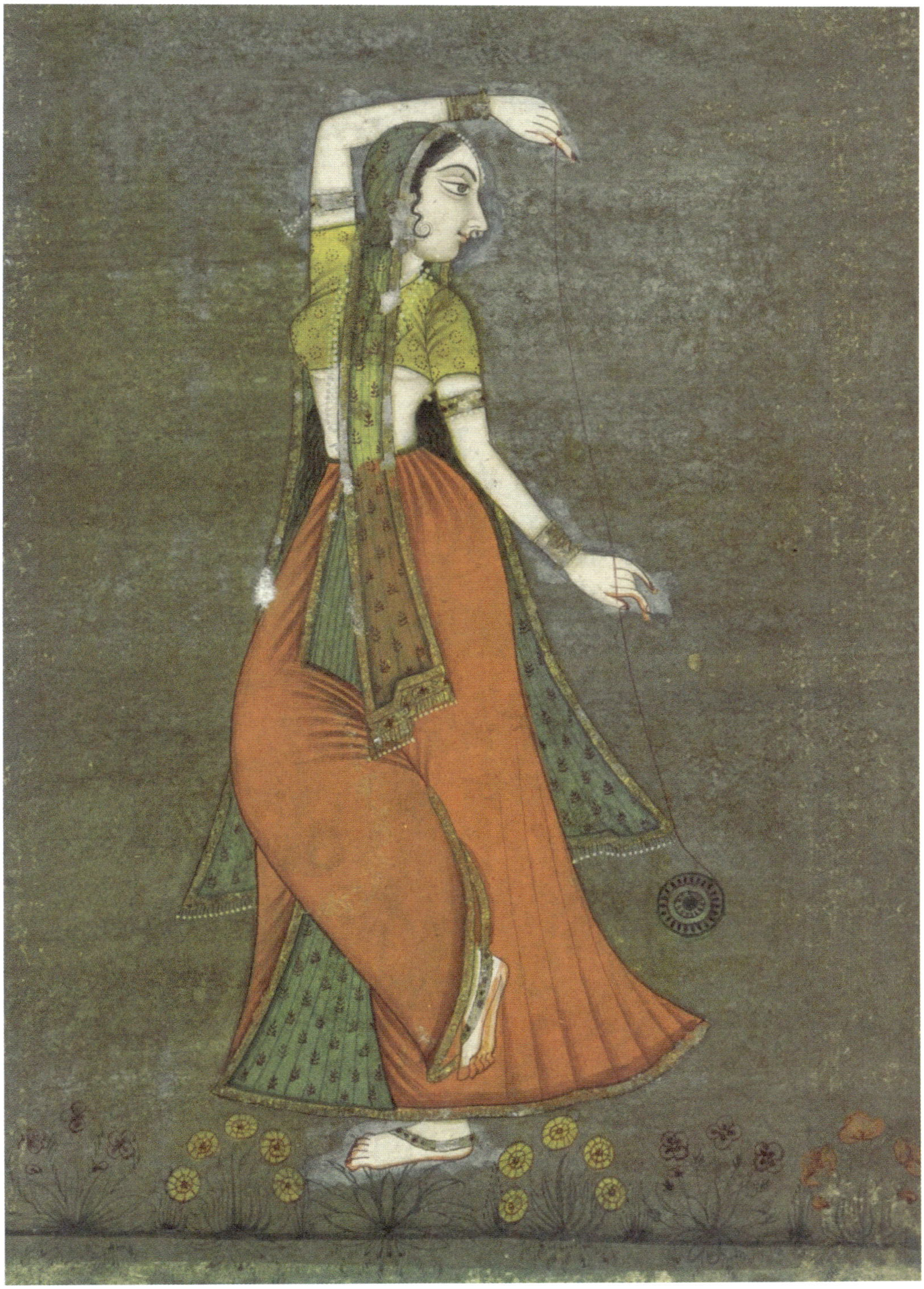

Woman playing with a yo-yo, Indian miniature painting, c. 1680–1699.
Miniature paintings often depict both leisure activities and daily life.

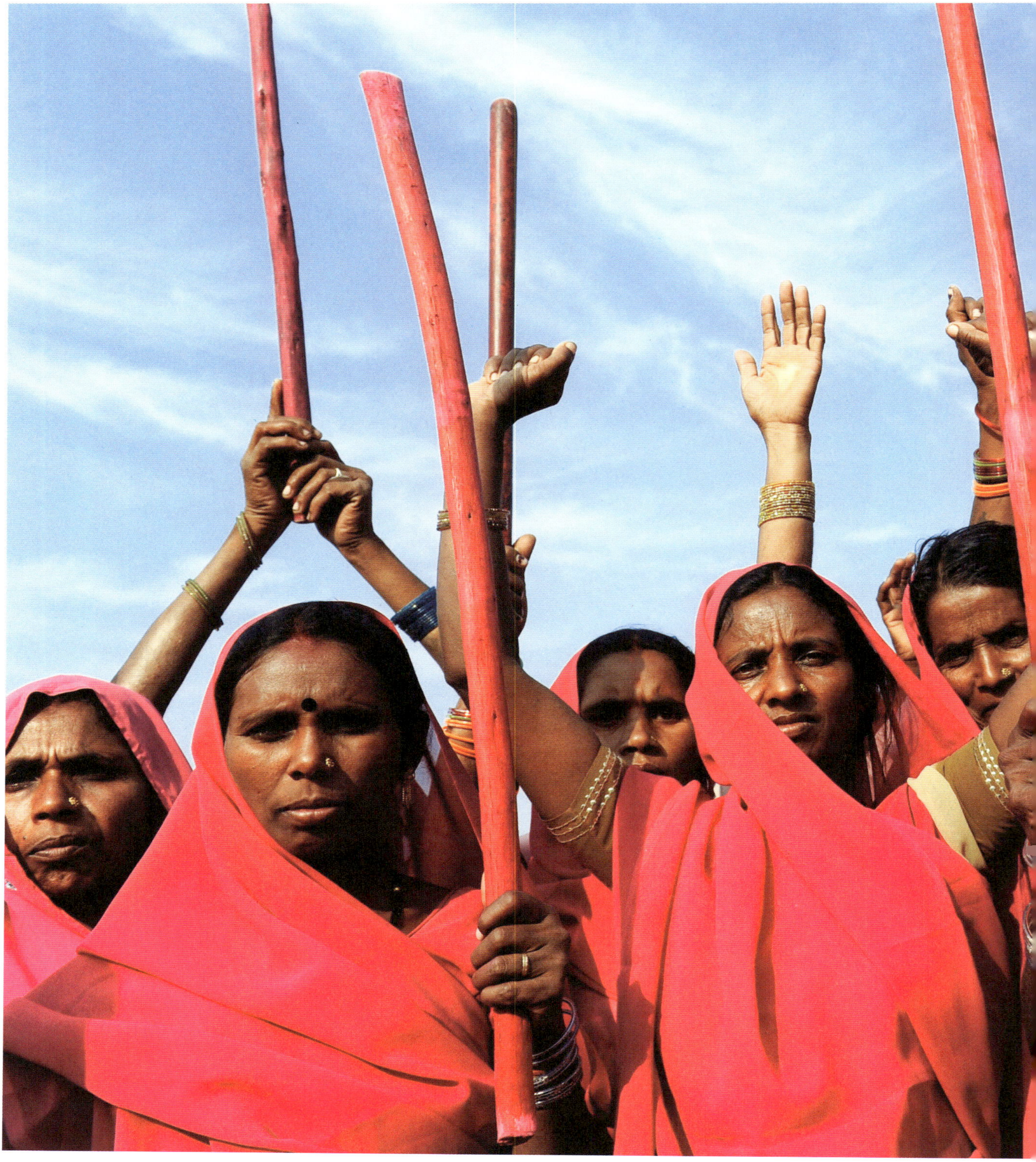

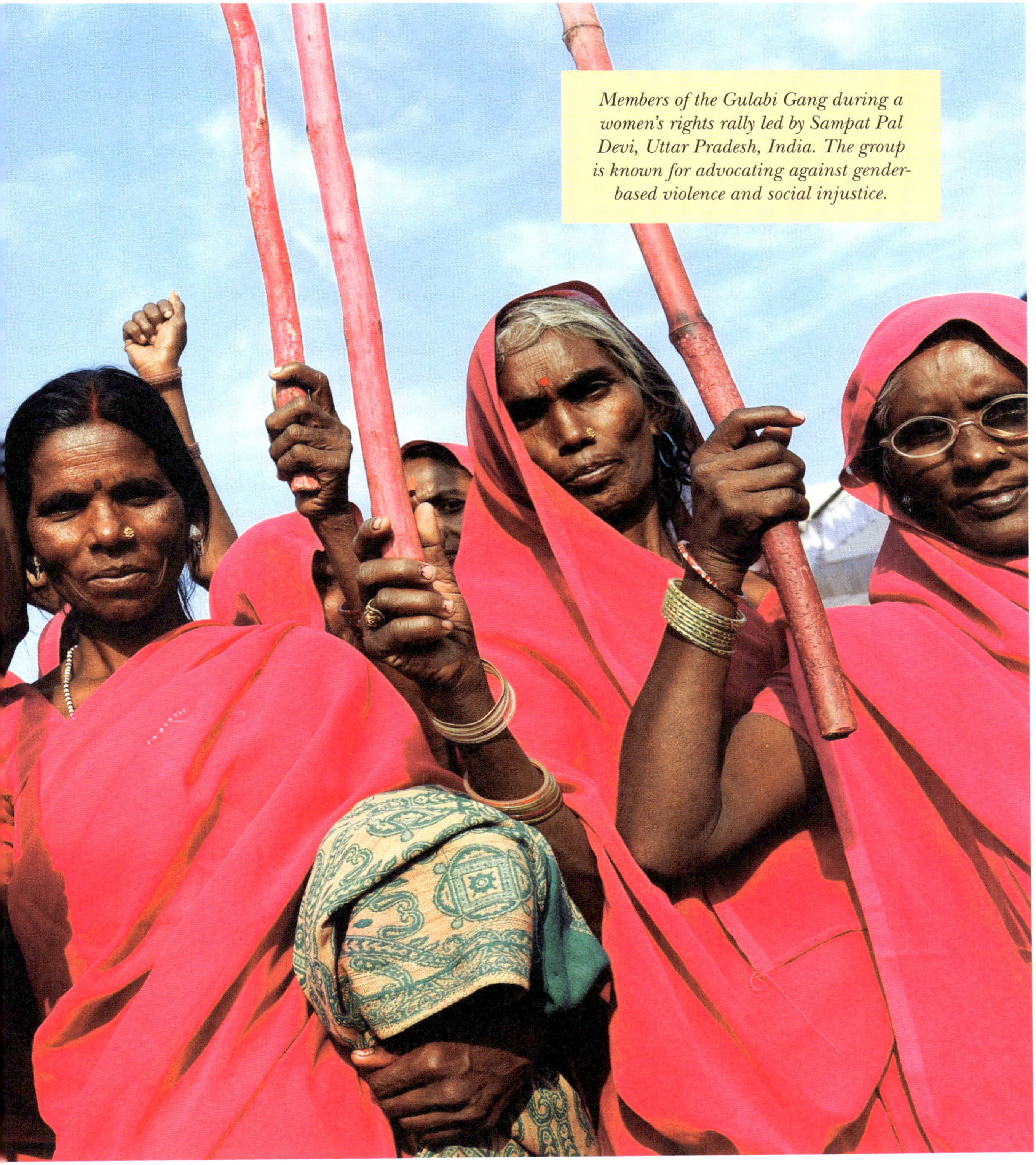

Members of the Gulabi Gang during a women's rights rally led by Sampat Pal Devi, Uttar Pradesh, India. The group is known for advocating against gender-based violence and social injustice.

A Living Fabric

What unfolds is a portrait of resilience. The sari is no longer confined to ancestral chests or ceremonial mornings; it appears on Instagram feeds, in offices, on fashion runways, and at Pride marches. It is worn by artisans' daughters and corporate lawyers, by grandmothers and genderqueer youth alike. It carries the heritage of village looms alongside urban prints, blending ecological ideals with rebellious slogans.

In this swirl of continuity and change, the sari shows its greatest strength: adaptability. It is not a relic to be preserved under glass, nor a uniform to be enforced. It is a living language, constantly absorbing new words and accents. Draping a sari today is a way of inscribing oneself into a story that spans centuries, yet remains wide open to the future.

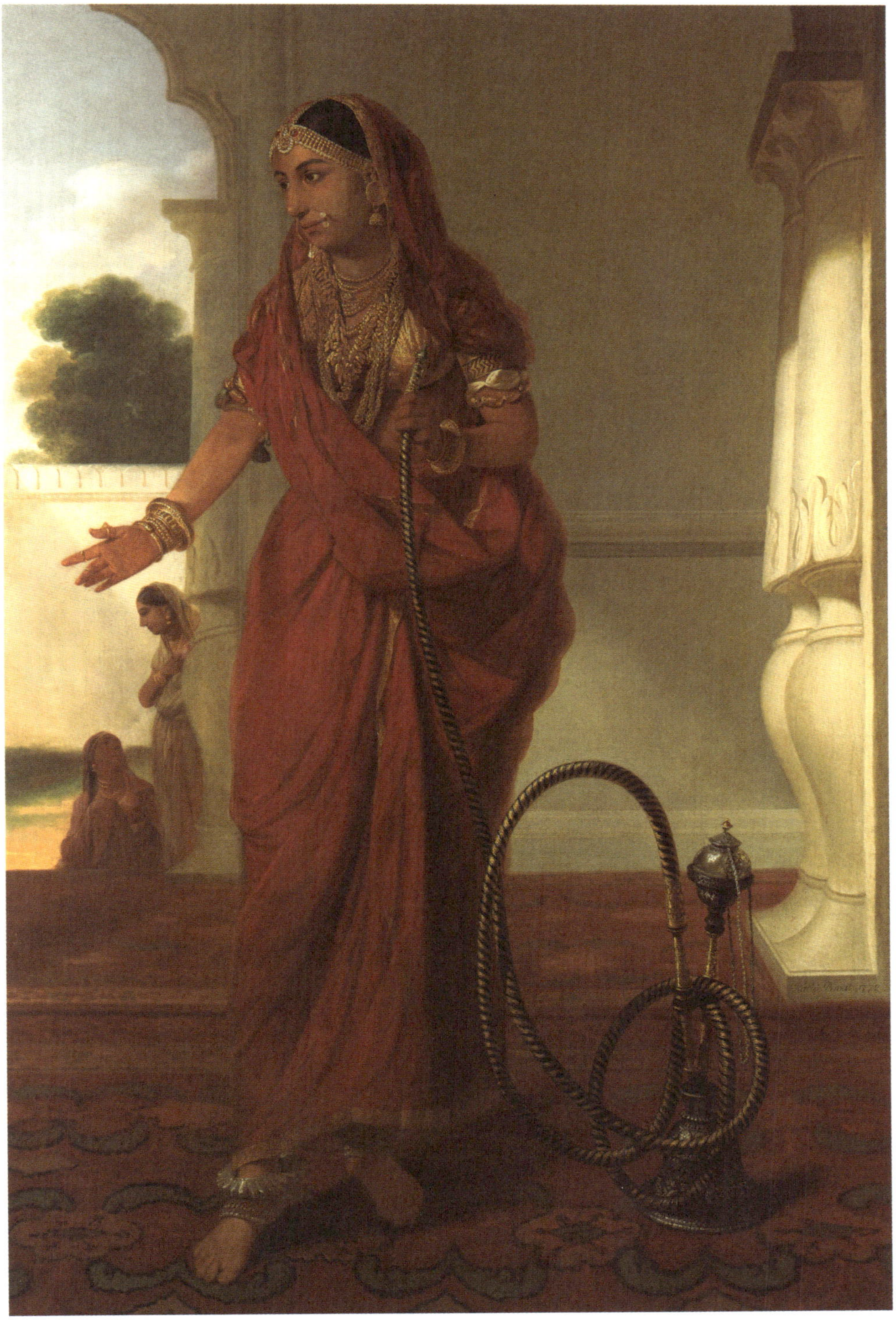

'Dancing Girl', by Tilly Kettle, 1772, oil on canvas.
Kettle was among the earliest British portrait painters to work in India.

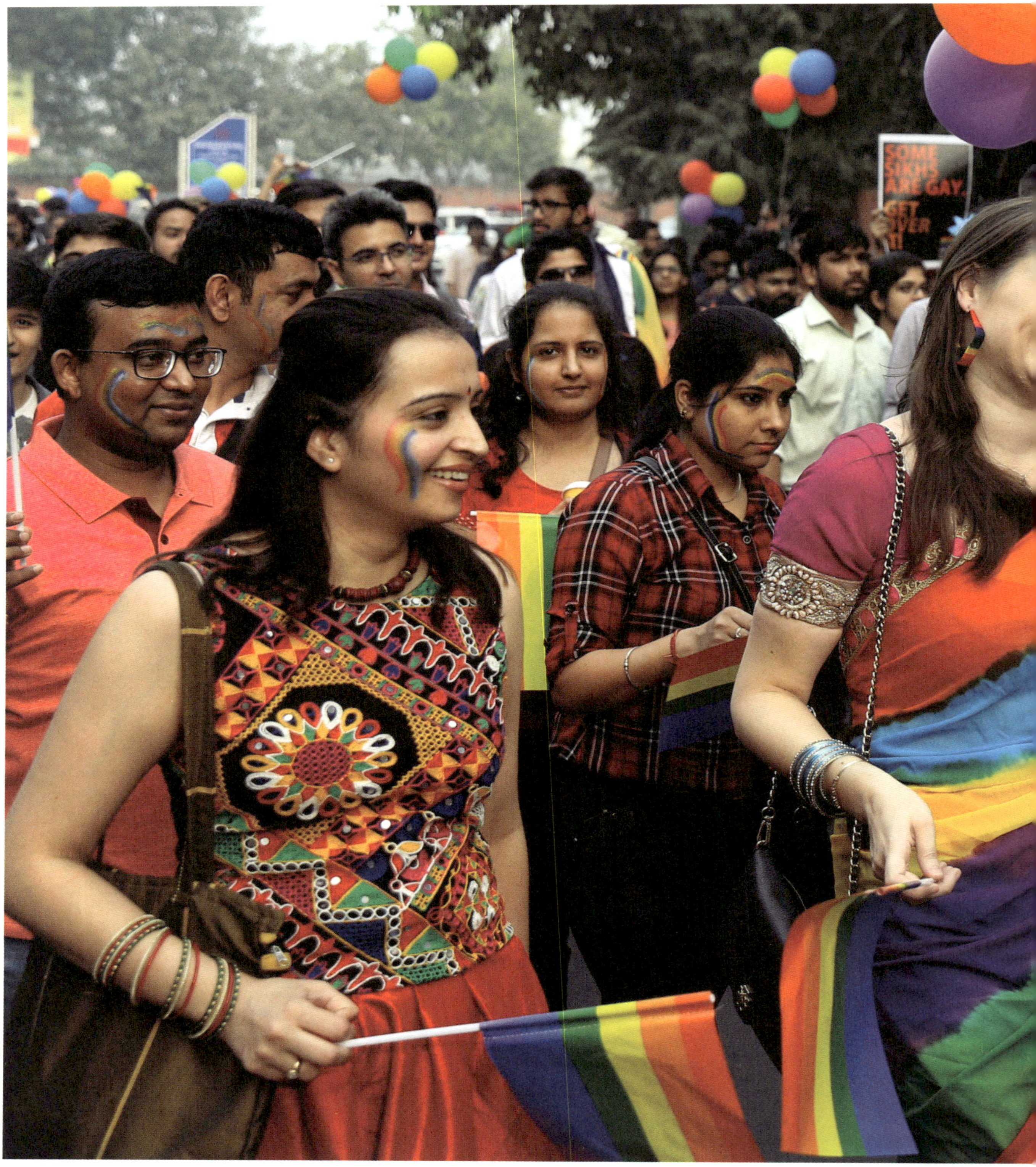
SOME SIKHS ARE GAY.
GET OVER IT!

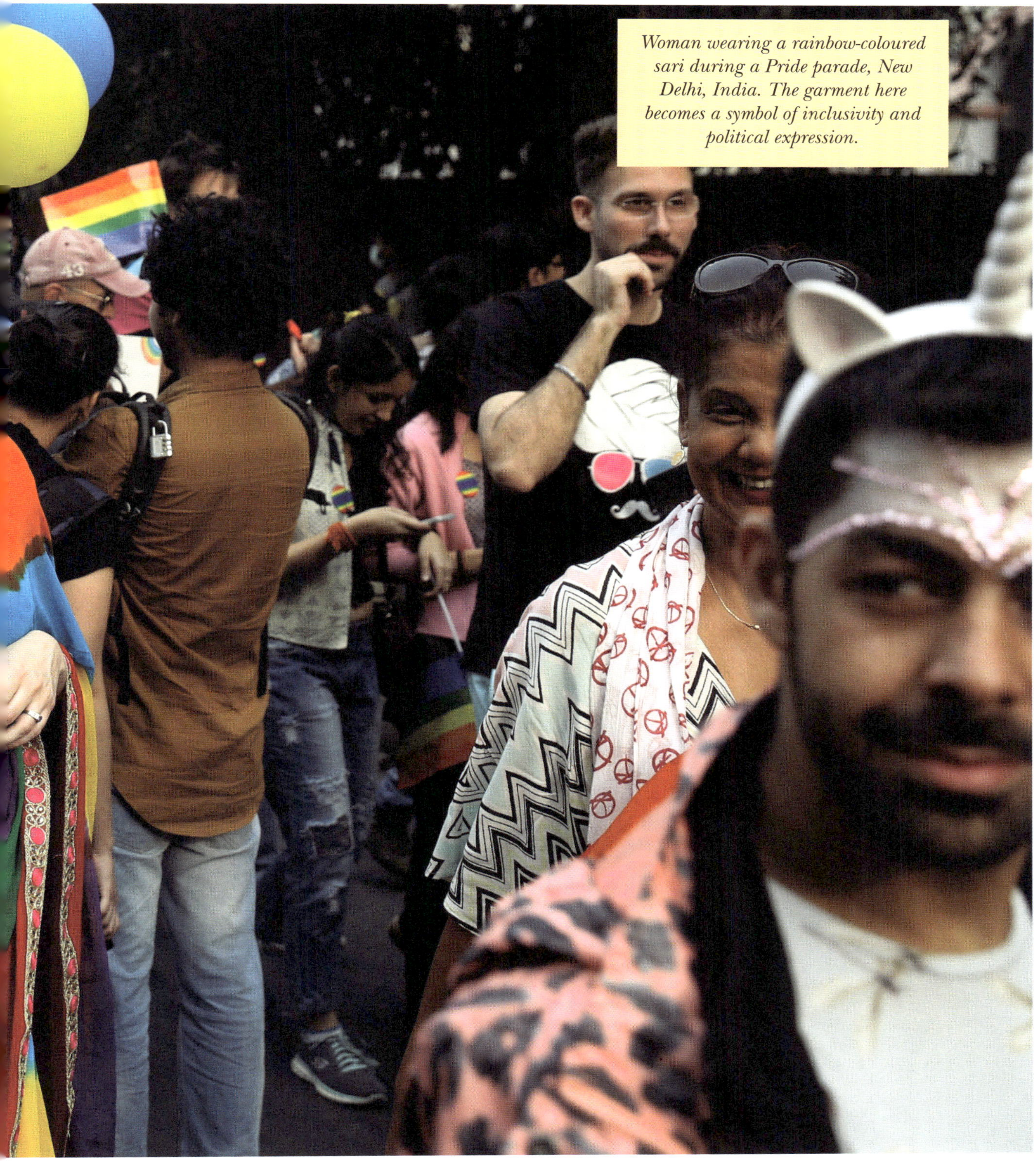

Woman wearing a rainbow-coloured sari during a Pride parade, New Delhi, India. The garment here becomes a symbol of inclusivity and political expression.

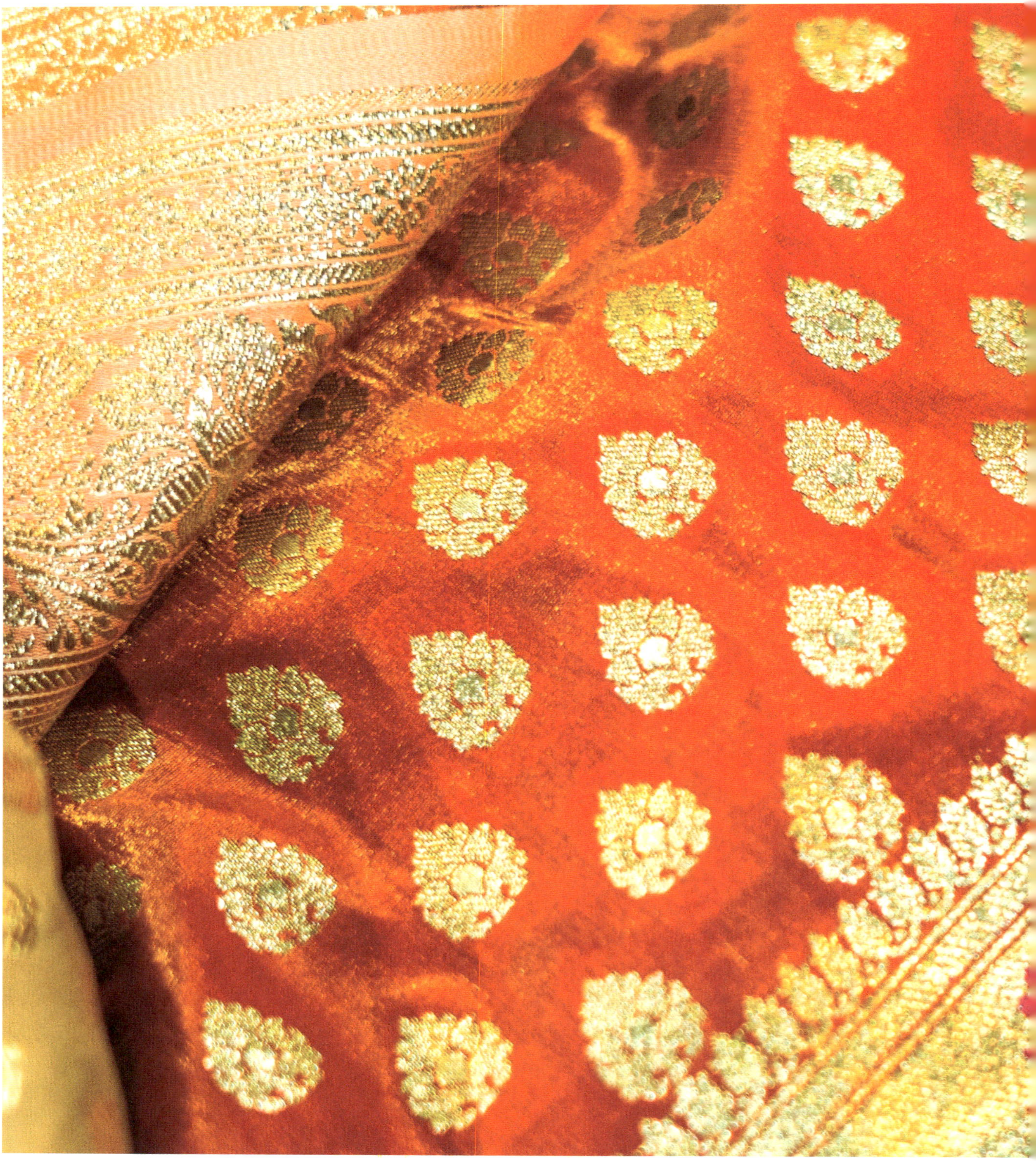

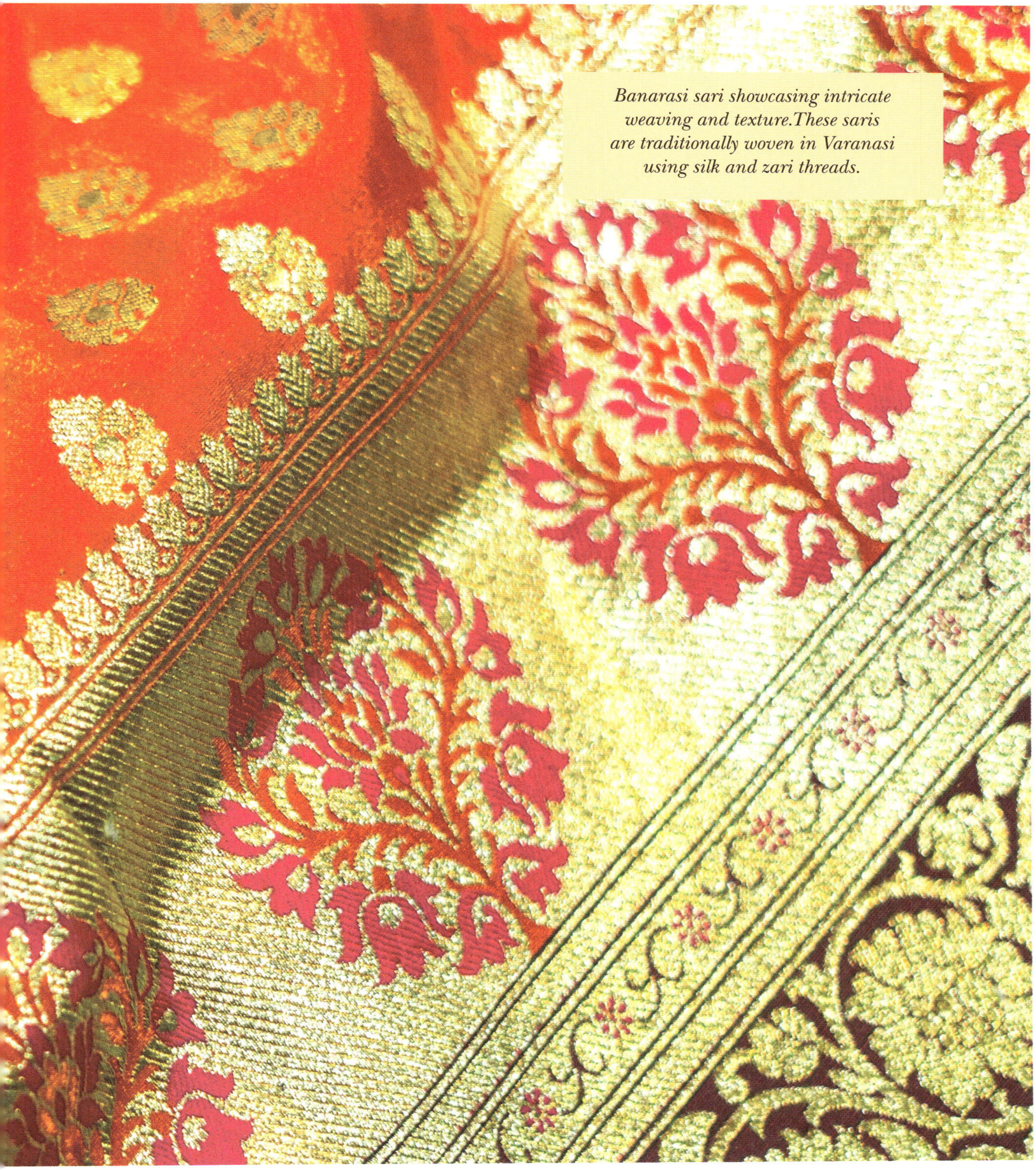

Banarasi sari showcasing intricate weaving and texture. These saris are traditionally woven in Varanasi using silk and zari threads.

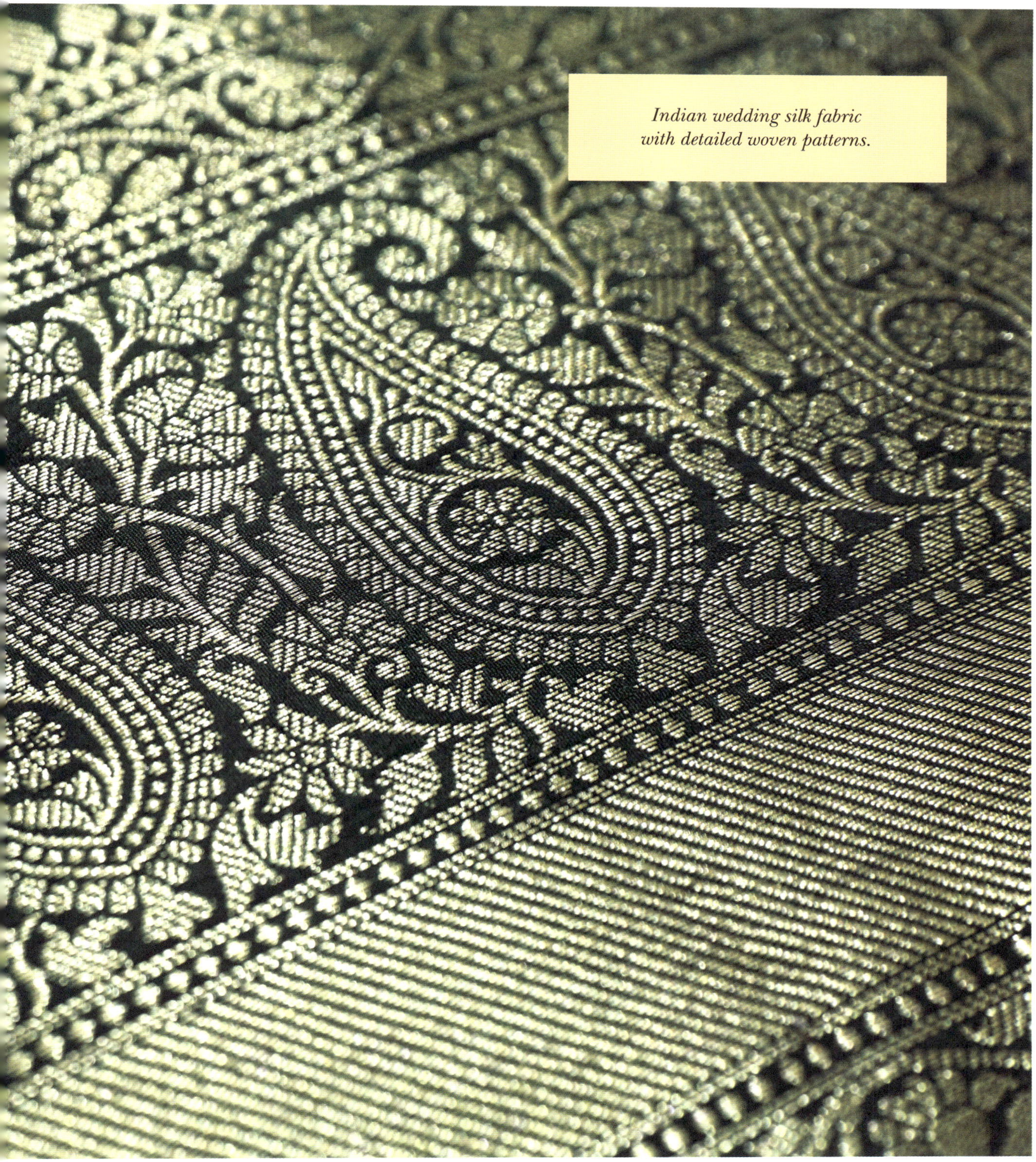

Indian wedding silk fabric with detailed woven patterns.

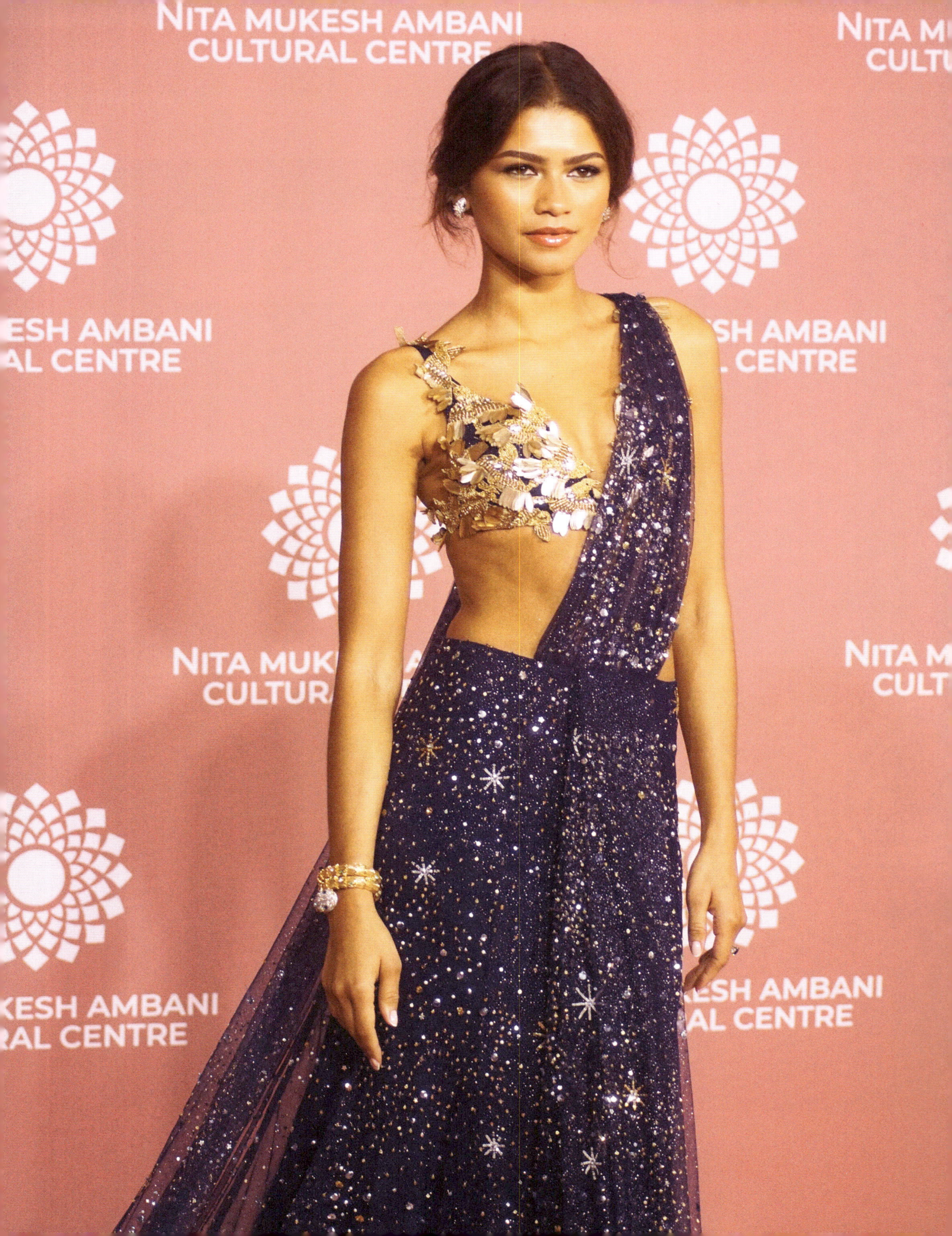
NITA MUKESH AMBANI
CULTURAL CENTRE

CHAPTER 6

अंतरराष्ट्रीय पहचान

International Recognition

For centuries, the sari existed as an intimate garment of the subcontinent – woven in villages, draped in households, and exchanged through rituals. Yet in the past century, and more dramatically in the last few decades, the sari has stepped onto a new stage: the global runway. From Paris to New York, from Hollywood red carpets to New York's Met Gala, its folds have become both spectacle and statement. Once confined to the private rhythms of Indian life, the sari now engages in dialogue with global couture.

This recognition did not happen overnight. It came through creative encounters: between designers and traditions, between celebrities and stylists, between the sari's timeless adaptability and the world's hunger for reinvention.

Zendaya at the launch of the Nita Mukesh Ambani Cultural Centre (NMACC), Mumbai, India, 2023. Her appearance highlights the global influence of Indian-inspired couture.

Icons in 'Six Yards'

When American actress Zendaya appeared at the opening of the Nita Mukesh Ambani Cultural Centre in Mumbai in 2023, her sari was not simply an outfit. Designed by Rahul Mishra and hand–embroidered over 3000 hours, the shimmering blue drape fused tradition with contemporary couture. It honoured India's artisanal heritage while marking Mishra's own milestone as the first Indian designer to join the official Paris Haute Couture calendar. In that moment the sari became both a celebration of India and a conversation with the world.

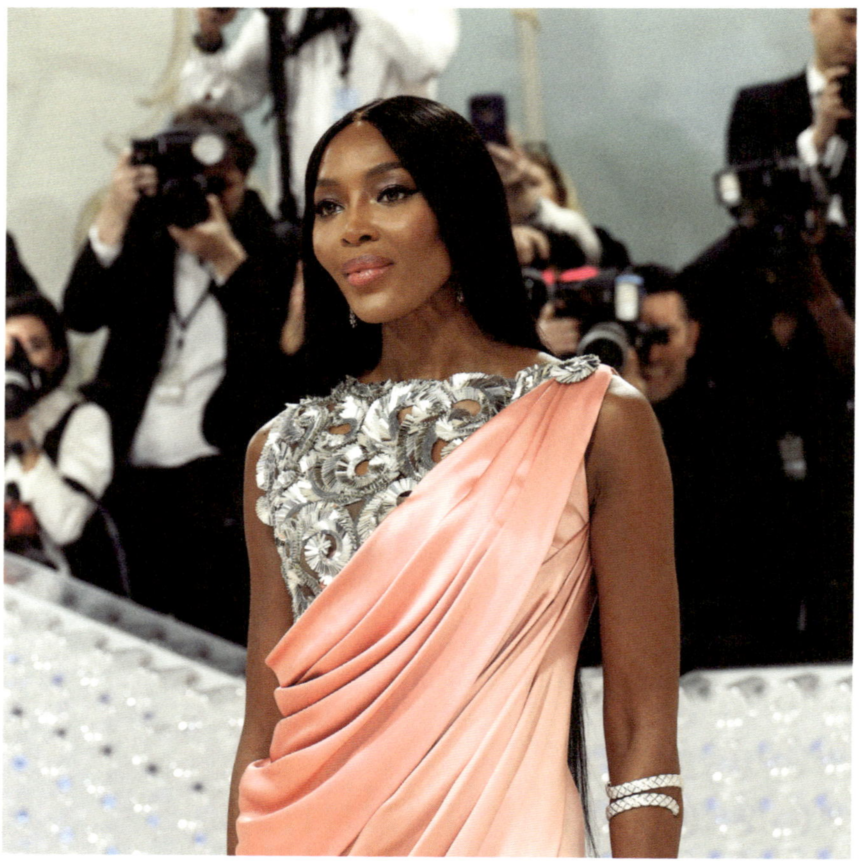

Naomi Campbell at the Met Gala, New York, 2023, wearing a sari-inspired Chanel gown.

At that year's Met Gala in New York, British model Naomi Campbell turned heads in a rare archival Chanel gown inspired by the drape of the sari. Though not a sari in the strict sense, it was an homage – an acknowledgment that this unstitched cloth continues to inspire even the most guarded archives of European fashion. For Campbell, the look was personal; for the garment, it stood as testament to how deeply the sari had became part of the language of global glamour.

The Designer's Muse

International designers have long flirted with the sari, sometimes clumsily, often brilliantly.

French designer Jean Paul Gaultier – irreverent, bold and endlessly fascinated with India – has returned to the sari repeatedly. In his Fall 2017

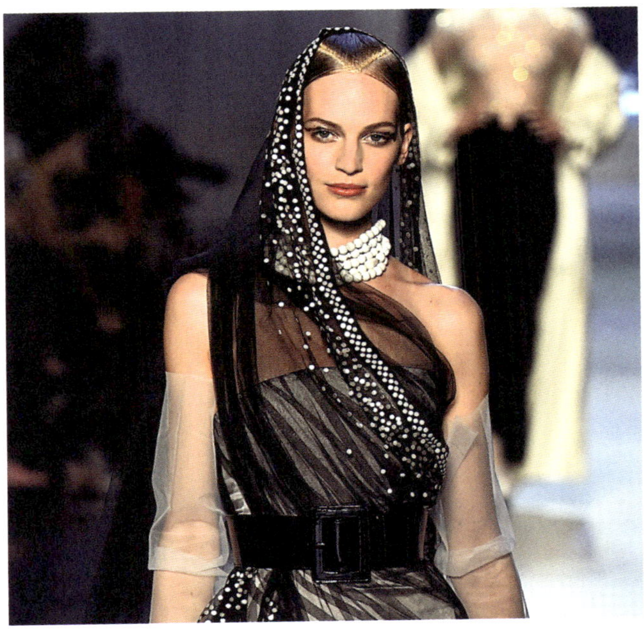

Model walking the runway at Jean Paul Gaultier Haute Couture Fall/Winter 2017–2018, Paris. Gaultier has frequently drawn inspiration from non-Western garments including the sari.

Haute Couture collection, he reshaped the sari into unexpected forms, including hybrids with tuxedos. Decades earlier, during his tenure as creative director at Hermès, the house's 2008 ready-to-wear show featured sari-inspired designs on the Paris runway – flowing fabrics and draped forms unmistakably rooted in South Asian heritage.

British designer Alexander McQueen, whose work often combined history with provocation, paid homage in his Fall 2008 collection with a red silk sari reimagined in a new silhouette. It was a rare gesture: a designer so deeply anchored in his Scottish identity choosing to honour Indian heritage. In McQueen's hands, the sari was never mimicry – it was acknowledgement.

Spanish designer Cristóbal Balenciaga, decades earlier in the 1960s, had explored what he called the 'sari dress'. In pink silks and sculptural

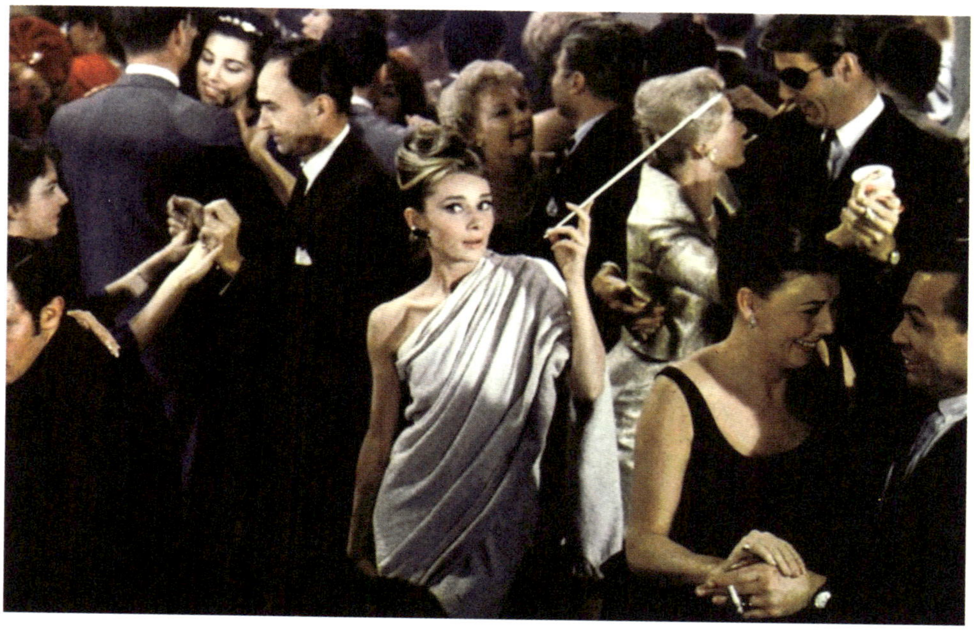

Scene from 'Breakfast at Tiffany's', featuring Audrey Hepburn in a sari-inspired drape, 1961. The look is one of the early references to South Asian draping in Hollywood cinema.

folds, his designs were reinterpretations rather than replicas. American star Elizabeth Taylor wore one of these creations in 1964 at Paris' Gala of Lido, cementing the garment's crossover into Hollywood legend.

Even Givenchy, a name is etched into cinematic fashion history through Audrey Hepburn, found himself drawn to the sari's form. In the 1961 film *Breakfast at Tiffany's*, Hepburn wore what was technically a draped bedsheet, but the reference was unmistakable. Though not 'authentic', it became iconic: one of the earliest representations of sari draping in a Hollywood film.

Beyond the Runway

What do all these moments add up to? Not simply celebrity costumes or fashion experiments, they are evidence of how the sari has entered the global imagination. Seeing it on Zendaya or Naomi Campbell transforms the sari from 'exotic dress', into haute couture. Watching it inspire designers across decades – from Balenciaga's ateliers to Gaultier's runway – is to witness the sari's remarkable adaptability across cultures and centuries.

The sari, after all, has always been more than a garment. In India, it represents ritual, rebellion, and remembrance. On global platforms, it becomes a dialogue – between East and West, tradition and innovation, and history and reinvention.

The sari no longer sits quietly in cupboards lined with naphthalene balls. It strides the red carpet, commands the gaze of cameras and pushes the boundaries of fashion. Its recognition is not merely international – it is inevitable.

CONCLUSION

छह गज, अनगिनत कहानियाँ

Six Yards, Infinite Lives

The sari is never only fabric. It is memory, devotion, identity and resilience. To follow its journey across our land is to trace the country's own story – woven in warp and weft, carried from generation to generation like a sacred trust. From the temple looms of Kanchipuram to the backyards of Assam, from desert dyes in Gujarat to the translucent air of Chanderi, each sari tells of rivers, soils and skies. Each drape is both local and universal, born of its region yet belonging to everyone who wears it.

Across centuries, the sari has endured. It has outlived empires, weathered colonial rule and withstood laws that tried to dictate what women could or could not be. It has survived monsoons, droughts and the shifting sands of taste. And yet, every time it seemed it might be folded away, it re-emerged – adapted, reinvented, renewed.

The sari has always been more than a garment. It is made and remade by human hands: spun by weavers, dyed with earth and leaf, embellished with thread and story. It is bought not merely as fabric but as a blessing: for a bride's trousseau, a festival morning, a farewell gift. It is preserved in trunks and cupboards, wrapped in muslin and naphthalene, its folds heavy with the fragrance of jasmine, sandalwood or time itself. And when it is passed down – from mother to daughter, grandmother to granddaughter – it becomes more than cloth. It becomes a lineage.

Every sari carries two lives: the one lived by its weaver and the one lived by its wearer. Together, they form an unbroken dialogue across generations. A grandmother's wedding sari becomes a granddaughter's keepsake. A mother's daily cotton, worn thin with chores and laughter, becomes a relic of tenderness. A handloom bought at a village fair carries the story of an artisan who wove hope into every thread.

In modern times, the sari has shown us it can breathe with the present. It is worn by young professionals who drape it over sneakers, by activists who carry it as a protest, by designers who reinvent it in recycled fabrics and bold prints. It is genderless, ageless, timeless. In the sari, the past and future fold into one another like pleats.

To hold a sari is to hold continuity. It is the living proof of India's history: a tradition that has survived conquest and colonialism, globalization and modernity. It has endured because it is not static, but rather it shifts, bends and adapts while never losing its essence. The sari is not just India's costume; it is India's text, its archive, its testament.

As long as hands weave and hearts remember, the sari will continue to live. Not just in museums or runways, but in kitchens and courtyards, in classrooms and boardrooms, in protests and celebrations. Six yards of thread, infinite lives of meaning.

The sari is not merely worn. It is lived.

Sari Regions of India

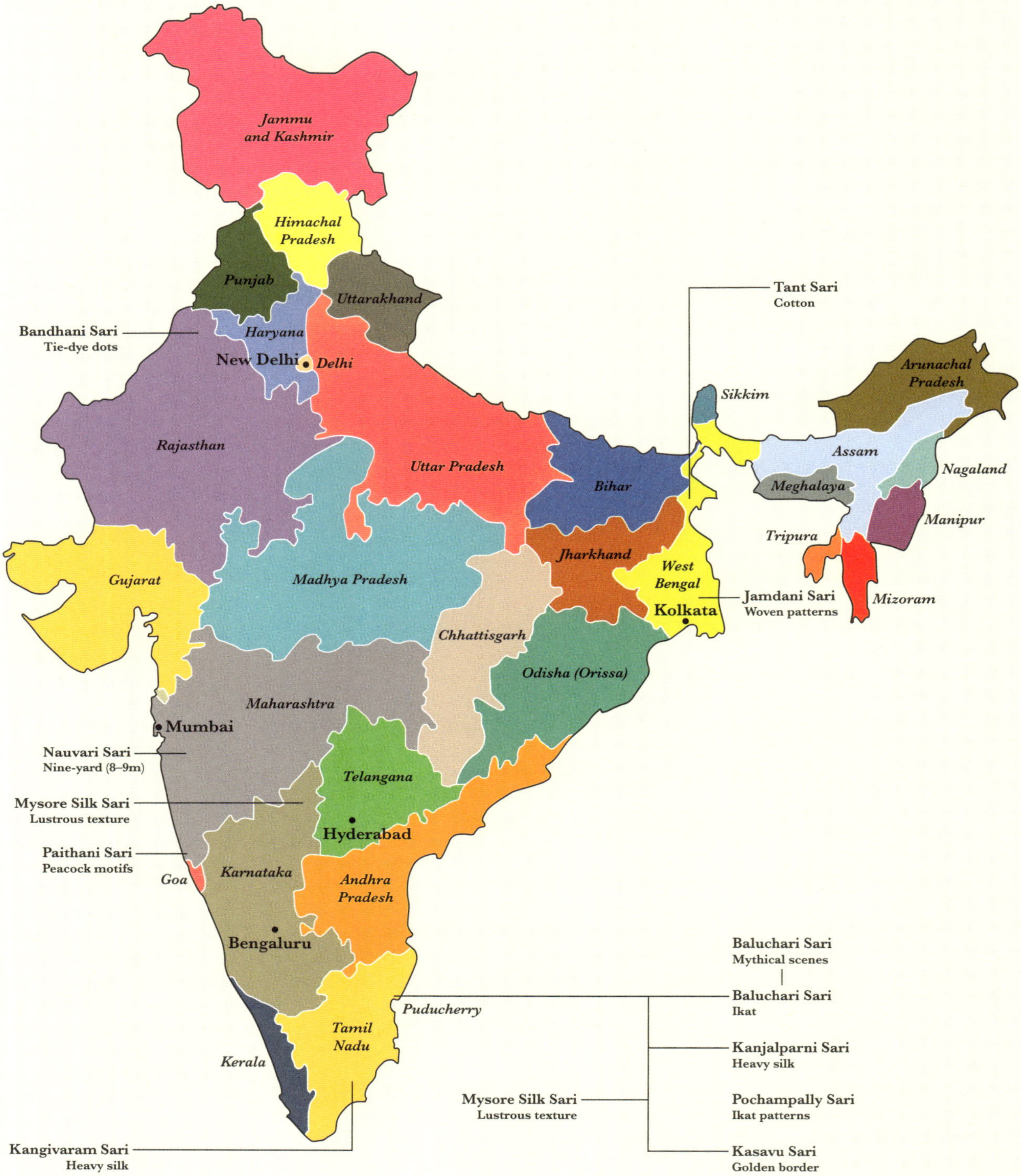

Bibliography

Websites:

National Geographic (https://www.nationalgeographic.com/history/article/the-story-of-the-sari-in-india)

Medium – the Origins of the Sari (https://medium.com/@zaildugal/the-origins-of-the-sari-503d4a998081)

International Journal of Home Science (https://www.homesciencejournal.com/archives/2019/vol5issue2/PartE/5-2-46-788.pdf)

Bharat Karigar Sarees (https://www.bharatkarigar.com/post/the-history-of-sarees-in-india)

Tulsi Silks (https://tulsisilks.co.in/about-us)

Seven Sarees (https://sevensarees.com/blogs/seven-sarees-blogs/her-story-of-a-saree)

Spain Industrial Design – Wordpress (https://spaindustrialdesign.wordpress.com/2020/12/20/banarasi-sari/)

Nazrana (https://nazranachikan.com/blogs/news/chikankari-sarees-a-guide-to-history-and-designs)

Dress 365 Days (https://www.dress365days.com/blogs/chikankari-articles/chikankari-sarees-a-guide-to-history-types-designs-and-care)

Fabric Lore (https://fabriclore.com/blogs/fabric-wiki/information-about-chanderi-fabric)

BongChong Sarees (https://bongchong.in/bandhej-sarees/)

Artnet News (https://news.artnet.com/art-world/the-offbeat-sari-exhibition-design-museum-london-2309033)

Runway Ready Sarees (https://www.runwayreadysarees.com.au/blogs/news/the-evolution-of-sarees-tradition-meets-modern)

CNN style (https://edition.cnn.com/style/how-the-sari-went-global)

WION (https://www.wionews.com/entertainment/lifestyle/news-met-gala-2023-highlights-naomi-campbell-dons-rare-saree-inspired-archival-chanel-gown-588069)

Manifest magazine (https://www.manifestmagazine.in/fashion-beauty/features/international-designers-inspired-by-sari)

ELLE India (https://elle.in/article/jean-paul-gaultier-sari-obsession/)

Jagran Josh (https://www.jagranjosh.com/general-knowledge/what-is-world-saree-day-and-when-is-it-celebrated-1703080932-1)

The Economic Times (https://economictimes.indiatimes.com/industry/cons-products/fashion-/-cosmetics-/-jewellery/how-rahul-mishras-designs-reflect-the-interwoven-beauty-of-nature-and-humanity/articleshow/119188649.cms?from=mdr)

The Indian Express (https://indianexpress.com/photos/lifestyle-gallery/6-indian-fashion-designers-practicing-sustainable-fashion-10275038/)

Dhakeswari Bastralaya (https://dhakeswaribastralaya.com/styles-of-draping-a-saree)

Moni Gāthā (https://monidipa.net/2018/02/08/the-history-of-bengali-sarees)

The Times of India (https://timesofindia.indiatimes.com/life-style/fashion/style-guide/all-about-haku-patasi-the-nepalese-saree/articleshow/123434679.cms) (https://timesofindia.indiatimes.com/life-style/fashion/buzz/all-about-sri-lankas-most-popular-sari-the-kandyan/photostory/105018986.cms)

Books:

Saris: Splendour in Threads by Soha Parekh
Indian Saris by Vijai Singh Katiyar
Saris of India: Traditions and Beyond by Rta Kapur Chishti

Index

Acknowledgements

This book has been woven not only from threads of fabric, but from threads of memory, generosity and love. I wish to extend my heartfelt gratitude to The Registry of Sarees for giving me the space and resources to research and gain insights that shaped these pages. Their work in preserving and documenting the textile heritage of our land has been an anchor, and this book would not have found its rhythm without them. This is more than an informative piece – it is a story I hold close to my heart, one that belongs to my family as much as it does to me. Every sari in these pages echoes the ones I have seen worn, folded, gifted and passed down in my own home. To my family, whose love for this garment has been my first and greatest lesson, I owe every word.

And to the countless weavers, artisans and women whose lives and labours have kept the sari alive across centuries – I bow in gratitude.

This book is only a small attempt to honour the vast tapestry they continue to create.

Picture Credits

Alamy: 17 (CPA Media), 71 (Sabena Jane Blackbird), 86 (IndiaPicture), 93 (NurPhoto SRL), 94 (imageBROKER), 95 (ephotocorp), 105 (Balaji Srinivasan), 106 & 107 (Stuart Forster), 108 (imageBROKER), 109 (Dinodia Photos), 112/113 (Abdul Malek Babul), 119 (Matjaz Corel), 120 (Robert Harding), 121 (Tom Salyer), 126 (Robert Harding), 133 (Dinodia Photos), 141 (Raquel Mogad), 146 (Alexey Panferov), 151 (Luis Dafos), 155 (Dinodia Photos), 156/157 & 162/163 (imageBROKER), 164 (Robert Harding), 185 & 186 (Stuart Pearce), 187 (Archivist), 188 (Xinhua), 199 (Sipa US), 202/203 (Joerg Boethling), 206/207 (Associated Press), 216 (Pictorial Press)

Art Institute of Chicago: 18, 28, 36, 51, 53

Cleveland Museum of Art: 12 left, 14, 32, 43, 52

Dreamstime: 22 (ePhotocorp), 30/31 (Mitrarudra), 68 (Samrat35), 70 (Nevinates), 73 (Sayali90p), 136 (Surya Nair), 140 (Akashparmar870), 153 (Midhun Menon), 168 (Eduardo Lopez Coronado), 181 (Indiatraveler)

Getty Images: 5 (D Kart), 10 (hadynyah), 15 (Hulton), 33 (Pictures from History), 56 (Marji Lang), 58 (Himanshu Sharma), 59 (D Kart), 60 (hadynyah), 62 (Bloomberg), 63 (CR Shelare), 64 (SOPA Images), 65 (NurPhoto), 66/67 (AnnSteer), 69 (IndiaPictures), 72 (Creative-Family), 75 (IndiaPictures), 78 (Bloomberg), 79 (Science & Society Picture Library), 85 (IndiaPictures), 88 (Frank Bienewald), 96 (NurPhoto), 98 & 101 (AFP), 110 (Dibyangshu Sarkar), 122 & 128/129 (Mint), 139 & 142 (Tuul & Bruno Morandi), 143 (SOPA Images), 144 (Niharika Kulkarni), 145 (ZUMA Press), 147 (Sudip Biswas), 154 (Jeremy Woodhouse), 161 (R.Satich Babu), 166 (NurPhoto), 167 (Pacific Press), 177, 179 & 180 (Siempreverde22), 182/183 (Andrew Geiger), 195 (Indranil Mukherjee), 196 (Chandan Khanna), 212 (Prodip Guha), 214 (Mike Coppola), 215 (Victor Virgile)

J Paul Getty Museum: 26, 54

Los Angeles County Museum of Art: 12 right, 20, 23, 44, 49, 55

Metropolitan Museum of Art, New York: 13, 19, 21, 38, 39, 41, 42, 46, 50

Minneapolis Institute of Art: 170, 171, 173, 193

Public Domain: 99

Rijksmuseum, Amsterdam: 25, 118, 124, 201

Shutterstock: 76/77 (r-d-p), 81 (Ruma Dey Acharya), 82 (Vani Chutani), 83 (PradeepGaur), 84 (CRS PHOTO), 91 (Sharon Sam), 102 (mridulablog), 114 (jayk67), 123 (Vinayak Jagtap), 131 (Orapin Joyphuem), 132 (Snehal Jeevan Pailkar), 134 (Rashmi Kale), 135 (Dipak Shelare), 137 & 138 (Musical Mrudang), 148 (Pal Teravagimov), 149 (Storm Is Me), 150 (chetansoni), 152 (to_look_further), 159 (dinesh0507), 174 (Sumit Saraswat), 178 (Nabaraj Regmi), 208/209 (sdx15), 210/211 (Shyamalamuralinath)

Smithsonian American Art Museum, Washington: 35

Smithsonian Freer Gallery of Art, Washington: 24, 34

Wellcome Collection: 27, 29, 40, 47, 57, 115

Yale Center for British Art: 158, 205

Illustrations on pages 8 & 9 and map on page 220 by Patrick Mulrey